For my friendly adversary   6/28 2002

心 = heart

爰 = accepting

心 + 爰 = 愛 = love

Keep Fighting

-- Aaaaaaamen --

your adversarial friend

ALSO BY DENIS DE ROUGEMONT

Love Declared
The Devil's Share

LOVE IN THE WESTERN WORLD

LOVE
IN THE
WESTERN
WORLD

DENIS DE ROUGEMONT

TRANSLATED BY
MONTGOMERY BELGION

Schocken Books   New York

Library of Congress Cataloging-in-Publication Data
Rougemont, Denis de, 1906–
Love in the Western world.
Translation of: L'Amour et l'occident.
Reprint. Previously published: Princeton, N.J.:
Princeton University Press, 1983, c1956.
Includes index.
1. Literature, Medieval—History and criticism.
2. Courtly love in literature.   3. Love in literature.
4. Love—History.   5. Troubadours.   6. Albigenses.
I. Title.
PN682.C6R613   1990   306.7'09181'2   89-42547
ISBN 0-8052-0950-6

Manufactured in the United States of America
First Schocken Edition

Contents

Contents

Contents

Appendix INCONCLUSIVE AND SCIENTIFICO-POLEMICAL POSTSCRIPT

6

Preface to the 1956 Edition

I
t was at the suggestion of my English publisher that I undertook to revise this book.
    Three times five years have passed since it first appeared,
and there has been a war, and much has been experienced to put
my contentions to a stern test. I have forgotten nothing and have
learned a little; for that matter, I have learned more from life
than from reading my critics, as these have been far from mutual
agreement. Some of them have nevertheless swayed me. In this
new version I have replaced one or two wild flourishes of the
pen by a little analysis, even though I feel that this worsens my
case.

The historians deplored my insistence upon the disturbing relations which I noted between Cathars and Troubadours. They, for
want of evidence, do not find them disturbing. Several theologians, either Roman or Greek, complained with friendliness that
I contrast Eros with Agape in too uncompromising a fashion,[1]
one which does not allow for the intermediate kind of love without which we should be unable to live. To the historians I shall
reply simply that I was in quest of an existential *meaning*. Hence I
had no idea of poaching upon their preserves. The documents
which I quote, the juxtapositions which I propose, are intended to
serve less as evidence than as illustrations. However, as far back
as 1940 fresh research began to strengthen my theory. I have
taken advantage of this to rewrite nearly the whole of Book II,
which deals with the twelfth century, with Catharism, the
troubadours, and Tristan. That is what is mainly new.

To the critics who disputed the actual *meaning* which I thought

[1] Cf. in particular the excellent book by Father M. C. D'Arcy, S.J., *The
Mind and Heart of Love* (London, 1945), which is largely devoted to a critical
exposition of the standpoints represented by Anders Nygren in his *Eros and
Agape* and by the present book.

7

Preface

I was justified in putting on the facts, I am tempted to give way on a number of points. My original task was to clear the ground and mark decisive contrasts; I could not always qualify or draw distinctions. A chapter now added to Book VI, and innumerable corrections of detail, will show, I hope, that I have gained in realism.

My central purpose was to describe the inescapable conflict in the West between passion and marriage; and in my view that remains the true subject, the real contention of the book as it has worked out.

The topicality of my inquiry seems to have suffered in no way from the second world war. Particularly at the end of Book V, I mentioned the possibility of a conflict which might put an end to the problems propounded in this study. My fear very nearly proved right, and I need now but transfer it to the foreseeable results of an inter-continental atomic war. Furthermore, seven years spent in the United States have afforded me the opportunity of seeing that the passion myth—now degraded to mere romance —is not in sight of exhausting its effects. The cinema[1] propagates those effects the entire world over, and the statistics of divorce show us how strong they are. If our civilization is to endure, it will have to carry through a great revolution. It will have to recognize that marriage, upon which its social structure stands, is more serious than the love which it cultivates, and that marriage cannot be founded on a fine ardour.

The ways of such a revolution are not yet to be forecast. On that I dwell in Book VI. My ambition is confined to making readers sensitively alive to the presence of the myth, and thereupon to enabling them to detect its radiation into real life as much as into works of art. It will perhaps not be altogether in vain for a few minds to be brought to grow conscious of what is being implied around them. For if it is true that the mutations of the heart are matured, and indeed happen, in the unconscious, they begin with their epiphany in expression, whether that is written, plastic, or pictorial, even as a love affair with its first avowal.

D. de R.

[1] It is curious to note that several films have taken their plots from my account of passionate love. Cf. B. Amengual, *Le Mythe de Tristan au Cinéma* (Algiers, 1951).

Particulars 1982

The 'Inconclusive and Scientifico-Polemical Postscript' (a reversal of the famous Kierkegaard title) constitutes the main change in the present edition, more than forty years after its original publication. This text revives—because it can't be concluded—the long scholarly debate over the validity of my theses. But the book was not meant for the universities, where ironically it is widely used today as required reading (after having been unremittingly condemned decades ago). What about the public who reads me today? Will the new generations find answers to their problems? Have not these problems radically changed in the course of four decades rich in both political and moral revolutions?

'Everything changes except the human heart', say the old sages, but they are wrong. Metaphorically speaking, the human heart is strangely sensitive to variations in time and place. What we call 'passionate love' is unknown in India and China. They have no words to render this concept. A Hindi once said to a friend of mine: 'When we experience something resembling what Western novels describe, all we say is, "It's romance!"'

When I am asked: 'Does the word *love* express the same realities now as it did before?' I answer: 'What love, what realities, what before?' The European languages alone have included all these realities in one single word. The West is distinct from other cultures not only by its invention of passionate love in the twelfth century and the secular elaboration of conjugal love, but by its confusion of the notions of eros, agape, sexuality, passion. Classical Greek used at least sixteen different terms to designate love in all its forms: *erōs* for physical love, *agapē* for altrustic love, *philia* for tender or erotic feelings, etc.

9

Let us first try to define our own terms. Sexuality is the instinct which directs the individual to the objectives of the species. Eroticism is sexual pleasure for its own sake and not as a means for procreation. Amorous passion is infinite desire which takes as its object or pretext a finite individual. And true love, active love, that which seeks the welfare of the Other, designates the supreme end, the fulfillment of the whole person in the act of giving.

When our times are credited with having finally 'liberated love', formerly bound by 'the Judeo-Christian concept and its interdict', or when, on the contrary, people regret the 'unleashing of a sexuality which rejects all religious and bourgeois taboos'—the breadth of modern confusion in this domain is revealed.

It is dangerous to speak of the Christian conception of love without analysing its meaning. Before declaring it defunct, it would be prudent to study it and distinguish it from bourgeois and Victorian conceptions—more precisely from twelfth-century conceptions introduced by the troubadours and the romance of Tristan. There would have to be a distinction between love and sexuality, at least. Sexual intercourse as a means to procreation—not love as we understand it—was regulated by primitive peoples. There is not a single law in any country or period that has ever controlled or condemned love as such—or even named it.

From what should we 'liberate' love? True love has always been free, and even more, it is the active principle of all human freedom. Love is freedom itself. The only real obstacles to love are in ourselves: barrenness, spiritual wounds, the anxiety of pride turned into mistrust of others, and especially self-contempt. 'You will love the Lord your God and your neighbor as yourself', say the Old Testament and the Gospels. But what happens if one does not love oneself? To liberate love, be in love! It is the only and sufficient condition.

The sexual problem is quite another matter. We enjoy and suffer from sexual freedom more than any other civilization. The taboos of ancient and primitive religions have given way to our mild prejudices. It is precisely the existence—and not the absence—of near total sexual freedom which poses a serious problem to young Western generations. The inscription on the walls of the Sorbonne during the student riots of May

Particulars 1982

1968: 'Down with the Oedipus complex!' provides a measure of the confusion in which we live and the extreme naivete of a certain progressivism unaware of mental structures and the dangers risked in their violation—ever so much more serious than any legal sanction.

In addition, the legalization of sexual intercourse for fourteen-year olds and the decriminalization of incest—as will be brought to a referendum in Switzerland—would in addition be disastrous for our literature, which has always been nurtured by obstacles, like passion itself. Remember two masterpieces: Vladimir Nabokov's *Lolita* and Robert Musil's *The Man Without Qualities*.

What future is evolving in the unconscious of our times and in the signs which enable us to probe it? Ecology—the reaction to the agression of our technology against life and affectivity—was the big fad of the seventies. We are as yet unable to measure the changes it will bring about in the interaction between Western man and his natural and social environments.

'Only algebra and sensations were cultivated', wrote Paul Valéry of the prewar years. The postwar 'unleashed eroticism' was the fever—not the cure—of this intellectual illness of the European psyche. Once the fever dropped, circulation of female, then male, porno magazines decreased.

Beyond the 'liberties' of adolescence (which are nothing but a return to ancient custom), beyond the vindications and rebellions, a new idea of marriage, of fidelity, conceived as a free creation between *equals*, rather than constraint, seems to be quietly emerging in replies of young people to polls and surveys and in their social behaviour. A more convivial vision of community may be emerging, one with a new ethic of love, having as a goal the full and authentic freedom of a real person: *the control, not of others, but of oneself.*

D. de R.
October, 1982

II

Book I

THE TRISTAN MYTH

I

Behind the Vogue of the Novel

'My Lords, if you would hear a high tale of love and death . . .'[1]

We know we could listen to nothing more delightful; and this opening of Bédier's *Tristan* should serve accordingly as a model for the beginning of a novel. It must be an unerring art that can at once thrust us into the state of absorbed suspense thanks to which narrative imparts the illusion of veracity. Where does the spell come from? And why should our feelings go half-way to meet the emotional effect of such a profound rhetorical device? One thing the tremendous vogue of the romantic novel makes immediately clear: the chord that awakens in us the most sonorous echoes has for its tonic and dominant, so to speak, the words 'love' and 'death'. There are other and more occult grounds for thinking that this is one clue to the European mind.

Love and death, a fatal love—in these phrases is summed up, if not the whole of poetry, at least whatever is popular, whatever is universally moving in European literature, alike as regards the oldest legends and the sweetest songs. Happy love has no history. Romance only comes into existence where love is fatal, frowned upon and doomed by life itself. What stirs lyrical poets to their finest flights is neither the delight of the senses nor the fruitful contentment of the settled couple; not the satisfaction of love, but its *passion*. And passion means suffering. There we have the fundamental fact.

[1] Joseph Bédier, *The Romance of Tristan and Iseult*, translated by Hilaire Belloc (London, 1913).

15

Our eagerness for both novels and films with their identical type of plot; the idealized eroticism that pervades our culture and upbringing and provides the pictures that fill the background of our lives; our desire for 'escape', which a mechanical boredom exacerbates—everything within and about us glorifies passion. Hence the prospect of a passionate experience has come to seem the promise that we are about to live more fully and more intensely. We look upon passion as a transfiguring force, something beyond delight and pain, an ardent beatitude. In 'passion' we are no longer aware of that 'which suffers', only of what is 'thrilling'. And yet actually passionate love is a misfortune. In this respect manners have undergone no change for centuries, and the community still drives passionate love in nine cases out of ten to take the form of adultery. No doubt lovers can invoke numerous exceptions. But statistics are inexorable, and they confute our poetic self-deception.

Can we be in such a state of delusion, can we have been so thoroughly 'mystified', as *really* to have forgotten the unhappy aspect of passion, or is it that in our heart of hearts we prefer to what must seemingly fulfil our ideal of a harmonious existence something that afflicts and yet elevates us? Let me examine the contradiction more closely, notwithstanding that to do so *must* seem disagreeable, since it threatens to uncover what we would rather not see. To assert that passionate love is actually tantamount to adultery is to insist upon a fact which our cult of love both conceals and distorts; it exposes what by the cult is dissimulated, repressed, and left unnamed, so as to leave us free to give ourselves up ardently to something we should never dare claim as our due. In the reader's very objection to recognizing that passion and adultery are commonly indistinguishable in contemporary society, we have a first indication of the paradox that we now desire passion and unhappiness only on condition we need never admit wishing for them as such.

To judge by literature, adultery would seem to be one of the most remarkable of occupations in both Europe and America. Few are the novels that fail to alude to it; and the vogue of the others, how we make allowances for these, the very passion with which we sometimes denounce them—all that shows well enough what couples dream about in the grip of a rule that has turned marriage into a duty and convenience. Without adultery, what would happen to imaginative writing? Novels and plays subsist on the so-called 'breakdown of marriage'. Probably, also, they help to prolong the breakdown, on the one hand by extolling what religion regards as a crime and law as an infringement, and, on the other hand, by making fun of this and drawing from it an inexhaustible fund of situations either comic or shameless. Whether the subject is idealized by speaking of the divine rights of passion, refined away by means of a smart, worldly psychology, or mocked by the popularity which the eternal triangle enjoys in the theatre, we are constantly *betraying* how widespread and disturbing is our obsession by the love that breaks the law. Is this not the sign that we wish to escape from a horrible reality? To turn the situation into either a farce or something mystical is equally to confess that it is unbearable. Ill-assorted couples, the disappointed, the rebellious, the intense, the shameless, the unfaithful or the deceived (whether in fact or in dreams, in remorse or in terror, in the delight of revolt or the disquiet of temptation)—few men and women will fail to see that they belong to at least one of these categories. The word 'adultery' sums up one half of human unhappiness—renunciation, compromises, separations, neurasthenia, together with the irritating and petty confusion of dreams, obligations, and secret acquiescence. Although so many books are being produced, or perhaps on that very account, it sometimes seems as if nothing had yet been said about the reality of our unhappiness, and that some of the most ingenuous problems in this department have more often been solved than propounded.

For instance, once the existence of the ill has been recognized, must the institution of marriage bear the blame for it, or is there something fatal to marriage at the very heart of human longing? Has the so-called 'Christian' notion of marriage, as many people suppose, really brought about all this turmoil, or is there a notion of love abroad in the world which, although we do not yet realize it, renders the marriage bond intolerable in its very essence? It is obvious that Western Man is drawn to what destroys 'the happiness of the married couple' *at least as much* as to anything that ensures it. Where does the contradiction come from? If the breakdown of marriage has been simply due to the attractiveness of the forbidden, it still remains to be seen why we hanker after unhappiness, and what notion of love—what secret of our existence, of the human mind, perhaps of our history—this hankering must hint at.

2

The Myth

There is one great European myth of adultery—the Romance of *Tristan and Iseult*. In the midst of our chaotic conduct, and piercing the jumble of moral systems and immorality which the chaos fosters, there are purely dramatic moments when this mythical shape looms out like a watermark. It is then a bold and simple design, a kind of archetype of our most complex feelings of unrest. And as poets, in order to get away from the current linguistic confusion, are wont to seek the remote origin of a word—the thing or action which this word first denoted—so I wish to connect with this myth part of the disorder in contemporary manners. I am undertaking an *etymology of the passions*, which promises to be less inconclusive than actual etymology, because it is our lives, and not some theoretical science, that will supply its instant verification.

It may at once be asked if the Romance of *Tristan* is indeed a myth, and if in that case to try to analyse it is not to destroy its *charm*. But we are no longer at the stage of supposing that the mythical is tantamount to unreality or illusion. Too many myths now display their indisputable power over us. And yet abuse of the term has made a fresh definition needful. Speaking generally, a myth is a story—a symbolical fable as simple as it is striking—which sums up an infinite number of more or less analogous situations. A myth makes it possible to become aware at a glance of certain types of *constant relations* and to disengage these from the welter of everyday appearances.

More narrowly, a myth expresses the *rules of conduct* of a given social or religious group. It issues accordingly from whatever *sacred* principle has presided over the formation of this group. Symbolical accounts of the life and death of gods, legends accounting for either sacrifices or the origin of taboos, are examples of myths. It has frequently been noted that myths never have an author. The origin of a myth has to be *obscure*, and so to some extent has its meaning. A myth stands forth as the entirely anonymous expression of collective—or, more exactly, of common—facts. Therefore, a work of art—whether poem, tale, or novel—differs radically from a myth. The validity of a work of art depends on nothing but the talent of its author. What matters about it is exactly what does not matter as regards a myth—its 'beauty' or its 'verisimilitude', together with all its qualities of singular success, such as originality, skill, style, etc. *But the most profound characteristic of a myth is the power which it wins over us, usually without our knowing.* If a story, an event, or some leading human figure may turn into a myth, it is precisely by virtue of coming to hold sway over us as though against our will. A work of art, as such, never exerts, properly speaking, any *compulsion* upon its spectators or auditors. However splendid and powerful it may be, it is always open to criticism and can always be enjoyed on individual grounds. With a myth it is otherwise. The statement of a myth disarms all criticism, and reason, if not silenced, becomes at least ineffective.

I propose to consider *Tristan*, not as a piece of literature, but as typical of the relations between man and woman in a particular historical group—the dominant social caste, the courtly society, saturated with chivalry, of the twelfth and thirteenth centuries. The group in question was indeed long ago dissolved. Yet its laws remain our laws in an unsuspected and diluted form. Profaned and repudiated by our official legal codes, these laws have become the more compelling in that they wield no power over us except in our *dreams*.

The Tristan legend has many features indicative of a myth. First of all these is the fact that the author—supposing the legend to have had one, and one only—is entirely unknown. The five 'original' versions that have come down to us are artistic rearrangements of an archetype it is impossible to trace.[1]. Another sign of the mythical in the Tristan legend is its making use of a *sacred* principle.[2] The advance of the action, and the effects which

---

[1] Critical comparision makes it easy to eliminate the individual vagaries of the five authors. When I come below (Chap. 5) to analyse the content of the legend, I shall neglect such variations, because they are very easily accounted for by ephemeral circumstances or else by the personal tastes of each writer.

[2] In order to forestall misconception, I must insist that I am concerned only with the Tristan legend as *written*. That alone is what I refer to wherever I speak of the original myth. No doubt much can be made out of the sacred attri-

this action was intended to have on an auditor, depend (to an extent I hope to make clear) on a set of rules and ceremonies which are no other than those of the custom of medieval chivalry. And the 'orders' of chivalry were often called 'religions'. 'A religion' is what Chastellain, the fifteenth-century Burgundian chronicler, calls the Order of the Golden Fleece—the latest of such orders in point of time—and he refers to it as a sacred mystery, notwithstanding that he wrote at a period when chivalry was no more than a survival.[1] Finally, the very *obscurity* which we find in the legend denotes its deep relation to a myth.

---

butes of the characters of Tristan and Iseult (or Essylt) in Celtic mythology. And unquestionably many details of the bardic oral tradition were incorporated with the legend (cf. Book II, Chap. 12, below). But it is equally certain that none of the five authors—neither Béroul, Thomas, Eilhart, nor the author of the *Roman en prose*, nor the author of *La Folie Tristan*—had been initiated to this tradition. Not one of them is aware of the sacred and symbolical significance originally inhering in the characters whose loves he relates. Moreover, the myth of passionate love is all contained in the legend as this was set down by twelfth-century poets after they had endowed it with a new significance, and *that alone is what is still active within us today.*

[1] J. Huizinga, in *The Waning of the Middle Ages*, translated by F. Hopman (London, 1924), says (p. 56):
'Medieval thought in general was saturated in every part with the conceptions of the Christian faith. In a similar way and in a more limited sphere, the thought of all those who loved in the circles of court or castle was impregnated with the idea of chivalry. . . : This conception even tends to invade the transcendental domain. The primordial feat of arms of the archangel Michael is glorified by Jean Molinet as "the first deed of knighthood and chivalrous prowess that was ever achieved". From the archangel "terrestrial knighthood and human chivalry" take their origin, and in so far are but an imitation of the host of the angels around God's throne.'
Again (p. 57):
'The conception of chivalry constituted for these authors [Froissart, Monstrelet, d'Escouchy, Chastellain, La Marche, etc.] a sort of magic key, by the aid of which they explained to themselves the motives of politics and history. . . . What they saw about them looked primarily mere violence and confusion. War . . . tended to be a chronic process of isolated raids and incursions; diplomacy was mostly a very solemn and very verbose procedure, in which a multitude of questions about juridical details clashed with some very general traditions and some points of honour. All notions which might have enabled them to discern in history a social development were lacking to them. Yet they required a form for their political conceptions, and here the idea of chivalry came in. By this traditional fiction they succeeded in explaining to themselves, as well as they could, the motives and the course of history, which thus was reduced to a spectacle of the honour of princes and the virtue of knights, to a noble game with edifying and heroic rules.'

The Myth

As a rule, the obscurity of a myth does not reside in its form of expression.[1] The obscurity belongs in part to the mystery of the origin of the myth, and in part to the vital import of what the myth symbolizes. If this were not obscure, or *if there were no reason to conceal its origin and its bearing so that it might escape challenge*, a myth would lack a *raison d'être*. A law, a moral treatise, or even some little tale able to serve as a mnemonic summary, would do instead. No myth arises so long as it is possible to keep to the obvious and to express this obvious openly and directly. On the contrary, a myth arises whenever it becomes dangerous or impossible to speak plainly about certain social or religious matters, or affective relations, and yet there is a desire to preserve these or else it is impossible to destroy them. There is, for example, no need of myths nowadays in order to set forth scientific truths, which we deal with from an entirely 'lay' standpoint and which therefore have everything to gain from individual criticism. *But a myth is needed to express the dark and unmentionable fact that passion is linked with death*, and involves the destruction of any one yielding himself up to it with all his strength. For we have wanted to preserve passion and we cherish the unhappiness that it brings with it; and yet at the same time both passion and unhappiness have stood condemned in the sight of official morals and in the sight of reason. Hence, thanks to the obscurity, we have been able to receive and enjoy imaginatively the disguised content of the myth, and yet have not grown sufficiently aware of the nature of this content to be confronted by the contradiction. In this way certain human facts which are, we either realize or suspect, fundamental, have escaped challenge. The myth *expresses* those realities to the extent exacted by our instinct, but it also veils them to the extent that broad daylight and reason[2] might imperil them.

The origins of the mythical romance of *Tristan* are unknown or but half-known, its nature was once *sacred*, and it veils what it is disclosing, so that it may be wondered if it fully possesses the *compelling* features of a true myth. The question is not to be shirked. It carries us into the heart of the problem and shows the

---

[1] Here the form of expression is the language of the poem; and we know that this is extremely simple.

[2] The kind of reason I have in mind here is the 'profaning' activity that operates at the cost of what is collectively sacred and emancipates the individual from the compulsions which this exerts. Although rationalism has been raised to the status of an official doctrine, we ought not to forget its strictly *sacrilegious* anti-social, and 'disruptive' power.

problem to be important for the present day. In the thirteenth century the rules of chivalry did indeed operate with absolute compulsion, but in the romance they are introduced only as a *mythical obstacle* and as *ritualistic figures* of rhetoric. They provide the tale with pretexts for renewals of impetus, and, above all, the tale would not, without them, have been accepted unquestioningly by its audiences. It has to be recognized that these social 'cere-monies' are means of obtaining allowance for an anti-social *content*, and this content is passion. In this context, indeed, the word 'content' acquires its full force. The rules of chivalry liter-ally 'contained' the passion of Tristan and Iseult; and only on that condition was the passion open to being expressed in the twilight of a myth. Because, in being the passion that wants Darkness and triumphs in a transfiguring Death, it must represent, for any society whatsoever, a threat overwhelmingly intolerable. The social groups then in existence had therefore to be capable of with-standing it by means of a strongly framed structure, so that while obtaining an outlet it nevertheless did not do too much damage.

Let the social bonds subsequently slacken, or the social group disintegrate, and the myth must cease to be such in the strict sense. But what it then loses in compelling force and ability to be com-municated in a veiled and tolerable guise, it gains in occult in-fluence and in lawless violence. *Pari passu* with the loss of the last virtues of chivalry, even in the profaned guise of good form—the conventions to be observed by gentlemen—the passion 'con-tained' in the original myth spread out into everyday life, invaded the subconscious, and invoked or, if necessary, invented new com-pulsions. For, as will be shown presently, it was not only the nature of society, but also the very ardour of the dark passion, that required the avowal to be *masked*.

The myth itself, in the strict sense, was formed in the twelfth century, at the very time the leading caste was making a great effort to establish social and moral order. The intention was, indeed, 'to contain' the surges of the destructive instinct; for religion, in attacking this instinct, had been exacerbating it. Con-temporary chronicles, sermons, and satires show that in this cen-tury there occurred an early 'breakdown of marriage', and the breakdown made a vigorous reaction imperative. The achievement of the Romance of *Tristan* was thus to set passion in a framework within which it could be expressed in symbolical satisfactions.[1] Let such a framework disappear, and passion will nevertheless subsist. It will still be as dangerous to the life of society, and will still drive society to attempt a corresponding restoration of order. Hence, not the myth in its original guise, but *that need of a myth* which the Romance met, remains historically permanent.

Enlarging my definition, I shall henceforth intend by the term 'a myth' this permanence of a type of relations together with the corresponding reactions. The myth of Tristan and Iseult I shall consider to be, not merely the Romance, but the peculiarity which the Romance illustrates—something the influence of which has gone on extending all the way down to our own day. The myth that has been agitating us for eight hundred years as spell, terror, or ideal, is at one and the same time a passion sprung from dark nature, an energy excited by the mind, and a pre-established potentiality in search of the coercion that shall intensify it. In having shed its original guise, it has merely become more dangerous. Fallen myths can distil venom even as the dead truths alluded to by Nietzsche.

3

Topicality of the Myth, or Reasons for its Analysis

There is no need to have read Béroul's *Tristan* or M. Bédier's, and no need to have heard Wagner's opera, in order to undergo in the course of everyday life the nostalgic dominion of such a myth. It is manifested in the majority of novels and films, in the popularity these enjoy with the masses, the acceptance

---

[1] Rather with the same aim and to the same effect, the Church took paganism into its ritual.

which they meet with in the hearts of middle-class people, from poets, from ill-assorted couples, and from the seamstresses who dream of having a miraculous love-affair. The myth operates wherever passion is dreamed of as an ideal instead of being feared like a malignant fever; wherever its fatal character is welcomed, invoked, or imagined as a magnificent and desirable disaster instead of as simply a disaster. It lives upon the lives of people who think that love is their fate (and as unavoidable as the effect of the love-potion is in the Romance); that it swoops upon powerless and ravished men and women in order to consume them in a pure flame; or that it is stronger and more real than happiness, society, or morality. It lives upon the very life of the romanticism within us; it is the great mystery of that religion of which the poets of the nineteenth century made themselves the priests and prophets.

Of this influence, and that it is the influence of a myth, there is immediate evidence, evidence provided in this very place by the reader's reluctance to face squarely what it is I am proposing to do. The Romance of Tristan is 'sacred' for us precisely to the extent that it seems 'sacrilegious' on my part to attempt to analyse it. No doubt the charge of sacrilege now has a very mild quality. In primitive societies it resulted, not in the reluctance which I anticipate, but in the execution of the guilty person. The sacred which is involved here amounts to no more than an obscure and weak survival. The only risk I run is that the reader may close the book at this point, and not open it again. True, the unconscious intent of such an act does not fall short of getting me put to death, but the intent is without effect. However, supposing you spare me, dear Reader, am I to conclude that the passion is not sacred for you? Possibly people are nowadays as feeble in passion as in acts of reproof. In the absence of open foes, perhaps it is against themselves that writers must show the daring which is being demanded of them, and perhaps it is only the enemy in our own breasts that we can really contend with.

I confess I was vexed to find one commentator describing the Tristan legend as 'an epic of adultery'. The phrase may be accurate enough in respect of the dry bones of the Romance. That does not make it any the less vexatious and 'prosaically' narrow. I doubt if it can be maintained that the real subject of the legend is the moral fault. How assert that Wagner's *Tristan*, for example, is no more than an opera about adultery? For that matter, is adultery

but a nasty word, or a breach of contract? Adultery is that too, and in all too many cases no more than that. But it often is a great deal more—a passionate and tragic atmosphere beyond good and evil, and a drama either lofty or dreadful; in short, a drama—a *romance*. And 'romanticism' derives from 'romance'.

The problem expands splendidly—and my case worsens proportionately. I shall set out my reasons for going on, and it can then be decided if they are diabolical. First, social confusion has now reached a point at which the pursuit of immorality turns out to be more exhausting than compliance with the old moral codes. The cult of passionate love has been *democratized* so far as to have lost its aesthetic virtues together with its spiritual and tragic values; and we are left with a dull and diluted pain, something unclean and gloomy. In profaning the falsely sacred causes of this, I cannot believe that we have anything to lose. The literature dealing with passion, the advertising which passion gets, the business-like 'vogue' of what used to be a religious secret—all that needs to be attacked and made war upon, if only to rescue the myth from being abused in its excessive popularization. And whatever sacrilege we may thereby commit will not matter; for poetry has other outlets.

My second reason is a desire to be quite clear about contemporary life. I fasten upon the Tristan myth because it enables me to offer a *simple explanation* of our present confusion and at the same time to set forth certain *permanent relations* which the scrupulous vulgarities of current psychologies submerge. Furthermore, I can lay bare a particular *dilemma*, the stern reality of which we are in process of overlooking as a result of our frenzied living, the state of our culture, and the purr of current moral doctrines.

To raise up the myth of passion in its primitive and sacred vigour and in its monumental integrity, as a salutary comment upon our tortuous connivances and inability to choose boldly between the Norm of Day and the Passion of Night—such is my first purpose. It means raising up that image of the Dying Lovers which is excited by the disturbing and vampire-like crescendo of Wagner's second act. And what I aim at is to bring the reader to the point of declaring frankly, either that 'That is what I wanted!' or else 'God forbid!'

I am not certain that complete self-awareness is useful either in a general way or *per se*. I do not hold that practical truths can be made plain in the market place. But whatever the 'usefulness' of

my undertaking, we who dwell in the Western world are destined
to become more and more aware of the illusions on which we
subsist. And possibly it is the job of philosophers, moralists, and
creators of ideal forms, simply to increase our self-awareness—
the consciousness which is of course also a bad conscience.

With that I pass to the promised analysis. Remaining deaf and
blind to the 'charms' of the tale, I am going to try to summarize
'objectively' the events it relates and the reasons which it either
gives for these events or very oddly omits.

4

What the Tristan Romance[1] Seems
to be About

Amors par force vos demeine!—BÉROUL.

Tristan is born in misfortune. His father has just died, and
Blanchefleur, his mother, does not survive his birth. Hence
his name, the sombre hue of his life, and the lowering
stormy sky that hangs over the legend. King Mark of Cornwall,
Blanchefleur's brother, takes the orphan into his castle at Tintagel
and brings him up there.

[1] In summing up the chief episodes of the Romance, I shall make use (except
here and there) of M. Bédier's *Concordance* (contained in his study of Thomas's
poem) for the five twelfth-century versions—those by Béroul, Thomas and
Eilhart together with *La Folie Tristan* and *Le Roman en prose*. The later versions
by Gottfried of Strasbourg, or by German, Italian, Danish, Russian, Czech, and
other imitators, are all derived from those five. I also take into account the more
recent critical undertakings of Messrs. E. Muret and E. Vinaver.

What the Tristan Romance Seems to be About

Tristan presently performs an early feat of prowess. He vanquishes the Morholt. This Irish giant has come like a Minotaur. to exact his tribute of Cornish maidens or youths. Tristan is of an age for knighthood—that is, he has just reached puberty—and he obtains leave to fight him. The Morholt is killed, but not before he has wounded Tristan with a poisoned barb. Having no hope of recovery, Tristan begs to be put on board a boat that is cast adrift with neither sail nor oar. He takes his sword and harp with him.

He lands in Ireland. There is only one remedy that can save him, and, as it happens, the Queen of Ireland is alone in knowing its secret. But the giant Morholt was this queen's brother, and so Tristan is careful not to disclose his name or to explain how he has come by his wound. Iseult, the queen's daughter, nurses him and restores him to health. That is the Prologue.

A few years later a bird has brought to King Mark a golden hair. The king determines to marry the woman from whose head the hair has come. It is Tristan whom he selects to go in quest of her. A storm causes the hero to be cast ashore once again in Ireland. There he fights and kills a dragon that was threatening the capital. (This is the conventional motif of a virgin delivered by a young paladin.) Having been wounded by the dragon, Tristan is again nursed by Iseult. One day she learns that the wounded stranger is no other than the man who killed her uncle. She seizes Tristan's sword and threatens to transfix him in his bath. It is then that he tells her of the mission on which he has been sent by King Mark. And Iseult spares him, for she would like to be a queen. (According to some of the authors, she spares him also because she then finds him handsome.)

Tristan and the princess set sail for Cornwall. At sea the wind drops and the heat grows oppressive. They are thirsty. Brengain, Iseult's maid, gives them a drink. But by mistake she pours out the 'wine of herbs' which the queen, Iseult's mother, has brewed for King Mark and his bride after they shall have wed. Tristan and Iseult drink it. The effect is to commit them to a fate from 'which they can never escape during the remainder of their lives, *for they have drunk their destruction and death*'. They confess that they are now in love, and fall into one another's arms.

(Let it be noted here that according to the archetypal version, which Béroul alone has followed, the effect of the love-potion is

27

limited to three years.[1] Thomas, a sensitive psychologist and highly suspicious of marvels, which he considers crude, minimizes the importance of the love-potion as far as possible, and depicts the love of Tristan and Iseult as having occurred spontaneously. Its first signs he places as early as the episode of the bath. On the other hand, Eilhart, Gottfried, and most of the others attribute un-limited effect to the magic wine. Nothing could be more significant than these variations, as we shall see.)

Thus the fault is perpetrated. *Yet Tristan is still in duty bound to fulfil the mission with which King Mark has entrusted him.* So, not-withstanding his betrayal of the king, he delivers Iseult to him. On the wedding night Brengain, thanks to a ruse, takes Iseult's place in the royal bed, thus saving her mistress from dishonour and at the same time expiating the irretrievable mistake she made in pouring out the love-potion.

Presently, however, four 'felon' barons of the king's go and tell their sovereign that Tristan and Iseult are lovers. Tristan is banished to Tintagel town. But thanks to another trick—the episode of the pine-tree in the orchard—Mark is convinced of his innocence and allows him to return to the castle. Then Frocin the Dwarf, who is in league with the barons, lays a trap in order to establish the lovers' guilt. In the spear-length between Tristan's bed and the queen's he scatters flour, and persuades Mark to order Tristan to ride to King Arthur at Carduel the next morning at dawn. Tristan is determined to embrace his mistress once more before he rides away. To avoid leaving his foot-marks in the flour he leaps across from his own bed to the queen's. But the effort reopens a wound in his leg inflicted the previous day by a boar. Led by Frocin, the king and the barons burst into the bedchamber. They find the flour blood-stained. Mark is satisfied with this evidence of adultery. Iseult is handed over to a party of a hundred lepers, and Tristan is sentenced to the stake. On the way to

---

[1] Verses 2137-2140:

> A conbien fu determinez
> Li lovendrins, li vin herbez:
> La mere Yseut, qui le bolli,
> A trois anz d'amistié le fist.

The quotation is from Béroul, as are those in Chapter 8, below. I follow A. Ewert's text (*The Romance of Tristan* (Oxford, Blackwell, 1939)), which is later than E. Muret, and I am also indebted to Ewert's glossary for my trans-lations. 'For how long was the love potion, the herb wine? Mother Yseut, who brewed it, made it to three years of love.'—Translator's Note.

execution, however, he is allowed to go into a chantry on the cliff's edge. He forces a window and leaps over the cliff, thus effecting his escape. He rescues Iseult from the lepers, and together they go and hide in the depths of the Forest of Morrois. There for three years they lead a life 'harsh and hard'. It happens one day that Mark comes upon them while they are asleep. But on this occasion Tristan has put between Iseult and himself his drawn sword. Moved by this evidence of innocence, as he supposes it to be, the king spares them. Without waking them, he takes up Tristan's sword and sets his own in its place.

At the end of three years the potency of the love-potion wears off (according to Béroul and the common ancestor of the five versions). It is only then that Tristan repents, and that Iseult wishes she were a queen again. Together they seek out the hermit Ogrin, through whom Tristan offers peace to the king, saying he will surrender Iseult. Mark promises forgiveness. As the royal procession approaches, the lovers part. But before this happens Iseult has besought Tristan to stay in the neighbourhood till he has made certain that Mark is treating her well. Then, with a final display of feminine wiles, she follows up her advantage in having persuaded Tristan to agree to this, and declares she will join him at the first sign he makes, for nothing shall stop her from doing his will, 'neither tower, nor wall, nor stronghold'.

They have several secret meetings in the hut of Orri the Woodman. But the felon barons are keeping watch and ward over the queen's virtue. She asks and is granted 'a Judgement of God'. Thanks to a subterfuge, the ordeal is a success. Before she grasps the red-hot iron which will not harm one who has spoken the truth, she swears that no man has ever held her in his arms except the king and a poor pilgrim who has just carried her ashore from a boat. And the poor pilgrim is Tristan in disguise.

However, fresh adventures carry Tristan far away from Iseult, and he then comes to suppose that she no longer loves him. So he agrees to marry 'for her beauty and her name'[1] another Iseult, Iseult 'of the White Hand'. And indeed this Iseult remains unstained, for after their marriage Tristan still sighs for 'Iseult the Fair'.

At last, wounded by a poisoned spear and about to die, Tristan sends for the queen from Cornwall, she who alone can save his life. She comes, and as her ship draws near it hoists a white sail

[1] 'Pur belté e pur nun d'Isolt' (Thomas).

as a sign of hope. But Iseult of the White Hand has been on the look-out, and, tormented by jealousy, she runs to Tristan and tells him that the sail is black. Tristan dies. As he does so, Iseult the Fair lands, and on arriving at the castle, she lies down beside her dead lover and clasps him close. Then she dies too.

5

Some Riddles

Thus summarized, and with all the 'charm' destroyed, the most absorbing of poems appears, on cool consideration, to be straightforward neither in its matter nor in its progression. I have passed over numerous accessory episodes, but over none of the motives alleged for the central action. Indeed, these motives I have rather stressed. They have been seen not to amount to much. Tristan delivers up Iseult to the king, *because* bound by the fealty of a knight. At the end of the three years spent in the forest, the lovers part, *because* the love-potion has lost its potency. Tristan marries Iseult of the White Hand '*for her beauty and her name*'. If these 'reasons' are discounted—although we shall return to them—the Romance turns out to depend on a series of puzzling contradictions.

I have been struck by the passing comment of one recent editor of the legend. All through the Romance Tristan is made to appear the physical superior of all his foes and particularly of the king. It follows that no external power prevents him from carrying off Iseult and thus fulfilling his fate. The manners of the time sanctioned the rights of the stronger; they made these rights divine without qualification; and this was especially the case with a man's rights over a woman. *Why does Tristan not take advantage of these rights?*

Put on the alert by this first question, our critical suspicions lead us to discover other riddles, no less curious and obscure. *Why has the sword of chastity been placed between the two sleepers in the forest?* The lovers have already sinned, and they refuse to repent just then. Furthermore, they do not expect that the king will discover them. Yet in all five versions there is neither a line nor a word to explain the sword.[1] Again, *why does Tristan restore the queen to Mark*, even in those versions where at that time the love-potion is still active? If, as some say, the lovers part because they now sincerely repent, why do they promise one another to meet again in the moment they undertake to part? And why later does Tristan go forth upon fresh adventures when he and Iseult have made a tryst in the forest? Why does the guilty queen ask for 'a Judgement of God'? She must know that the ordeal is bound to go against her. It is only successful thanks to a trick improvised at the last moment; and this trick, it is implied, deceives God Himself, since the miracle ensues.[2] Moreover, the judgement having gone in the queen's favour, her innocence is thereupon taken for granted. But if she is innocent, so is Tristan; and it becomes quite impossible to see what prevents his return to the king's castle, and *hence to Iseult's side.*

At the same time it is surely very odd that thirteenth-century poets—so punctilious in matters of honour and suzerain fealty—should let pass without a word of comment so much thoroughly indefensible behaviour. How can they hold up Tristan as a model of chivalry when he betrays his king with the most shameless cunning, or the queen as a virtuous lady when she is not only an adulteress, but does not shrink from committing an astute blasphemy? On the other hand, why do they call 'felons' the four barons who defend Mark's honour and who, even if actuated by

---

[1] It is true that in Bédier's edition of Thomas's poem (Vol. I, p. 240), the king's huntsman is said to have gone to the lovers' retreat, where he has seen 'Tristan' lying asleep, and across the cave was Iseult. The lovers were resting from the great heat, and lay apart from one another because . . . .' At this point the text breaks off! And Bédier notes: 'An unintelligible passage.' What diabolical agency can have partly destroyed *the one text* likely to have solved the riddle?

[2] Gottfried of Strasbourg brazenly insists:
'Twas thus made manifest
And averr'd before all
That Christ most glorious
Will mould like cloth for garments.
. . . He complies with ev'ry one's wish,
Whether honest or deceitful.
He ever is as we would have Him be.

jealousy, neither deceive nor betray (which is more than can be said of Tristan?

Even the validity of what few motives are mentioned remains open to question. For if the rule of suzerain fealty required that Tristan should deliver to Mark the betrothed he had been to fetch,[1] his compliance with this rule must seem both very belated and hardly sincere, inasmuch as once he has delivered up Iseult he knows no rest till he has contrived to get back into the castle and is with her again. And as the love-potion was brewed for Mark and his queen, it must be wondered why its potency is not permanent. Three years of married bliss are not much. And when Tristan marries another Iseult 'for her beauty and her name', but does not touch her, it is surely obvious that nothing has compelled him either to marry or to be guilty of his insulting chastity, and that by marrying a woman whom he cannot make his wife he has put himself into a position from which the only way out is death.

6

Chivalry v. Marriage

The Romance of *Tristan and Iseult* brings home to us the antagonism which grew up in the second half of the twelfth century between the rule of chivalry and feudal custom. Perhaps the extent to which the Arthurian romances reflect and foster this antagonism has not hitherto attracted the notice it deserves. In all likelihood, courtly chivalry was never more than an ideal. The earliest writers to mention it commonly lament its decay, but in doing so they overlook that in the form which they would like it to assume it has only just come into existence in their dreams. It is of the essence of an ideal that its decay should be

[1] But to whom he had won a full title *himself* by delivering her from the dragon, as Thomas does not omit to stress.

Chivalry v. Marriage

lamented in the very moment it is clumsily striving for fulfilment. Moreover, to contrast the *fiction* of some ideal of living with tyrannical reality is precisely something possible in a romance. A preliminary answer to several of the riddles propounded by the legend can be sought in this direction. Once it is granted that Tristan's experience was intended to illustrate a conflict between chivalry and feudal society—and hence a conflict between two kinds of *duty* and even between two 'religions'[1]—a number of episodes are made intelligible. At any rate, even if not disposing of every difficulty, the hypothesis significantly delays a solution.

Arthurian romance, which supplanted the *chanson de geste* with astonishing swiftness in the middle of the twelfth century, differs from this *chanson* in that it allots to a woman the part formerly taken by a suzerain. An Arthurian knight, exactly like a troubadour of the South, regarded himself as the vassal of some chosen Lady, when, actually, he remained the vassal of a lord; and this gave rise to a number of conflicting claims of which the Romance supplies examples.

Let me go back to the three 'felon' barons. According to feudal morals, it was the duty of a vassal to warn his lord of anything that might endanger the latter's rights or honour. He was a 'felon' if he did not. Now, in *Tristan* the barons go and tell King Mark how Iseult is behaving. They should therefore be considered feal and true. If, then, the author refers to them as 'felons', he must evidently do so in virtue of some other code, which can only be the code of southern chivalry. For instance, according to a well-known judgement delivered by the Gascon courts of love, whosoever discloses the secrets of courtly love is a felon. The single instance is enough to show that the authors of the different versions of the Romance were deliberately siding with 'courtly' chivalry against feudal law. But there are further grounds for thinking so. Alone the view of fidelity and of marriage that was adopted in courtly love will explain some of the striking contradictions in the tale.

According to the theory officially received, courtly love arose as a reaction to the brutal lawlessness of feudal manners. It is well known that the nobles in the twelfth century made of marriage simply a means of enriching themselves, either through the annexation of dower estates or through expectations of inheritance. When a 'deal' turned out badly, the wife was repudiated. The

[1] As was hinted at on p. 20, above.

33

plea of incest was exploited in curious ways, and in the face of it the Church was powerless. To allege a consanguinity of even the fourth degree, no matter on what slender evidence, was enough to secure an annulment. In order to counteract these abuses, which led to much quarrelling and to warring, courtly love established a *fealty* that was independent of legal marriage and of which the sole basis was love. It was even contended—for example, in the famous judgement delivered by a court of love in the house of the Countess of Champagne[1]—that love and marriage were incompatible. If such is the view of both Tristan and the author of the Romance, the sense given to the terms 'felony' and 'adultery' is thereby justified—indeed, more than justified, extolled, inasmuch as it implies an intrepid loyalty to the higher law of the *donnoi* or courtly love. (*Donnoi*, or *domnei*, is the Provençal name for the vassal-relation set up between a knight-lover and his lady, or *domina*.)

As has been said, this loyalty was incompatible with the fidelity of marriage. The Romance misses no opportunity of disparaging the social institution of marriage and of humiliating husbands—e.g. the king with horse's ears who is always being so easily deceived—as well as of glorifying the virtue of men and women who love outside, and in despite of, marriage. This courtly loyalty, however, displays one curious feature. It is opposed to the 'satisfaction' of love as much as to marriage. 'Of *donnoi* he knows truly nothing who wants fully to possess his lady. *Whatever turns into a reality is no longer love.*'[2] Here is something that puts us on the track of a preliminary explanation of such episodes as that of the sword of chastity, of Iseult's return to her lord after staying in the Forest of Morrois, and even of Tristan's nominal marriage.

The 'claims of passion', as understood today, would entitle Tristan to carry off Iseult as soon as he and she had drunk the love-potion. Instead he delivers her to Mark, and he does so because

---

[1] The judgement reads as follows: 'We declare and affirm, by the tenour of these presents, that love cannot extend its rights over two married persons. For indeed lovers grant one another all things mutually and freely, without being impelled by any motive of necessity, whereas husband and wife are held by their duty to submit their wills to each other and to refuse each other nothing.

'May this judgement, which we have delivered with extreme caution, and after consulting with a great number of other ladies, be for you a constant and unassailable truth, Delivered in this year 1174, on the third day before the Kalends of May, Proclamation VII.'

Claude Fauriel, *Histoire de la poésie provençale* (Paris, 1846), I, p. 512.

the rule of courtly love did not allow a passion of this kind 'to turn into a reality', to result in the 'full possession of his lady'. Accordingly, Tristan chooses to respect feudal fealty, which is thus made to disguise and equivocally to abet courtly fealty. He chooses quite freely; for, as was noted above, being stronger than the king and the barons, he could—*on the feudal plane upon which he puts himself*—resort to the right of force.

What a strange love (it will be thought) that thus conforms to laws whereby it stands condemned in order the better to preserve itself! Whence arises this preference for whatever *thwarts* passion, hinders the lovers' 'happiness', and parts and torments them? To reply that so courtly love required is only to reply super-ficially; for this still leaves it to be ascertained why love of this kind is preferred to the other, the love that gets 'fulfilled' and 'satisfied'. With the help of the highly plausible theory that the Romance illustrates a conflict between 'religions', we have been able to specify and set forth the main difficulties raised by the plot; but really we have only succeeded in deferring a solution of the problem.

7

The Love of the Romance

In my summary of the legend, one thing in particular must have struck us. The two codes that come into play—chivalry and feudal morals—are respected by the author *only in those situations where his respecting them makes it possible for the tale to move forward again*.[1] In itself this explains nothing. It is all too easy to dispose

---

[1] I should make this quite clear. 1. The codes are respected each in turn as the result of a secret calculation; for if either was chosen to the entire exclusion of the other, the situation would be resolved too soon. 2. The codes are not always respected: for instance, when the lovers sin together as soon as they have drunk

of every one of our questions by saying: Events happen thus because *otherwise* there would be no story. Such a reply will appear convincing only owing to a lazy custom of literary criticism. Actually, it answers nothing. It simply raises the fundamental question: Why has there to be a story? And *this* story in particular? There is an unconscious wisdom in calling such a question ingenuous, for it is not asked without peril. In fact, it carried us into the heart of the problem; and undoubtedly it involves far more than the particular case of this myth.

If, by an effort of abstraction, we place ourselves outside the process common to both novelist and reader so that we can over-hear the intimate dialogue that goes on between them, we see that a tacit convention, or, rather, a mutual *encouragement*, unites them. They both wish the novel to go on, or, as the saying is, to rebound. Suppress that *wish*, and there can be no verisimilitude whatsoever. This is exemplified in scientific history. The reader of a 'serious' book is all the more exacting for being aware that neither his wishes nor the author's fancies can govern the sequence of events. Suppose, instead, these wishes to operate un-checked, and then nothing is too far-fetched. That is the situation for fiction. Between the two extremes there are as many levels of verisimilitude as there are plots. Or, if you like, what shall be verisimilitude in any given piece of literary fiction depends on the nature of the passions which this piece of fiction is intended to please. In short, a reader pays no need to distortions or to twist-ings of the 'logic' of current observation so long as the licence thus taken produces the *pretexts* necessary to the passion which he longs to feel. Hence it is in the kink of 'tricks of the trade' employed by the author that the real plot of a given piece of fiction is disclosed, and a reader condones these tricks precisely to the extent that he shares the author's intentions.[1]

I have shown that the external barriers to the fulfilment of Tristan's love are in one sense arbitrary, and, after all, only fictional contrivances. And it follows from what has just been said about verisimilitude that it is precisely the arbitrary character

the love-potion they are committing a sin according to courtly love just as much as according to Christian and feudal morality. But were it not for that first fault there would be no romance at all.

[1] The twentieth-century detective story is the best illustration of this. Veri-similitude there becomes a function of the amateur's 'technical' pleasure and is nothing else.

of the obstructions introduced into a tale that may show what this tale is really about and what is the real nature of the passion it is concerned with. In this respect everything, it must be realized, is symbolical. Everything holds together and is connected after the manner of a *dream*, and not in accordance with our lives. This is equally true of the pretexts devised by the author, the conduct of his two leading characters, and the secret inclinations which he assumes to exist in his reader. The events narrated are but images or projections of a longing and of whatever runs counter to this longing, excites it, or merely protracts it. Everything the knight and princess do betrays that they act in virtue of a necessity they are unaware of—and that perhaps the author has been unaware of too—but *that is stronger than the need of their happiness*. Objectively, not one of the barriers to the fulfilment of their love is insuperable, and yet each time they give up. It is not too much to say that they never miss a chance of getting parted. When there is no obstruction, they invent one, as in the case of the drawn sword and of Tristan's marriage. They invent obstructions as if on purpose, notwithstanding that such barriers are their bane. Can it be in order to please author and reader? It is all one; for the demon of courtly love which prompts the lovers in their inmost selves to the devices that are the cause of their pain is the very demon of *the novel* as we in the West like it to be.

What, then, is the legend really about? The partings of the lovers? Yes, but in the name of passion, and for love of the very love that agitates them, in order that this love may be intensified and transfigured—at the cost of their happiness and even of their lives.

The secret and disturbing significance of the myth is beginning to loom out—the *peril* it at once expresses and veils, the passion to which to yield is like a swoon. But it is too late to turn away. We are affected, we are under the spell, we grow alive to the 'exquisite anguish'. It would be idle to condemn; swooning cannot be condemned. But is it not a philosopher's passion to meditate in the act of swooning? Perhaps knowledge is but the effort of a mind that resists the headlong fall and holds back in the midst of temptation.

8

The Love of Love

'De tous les maux, le mien diffère; il me plaît; je me réjouis de lui; mon mal est ce que je veux et ma douleur est ma santé. Je ne vois donc pas de quoi je me plains; car mon mal me vient de ma volonté; c'est mon vouloir qui devient mon mal; mais j'ai tant d'aise à vouloir ainsi que je souffre agréablement, et tant de joie dans me douleur que je suis malade avec délices.'—CHRESTIEN DE TROYES.[1]

It is only 'silly' questions that can enlighten us; for behind whatever seems obvious lurks something that is not. Let us then boldly ask: Does Tristan care for Iseult, and she for him? The lovers do not seem to be brought together in any normal *human* way. On the contrary, at their first encounter they confine themselves to having ordinary polite relations; and later, when Tristan returns to Ireland to fetch Iseult, the politeness, it will be remembered, gives place to open hostility. Everything goes to show that they would never have chosen one another were they acting *freely*. But no sooner have they drunk the love-potion than passion flares between them. Yet that any fondness supervenes to unite them as a result of the magic spell I have found, among the thousands of lines of the Romance, only a single indication. When, following Tristan's escape, it has been told how they have gone to live in the Forest of Morrois, there occur these lines:

> Aspre vie meinent et dure:
> Tant s'entraiment de bone amor
> L'un por l'autre ne sent dolor.[2]

---

[1] 'From all other ills doth mine differ. It pleaseth me; I rejoice at it; my ill is what I want and my suffering is my health. So I do not see what I am complaining about; for my ill comes to me by my will; it is my willing that becomes my ill; but I am so pleased to want thus that I suffer agreeably, and have so much joy in my pain that I am sick with delight.'

[2] 'Harsh life led they and hard, so entertaining good love for one another. One by the other was ne'er exposed to pain.'

The Love of Love

If it should be imagined that poets in the Middle Ages were less emotional than we have grown to be and felt no need to insist on what goes without saying, let the account of the three years in the forest be read attentively. Its two finest passages—which are no doubt also the most profound passages in the whole legend—describe the lovers' two visits to the hermit Ogrin. The first time they go to see him, it is in order to make confession. But instead of confessing their sin and asking for absolution, they do their best to convince him that they are not to blame for what has befallen, since after all *they do not care for one another!*

> Q'el m'aime, c'est par la poison
> Ge ne me pus de lié partir,
> N'ele de moi——[1]

So speaks Tristan, and Iseult says after him:

> Sire, por Deu omnipotent,
> Il ne m'aime pas, ne je lui,
> Fors par un herbé dont je bui
> Et il en but: ce fu pechiez.[2]

They are thus in a thrillingly contradictory position. They love, but not one another. They have sinned, but cannot repent; for they are not to blame. They make confession, but wish neither to reform nor even to beg forgiveness. Actually, then, like all other great lovers, they imagine that they have been ravished 'beyond good and evil' into a kind of transcendental state outside ordinary human experience, into an ineffable absolute irreconcilable with the world, but that they feel to be *more real than the world.* Their oppressive fate, even though they yield to it with wailings, obliterates the antithesis of good and evil, and carries them away beyond the source of moral values, beyond pleasure and pain, beyond the realm of distinctions—into a realm where opposites cancel out.

Their admission is explicit enough: 'Il ne m'aime pas, ne je lui.' Everything happens as if they could neither see nor recognize one another. They are the prisoners of 'exquisite anguish'

---

[1] 'If she loves me, it is by the poison which holds me from leaving her and her from leaving me.'

[2] 'Lord, by almighty God, he loves me not, nor I him; except for a herb potion which I drank and which he drank; it was a sin.'

owing to something which neither controls—some alien power independent of their capacities, or at any rate of their conscious wishes, and of their being in so far as they are aware of being. Both characters, the man as much as the woman, are depicted physically and psychologically in an entirely conventional and rhetorical manner. He is 'the strongest'; she, 'the most beautiful'; he, the knight; she, the princess; and so on. It is impossible to believe that any human feeling can grow between two such rudimentary characters. The friendship mentioned in connexion with the length of time the effect of the love-potion lasts is the opposite of a true friendship; and, what is still more striking, if moral friendship does at last appear, it is at the moment their passion declines. And the immediate consequence of their nascent friendship, far from being to knit them more closely together, is to make them feel that they have everything to gain from a separation. This last point deserves to be considered more closely.

> L'endemain de la saint Jehan
> Aconpli furent li troi an.[1]

Tristan is out in the forest after game. Suddenly he is reminded of the world. He sees in his mind's eye King Mark's castle. He sighs for 'the vair and grey' and for the pomp of chivalry. He thinks of the high rank he might hold among his uncle's barons. He thinks too of his beloved—apparently for the first time! But for him she might be 'in fine rooms . . . hung with cloth of silk'. Simultaneously Iseult is filled with similar regrets. In the evening they are together and they confess to one another what is newly agitating them—'en mal uson nostre jovente'. It does not take them long to agree to part. Tristan talks of making off to Brittany. But first they will seek out Ogrin the Hermit and beg his forgiveness—and at the same time King Mark's forgiveness of Iseult.

It is at this point that there occurs a highly dramatic short dialogue between the hermit and the two penitents:

> Amors par force vos demeine![2]
> Conbien durra vostre folie?
> Trop avez mené ceste vie.

---

[1] 'On the morrow of St John's Day, the three years were accomplished.'

[2] 'Love by force dominates you. How long will your folly last? Too long you have been leading this life.' *Amors par force vos demeine*—the most poignant description of passion ever penned by a poet! We must pause to admire it. In a

The Love of Love

So Ogrin admonishes them.

> Tristan li dist: or escoutez[1]
> Si longuement l'avons menee
> Itel fu nostre destinee.

On top of this comes one more feature. When Tristan hears that the king agrees to Iseult's return:

> Dex! dist Tristan, quel departie![2]
> Molt est dolenz qui pert s'amie!

It is with his own pain that he commiserates; not a thought for 's'amie'! And she too, we are made to feel, finds it much more pleasant to be back with the king than she ever did with her lover—happier in the unhappiness of love than she ever was in the life they led together in the Morrois.

For that matter, later on—as we have seen—passion seizes the lovers again, notwithstanding that the effect of the love-potion has worn off, and this time they are so carried away that they die —'he by her, she by him'. The seeming *selfishness* of their love is enough to account for the many 'chance' happenings and tricks of fate that obstruct their attainment of happiness. But this selfishness, in its profound ambiguity, still wants explaining. Selfishness, it is said, always ends in death. But that is as a final defeat. Theirs, on the contrary, requires death for its perfect fulfilment and triumph. To the problem this raises there is only one answer worthy of the myth.

Tristan and Iseult do not love one another. They say they don't, and everything goes to prove it. *What they love is love and being in love.* They behave as if aware that whatever obstructs love must ensure and consolidate it in the heart of each and intensify it infinitely in the moment they reach the absolute obstacle, which is death. Tristan loves the awareness that he is loving far more than he loves Iseult the Fair. And Iseult does nothing to hold Tristan. All she needs is her passionate dream. Their need of one another is in order to be aflame, and they do not need one another

---

single line the whole of passion is summed up with a vigour of expression making all romanticism look pallid! Shall we ever recover this sturdy 'dialect of the heart'?

[1] 'Tristan quoth to him: "Now hearken, if for long we have been leading this life, that is because it was our destiny."'

[2] 'God!' quoth Tristan, 'What a fate! Wretched he who loseth his mistress.'

as they are. What they need is not one another's presence, but one another's absence. *Thus the partings of the lovers are dictated by their passion itself*, and by the love they bestow on their passion rather than on its satisfaction or on its living object. That is why the Romance abounds in obstructions, why when mutually encouraging their joint dream in which each remains solitary they show such astounding indifference, and why events work up in a romantic climax to a fatal apotheosis.

The duality is at once irrevocable and deliberate. 'Mot est dolenz qui pert s'amie,' Tristan sighs: and yet he then already sees, glimmering in the depths of the approaching night, that hidden flame which absence rekindles.

9

The Love of Death

But we must push on further still. Augustine's *amabam amare* is a poignant phrase with which he himself was not content. I have repeatedly referred to *obstruction*, and there is the way in which the passion of the two lovers *creates obstruction*, its effects coinciding with those of narrative necessity and of the reader's suspense. Is this obstruction not simply a *pretext* needed in order to enable the passion to progress, or is it connected with the passion in some far more profound manner? If we delve into the recesses of the myth, we see that this obstruction is what passion really *wants*—its true object.

I have shown that the Romance is given its motive power by the repeated partings and reunions of the lovers. For convenience, here once more, briefly, is what happens. Tristan, having landed in Ireland, meets Iseult and then parts from her without being in love. He turns up in Ireland again, and this time Iseult wants to kill him. They take ship together and drink the love-potion, and then sin. Next, Iseult is delivered up to Mark, and Tristan is banished from the castle. He and Iseult meet under a pine-tree, their talk being overheard by Mark. Tristan comes back to the castle, and Frocin and the barons discover evidence of his crime. They are parted. They meet again, and for three years go to live in the forest. Then, once more, they part. They meet at the hut of Orri the Woodman. Tristan goes away. He comes back, disguised as a poor pilgrim. He goes away again. The separation this time is prolonged, and he marries Iseult of the White Hand. Iseult the Fair is about to rejoin him when he dies. She dies too. More briefly still: They have one long spell together ('L'aspre vie'— 'The harsh life'), to which corresponds a lengthy separation—and Tristan's marriage. First, the love-potion; lastly, the death of both. In between, furtive meetings.

They are led to part so often either by adverse external circumstances or by hindrances which Tristan devises; and it is to be noted that Tristan's behaviour varies according to which kind of cause is operating. When social circumstances—for example, Mark's presence, the barons' suspiciousness, the Judgement of God—threaten the lovers, Tristan leaps over the obstruction (this is symbolized by his leap from his own bed to the queen's). He then does not mind pain (his wound reopens) nor the danger to his life (he knows he is being spied upon). Passion is then so violent—so brutish, it might be said—that in the intoxication of his *déduit* (or delight) he is oblivious to pain and perils alike. Nevertheless, the blood flowing from his wound betrays him. This is the 'red stain' that apprises the king of what is happening. And it also apprises the reader of the lovers' secret—that they are seeking peril for its own sake. But so long as the peril comes from without, Tristan's prowess in overcoming it is an affirmation of life. At this stage Tristan is simply complying with the feudal practice of knights. He has to prove his 'valour' and show he is either the stronger or the more wily. We have seen that if he persevered in this direction he would carry off the queen, and that established law is only respected here because this gives the tale an excuse to rebound.

But the knight's demeanour becomes quite different when nothing external any longer separates the two lovers. Indeed, it becomes the opposite of what it has been. When Tristan puts his drawn sword between himself and Iseult although they are lying down fully clothed, this is again prowess, but on this occasion against himself, *to his own cost*. Since he himself has set up the obstruction, it is no longer one *he can overcome!* It must not be overlooked that the hierarchy of events corresponds closely to the hierarchy of both the story-teller's and the reader's *preferences*. The most serious obstruction is thus the one preferred above all. It is the one must suited to intensifying passion. At this extreme, furthermore, the wish to part assumes an emotional value *greater than that of passion itself*. Death, in being the goal of passion, kills it.

Yet the drawn sword is not the ultimate expression of the dark desire and of the actual *end* of passion (in both senses of the word 'end'). The admirable episode of the exchange of swords makes this clear. When the king comes upon the lovers lying asleep in the cave, he substitutes his own sword for that of his rival. The meaning of this is that in place of the obstruction which the lovers have wanted and have deliberately set up he puts the sign of his social prerogative, a legal and objective obstruction. Tristan accepts the challenge, and thereby enables the *action* of the tale to rebound. At this point the word 'action' takes on a symbolical meaning. Action prevents 'passion' from being complete, for passion is 'what is suffered'—and its limit is death. In other words, the action here is a fresh postponement of passion, which means a delaying of Death.

There is the same shift as regards the two marriages in the Romance, that of Iseult the Fair to the king and that of Iseult of the White Hand to Tristan. The first is an obstruction in fact. The concrete existence of a *husband* symbolizes its character, husbands being despised in courtly love. Making the obstruction that leads to adultery a husband is unimaginative, the excuse most readily thought of, and most in keeping with everyday experience.[1] See how Tristan shoves the husband aside, and enjoys making sport of him! But for the existence of a husband, the love of Tristan and Iseult would not have lasted beyond three years! And old Béroul showed his good sense in limiting the effect of the love-potion to that length of time:

> La mere Yseut, qui le bolli,
> A trois anz d'amistié le fist.

But for the existence of a husband, the lovers would have had to get married; and it is unbelievable that Tristan should ever be in

---

[1] Romanticism was later on to devise more refined excuses.

a position to marry Iseult. She typifies the woman a man does not marry; for once she became his wife she would no longer be what she is, and he would no longer love her. Just think of a Mme Tristan! It would be the negation of passion—at least of the passion we are concerned with here. The spontaneous ardour of a love crowned and not thwarted is essentially of short duration. It is a flare-up doomed not to survive the effulgence of its fulfilment. But its *branding* remains, and this is what the lovers want to prolong and indefinitely to renew. That is why they go on summoning fresh perils. But these the knight's valour drives him to overcome, and so he has to go away, in quest of more profound and more intimate—and it even seems, more interior—experiences.

When Tristan is sighing quietly for his lost Iseult, the brother of Iseult of the White Hand thinks his friend must be in love with his sister. This confusion—produced by identity of name—is the sole 'cause' of Tristan's marrying. It is obvious that he could easily have cleared up the misunderstanding. But here again honour supervenes—of course, as a mere pretext—to prevent him from drawing back. The reason is that he foresees, in this new ordeal which is *self-imposed*, the opportunity of a decisive advance. This merely formal marriage with a woman he finds beautiful is an obstruction which he can remove only by achieving a victory *over himself* (as well as over the institution of marriage, which he thus damages from within). This time his prowess goes against him. His chastity now he is married corresponds to the placing of the drawn sword between himself and the other Iseult. But a self-imposed chastity is a symbolical suicide (here is the hidden meaning of the sword)—a victory for the courtly ideal over the sturdy Celtic tradition which proclaimed its pride in life. It is a way of purifying desire of the spontaneous, brutish, and active elements still encumbering it. 'Passion' triumphs over desire. Death triumphs over life.

Hence Tristan's inclination for a *deliberate obstruction* turns out to be a desire for death and an advance in the direction of Death! But this death is for love, a deliberate death coming at the end of a series of ordeals thanks to which he will have been purified; a death that means transfiguration, and is in no way the result of some violent chance. Hence the aim is still to unite an external with an internal fate, which the lovers deliberately embrace. *In dying for love they redeem their destiny and are avenged for the*

45

love-potion. So that at the last the struggle between passion and obstruction is inverted. At this point the obstruction is no longer serving irresistible passion, but has itself become the goal and end wished for for its own sake. Passion has thus only played the part of a purifying ordeal, it might almost be said of a penance, in the service of this transfiguring death. Here we are within sight of the ultimate secret.

The love of love itself has concealed a far more awful passion, a desire altogether unavowable, something that could only be 'betrayed' by means of symbols such as that of the drawn sword and that of perilous chastity. Unawares and in spite of themselves, the lovers have never had but one desire—the desire for death! Unawares, and passionately deceiving themselves, they have been seeking all the time simply to be redeemed and avenged for 'what they have suffered'—the passion unloosed by the love-potion. In the innermost recesses of their hearts they have been obeying the fatal dictates of a wish for death; they have been in the throes of *the active passion of Darkness*.

10

The Love-Potion

And thereupon we perceive, now that it is half-disclosed, what caused the *myth* to take from and the very necessity whereby it was brought forth. So dreadful and unutterable is the real meaning of passion that not only are those persons who undergo it unable to grow aware of its end, but also writers wishing to depict it in all its marvellous violence are driven to employ the *deceptive* language of symbols. I shall set aside for the moment the question whether or not the authors of the five original poems were aware of what they were writing about. In all fairness, it is first imperative to make plain what I wish to imply by the word 'deceptive' which I have just used.

Thanks to the popularization of psycho-analysis, we now commonly take it for granted that the existence of a repressed wish is invariably manifested, though in such a way as to disguise the true nature of this wish. A forbidden passion or a shameful love finds expression in the symbols of a hieroglyphic language which consciousness leaves undeciphered. The language is essentially equivocal; in both senses of the verb, it 'betrays' what it wishes to say without saying it. A single gesture or a single metaphor may thus express at one and the same time both the object of a wish and what condemns the wish. The prohibition is thus recognized, and the object is not, and yet the latter is being alluded to. In this way irreconcilable demands are to some extent simultaneously satisfied. Two needs—that of speaking of what delights, and that of avoiding to decide whether the delightful is good or bad— and two instincts—that of courting danger and that of taking care—are all four gratified. If anybody using this language is asked why the predilection for this or that apparently weird image, the answer will be that 'it's perfectly natural', that 'he hasn't the remotest idea', or that 'he doesn't think it matters'. If the person questioned is a poet, he will drag in inspiration or poetic licence. In no circumstances will he any hesitation in showing that he is in no way *responsible*.

Now, consider the problem that must have confronted the author of the original Romance. The symbolical material available in the twelfth century for concealing what had also to be expressed was magic, on the one hand, and the rhetoric of chivalry on the other. How convenient are these forms of expression is something immediately obvious. Magic persuades without giving reasons, and is perhaps persuasive to precisely the extent that it withholds reasons. Like all rhetoric, the rhetoric of chivalry is a means of passing off the most obscure statements as 'natural'. It was an ideal mask; for it ensured secrecy all right, and also ensured that the approval of the reader would be *unconditional*. Chivalry was the rule which the leading caste was hoping to employ to check the wildest 'follies' that were felt to be threatening the framework of its society. The customs of chivalry were thus bound to supply the Romance with its armature. And I have repeatedly indicated how the prohibitions of chivalry prove to be 'perfect pretexts' for the progression of the narrative. Magic

comes in because the passion which has to be depicted has a fascinating violence not to be accepted without qualms. Passion
appears uncouth in its effects. The Church proscribes it as sinful,
and common sense looks upon it as a morbid excess. It is thus not
open to admiration till it has been freed from every kind of visible
connexion with human responsibility. That is why it was indispensable to bring in the love-potion, which acts willy-nilly, and—
better still—is drunk by mistake.[1]

The love-potion is thus an *alibi* for passion. It enables each of the
two unhappy lovers to say: 'You see, I am not in the least to
blame; you see, it's more than I can help.' Yet, thanks to this deceptive necessity, everything they do is directed towards the fatal
fulfilment they are in love with, and they can approach this fulfilment with a kind of crafty determination and a cunning the more
unerring for not being open to moral judgement. Our least cal-
culated actions are sometimes the most effective. A stone which
we throw 'without aiming' hits the mark. Actually, we aimed at
the mark all right, but consciousness was not given time to inter-
fere and deflect our spontaneous movement. That is why the
finest passages in the Romance are those where the authors did
not see how to dilate upon events and wrote as if in perfect innocence. There would be no myth and no romance if Tristan and
Iseult were able *to say* what is the end they are making ready for
in the depths—indeed, in the abyss—of their wills. Who would
dare admit that he seeks Death and detests offensive Day, that
what he longs for with all his being is the annihilation of his
being.

Much later on poets arose who did dare to make this crowning
avowal. But the masses said of them: 'They are mad!' And the
passion which most novelists wish to please in the reader is seemingly something weaker. It is unlikely ever to be driven to proclaim itself by undeniable excess, by a death in which it would be
manifested beyond any possible repentance! Some of the mystics
have gone further than avowal. They have understood and explained. But if they were able to face 'the Dark Night' with a
most strict and lucid passion, it was because, through faith, they
had won a pledge that an altogether personal and 'luminous'
Will would take the place of theirs. Their will power was not

[1] Thomas, who seeks to minimize the part played by this magical influence,
is driven to making passion less inhuman and hence more tolerable to a moralist.
Inferior in this respect to Béroul, he is the first writer to degrade the myth.

The Love-Potion

seized upon by the nameless god of the love-potion, a blind force or Nothingness, but by the God who promises His grace, and 'the living flame of love' that burns in the 'deserts' of the Night.

But Tristan can make no avowal. His longing is as if he had it not. He confines himself inside an unverifiable and unjustifiable 'truth', from any understanding of which he recoils with horror. He has his excuse ready, and it is pervasively specious: it is the poison which 'par force le demeine'. And yet, that he has chosen his fate, and willed and welcomed it in a dark and complete assent, is betrayed by everything he does, down to his desperate flight, a sublime coxcombry! And at the same time it is essential to the exemplary grandeur of his life that he should be unaware of this fate. Night has its reasons which are not those of Day, and they cannot be made known to Day.[1] Day they despise. Tristan has delivered himself over to a madness that must rob him of wisdom, 'truth', and life itself. He has travelled beyond our pleasure and pain. He is hastening forward to the supreme moment in which delight is all concentrated on *foundering*.

Night cannot be described in the language of Day. But this particular form of desire has not lacked, and has indeed produced, an 'artful music'. Arise, deep-sounding tempests of Tristan and Isolde's death! The hero sings:

> Old tune so full of sadness
> That sing'st thy sad complaint.
> Through evening breezes came that strain,
> as once my father's death I learned in childhood;
> through morning twilight, sadder sounding,
> as to me my mother's fate was told.

[1] In Wagner's drama, when the king surprises the lovers and asks 'for the undiscovered deep and secret cause of all', Tristan replies (F. Jameson's translation of the poem):
> King Marke, that *I can never tell thee*;
> and what thou ask'st that canst thou ne'er discover.

Later, when dying, Tristan says too:
> Where I awoke I stayed not;
> yet where I tarried, that *I can never tell thee* . . . .
> It was where I had been for ever,
> Where I for aye shall go;
> the boundless realm of night's domain.
> There one thing alone is ours:
> deep, eternal, all forgetting! . . .
> This terrible yearning wasting my heart;
> *if I could name it, if thou couldst know it!*

49

He who begot me died, she dying gave me birth.
The olden ditty's mournful plaint,
E'en so to them its numbers came,
that strain that asked, that asks me still.
what fate for me was chosen,
when there my mother bore me,
what fate for me?
The olden ditty once more tells me:
'tis yearning and dying! . . .
                    Yearning now calls.
for death's repose.

He may curse his stars and his birth, but the music is indeed artful, and its notes make known tremendously the lovely secret. It is he who has willed his own fate.

The terrible draught that this anguish has brought,
'tis I myself by whom it was wrought! . . .
          What I have drunken,
what day by day has gladdened my spirit.

I I

Unhappy Mutual Love

Passion means suffering, something undergone, the mastery of fate over a free and responsible person. To love love more than the object of love, to love passion for its own sake, has been to love to suffer and to court suffering all the way from Augustine's *amabam amare* down to modern romanticism. Passionate love, the longing for what sears us and annihilates us in its triumph—there is the secret which Europe has never allowed to be given away; a secret it has always repressed—and preserved! Hardly anything could be more tragic; and the way passion has persisted through the centuries should cause us to look to the future with deep despondency.

Here let me note a feature which will presently call for consideration. Both passion and the longing for death which passion disguises are connected with, and fostered by, a particular notion of how to reach understanding which in itself is typical of the Western *psyche*. Why does Western Man wish to suffer this passion which lacerates him and which all his common sense rejects? Why does he yearn after this particular kind of love notwithstanding that its effulgence must coincide with his self-destruction? The answer is that he reaches self-awareness and tests himself only by risking his life—in suffering and on the verge of death. The third act of Wagner's drama represents far more than a romantic disaster; it represents the *essential disaster* of our sadistic genius—the repressed longing for death, for self-experience to the utmost, for the revealing shock, a longing which beyond question manifests the most tenacious root of the war instinct we nourish.

From this tragic extreme—illustrated, avowed, and evidenced by the myth in its pristine purity—let us step down to passionate experience as men undergo it today. The tremendous success of the Tristan Romance shows, whether we like it or not, that we have a secret preference for what is unhappy. According to the sturdiness of our spirit, this unhappiness may be the 'delightful sadness' and spleen of nineteenth-century decadence, a transfiguring torment, or a challenge which the mind flings down to the world. But in any case, what we pursue is what promises to uplift and excite us, so that in spite of ourselves we shall be transported into the 'real life' spoken of by poets. But this 'real life' is an impossible one. What is heralded by the sky with high-riding clouds and by the empurpled heroic sunset is not Day; it is Night! 'Real life is *elsewhere*,' Rimbaud said. 'Real life' indeed is but another name for Death, and the only name we have dared *to invoke* it by—even while we were pretending to fend it off. Why is it that we delight most of all in some tale of impossible love? Because we long for the *branding*; because we long to grow *aware* of what is on fire inside us. Suffering and understanding are deeply connected; death and self-awareness are in league;[1] and European romanticism may be compared to a man for whom

[1] On this alliance Hegel was able to ground a general explanation of the human mind, and also of human history.

sufferings, and especially the sufferings of love, are a privileged mode of understanding.

Of course, this is only true of the best romantics among us. Most people do not bother about understanding or about self-awareness; they merely go after the kind of love that promises the most *feeling*. But even this has to be a love delayed in its happy fulfilment by some obstruction. Hence, whether our desire is for the most self-conscious or simply for the most intense love, secretly we desire obstruction. And this obstruction we are ready if needs be to invent or imagine.

This seems to me to explain much of our psychological nature. Unless the course of love is being hindered there is no 'romance'; and it is romance that we revel in—that is to say, the self-conciousness, intensity, variations, and delays of passion, together with its climax rising to disaster—not its sudden flaring. Consider our literature. The happiness of lovers stirs our feelings only on account of the unhappiness which lies in wait for it. We must feel that life is imperilled, and also feel the hostile realities that drive happiness away into some beyond. What moves us is not its presence, but its nostalgia and recollection. Presence is inexpressible and has no perceptible duration; it can only be a *moment* of grace —as in the duet of Don Giovanni and Zerlina. Otherwise we lapse into a picture-postcard idyll. Happy love has no history—*in European literature*. And a love that is not mutual cannot pass for a true love. The outstanding find made by European poets, what distinguishes them first and foremost among the writers of the world, what most profoundly expresses the European obsession by suffering as a way to understanding, is the secret of the Tristan myth; passionate love at once shared and fought against, anxious for a happiness it rejects, and magnified in its own disaster—*unhappy mutual love*.

Let us pause at this description of the myth.

The love is *mutual* in the sense that Tristan and Iseult 'love one another', or, at least, believe that they do. Certainly their mutual fidelity is exemplary. But *unhappiness* comes in, because the love which 'dominates' them is not a love of each for the other as that other really is. They love one another, but each loves the other *from the standpoint of self and not from the other's standpoint*. Their unhappiness thus originates in a false reciprocity, which disguises a twin narcissism. So much is this so that at times there pierces through their excessive passion a kind of hatred of the beloved.

Unhappy Mutual Love

Long before Freud and modern psychology Wagner saw this. 'By me chosen, lost by me!' Isolde sings in her frantic love. And the sailor's opening song from the mast-head predicts the inevitable fate of them both:

> Westward sweeps the eye, eastward on we fly.
> The wind so wild blows homeward now:
> my Irish child, where tarriest thou?
> Sighs from thy heart ascending,
> help to our sails are lending!
> Sigh, ah sigh, wind so wild!
> Sigh, ah sigh now, my child!
> O Irish maid, thou wayward, winsome maid!

Their passion is twice unhappy in that it flees from both reality and the Norm of Day. The essential unhappiness of this love is that what they desire they have not yet had—this is Death—and that what they had is now being lost—the enjoyment of life. And yet, far from this loss being felt as privation, the couple imagine that they are now more fully alive than ever and are more than ever living dangerously and magnificently. The approach of death acts as a goad to sensuality. In the full sense of the verb, it aggravates desire. Sometimes even, it aggravates desire to the point of turning this into a wish to kill either the beloved or one-self, or to founder in a twin downrush.

> Hear now my will, ye craven winds! [Isolde begins by
> singing]
> come forth to strife and stress of the storm!
> to turbulent tempests' clamour and fury!
> Drive from her dreams this slumbering sea;
> wake from the depths all her envious greed!
> Destroy now this insolent ship,
> let its wreck be sunk in her waves!
> All that hath life and breath upon it,
> I leave to you winds as your prize!

Drawn to a death remote from the life that has been spurring them on, the lovers are doomed to become the voluptuous prey of conflicting forces that will cast both into the same headlong swoon. For they can never be united till, bereft of all hope and of all possible love, they reach the heart of utter obstruction and experience the supreme exaltation which is destroyed in being fulfilled.

12

Old Tune so Full of Sadness

In summarizing the Romance from an objective standpoint, we were led to detect in it a number of contradictions; and in supposing that the author really intended to illustrate how the rule of chivalry conflicted with feudal custom we were led to see how these contradictions came about. Thereupon we set out to find the real theme of the legend. The author sides with the rule of chivalry, and in doing so betrays a sense of story-telling. This in turn betrays a hankering after love for its own sake, which implies a secret quest of the obstruction that shall foster love. But this quest is only the disguise of a love for obstruction *per se*. Now, it turns out that the ultimate obstacle is death, and at the close of the tale death is revealed as having been the real end, what passion has yearned after from the beginning, the avenging of a fate that, having been suffered, is now at last redeemed.

Although the secrets disclosed by an analysis of the myth are of considerable import, the inward private assurances of what is their nature are likely to be rejected by our ordinary consciousness. My description has necessarily had to follow the meanderings of the internal logic of the Romance, and I realize that its dryness may seem vaguely damaging. I shall be consoled if the results are correct. With proof to the contrary I shall be ready to admit that some of the conjectures are questionable. It remains that my interpretation has enabled us to come upon some fundamental relations where they were in process of being formed, and that these relations subtend our fate. In so far as *passionate love* endows the myth with a new youth through its effect upon our own lives, it is henceforth impossible to overlook how it stands for a radical condemnation of *marriage*. The ending of the myth shows that

54

passion is an *askesis*,[1] and that as such it is all the more effectively in opposition to earthly life that it takes the form of desire, and that, as desire, it simulates fate.

Incidentally, I have mentioned that such a love is profoundly connected with our liking for *war*.

Furthermore, if passion and the need of passion are indeed aspects of our Western way of coming to understand, we must consider—at least interrogatively—the existence of one more relation, which may ultimately turn out to be the most fundamental of all. We must ask ourselves if to understand through suffering is not the capital feature as well as the daring element in our most self-conscious *mysticism*. The two passions—the erotic (in a higher sense) and the mystical—speak one same language, whether because either is cause or effect of the other or because they have had a common origin—and perhaps both sound to our ears the same 'old tune so full of sadness' which Wagner's drama orchestrates:

> That strain that asked, that asks me still,
> what fate for me was chosen . . .
> what fate for me?
> The olden ditty once more tells me:
> 'tis yearning and dying!

Thanks to a 'physiognomical' examination of the shape and structure of the Romance, I have succeeded in setting forth the original content of the myth in all its harsh and noble purity. Two ways now beckon—one leading back to the historical and religious background of the myth, the other down from the myth to our own time. Let us take each way in turn without presuppositions. Here and there I shall pause to verify this or that clearly localized origin or this or that unforeseen consequence of the *relations* which have now been laid bare.

[1] The word '*ascèse*', though not included in standard dictionaries, has lately become very popular with French religious writers. The word is a French adaptation of the Greek ἄσκησις = exercise, training, practice. It serves to indicate a religious preparation and training. The author is anxious to emphasize the severity and deprivation involved. Being a neologism, it will here be rendered throughout by 'askesis'—Translator.

Book II

THE RELIGIOUS ORIGINS

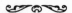

I

The Natural and Sacred 'Obstruction'

People are all more or less materialists today, for they are the
heirs of the nineteenth century. They need only be shown
some crude mimicry of 'mental' events in nature or in
instinct, and they will fancy that the 'mental' has been explained.
It is whatever is lower that we take to be more real. The superstition
of our time expresses itself in a mania for equating the sublime
with the trivial and for quaintly mistaking a merely necessary condition for a sufficient cause. The mania usurps the name of 'scienti
fic integrity', and is defended on the ground that it emancipates
the mind from delusions about 'spirit'. Yet it is difficult to see
how there can be any emancipation in 'explaining' Dostoievsky
by epilepsy or Nietzsche by syphilis. To deny the existence of
mind is a curious way of ensuring its freedom. But however
much I protest beforehand, no sooner do I admit that in instinct
and sex there are spontaneous reactions analogous in some respects
to those occurring in the passion of the Tristan myth than many
people will suppose that this settles the matter so far as I am concerned. They are bound to think that the *obstruction* which has so
often cropped up in the course of my analysis of the myth is something altogether natural. To delay pleasure is the most elementary
of the wiles of desire; and man is 'so made' as sometimes to subject himself to a semi-instinctive continence for the benefit of the
species. Lycurgus, the Spartan legislator, required newly married
husbands to remain continent for a considerable time. Plutarch
says[1] his reason was that 'it kept their bodies in strength and better
state, to bring forth children', and that 'it continued also in both
parties a still burning love and a newe desire of the one to the

[1] North's translation.

59

other'. Likewise feudal chivalry, it will be said, looked upon chastity as an instinctive obstacle to the assertion of instinct, and extolled it in order that warriors might be the better fitted to show valour.

But it is only in relation to life that discipline of this sort can have any value; not in relation to the mind. Such discipline yields to its own success; it aims at nothing ulterior. The eugenics of Lycurgus were in no way ascetic; on the contrary, he aimed at the better propagation of the species. The processes which secure the perpetuation of life cannot be anything more than the physiological *concomitant* of the reactions of passion. Of course, passion has to make use of the body and to obey its laws. But to recognize in what the laws of the body consist does nothing to explain, for example, why Tristan loves as he does. In fact, the recognition serves but to render more conspicuous the presence of some additional and 'alien' factor, a factor having the power to make instinct turn away from its natural goal and to transform desire into *limitless* aspiration, into something, that is to say, which does not serve, and indeed operates against, biological ends. The same can be said of suggestions that the motives of behaviour characteristic of the Romance originated in the sacred customs and taboos of primitive peoples. Nothing is easier than to connect the distant *quest* of a bride with the custom of nuptial abduction observed among exogamic tribes, and to imagine that *prowess* was encouraged because it was an undisguised sublimation of much older customs inspired by nature in order to achieve biological selection. Even the *longing for death* can be assimilated to *the death instinct* that Freud and the latest biologists refer to.

But nothing in all this will explain the belated appearance of the myth, still less its localization in European history. Antiquity has left no record of an experience akin to the love of Tristan and Iseult. It is well known that the Greeks and Romans looked on love as a sickness—the expression is Menander's—whenever it went, no matter how little, beyond the sensual pleasure which was considered to be its natural expression. Plutarch calls love 'a frenzy'. 'Some have believed it was a madness. . . . Thus those who are in love must be forgiven as though ill.' We are thus led to ask whence arose the glorification of passion, which is precisely that feature of the Romance which we find moving. To speak of a deflexion of instinct is to say nothing, inasmuch as what we want to know is indeed how the deflexion was caused.

2

Eros, or Boundless Desire

Plato, alike in the *Phaedrus* and in the *Symposium*, speaks of a frenzy that, spreading from the body, infects the spirit with malignant humours. This is not love as he commends it. But there is, he says, another kind of frenzy or delirium which is neither conceived nor born in a man's soul except by the inspiration of heaven. It is alien to us, its spell is wrought from without; it is a transport, an infinite rapture away from reason and natural sense. It is therefore to be called *enthusiasm*, a word which actually means 'possessed by a god', for the frenzy not only is of heavenly origin, but culminates at its highest in a new attainment of the divine.

Such is Platonic love.[1] It is 'a divine delirium', a transport of the soul, a madness and supreme sanity both. A lover with his beloved becomes 'as if in heaven'; for love is the way that ascends by degrees of ecstasy to the one source of all that exists, remote from bodies and matter, remote from what divides and distinguishes, and beyond the misfortune of being a self and even in love itself a pair.

Eros is complete Desire, luminous Aspiration, the primitive religious soaring carried to its loftiest pitch, to the extreme exigency of purity which is also the extreme exigency of Unity. But absolute unity must be the negation of the present human being in his suffering multiplicity. The supreme soaring of desire ends in

[1] I am, of course, aware that Socrates is made to say in the *Phaedrus* that the greatest satisfaction of the lover comes, not from physical fulfilment, but from consciousness of the joint attainment by lover and beloved of self-mastery; and in the *Symposium* that erotic passion at its highest is a delight in beauty of every kind, so that the lover who has ascended high enough will descry the supreme, eternal, self-same, and perfect beauty, the reality and substance of that in which everything else called beauty is a participant. But I am concerned above all with what European culture generally has preserved of Plato.

non-desire. The erotic process introduces into life an element foreign to the diastole and systole of sexual attraction—a desire that never relapses, that nothing can satisfy, that even rejects and flees the temptation to obtain its fulfilment in the world, because its demand is to embrace no less than the All. It is *infinite transcendence*, man's rise into his god. And this rise is *without return*.

Little has so far been discovered about the antecedents of Platonism, but they are certainly Iranian and Orphic. And through Plotinus the Platonic doctrine of love was transmitted to the medieval world. That is how the East came to brood over our lives and hence to stir up some very ancient memories. For from the depths of the West the voices of Celtic filids and bards arose in answer. It was perhaps an echo, or some ancestral harmony—all our races come from the East—or perhaps human nature is given everywhere and at all times to divinizing its Desire. I cannot pronounce upon the theory according to which the most ancient of Celtic myths are akin to the Greek—the quest of the Holy Grail being regarded as another form of the quest of the Golden Fleece, the Pythagorean theories of reincarnation as another version of druidical beliefs about immortality. But, whatever that theory may be worth, recent investigation has detected general convergences in support of the view that the religious beliefs of East and West had a common source.

The Celts spread over Europe from the Atlantic to the Black Sea long before the Romans embarked upon their conquests. But the Celts were not a nation. They were loosely held together by a civilization or culture which had its spiritual centre in the sacerdotal college of the druids. The college had not emanated from small tribes; it was 'a kind of international institution' and served every people of Celtic race from the remote corners of Britain and Ireland across to Italy and Asia Minor. The travels and meetings of druids 'cemented the union of Celtic peoples and their feeling of being related'.[1] The druids were grouped in brotherhoods, and had very wide powers. They were soothsayers, magicians, medicine-men, priests, and teachers all in one. They set nothing down in writing, but by word of mouth, in gnomic verses, they taught pupils for whom the course of instruction lasted twenty years.[2]

[1] H. Hubert, *Les Celtes* (Paris, 1932), II, pp. 227, 229, 274. The best general study of Celtic civilization, history and archaeology.

[2] H. d'Arbois de Jurainville, *Cours de littérature celtique*, I, pp. 1-65.

The sacerdotal college of the druids was not unique. Iranian magi, Indian brahmans, Roman pontiffs and flamens, have been credited with identical institutions; and that 'flamen' is the same name as 'brahman' indicates that the functions of each of these various kinds of priests were fundamentally akin.[1]

However, as regards the Celts, there is no doubt that they believed in a life after death. They pictured that life to themselves as one filled with adventure—very like the life led on earth, but purified. They even supposed that some of their heroes were enabled *to return* from the hereafter, and under other names to mingle with the living. It is through this central doctrine of soul survival that the Celts are akin to the Greeks. But every doctrine of immortality implies a tragic preoccupation with death. The Celts, according to Hubert,[2] 'certainly elaborated a metaphysic of death. They had meditated on death a great deal. It had grown into a familar companion, *whose disturbing nature*, however, *they deliberately disguised.*' And Hubert remarks further that in Celtic mythology 'the notion of death is found to predominate over all things, and *everything discloses it*'. These statements invite juxtaposition with what I have said above about the Tristan myth, which both veils and expresses a longing for death.

Celtic gods, furthermore, formed two opposite sets, *light* and *dark*. It is important to stress this fundamental *dualism* in the religion of the druids. For that is where Iranian, Gnostic and Hindu myths converge upon the basic religion of Europe. From India to the shores of the Atlantic, though in the most varied forms, there is expressed the same mystery of Day and Night and the same mystery of the *fatal* struggle going on between them inside men's breasts. There is a god of uncreated and timeless Light, and there is a god of Darkness, the author of evil, who holds sway over all visible Creation. Centuries before Manes appeared, this opposition had already been established in Indo-European mythologies. The Iranian couple formed by Ahura Mazda and Ahriman is the classic instance.

Of direct interest for our purpose, Woman in the eyes of the druids was a being divine and prophetic. She is typified by the Germanic Velleda, who in Chateaubriand's *Martyrs* appears by night to a Roman general lost in reverie. 'Do you know', she says to him, 'that I am a sprite?' Eros has taken the guise of

[1] J. Vendryès, *Mémoires de la société linguistique*, XX, 6, 265.
[2] H. Hubert, op. cit., I, p. 18, and II, p. 328.

Woman, and symbolizes both the other world and the nostalgia which makes us despise earthly joys. But the symbol is ambiguous, since it tends to mingle sexual attraction with *eternal* desire. The Essylt mentioned in sacred legends as being both 'an object of contemplation and a mystic vision' stirred up a yearning for what lies beyond embodied forms. Although she was beautiful and desirable for herself, it was her nature to vanish. 'The Eternal feminine leads us away,' Goethe said, and 'Woman is man's goal,' according to Novalis.

Thus the yearning for Light was symbolized by the nocturnal attraction of sex. In the eyes of the flesh, uncreated broad Day was but Night, even as our day corresponded for the god dwelling beyond the stars to the realm of Dispater, the Father of Shadows. There is a kinship here with the yearning *to founder* shown by the Wagnerian Tristan, although in the case of that particular Tristan he yearns to founder only in order that he may rise again into a Heaven of Light. The 'Night' he sings of is Uncreated Day. And his passion is the cult of Eros—the desire that despises Venus even when in the throes of sensuality and he imagines he is in love with an actual fellow being. There has been too much talk about Nirvana and Buddhism in connexion with Wagner's opera. The pagan background of the West was more than ample for the needs of a magician who wished to brew his love-potion with active ingredients. For that matter, it is significant that the original Celtic cult should have survived both the Roman conquest and the Germanic invasions. 'The Gallo-Romans were mostly Celts in disguise, so that after the Germanic invasions Celtic fashions and inclinations reappeared in Gaul.'[1] Both Romanesque art and the Romance languages witness to the wealth of the Celtic inheritance. Later on, it was thanks to the monks in Britain and Ireland—the two countries where the bardic legends had been preserved, and preserved, as it happens, by the clergy—that Europe was evangelized and brought back to the study of letters. This carries us to the threshold of the period in which the Tristan myth sprang up.

However, closer to us than either Plato or the druids, a kind of Indo-European unity may be seen looming out like a watermark upon the background of medieval heresies. As early as the third century, there spread over the geographical and historical area that is bounded by India on the one hand and by Britain on the

[1] Hubert, op. cit., I, p. 20. In the same way, the Gallic gods were given Latin names, but were not otherwise altered.

Eros, or Boundless Death

other, a religion that syncretized all the myths of Night and Day, a religion which had been elaborated first in Persia and then by the Gnostic and Orphic sects. This religion actually spread underground, and it is known as Manichaeism. The very difficulty there is today in describing it must be held to indicate something of its deepest nature and the extent of its human importance. For one thing, everywhere the authorities and orthodoxies persecuted it with incredible violence. It was pretended to see in it the gravest of social perils. Its followers were slaughtered, its writings scattered and burned, so that the evidence on which it has been judged originated most often from its foes. The doctrine of the Persian prophet Manes assumed forms that varied widely according to what beliefs were already established among the peoples to whom it spread—Christians, Buddhists, or Mohammedans. In a Manichaean hymn recently retrieved and translated, Jesus, Manes, Ormuzd, and Sakyamuni are invoked one after the other, and finally so is Zardusht—that is to say, Zarathustra or Zoroaster. And there is reason to suppose, furthermore, that the existence of Celtic survivals in the French area of Languedoc provided certain Manichaean sects with a particularly favourable soil.

For the understanding of what is to follow, two points in particular need to be stressed.

1. The fundamental dogma of all Manichaean sects is that the soul is divine or angelic, and is *imprisoned* in created forms—in terrestrial matter, which is Night. In the hymn called *The Soul's Fate*, a disciple of the saviour Manes causes his spiritual self to lament:

> I came out of light and the gods.
> Here in exile am I from them kept apart.
>
> . . . . .
>
> I am a god, of the gods I was born.
> But now I am made to know pain.

The soul's impulse to seek the Light has a kinship with the 'reminiscence of Beauty' referred to in the Platonic dialogues, and also with the nostalgia felt by the Celtic hero when, having come back to earth from heaven, he recalls the existence of the isle where the immortals dwell. But the impulse is constantly being checked by the jealousy of Venus (who, in the hymn just quoted, goes by the name of Dibat). Even after a lover has become possessed by the yearning for light, Venus wants him to remain within dark matter.

Hence there ensues the struggle between sexual love and Love, and it is a struggle displaying the fundamental *anguish* felt by fallen angels while confined in bodies all too human.

2. It has recently been shown[1]—and this is very important for what we are seeking to find out—that the structure of the Manichaean faith was '*in essence lyrical*'. In other words, the nature of this faith made it unamenable to rational, impersonal, and 'objective' exposition. Actually, it could only come to be held in being experienced, and the experience of it was one of combined dread and enthusiasm—that is to say, of invasion by the divine—which is essentially poetic. The cosmogony and theogony of this faith became 'true' for a believer only when certitude was induced by his recital of a *psalm*. So Tristan, it will be recalled, cannot state his secret, only sing it.

Every dualistic—let us say, every Manichaean—interpretation of the universe holds the fact of being alive in the body to be the absolute woe, the woe embracing all other woes; and death it holds to be the *ultimate* good, whereby the sin of birth is redeemed and human souls return into the One of luminous indistinction. We may already attain to Light while here below through a gradual ascent which is achieved in the progressive death of a deliberate *askesis*. But the goal and the end of the spirit is also the end of limited life, of physical life obscured by immediate multiplicity. Eros, object of our supreme Desire, intensifies all our desires only in order to offer them up in sacrifice. The fulfilment of Love is the denial of any particular terrestrial love, and its Bliss of any particular terrestrial bliss. *From the standpoint of life*, it is this Love which is the absolute woe.

There we have the broad Eastern and Western background of paganism out of which the Tristan myth sprang. It has now to be asked how indeed the myth should have come out of this background; what prohibitions and perils compelled this doctrine to put on veils and no longer to proclaim itself except in deceptive symbols, no longer to allure us except by means of the spell and secret incantation of a myth.

[1] H. Corbin, 'Pour l'hymnologie manichéenne' (*Yggdrasil*, Aug. 1937).

3

Agape, or Christian Love

The Gospel according to Saint John opens as follows:
'In the beginning was the Word, and the Word was with God, and the word was God. . . . In him was life; and the life was the light of men. And the light shinetn in darkness; and the darkness comprehended it not.'
This might seem to be another expression of the eternal and relentless dualism according to which terrestrial Night and transcendent Day are irrevocably hostile to one another. But no. The Gospel continues:
'And the Word was made flesh, and dwelt among us, (and we beheld his glory, the glory as of the only begotten of the Father,) full of grace and truth.'
The incarnation of the Word in the world—and of Light in Darkness—is the astounding event whereby we are delivered from the woe of being alive. And this event, in being the centre of the whole of Christianity, is the focus of that Christian love which in Scripture is called *agape*.

The event is unique, and not to be believed 'naturally'. That the Incarnation occurred is the radical negation of every kind of *religion*—the ultimate offence, not only to our reason, which is unable to countenance the absurd running together of the infinite and the finite, but also and especially to any natural religious disposition. Every known religion tends *to sublimate* man, and culminates in condemning his 'finite' life. Our desires are intensified and sublimated by the god Eros through being embraced in a single Desire whereby they are abolished. The final goal of the process is to attain what is not life—the death of the body. Night and Day being incompatible, and men being deemed creatures of Night, men can only achieve salvation by ceasing to be, by being 'lost' in the bosom of the divine. But in Christianity, thanks

67

The Religious Origins

to its dogma of the incarnation of the Christ in Jesus, this process is completely inverted. Death, from being the last *term*, is become the first condition. What the Gospel calls dying to self is the *beginning* of a new *life* already *here below*—not the soul's flight out of the world, but its return in force into the midst of the world. It is an immediate recreation, a reassertion of life—not of course of the old life, and not of an ideal life, but of our present life now repossessed by the Spirit. God—the real God—has been made man—a real man. Darkness as 'comprehended' the light in the person of Jesus Christ. And every man born of woman who *believes* this is born again of the spirit here and now—dead to himself and dead to the world in so far as self and the world are sinful, but restored to himself and to the world in so far as the Spirit wants to save them.

Thereupon to love is no longer to flee and persistently to reject the act of love. Love now still begins beyond death, but from that beyond it returns to life. And, in being thus converted, love brings forth our *neighbour*. Eros had treated a fellow-creature as but an illusory excuse and occasion for taking fire; and forthwith this creature had had to be given up, for the intention was ever to burn more fiercely, to burn to death! Individual beings were but so many defects and eclipsings of the one and only Being; and as such none was susceptible of being really loved. Salvation lay *hereafter*, and a religious-minded person forsook the creatures from whom his god had turned away. But the Christian God has not forsaken us. He alone, among all gods known to us, has not turned away. Quite the contrary, '*He first loved us*'—loved us as we are and with our limitations; and these He even went so far as to put on, making Himself as one of us. In thus putting on, though without sin and without self-division, the garment of sinful and manifold men, the Love of God has opened an entirely new way to us—the way of *holiness*. And the way is the contrary of the sublimation that had been an illusory flight out of the concreteness of life. To love according to this new way is a positive act and an act of transformation. Eros had pursued infinite becoming. Christian love is obedience in the present. For to love God is *to obey* God, Who has commanded us to love one another. *To love your enemies* is to shed selfishness and the desirous and anxious self; it means the death of the solitary human being, but it also means the birth of our neighbour. In reply to the ironical question: 'Who is my neighbour?' Jesus answered: 'Whoever has need of

68

you.' From that moment every human relation has been given a new *direction* in being given a new *meaning*.

The symbol of Love is no longer the infinite *passion* of a soul in quest of light, but the *marriage* of Christ and the Church. And in this way human love itself has been transformed. Whereas, according to the doctrines of mystical paganism, human love was sublimated so thoroughly as to be made into a god even while it was being dedicated to death, Christianity has restored human love to its proper status, and in this status has hallowed it by means of marriage. Such a love, being understood according to the image of Christ's love for His Church (Ephesians, v. 25), is able to be truly mutual. For its object, from having been the actual notion of love and the exquisite and fatal branding of love ('It is better', Saint Paul says, 'to marry than to burn'), has become the other *as he or she really is*. And, in spite of the hindrance of sin, human love is a happy love, since already here below it can by obedience attain to the fullness of its own status.

When pursued to its logical extreme, the dualism of Night and Day had resulted, *from the standpoint of life*, in the ultimate misfortune—death. Christianity is a fatal misfortune only for the man who is parted from God, but it is a newly creative and blessed misfortune *already in this life* for the believer who 'takes the cup of salvation'.

4

East and West

It is the duty of a writer who refers to East and West in any but a geographical sense to define his terms. By 'East' I mean in this book an attitude of the human mind which has reached its highest and purest expression in the direction of Asia; this mystical attitude is dualistic as regards the world and monistic as regards fulfilment. 'Eastern' *askesis* is directed to negation of the Many and to absorption into the One; it looks to a *complete fusion* with a god, or, lacking a god (as in the case of Buddhism), with the universal One of Being. All that assumes the availability of a Wisdom, of a technique of progressive illumination—as with Yoga, for example—an *ascent* for the individual towards that Unity in which he will be lost. By 'West' I mean a religious attitude which actually reached us from the Near East, but has been supreme solely in the West. According to this attitude, God and man are divided by a fundamental abyss—or, as Kierkegaard calls it, by 'an infinite qualitative difference'. This attitude accordingly does not look to any absorption or union in substance; but only to a communion, the model of which is the *marriage* of the Church and her Lord. And that assumes a sudden illumination or conversion, a *descent* of Grace, from God to man. No doubt the 'Western' attitude has often been found in the East, and *vice versa*. But that is immaterial.

Now Eros, it will be recalled, requires union—that is, the complete absorption of the essence of individuals into the god. The existence of distinct individuals is considered to be a grievous error, and their part is to rise progressively till they are dissolved in the divine perfection. Let not a man attach himself to his fellow-creatures, for they are devoid of all excellence, and in so far as they are particular individuals they merely represent so many deficiencies of Being. There is no such thing as our neighbour. And the intensification of love must be at the same time a lover's *askesis*, whereby he will eventually escape out of life.

Agape, on the contrary , is not directed to a union that can only occur after life is over. 'God is in heaven, and thou art on earth.' And thy fate is being decided here below. Sin consists not in having been born, but in having lost God by becoming independent. And God is not to be found again by means of a limitless *elevation* of desire. However much our eros may be sublimated, it can never cease to be self. Orthodox Christianity allows no room either to illusion or to human optimism. But that does not mean that it condemns us to despair.

For we have had the Good Tidings—the tidings that God is seeking us. And He finds us whenever we hearken to His voice, and answer by obeying Him. God seeks us, and He has found us, thanks to His Son Who came *down* as far as us. The Incarnation is the historic sign of a renewed creation, wherein a believer is reinstated thanks to his very act of faith. Thereupon, forgiven and hallowed—that is to say, reconciled—he is still a man; there has been no divinization—but he no longer lives for himself alone. 'Thou shalt love the Lord thy God, and thy neighbour as thyself.' It is in loving his neighbour that a Christian is fulfilled and truly loves himself.

Agape brings no fusion or ecstatic dissolving of the self in God. The divine love is the *beginning* of a new life, a life created by the act of communion. And for a real communion there are certainly required two participants, each present to the other. It is thus that each is the other's neighbour. And since *agape* is alone in recognizing the existence of our neighbour—*Eros* failing to do so— and is the love of this neighbour, not as an excuse for self-exaltation, but as an acceptance of him or her in the whole concrete reality of his or her affliction and hope, it seems legitimate to infer that the kind of love called *passion* must have arisen usually among peoples who adored Eros, and that, on the contrary, Christian peoples—historically speaking, the inhabitants of the Western Continent of Europe—must have remained strangers to passion, or at least must have found it incredible. But history compels us to acknowledge that exactly the opposite has happened.

In the East,[1] and also in the Greece of Plato, human love has usually been regarded as mere pleasure and physical enjoyment. Not only has passion—in the tragic and painful sense of the word —seldom been met with there, but also and especially it has been despised in the eyes of current morals and treated as a sickness or frenzy. 'Some think it is a madness,' Plutarch says. In the West, on the contrary, it was marriage which in the twelfth century became an object of contempt, and passion that was glorified

---

[1] And by the 'East' I mean a certain kind of attitude to both the whole of life and the world which was characteristic chiefly not of Persia, Islam, Arabia, or Judaism, which are directly connected with Western religious cycles, but of India, China, Tibet, Japan, and so on. The Chinese have married young, unions being arranged by the parents, and for them the problem of love does not arise. 'The attitude of a European, who wonders all his life: "Is it love or not? Do I really love this woman, or is it affection that I feel for her? Do I love God or do I merely want to love God? Am I in love with her or am I in love with love?"— to a Chinese psychiatrist that attitude might well appear as symptomatic of insanity. We are mad without knowing it. Our whole life is founded upon passion, and we want peace and tranquillity! I am myself the maddest of all madmen, alas! But at least now I know it.' So writes Leo Ferrero in his book, *Désespoirs*.

precisely because it is preposterous, inflicts suffering upon its victims, and wreaks havoc alike in the world and in the self.

As a result of identifying the religious components whose presence we had detected in the myth, we find ourselves confronted by a flagrant contradiction between doctrine and manners. Perhaps it is this very contradiction that can account for the myth.

5

Reaction to Christianity in European Manners

I offer the following scheme for the sake of clarity.

	Doctrine	*Theoretical Application*	*Historical Fulfilment*
Paganism	Mystical union (Blissful divine love)	Woeful human love	Hedonism; passion rare and despised
Christianity	Communion (but no union of essence)	Love of our Neighbour (Blissful marriage)	Painful clashes, intense passion

Psychologically, the paradoxes of this scheme are pretty easily accounted for. Neither during Plato's own lifetime nor in the course of the ensuing few centuries did Platonism become popular; it remained an esoteric wisdom. Esoteric likewise to some extent were the Celtic mysteries, and the Manichaean entirely so.

Thereupon, Christianity triumphed. Under Constantine and under the Carolingian emperors its doctrines became the apanage of princes and ruling caste, who forced them upon all the peoples of the West. This, of course, meant the repression of the old pagan beliefs, which became the hope and refuge of natural inclinations frowned upon and not disposed of by the new rule. In the eyes of the Ancients, marriage, for example, was a utilitarian institution of limited purpose. If not adultery as understood today, at least concubinage was allowed by custom, for slaves could be both used and abused.[1] But Christian marriage, inasmuch as it is a sacrament, imposed on the natural man a constancy which he found unbearable. Any one compulsorily converted came under the restraints of the Christian code, but lacked the support of any actual faith. Inevitably the barbarian blood of such people must have rebelled, and they were all disposed to welcome a revival of the pagan mysteries in Catholic guise, since this brought a promise of 'emancipation'. Hence it was that the secret doctrines of which we have been investigating the antecedents had no real hold on the West except during the centuries they were banned by official Christianity. So it was that passionate love—a terrestrial form of the cult of Eros—came to invade the psyche of those members of the leading caste who had only simulated conversion and felt the marriage rule as a restriction. Yet devotion to a god who was anathema to the Church could not be avowed in the light of day. It took esoteric forms and flourished in the guise of secret heresies more or less orthodox in appearance. At the beginning of the twelfth century these heresies spread quickly. On the one hand, they wormed their way among the clergy, and a little later were manifested in many subtle and complicated ways in the great mystical revival. On the other hand, they drew a ready response out of the depths of the spirit of the age. They were able to penetrate the feudal world, which was not invariably aware of the source and mystic significance of a set of values it treated as fashionable and which it adapted to the purposes of its own amusement. Before long a religion that rejected the Incarnation as something too materialistic had itself taken on a materialist tinge!

It has been typical of the West as regards religion to keep the letter while betraying the spirit. Here is one instance. Plato linked Love and Beauty, although what he called Beauty was above all

[1] In Roman law, slaves were not persons: *Persona est sui iuris; servus non est persona.*

The Religious Origins

the intellectual essence of uncreated perfection—the form of all excellence. According to José Ortega y Gasset,[1] 'it is impossible to tell to what deep levels of the Western mind Platonic notions have penetrated. The simplest sort of person regularly employs expressions and betrays views which are derived from Plato.' But such a person distorts these expressions and views in a direction suited to his Western nature; and it is in this way that popular Platonism has led us into a grievous error—the error of supposing that love is first and foremost a matter of *physical* beauty, when, actually, this beauty is but an attribute bestowed by a lover on the chosen object of his love. Daily experience shows well enough that 'love beautifies its object' and that 'official' beauty is no pledge of being loved. But the degenerate Platonism by which we are obsessed blinds us to the reality of the object as it is according to *its own* truth—or else renders it little likeable. And it sends us in pursuit of chimeras that exist only inside ourselves. It may well be asked why an error due to misunderstanding Plato should have succeeded so well and have endured invincibly. The error awakens obscure responses in every human being's heart, and in particular in the heart of every European. We have seen that as far back as the Celts, the druidical cult turned Woman into a prophetic being, 'the eternal feminine' and 'man's goal'; in this way it sought to materialize the divine urge and to endow it with a corporeal hypostasis. Moreover, Freud has now made us aware that a man's 'type of woman', that image which he bears graven upon his heart and instinctively turns into a definition of feminine beauty, may be but a 'mother fixation' haunting the recesses of his memory.

Assuming that we have now distinguished the causes of the curious contradiction between teaching and manners that grows visible in the twelfth century, it becomes possible to formulate a preliminary inference. *The cultivation of passionate love began in Europe as a reaction to Christianity (and in particular to its doctrine of marriage) by people whose spirit, whether naturally or by inheritance, was still pagan.*

But this would be mere theory and highly disputable were it not that we are in a position to trace the historical ways and means to the rebirth of Eros. We have already settled on a date. The earliest passionate lovers whose story has reached us are Abélard and Héloïse, who met for the first time in 1118! And it is in the

[1] *Über die Liebe* (Berlin, 1933).

74

middle of this same century that love was first recognized and encouraged as a passion worth cultivating. Passionate love was then given a name which has since become familiar. It was called *cortezia*, or courtly love.

6

Courtly Love: Troubadours and Cathars

That all European poetry has come out of the Provencal poetry written in the twelfth century by the troubadours of Languedoc is now accepted on every side. This poetry magnified unhappy love. M. Charles Albert Cingria remarks:[1]

'Between the eleventh and twelfth centuries, poetry—whether Hungarian, or Spanish, Portuguese, German, Sicilian, Tuscan, Genoese, Pisan, Picard, Champagne, Flemish, English, etc.—was at first Languedoc; which is to say, that the poet, who had to be a troubadour, was compelled to speak the troubadour language which was never other than Provençal.

'The whole of the Occitanian, Petrarchian, and Dantesque lyric has but a single theme—love; and not happy, crowned, and satisfied love (the sight of which yields nothing), but on the contrary love perpetually unsatisfied—and but two characters: a poet reiterating his plaint eight hundred, nine hundred, a thousand times; and a fair lady who ever says "No".'

No European poetry has been more profoundly *rhetorical*, not only in in its verbal and musical forms, but also—paradoxical as it may seem—in its actual inspiration, which it obtained from a fixed system of rules which was codified as the *leys d'amor*. But it is likewise true that no rhetoric has been more productive of high-flown

[1] *Mesures*, No. 2 (Paris, 1937). The Provençal mentioned there was in reality the dialect of the county of Toulouse.

fervour. What it quickens with noble emotion is love outside marriage; for marriage implies no more than a physical union, but 'Amor'—the supreme Eros—is the transport of the soul upwards to ultimate union with light, something far beyond any love attainable in this life. That is why Love now implies chastity. 'E d'amor mou castitaz', sang the Toulouse troubadour, Guilhem Montanhagol. 'Out of love comes chastity.' Love further implies a ritual—the ritual of *domnei* or *donnoi*, love's vassalage. It is by the beauty of his musical homage that a poet wins his *lády*. On his knee he swears eternal constancy to her, as knights swore fealty to their suzerain. He receives from her a golden ring and a chaste kiss on his brow. Thereupon the 'lovers' are bound by the rules of *cortezia*: secrecy, patience, and moderation—the last not being altogether synonymous with chastity, but meaning rather restraint.... And especially a man has to be the *servente* of a woman.

Whence came this notion of a love 'perpetually unsatisfied' and whence too that of singing with plaintive enthusiasm the praises of 'a fair lady who ever says "No"'? And how is it that such consummate poesy was at hand ready to serve the new passion? The miraculous character of the twin birth cannot be too greatly stressed. Within no more than about twenty years there were established together, on the one hand, a vision of woman entirely at variance with traditional manners—woman was set *above man*, and became his nostalgic ideal—and on the other hand, a new but fully developed poetry of an extremely complex and refined character—a poetry equally unknown to Antiquity, and to the few centuries of Romanic literary vigour that had followed the Carolingian Renaissance. Either both these things 'dropped out of the sky'—that is to say, medieval society was suddenly and collectively inspired with them—or else they had some definite historical cause. On the first assumption, we must ask why the inspiration came at that particular time and in that particular area; and on the second assumption, why the historical cause should have remained a mystery ever since. The most curious feature of the business is that whenever the most serious authorities happen to refer to it they betray that they are at a loss and at once determine to say nothing.

It is generally recognized today that both Provençal poetry and the notion of love which informs its themes, far from being accounted for by conditions prevailing at the time, seem to have been in flat contradiction to them. 'Evidently', according to M.

Courtly Love: Troubadours and Cathars

Jeanroy,[1] 'the poetry did not reflect the actual state of affairs, for the position allotted to woman in feudal institutions of the South was quite as lowly and dependent as in those of the North.' If it is thus 'evident' that the troubadours were not depicting the conditions around them, they must have obtained their notion of love from *elsewhere*. The same must be true, for that matter, of their art, their poetic technique. 'An extremely original creation,' M. Jeanroy writes, notwithstanding that each poet when he takes them singly he reproaches with having displayed no originality of any kind and with having merely refined on forms already fixed and on commonplaces. Yet one of them at least must have *created* the forms! Yet whenever some historian ventures on a theory of how courtly rhetoric came into being, the authorities turn on him with biting irony. Sismondi attributed the origins of emotional mysticism to the Arabs: his theory was disdainfully rejected as monstrous.[2] Diez discerned resemblances in the rhythms and pauses of Arab and Provençal lyric poetry: we are told he must not be taken seriously. Brinkmann and others suggested that Latin poetry of the eleventh and twelfth centuries may have provided models: but this, it is said, cannot be listened to, because the troubadours, it seems, were not sufficiently educated to have been aware of this poetry. Thus, no matter what explanation is offered, the authorities are apparently determined to pooh-pooh any attempt to give a meaning to what they have devoted their lives to studying. It is true that Wechssler, in a famous book,[3] supposed everything was going to be cleared up when he announced that he had found underlying Provençal poetry certain *religious* influences, of a neo-Platonist and debased Christian nature. But he was at once stigmatized 'a doctrinaire' —the most damaging of insults—and several Frenchmen implied that as he was both a professor and a German he was hardly fitted to form an opinion on a matter connected with the limpid and elegant genius of Southern France.

We thus have, on the one hand, a queer historical phenomenon, and, on the other hand, very learned refutations of whatever may claim to account for it. One professor writes: 'To look upon those love songs which form three-fourths of Provençal poetry as being a faithful reflection of reality is quite as impossible as to regard

[1] A. Jeanroy, Introduction to *Anthologie des Troubadours* (Paris, 1927).
[2] A. Jeanroy, op. cit., I, p. 69.
[3] E. Wechssler, *Das Kulturproblem des Minnesangs* (Halle, 1909).

The Religious Origins

them as being a bundle of set phrases devoid of meaning.' No doubt. But thereupon the professor declares that as 'a scrupulous historian' he takes care not to commit himself. That amounts to saying that the lyric poetry of courtly love, with which he is concerned, remains for him, till he learns to the contrary, 'a bundle of set phrases devoid of meaning'. Excellent 'material', it is true, for a self-respecting philologist who does not intend to force a text, even by means of the least attempt to understand it.

For my part, I cannot rest content with such a scrupulous attitude. I cannot believe that the troubadours were so simple as merely to repeat forms picked up anyhow. Following E. Aroux and Péladan,[1] I wonder if the clue to the secret of all this poetry is not to be sought nearer at hand than any one has so far looked for it—much nearer, on the spot, and in the environment of the poets. I do not mean the purely 'social' environment in the modern sense, but in the religious atmosphere which happened to determine the formal behaviour—including the social usages—of that environment.

One great historical event stands out in the Provençal twelfth century. Simultaneously with the lyrical surge of the *domnei*, and in the same provinces and among the same classes, there also arose a great heresy. Historians have declared that the Catharist religion was as powerful a menace to the Church as Arianism had been earlier. It has even been asserted that, notwithstanding the bloody Albigensian crusade, or on account of it, this religion won millions of secret converts in Europe during the thirteenth century and afterwards up to the Reformation.

The exact origin of the Heresy can be attributed to the Neo-Manichaean sects of Asia Minor and to the Bogomil churches of Dalmatia and Bulgaria. The Pure or Cathars[2] were affiliated with the great Gnostic streams that flowed across the first millennary of Christianity. It is well known that the Gnosis, like the doctrine of Mani (or Manes), thrust down its roots into the dualist religion of Persia. What was the Catharist doctrine? For a long time it went on being repeated that 'nobody would ever know', and this for the good reason that the Inquisition had burned all the liturgical books and doctrinal treatises of the Heresy, and that the only

[1] Eugène Aroux, *Dante, pasteur de l'église albigeoise de Florence* (1856); Joséphin Péladan, *Le Secret des troubadours* (1906).
[2] 'Cathar' is from the Greek καθαρὸς, spotless.

78

surviving testimony consisted of the answers of the accused during interrogation, these, however, having probably been extorted by the judges and deformed by the clerks who wrote them down. Actually, the discovery and publication in 1939 of a theological work of the Cathars—late, it is true—the *Book of the Two Principles*,[1] coming on top of the restoration of the New Testament and of rituals used by the Heretics,[2] enables us at the present day to understand generally and in a number of variations what were the dogmas of the 'Church of Love', as the Heresy is sometimes called, although known mostly as the Albigensian heresy.[3]

Underlying the attitude of the Cathars, or, more generally, underlying Dualism, there has ever been, alike in the most various religions and in the minds of millions of individual men, the problem of Evil—evil as the spiritually-minded man experiences it in the world—and of course that problem is one always tragically present. To the problem of Evil Christianity offers an answer at once dialectical and paradoxical. It is an answer summed up in the two words 'Freedom' and 'Grace'. More pessimistic and more solidly logical, Dualism declares Good and Evil to exist in absolute heterogeneity. There are two worlds, and two creations. In effect, God is Love, but the world is evil. Hence God cannot be the creator of the world, of its darkness, and of the sin which coils itself about us. His creation was first spiritual and then one of souls. It was completed and also perverted in the material order by the Rebel Angel, the Great Arrogant, the Demiurge—that is to say, by Lucifer or Satan. The latter tempted the Souls or Angels, saying 'It is better to be down below, where you will be able to do both good and evil, than up above, where God allows you only to do good.'[4] The better to seduce Souls, Lucifer showed them 'a woman of dazzling beauty, who inflamed them with desire'. Then he left heaven with her, in order to descend into

---

[1] *Liber de duobus Principiis*, A. Dondaine, O.P., editor (Rome, 1939).

[2] Cf. Döllinger's publication, *The Secret Supper* (Munich, 1890).

[3] Three important works on Catharism have appeared recently. They are: Déodat Roché, *Etudes manichéennes et cathares* (1952); René Nelli, Charles Bru, Canon de Lagger, D. Roché, L. Sommariva, *Le Catharisme* (1953); Arno Borst, *Die Katharer* (1953). The third is in many respects in opposition to the other two, but all three, taken together, throw a strong light on the precise nature of the Heresy as well as on its evolution and complexities.

[4] Cf. the Catharist Prayer quoted by Döllinger. It should be noted that man's freedom, the faculty to do either evil *or* good, would thus have originated not in God but in the Devil.

matter and into sensible manifestation. The Angel-Souls, having followed Satan and the woman of dazzling beauty, were ensnared in material bodies even though these were and remained *foreign* to them. (This notion strikes me as throwing light upon a fundamental human sentiment or feeling, one that is still met with nowadays.) A soul is then parted from its spirit, which remains in heaven. Tempted by the prospect of freedom, a soul actually becomes the prisoner of a body with terrestrial appetites and subject to the laws of procreation and death. But Christ came among us to show the way back to the Light. The Dualist Christ, like that of the Gnostics and of Manes, was not really incarnated; he but took the appearance of a man. Such is the great Docetist heresy ('Docetist', from the Greek δόκησις = apparition) which, from Marcion to our own day, expresses our quite 'natural' refusal to countenance the scandal of a Man-God. The Cathars therefore rejected the dogma of the Incarnation, and *a fortiori* its Roman translation in the sacrament of the mass. They replaced it with a supper of brotherhood which symbolized purely spiritual events. They also rejected baptism by water, and recognized only baptism by the consolatory Spirit: the *consolamentum* was the major rite of their Church. It was given at initiation ceremonies to brethren who undertook to renounce the world and solemnly promised to devote themselves to God alone, never to lie or take an oath, never to kill, or eat of, an animal, and finally ever *to abstain, if married, from all contact with a wife.* It seems that initiation was preceded by a fast of forty days,[1] and that another of the same length followed. (Later, in the thirteenth century, the ritual fast or *endura* was to result in the voluntary death of some of the Pure, death for the love of God, the consummation of supreme detachment from any material law.) The *consolamentum* was administered by bishops, and included the imposition of hands, amid a circle of the Pure, and then the Kiss of Peace was exchanged by the brethren. Thereupon, the fresh initiate became an object of veneration for ordinary believers who had not yet been 'consoled'; he was entitled to their 'salute' —that is to say, to three 'bows'.

[1] The number forty is archetypal. Jesus was forty days in the wilderness. The Hebrews wandered for forty years between Egypt and the Promised Land. The Flood was brought about by a rainfall that lasted forty days. In Buddhist Tantrism the 'service' of the Woman is broken up into trials or ordeals of forty days, etc., etc. Forty is the number for an ordeal or trial.

Courtly Love: Troubadours and Cathars

I have mentioned the part assigned to Woman as the Devil's lure to draw souls down into bodies. In return—one might say, in order to get even—a feminine principle, held to have pre-existed material creation, occupied in Catharism an analogous part to that of the Sophia-Pistis of Gnosticism. To the woman who was instrumental in the perdition of souls there corresponded Maria, symbol of the pure saving Light, intact (immaterial) Mother of Jesus, and (it would seem) the all-gentle Judge of released spirits.

The Manichaeans had for centuries the same sacraments as the Cathars: the laying on of hands, the Kiss of Peace, and the veneration of the Elect (or Pure). It is important here to mention that Manichaean veneration is addressed to the 'Form of Light', and that this represents in every man *his own spirit* (which has stayed in heaven, beyond terrestrial manifestation) and welcomes the homage of his soul by a salute and a kiss. Hell being the prison of matter, Lucifer, the Rebel Angel, can reign there only for the length of *time* that the 'error' of souls persists. At the end of the cycle of their ordeals—comprising for men who have not yet been illumined several lives, physical and other—creation will return to the unity of the Original Spirit, the sinners borne off by Satan will be saved, and Satan himself will once again bow in obedience to the Most High.

Catharist dualism issues in an eschatological monism, whereas our Christian orthodoxy, inasmuch as it decrees the eternal damnation of the Devil and of hardened sinners, becomes ultimately dualistic, even though, contrary to Manichaeism, it professes the idea of a single creation, accomplished entirely at the hands of the Deity, and one that began by being entirely good. There is a final feature to be noted. As with so many eastern religions and sects—Jainists, Buddhists, Essenes, and Gnostic Christians—the Catharist Church consisted of two groups: the Perfect (*perfecti*),[1] who had received the *consolamentum*, and the mere Believers (*credentes* or *imperfecti*). The latter alone were allowed to marry and to go on living in a world which the Pure condemned, and this without having to comply with all the precepts of esoteric morality: bodily mortifications, contempt for creation, the severance of all worldly ties.

[1] Incidentally, the name 'Perfect' is to be found nowhere but in the records of the Inquisition. The term 'Goodmen' (or, more simply, 'Christians') seems to have been used by the Cathars themselves, and 'Perfect' seems to have been ironical.

Saint Bernard of Clairvaux, quoted by Rahn, was able to say of the Cathars, notwithstanding that he fought them with all his might: 'No sermons are more thoroughly Christian than theirs, and their morals are pure.' His testimonial makes up to some extent for the slanders of the Inquisition. It is nevertheless odd to find a saint describing as 'Christian' a form of preaching in which several of the fundamental dogmas of his church were rejected. As for the purity of the morals of the Cathars, it has just been shown that they professed beliefs entirely contrary to those upon which true Christian morality is based. *The condemnation of the flesh, which is now viewed by some as characteristically Christian, is in fact of Manichaean and 'heretical' origin.* For it must be borne in mind that when Saint Paul speaks of the 'flesh' he means not the physical body but the *whole* of the unbelieving man—body, mind, faculties, and desires—and hence his *soul* too.

The Albigensian crusade, led by the Abbot of Citeaux at the beginning of the thirteenth century, resulted in the destruction of the towns inhabited by the Cathars, in the burning of their books, the slaughter and burning of the mass of the people who loved them, and the violation of their sanctuaries and supreme High Place, the famous Castle of Montségur. The highly refined civilization of which they were the austere and secret spirit was brutally devastated. Nevertheless, to that culture and its fundamental doctrines we still pay tribute. We are its debtors, as I hope to show, far more than we realize.

7

Heresy and Poetry

Should the troubadours be regarded as having been Believers of the Catharist Church and the bards of its heresy? This view, which I shall call the maximum view in contrast to the one which I feel I myself am authorized to adopt,[1] was put forward by

---

[1] It is set forth on page 101 and is discussed at greater length in Chapter 10.

a succession of venturous spirits such as Otto Rahn, and, in my opinion, they damaged it by trying to make it too plain at a historical rather than a spiritual level. Yet it is a view singularly irritating and stimulating, for it seems as impossible to reject as to accept, as impossible to demonstrate as to deny utterly, and this is due to the very essence of the phenomenon that it seeks to account for—an affair both historical and archetypal, both psychical and mystical, both concrete and symbolic, or, if you prefer, literary and religious.

The data are roughly as follows. On the one hand, the Catharist heresy and courtly love developed simultaneously in the twelfth century and also coincided spatially in the south of France.[1] How suppose that the two movements were entirely unconnected? For them not to have entered into relations would surely be the strangest thing of all! But, on the other hand, and weighting the opposite side of the scales, how could there be a connexion between those sombre Cathars, whose asceticism compelled them to shun all contact with the opposite sex,[2] and the bright troubadours, joyful and up to any folly, who turned love, the spring, dawn, flowery gardens, and the Lady, all into song? Our modern rationalism is entirely at one with the Romanist scholars who declare unanimously that Cathars and troubadours had nothing in common! But the irrepressible intuition of those venturous spirits to whom I referred above answers, with the approval of our common sense, 'Show us, then, how Cathars and troubadours were able to rub elbows day after day, without making one another's acquaintance, and how they could live in two completely watertight worlds amid the great psychical revolution of the twelfth century!' To refuse to understand the Heresy and courtly love each by means of the other and with but one movement of

[1] The first troubadour, William of Poitiers, died in 1127. The earliest references to an *organized* and public Catharist Church date from 1160. But already in 1145, according to Borst, Catharism was found to have spread in Bulgaria and England! The name appears that year in Germany and two years later in Languedoc. Arno Borst infers that Catharism invaded Europe in a couple of years! He is surprised. I do not believe it. Under other names, or even without name, Catharism existed in people's minds much earlier than 'historical' texts. Its doctrines were condemned in France as early as the eleventh century— at Orleans, in Poitou, Périgord, and Aquitaine; that is to say—and let us not fail to notice it—in the very places where the first troubadours appeared!

[2] This went so far as to prevent a Perfect from sitting on a bench if a woman had recently left it. Yet many women of the nobility were Cathars and the troubadours dedicated to them their lays.

the mind looks very much like refusing to understand each of them one by one.

What is there in favour of the 'venturous' view?

Raimon V, Count of Toulouse and Suzerain of Languedoc, wrote in 1177: 'The heresy has penetrated everywhere. It has sown discord in every family, dividing husband from wife, son from father, a man's wife from his mother. Even priests yield to the temptation. The churches are abandoned and falling into ruin. . . . The most important people on my estates have been corrupted. The crowd has followed their example and has given up the (Catholic) faith, so that I no longer dare to undertake anything.' How suggest that the troubadours lived and sang in such a world as is pictured there without caring what went on in the heads and hearts of the noblemen on whose bounty they lived? In reply to that question we are told that the first troubadours were seen in Poitou and the Limousin while the Heresy had its centre more to the southward—in the county of Toulouse. But we find that the language which the troubadours of the Limousin employed from the beginning is the language of the county of Toulouse! And the same language was soon being used by troubadours in other parts of Europe. It is also contended that the courts most often named by troubadours as making them particularly welcome were those of nobles who remained orthodox. But that does not hold for all of them. Far from it, as will be seen presently. Moreover, quite possibly the presence of troubadours at such courts is a sign of heretical tendencies in them. Here is the beginning of a song by Peire Vidal:

'My heart rejoices on account of the agreeable and sweet renewal, and on account of the Castle of Fanjeaux, which seems Paradise to me; for love and joy are confined there, as well as all that is due to honour, and sincere and perfect courtesy.'

Who would dare to say, or even to think for a moment, that those lines sound Catharist? Yet what is this Castle of Fanjeaux? One of the mother-houses of the Cathars! The most famous of heretical bishops, Guilabert of Castres, directed it in person from 1193, and the poem quoted above may be ascribed to about 1190. It is in the same castle that Esclarmonde of Foix, the highest of heretical ladies, received the *consolamentum*! The second verse of Vidal's song speaks solely of the ladies:

'I have no enemy however mortal whose true friend I do not become if he speaks to me of the ladies and does them honour and praise. And as I am not in the midst of them, but am going to another country, I utter my plaint, I sigh and I languish.'

The reader may well wonder if Peire Vidal can be more than an amusing gallant, a flatterer of the wealthy women who formed his 'public'. But the rest of the poem is disturbing. He lists the houses in which he has been made welcome and the places from which, alas! he has to take leave so as to get to Provence: the castles of Laurac, Gaillac, Saissac, and Montreal; the counties of the Albigenses and of Carcasses, 'where the knights and women of the country are courtly', and he refers to 'Dame Louve, who has so completely conquered me that, by God and my faith! her gentle laughter lingers in my heart!' Now we happen to know that *every one* of those castles was a well-known focus of the Heresy; that they were even 'Heretics' Houses' (convents of a kind); that the counties named were notoriously Catharist; and that the 'Louve' is Countess Stéphanie, alias La Loba, who belonged to a group of active heretics! The poem, entitled in a modern anthology in all innocence, 'Thanks for Gracious Moments of Hospitality', thus acquires the unexpected character of a kind of pastoral letter! And yet I read it over again and rub my eyes. Can this really be an instance of 'pure coincidences'? The doubt and the question recur *ad infinitum*.

It is again a 'pure coincidence', perhaps, that the troubadours, like the Cathars, extolled (without always practising) the virtue of chastity; that, like the Pure, they received from their lady but a single kiss of initiation; that they distinguished two stages in the *domnei* (the *pregaire*, or prayer, and the *entendaire*), as the Church of Love distinguished between Believers and Perfect. The troubadours scoffed at the marriage bond which the Cathars called the *iurata fornicatio*. They reviled the clergy and the clergy's allies, the members of the feudal caste. They liked best to lead the wandering life of the Pure, who set off along the road in pairs. And in their verse are expressions taken from Catharist liturgy.

It would be only too easy to go on finding similar 'coincidences'. But what of the arguments on the other side? Not all the troubadours, I shall be told, were supporters of the Heresy. A number ended their days in a convent cell. No doubt. And, moreover, Folquet of Marseilles turns out to have taken part in the Albigensian crusade. But on that very account he was considered a traitor, and one day was brought before Pope Innocent III and charged with having caused the death of five hundred thousand persons. As far as that goes, even if it could be shown that certain troubadours in particular never suspected the existence of a close connexion between the themes of their poems and Catharist doctrine, that would not show that the *origin* of the poetry was not Catharist. The troubadours, it should be borne in mind, displayed an admirable unanimity in composing their *coblas* and their *sirventes*. They all obeyed the same rhetorical canon. It is easy enough for poetry—and possibly very beautiful poetry—to be written with commonplaces of the time and for the poet concerned not to suspect the source of those commonplaces. Beauty apart, is this not indeed usual? And if it is objected that the troubadours, in the poems that have come down to us, never refer to their beliefs, the obvious answer is that the Cathars had to promise, on initiation, never to betray their faith, no matter what kind of death might seem to be in store for them. Thus the records of the Inquisition contain not a single admission about the *minesola* (or *malisola* or again *manisola*), the highest initiation ceremony of the Pure. We should also give due weight to how often the Courts of Love discussed the question, 'Can a married knight be true to his lady?' For all the troubadours had to undergo the semblance of a 'marriage' with the Church of Rome—they were clerks—while serving in their 'thoughts' another Lady—the Church of Love. . . . Bernard Gui, in his *Manuel de l'Inquisiteur*, shows that although the Cathars venerated the Blessed Virgin, she was not, in their belief, a woman of flesh and blood, the Mother of Jesus, *but their Church*.

It will be said that some troubadours abjured the Heresy without giving up the *trobar*. But it would not astonish us at all to see a newly converted poet of today devote to the Virgin images which he had invented for the praise of others and had as his stock in hand. I shall be told that Peire of Auvergne did penance. But what better proof that he had been a heretic?

However, let us turn to the textual evidence, which exposes the rhetoric in its sheer nudity and transparence. There is the theme that *death* is preferable to earthly rewards:

> Far more it pleaseth me to die
> Than easy mean delight to feel.
> For what will meanly satisfy
> Nor can nor ought to fire my zeal.

Thus Almeric de Belenoi. 'What will meanly satisfy' would rid

him of his desire were it not that the ill he cherishes is love without
end, *joy d'amor*, the frenzy that prevails over all else.

> ... in fact this wild desire
> Is bound to be my death, no matter if I stay or go.
> For she who could deliver me, no pity will she show.
> ... and this desire
> Although it hath from frenzy sprung, it certainly prevails
> Above the others all.

If he does not wish to die yet, it is because he feels that he has not
yet become detached from desire, and feels that he would be
leaving his body out of despair—a 'mortal sin'; it is also that he is
still unaware

> how this may be his weal
> That ecstasy his soul shall softly steal.

Did not the Catharist doctrine require that life should be ended,
'not out of weariness nor out of fear or pain, but in a state of utter
detachment from nature'?[1]

Next here is the theme of *parting*, the leitmotiv of all courtly
love:

> Heaven! How doth it thus befall
> The farther off I am the more I long for her.

Then there is Guiraut de Bornheil, who prays to the *true* Light[2]
as he waits for the dawn of terrestrial day—the dawn that is going
to reunite him with his 'copain' (or comrade) of the road—and
hence of his trials in the world. We may wonder whether the two
'copains' are not soul and body—the soul bound to the body, but
hankering after spirit? And we may also remember that mission-
aries go forth in pairs.

> O high and glorious King, O Light and Brightness true!
> O God of Power, Lord, suppose it pleases you,
> Make my comrade welcome, and grant him all your aid.
> For him I have not seen since fell the night's dark shade,
> And soon will come the dawn.

[1] Déodat Roché, a living scholar intensely interested in Catharism (cf. his
Etudes manichéennes et cathares (1952) and *Le Catharisme* (1938)), insists likewise
that in the Catharist view there was a 'danger of flying too swiftly up to heaven',
and opposes Catharism to Buddhism on that truly capital point.

[2] When a troubadour uses the word 'true' before any of the words, 'God',
'Light', 'Faith', or 'Church', it may be a sign of Catharism. The Cathars took
care to speak the language of orthodoxy, adding that significant little qualification for the benefit of the initiate.

But by the time the troubadour reaches the end of his lay, has he betrayed his vows, or has he found in the bosom of night that true Light from which there must be no parting?

> Noble comrade mine, so happy am I where I stay,
> I never wish again to see the rise of dawn or day.
> The loveliest of maidens that a mother could e'er bear
> I now hold closely in my arms, so I no longer care
> What happens to the envious or the dawn.

The nightingale was cheerfully giving throat to the trill that later on, in the second act of *Tristan*, provided Wagner with Brengain's sublime cry:

> Habet acht! Habet acht!
> Schon weicht dem Tag die Nacht![1]

But Tristan has his answer: 'Ever hold us, O night!' There is a parallel in the beginning of another (anonymous) 'Dawn':[2]

'In a garden, in a hawthorn nook, the lady has held her lover in her arms till the watchman cried: "God! It's the dawn! How quickly it comes!" "How I should like, my God, that night should not end, that my friend could stay by me, and that never the watchman called the rise of dawn! God, it's the dawn! How quickly it comes!"'

But in no poem is it clear whether the 'Fair Lady who ever says "No!"' is a woman or a symbol. The troubadours all swear that they will never betray the *secret* of their mighty passion, as if it were a faith, and one that had been imparted to them by initiation.

'Cease, I tell you, in the name of Love and in my own name, treacherous accusers, steeped in every kind of malice, cease asking who is she, and which her country, whether near or far. This I shall keep well hidden from you. I would rather perish than fail by so much as a word.'

What 'lady' could be worthy of such a sacrifice? And this cry of William of Poitiers:

> By her alone shall I be saved!

Or this invocation by Uc de Saint-Circ of a 'Dame sans merci':

[1] 'Have a care! Have a care!
Now Night gives way to Day!'
[2] 'Dawns' were an accepted kind of poem. It will readily be understood how appropriate they were for the purposes of a vision of the world in which Day and Night were hostile to one another.

Heresy and Poetry

'I do not wish God to aid me nor to give me joy and happiness except through you!'

If these are only rhetorical tropes, we must ask ourselves what attitude of mind produced them, and what kind of Love can have been their Platonic idea or form? In the song, 'Du moindre tiers d'Amour'—the tierce love of women—Guiraut de Calanson says of the two other tierce loves—the love of parents and heavenly love—

'To the second is suited nobility and thanks; and the first is so lofty that its powers hover above the sky.'

This one-in-three love, this feminine principle ('amor' in Provençal is of the feminine gender), which Dante presently found 'moving the sky and all the stars', seems indeed to be the Divinity-in-itself of the great heterodox mystics, the God of before the Trinity mentioned both in the Gnosis and by Meister Eckhart; and, more exactly still, the 'super-essential' God who, according to Bernard of Chartres (c. 1150!), 'resides above the heavens' and of whom 'Noys'—the Greek νοῦς—is the intellectual and *feminine* emanation. Nothing else would produce the uncertainty, the sense of dubiousness, which we cannot fend off as we read these love poems. The poems are about a real woman[1]—the physical *pretext* is there—but as in the Song of Songs the tone is truly mystical. Scholars keep on saying that this indicates something 'perfectly simple'—a fad for idealizing woman and natural love. But they do not say how the fad arose. Was it from some 'idealizing humour'?

Consider the lay by Peire de Rogiers:

> Bitter, bitter my distress must be,
> And never, never must my heart give up
> Its great and overwhelming grief for her,
> Nor I be granted e'en a passing hope
> Of joy however sweet, however good.
> Great joy could acts of prowess bring to me.
> I'll do none; all I know to want is SHE.

And the cry of Bernart of Ventadour:

'She has taken my heart, she has taken my self, she has taken me from the world, and then she has slipped away from me, leaving me with only my desire and my parched heart!'

[1] Generally referred to by a symbolic name or *senhal*, even as the Sufi mystics refer to God in their poems!

And next from Arnaut Daniel—a nobleman who turned wandering jongleur and whose poems, according to authorities on the Romance languages, are 'devoid of thought'—are two verses which seem to me to possess the very demeanour of negative mysticisim and to display its invariable metaphors.

'I love and seek her so eagerly that I believe the very violence of my desire for her would deprive me of all desire whatsoever could one lose aught by loving well. For her heart drowns mine in a never-diminishing flood. . . .

'I want neither the Roman Empire nor to be named its pope [and for a very good reason!], if I am not to be brought back to her for whom my heart is ablaze and cleft in twain. But if she has not solaced my anguish with a kiss before the New Year, she destroys me and I am damned.'

The intuition which directs this inquiry must be followed to the extreme end. If the Lady is not simply the Church of Love of the Cathars (as Aroux and Péladan considered they were entitled to think) nor the Sophia Maria of the Gnostic heresies (the Feminine Principle of Divinity), why should she not be the *Anima*, or, more precisely, man's *spiritual* element, that which the soul imprisoned in his body desires with a nostalgic love that death alone can satisfy?

In the *Kephalaia* or Chapters of Manes,[1] Chapter Ten tells how the elect person who has renounced the world receives the imposition of hands (among the Cathars the *consolamentum*, usually given at the approach of death); how he thus sees that he is 'ordained' in the Spirit of Light; how at the last, in the moment of death, the *Form of Light*, which is his spirit, appears to him and consoles him with a *kiss*; how his angel offers him its right hand and also *greets* him with the Kiss of Love; how finally the elect person venerates his own *Form of Light*, his *feminine Saviour*. Let us now recall that a troubadour lovesick with real love awaited from the Lady of his Thoughts—who was in essence unattainable, and put 'in too lofty a place for him'[2]—no more than a single kiss, a

---

[1] Discovered at the Fayum in Egypt in 1930 and published by C. Schmidt at Stuttgart in 1935.

[2] It is well known that one of the set themes of courtly rhetoric is the complaint that one 'loves in too lofty a place'. Scholars tell us that the poor troubadour, of socially low extraction, as a rule, fell in love with the wife of some high and mighty baron, who disdained him. No doubt that happened in a few cases. But it does not account for the same plaint being breathed in the poems of

single look, a single greeting. Geoffrey Rudel, after long being in love with the image of a woman he has never seen, beholds her at last after a sea passage and dies in the arms of the Countess of Tripoli as soon as she has bestowed upon him a single kiss of peace and a greeting. That is a legend, but a legend drawn from poems which unmistakably celebrate 'faraway love'. Other women are said to have been 'real'. Were they indeed more substantial than a psychical event?

Several writers have suggested that the *historical puzzle* could be solved by supposing that the Heretical Church was reduced to clandestine operation, and that the troubadours were its agents. From that puzzle we now pass to *the mystery of a strictly religious passion*, which involves a mystical view of man. That view in turn is strongly upheld by the very experience of the human spirit. Let us see if, by going between the points and limiting oscillations of our inquiry, we can get to the reality which usually lies intermediately, the reality of courtly lyric poetry, even though, because intermediate, it is by so much less 'clear' and less 'pure'.

8

Objections

There is a risk that the importance of the conclusions to which the two preceding chapters point will be judged by the number of objections to which those conclusions give rise. I hope to gain from criticism, and I do not want to repress it. But the reader will appreciate my dealing with the doubts that

---

Alfonso of Aragon, a most powerful king. For him, obviously, no woman in *this* world was too high. The real question is why the poet chooses to cast his love so high and chooses the unattainable.

have very likely come over him so far and my trying to dispel them.

There are, I think, four objections, and they are as follows:

1. The Religion of the Cathars is still imperfectly understood, and it is therefore at the very least premature to assume that this religion was the source, or a chief source, of courtly poems.

2. The troubadours never admitted being of this religion, and never stated that this religion was the subject of their poetry.

3. On the contrary, the love which they extol is but the idealization or sublimation of sexual desire.

4. Out of a confused mixture of Manichaean and Neo-Platonic doctrines operating upon a background of Celt-iberian traditions it is difficult to see how there could have arisen a rhetoric as highly elaborate as that of the troubadours.

With those objections I shall deal seriatim.

1. A RELIGION IMPERFECTLY UNDERSTOOD

If the Catharist religion were not known at all, then the problem of courtly lyric poetry would remain completely obscure, as the authorities on Romance languages allow. For my part, I cannot regard as absurd a poetic and morality of love out of which were to come in later centuries the most splendid of Western literary works. Furthermore, certain points about Catharist rites and beliefs have now been established beyond dispute. The origins of the Heresy are Manichaean. When we recall what was said above (II, 2) about the *essentially lyrical* character of Manichaean dogmas in general, it emerges that any small piece of additional information about this or that qualification or alteration to which the dogmas were subject in the Southern Church would not weigh much either for or against what I am contending. *What should be looked for in courtly rhetoric is not rational or precise equivalences of the dogma*, but the lyrical and psalmodic development of the fundamental symbolism. Likewise, to take a modern example, the 'Christian sentiment' which is discerned in the poetry of Baudelaire is not a term for term transposition of Catholic dogma. It is rather the manifestation of a certain and even of a definite sensibility which but for Catholic dogma could not be imagined, and to this are added elements of vocabulary and syntax which are unmistakably of liturgical origin. It is not going too far to suppose that the strains which we have noted in the work of the

92

Provençal poets stand in a similar relation to Neo-Manichaeism.[1]

For that matter, the heretical tonality of the set phrases and expressions in the rhetoric of courtly love becomes evident as soon as those phrases and expressions are compared with the clerical poetry of the period. A specialist as sceptical as Jeanroy does not fail to notice it. Writing of the abstract lyrical poetry of the troubadours of the thirteenth century and how it tends to fuse God and the Lady of Thoughts, he writes: 'It will be said that these are but rhetorical figures without consequence. Nevertheless the question is: Are not the theories which the troubadours developed with their grave intentness at the antipodes of Christianity? They must have noticed it. And why in their poems is there no hint of that internal rift, of that *dissidio*, which renders some of Petrarch's verses so full of pathos?'[2]

2. THE TROUBADOURS KEEP THE SECRET

To the theory that the troubadours were secretly Cathars several recent writers have objected that no courtly poet ever gave away the show, even after being converted to Catholic orthodoxy. That is to attribute to a man of the twelfth century a form of consciousness which he could not possibly have. If we try to place ourselves in the medieval atmosphere, it becomes clear that the absence of any symbolical meaning in a poem would have been something far more offensive then than it can be now. To a medieval man every thing meant some other things as in dreams, and this without any translation into concepts on hi, part. That is to say, he had no need to formulate the meaning of

---

[1] It is also credible that in many cases the correspondences of Catharist doctrine with courtly poems are very close. In a study of one of the last of the troubadours ('Peire Cardinal était-il hérétique?' in *Revue d'Histoire des Religions*, June 1938), Lucia Varga goes so far as to propose that some of the poems of the troubadours should be used as *sources* of the Heresy. In support, she quotes some verses by Peire Cardinal (or Cardenal) which reproduce the exact terms of a Catharist prayer published by Döllinger. For example, 'Give me the power to love those that thou lovest' (Cardenal) and 'Vouchsafe to us that we may love those that Thou lovest' (Prayer). But it must also be noticed that Peire Cardenal, a true Cathar, speaks reprovingly of the 'courtesy' in a poem where he says: 'I do not engage in stupid exploits. . . . I have got away from love.' I shall return to the theme of the poets of courtly love being compelled to tack between the twofold condemnation pronounced upon sexual love by the Perfect and upon idealized but adulterous love by the Catholics.

[2] *Poésie lyrique des troubadours*, II, p. 306.

the symbols he used nor to become fully conscious of them. He was innocent of the rationalism which causes people today to abstract and empty of all significant overtones the objects to which they attend.[1] One of the best historians of medieval manners, Huizinga, provides a pertinent instance of this in the behaviour of Suso the mystic.[2]

'Towards the end of the Middle Ages two factors dominate religious life: the extreme saturation of the religious atmosphere, and a marked tendency of thought to embody itself in images.

'Individual and social life, in all their manifestations, are imbued with the conceptions of faith. There is not an object or an action, however trivial, that is not constantly correlated with Christ or salvation. All thinking tends to religious interpretation of individual things; there is an enormous unfolding of religion in daily life. This spiritual wakefulness, however, results in a dangerous state of tension, for the presupposed transcendental feelings are sometimes dormant, and whenever this is the case, all that is meant to stimulate spiritual consciousness is reduced to appalling commonplace profanity, to a startling worldliness in other-worldly guise. . . .

'Even in the case of a sublime mystic like Henry Suso, the craving for hallowing every action of daily life verges in our eyes on the ridiculous. He is sublime when, following the usages of profane love, he celebrates New Year's Day and May Day by offering a wreath and a song to his betrothed, Eternal Wisdom, or when, out of reverence for the Holy Virgin, he renders homage to all womankind and walks in the mud to let a beggar-woman pass. But what are we to think of what follows? At table Suso eats three-quarters of an apple in the name of the Trinity and the remaining quarter in commemoration of "the love with which the heavenly Mother gave her tender child Jesus an apple to eat"; and for this reason he eats the last quarter with the paring, as little boys do not peel their apples. After Christmas he does not eat it, for then the infant Jesus was too young to eat apples. He drinks in five draughts because of the five wounds of the Lord, but as blood and water flowed from the side of Christ,

---

[1] For example, in the Middle Ages a man was too 'naïve' to be able to devote himself to any material he deemed absurd—that is, material which lacked a religious significance and a fixed position in the scheme of values he accepted.

[2] *The Waning of the Middle Ages*, op. cit., pp. 136–37.

he takes his last draught twice. This is, indeed, pushing the sancti-
fication of life to extremes.'

Must it be held that this is a drop from symbol into allegory? Certainly, but carried to an evident excess. Huizinga remarks some
pages later that the simple religious sense of the people did not
need to have its faith intellectually justified; the visible image of
holy things was enough to establish their reality. This shows that
in the eyes of the initiated and in those of sympathizers with the
Church of Love the 'secret' of the troubadours served as a *symbolical witness*. In the ordinary way it could not occur to any one
that the symbols were invalid unless expounded and accounted
for in non-symbolical fashion.

A contrary objection has been raised. How is it that no converted Cathar ever gave away the troubadours as being propa-
gators of the Heresy? That, however, is easily answered. Obviously
the troubadours were not looked upon as either preachers or mis-
sionaries; at most as Believers, and more often as merely sympathe-
tic and friendly. Anyhow, such distinctions were much less sharp
than they are now. The troubadours, for the benefit of a public in
which the majority favoured the Heresy, made up their lays about
a kind of love which happened to correspond (and to respond) to
a very difficult moral situation, the situation that had been produced both by the religious condemnation of sexuality by the
Perfect and by a natural revolt against the orthodox conception
of marriage which had recently been affirmed afresh in the Gre-
gorian reform. They had accordingly to protect themselves on
two flanks—against the severity of the Perfect and against the
severity of Catholics.

Nevertheless, it is easy to understand that the peculiar position
of heretics caused some poets to be very discreet in indicating that,
apart from the habitual symbolism which spoke for itself, their
work possessed an exact double meaning. Hence symbols were
sometimes vehicles of allegory as well, and took on a crypto-
graphic guise. This happened with the school of the *trobar clus*, to
which I have already referred. While on the subject of this school,
Jeanroy remarks:[1] 'Another way [of 'baffling the reader'] was
to put a sacred notion into profane dress, and to apply to divine
love phrases appropriated by custom to the expression of human
love.' He claims not 'to be able to unravel' the causes of this
'singular perversion of taste in a form of literature that had newly

[1] Op. cit., II, p. 16.

arisen.' The troubadour Alegret has, however, declared significantly:

'My verse must seem nonsense to fools who cannot understand it in two ways. . . . If some one wishes to challenge this line, let him come forward, and I shall show him how it was possible to put in two [*variant*, three] words with various meanings.'

There is no reason to suppose that the troubadours engaged in this skilful confusing of the sense (*entrebescar*, the Provençals called it, meaning 'to interweave') merely as a literary exercise for the purpose of 'puzzling their hearers with conundrums'. 'I interweave words rare, dark and colourful, pensively pensive,' Rambaut of Orange writes. And Marcabru says: 'Wise beyond doubt I hold him who divines what each word in my song means.' It is true that he adds—sally or precaution?—'Because I myself am hard put to it to light up my dark speech.'

How far a troubadour himself understood the deep purport of his symbols is something, indeed, that cannot be determined. After all, the general run of human beings are very little conscious of using metaphors.[1] What I quoted above about the artless way in which medieval people accepted symbolism needs to be borne in mind. Symbols were not translatable into prosaic and rational concepts. The question has therefore only to be asked concerning the *double* allegorical meaning. Furthermore, all this poetry was being produced in an atmosphere highly charged with passion. The happenings recorded in contemporary chronicles are among the wildest and most *surréaliste* is the history of European manners. A jealous lord killed his wife's favourite troubadour, and had the dead man's heart served up to her on a dish. The lady ate it without knowing what it was. Her lord having told her, 'Sir,' she said, 'you have given me such a delicious dish that never shall I partake of any other'; and she threw herself out of the window of the keep. In an atmosphere where such events were possible, poets, it will be agreed, can have had no difficulty in 'colouring' a symbolism originally dogmatic.

3. COURTLY LOVE IS BUT THE IDEALIZATION OF SEXUAL DESIRE

This is the most common view. Against it is the fact that

[1] If some inarticulate man copies the letters he sends to his beloved out of a text-book, it does not follow that the expressions he uses do not seem to him to express his true and sincere emotion.

medieval symbolism usually operated from high to low—from heaven to earth. That is enough to dispose of the modern theories to which the materialistic prejudice has given rise. But we must enter into detail. Against Wechssler,[1] who also insists that courtly lyrical poetry is an expression of the religious sentiment of the time,[2] Jeanroy writes:

'In these bold claims one error of fact is easily detected. It may be admitted that in time the lay was emptied of its initial content and became no more than a tissue of hollow set phrases. But from the beginning till the end of the twelfth century that was not so. In the poems of that period the expression of carnal desire is so strong and occasionally so brutal that it is really impossible to mistake the nature of the poets' aspirations.'

If that was so we may wonder why the author is embarrassed and almost irritable upon having to admit how ambiguous are the expressions of courtesy and their mystical undertones. He says: 'Unquestionably the religious ideas of a period generally influence the view taken of love, and so too the vocabulary of courtship is modelled on that of devotion. Once "adore" had become a synonym of "love", that first metaphor led to many others.' In the face of that passage, it is hard to understand why Jeanroy rejects without discussion Wechssler's writings, in which it is contended that the 'theories of love-making in the Middle Ages are but a reflection of the religious ideas of the period'. Why is he so anxious to maintain at all costs that the poems of the troubadours contain 'realistic' notations and exact descriptions of the beloved Lady when elsewhere the troubadours are reproached with having used only stereotyped epithets? Geoffrey Rudel, Prince of Blaye, states quite clearly that his Lady is a creation of his mind, and that she vanishes at dawn. Elsewhere it is 'a faraway princess' that he says he wishes to love. Yet M. Jeanroy is disturbed to find in Rudel's poems 'details that appear to plunge us into reality and that there is nothing to explain'. Here is an instance which he gives: 'I am in doubt on the subject of a certain thing and my heart is in suspense: it is that all that the brother refuses me I hear the sister grant to me.' On the other hand, Rudel describes his Lady: her body is *gras, delgat et gen*.[3] In the first sentence which Jeanroy interprets as yielding a biographical indication there is an evident mystical sense: 'What the body

---

[1] E. Wechssler, *Das Kulturproblem des Minnesangs*, 2 vols. (Halle, 1909), op. cit.
[2] But Catholic and not heretical.   [3] 'Plump, delicate, and pretty.'

denies me, the spirit grants' (That is one instance; there are still other meanings). And as for the 'realistic' epithets that are taken to apply to a 'real' Lady, epithets completely *identical* are to be found in thirty or so other poets! (It is not surprising that I forget which learned student of the period declared that it looked as though the poetry of the troubadours had been the work of a single author singing the praises of always *the same Lady*!) Where, then, is the 'strong and brutal' expression of an obviously carnal desire to be found? Is it in the crudity of certain terms? But such crudity was common and natural in the days before middle-class puritanism. The contention is anachronistic.

Here instead is a document that supports the symbolical theory. In a poem on women Rambaut of Orange says that if you want to win them you should be brutal, 'punch them on the nose' (this is crude enough, surely?), and force them, because that is what they like.

'As for me [he adds], I behave differently, because I do not care about loving. I do not want to be put to trouble for the sake of women, any more than if they were all my sisters; and so with women I am humble, obliging, frank and gentle, fond, respectful, and faithful. . . . I love nothing, except this ring, which is dear to me because it has been on a finger. . . . But I am going too far; stop, tongue! Because to say too much is worse than mortal sin!'

This same Rambaut of Orange, however, wrote admirable poems in praise of his Lady; and we saw earlier that a *ring* (such as Tristan and Iseult exchange) was the symbol of a constancy which happened not to be that of the body. Let me also stress the important fact that the courtly virtues of humility, frankness, respect, and fidelity to one's Lady are being expressly connected here with a rejection of physical love. Moreover, we shall see later[1] that in Dante the images are the more passionate and 'realistic' in proportion to Beatrice's progressive rise in the hierarchy of mystical abstraction, where she becomes first Philosophy, then Wisdom, and finally Divine Knowledge. And one more small fact is that in the twenty-sixth Canto of the *Purgatorio* two of the troubadours most ardent in praising the beauty of their Ladies, the Provençal Arnaut Daniel and the Tuscan Guido Guinicelli, are found in the sodomites' circle.[2]

[1] Book IV.
[2] Perhaps this is the place to mention that a courtly knight often gave his Lady the masculine title of *mi dons* (*mi dominus*), and in Spain *senhor* (*not*

Objections

But all this only compels us to recognize how complex is a problem of which I have so far deliberately stressed only one aspect, and that the most disputed. We have too long been supposing that *cortezia* was a mere idealization of the sexual instinct. At the same time it would be going too far to assert that the mystical ideal on which *cortezia* must have been founded was always and everywhere being invoked, *or that in itself it could have only one meaning*. Nearly always an emphasis on chastity is accompanied by lewd excess. Without stopping to consider the charges of debauchery often brought against the troubadours—little, actually, is known about their lives—I may recall that at the same time as the Gnostic sects contemned creation, and in particular sexual attraction, they erected on their contempt a peculiarly licentious set of morals. For example, the Carpocratians forbade procreation, and also divinized the spermatic fluid.[1] It is quite probable that the Cathars were given to similar excesses, and especially that their poorly disciplined disciples, the troubadours, were. Horrifying charges on this score are to be found in the records of the Inquisition. But these are often contradictory. At times they state that the Cathars looked upon the most gross sensual indulgence as harmless, and at others that they condemned marriage and also sexual intercourse, whether legitimate or not. Similar charges, we should remember, have been brought against every new religion, not excepting primitive Christianity. It is fair to quote the opinion of a Dominican who had occasion to search the archives of the Holy Office and who writes thus about the Cathars of Italy or Patarini:

'In spite of my careful examination of the indictments drawn by our brethren, I have not found that "consoled" heretics were guilty in Tuscany of monstrous acts or that they ever indulged, particularly between men and women, in sensual excesses.'

So far, then, the scheme which I put forward at the beginning

---

senhora). Andalusian and Arab troubadours did the same, and the greatest, the supremely mystical, were notoriously homosexual. However, I incline to think that here again, at least to begin with, all was religious symbol as much as or more than it was the translation of human relations. The narcissism inherent in any so-called Platonic love involves on the sexual plane obvious deviations into which it would be difficult to deny that some troubadours were tempted.

[1] Cf. the documents translated and expounded in Wolfgang Schultz, *Dokumente der Gnosis* (Jena, 1910), pp. 158–64.

of Chapter 5 needs to be qualified as follows. Although deflexions of passion—in the strict sense I have given to the word 'passion' —have a religious and mystical inspiration, they unquestionably encourage the sexual instinct *by the very fact that they seek to transcend it.*

All this leads me to assert confidently now, however hesitant I may have felt at the outset, that courtly lyrical poetry was *at least inspired* by the mysticism of the Cathars. This may look like a moderate contention, but, once it is granted, I think it implies and explains a great deal more.

So that we may better imagine how this *process of inspiration and influence* came to operate, let me offer a present-day analogy. I think it may be laid down that the data concerning *Surréalisme* and the influence of Freud's theories on this movement are fully determined and also are fully known (in the complete sense of 'known') to a number of persons now living. Let us suppose that in the future our civilization has been destroyed, and that at some date following its destruction a historian seeks to establish some of its details. Certain *surréaliste* poems have been found, and he is able to translate them and ascribe to them their correct date. He is further aware that more or less contemporaneously with *Surréalisme* there flourished a particular school of psychiatry. But no writings produced by this school survive. Fascism, which acceded to power soon afterwards, destroyed every one of them on the ground that they were Semitic. Nevertheless, the historian knows, thanks to booklets issued by adversaries of this school of psychiatry, that it put forward an erotic theory of dreams. The *surréaliste* poems that have been preserved and translated seem meaningless, and are open to the reproach of monotony—always containing the same set of erotic and bloodthirsty images and the same intense rhetoric, and it looks as if they must all have had one author, etc. But then some persons come along and suggest that the poems merely describe dreams, and that perhaps they *are* no more than dreams that have been set down in writing. The suggestion is treated with unconcealed scepticism by authorities on the twentieth century. Thereupon, a writer—one of those people not to be taken seriously—offers the theory that the whole of *Surréalisme* was produced under the influence of pyscho-analysis, and in support of this theory points to the coincidence of dates and the similarity of basic themes. The authorities on the twentieth century shrug their shoulders. 'Establish your theory by means of documents,' they say. 'You know very well there aren't any.' 'In that case, better to steer clear of coherent theories.

'Meanwhile, your common sense is enough to show you—

'(*a*) That the little we know about psycho-analysis does not entitle us to look upon this doctrine as having inspired documents we already possess. (It seems clear that Freud was above all a scientist, that he had a theory of *libido*, and that he was a determinist; whereas *Surréalisme* was above all a literary movement; none of its surviving poems contain the word "libido"); and these poems all lean towards idealisms and impulsiveness.)

'(*b*) That the *Surréalistes* never *stated* in any poem that they were disciples of Freud.

'(*c*) That the free will they extol is something every psycho-analyst was bound to deny.

'(*d*) Finally, that it is by no means apparent how a science having for its aim the analysis and cure of neuroses could have inspired a rhetoric of insanity, which must have been a challenge to science in general and to the science of psycho-analysis in particular.'

So, the future authorities on the twentieth century. It happens, however, that we—who are living in the twentieth century—know exactly how these improbable things actually occurred. We are aware that the men who promoted the *Surréaliste* movement had read Freud and that they looked on him with the greatest respect. We are aware that but for him their theories and their poesy would alike have been altogether different. We are aware that *surréaliste* poets felt no need and had no opportunity of referring to the *libido* in their writings. We are further aware that it was owing to *an initial misunderstanding* of the precise significance of Freud's (determinist and positivist) doctrines that the poets were led to seize on these doctrines as the subject-matter of their poesy—a most important point if all this is treated as analogical with what I am putting forward about the troubadours. And finally we are aware that it was only necessary for a few leaders of the movement to read Freud, and that the disciples were content to imitate the rhetoric of their masters.

Moreover, thanks to this analogy, it can be understood how a doctrine acts on poets less as a direct influence than by permeating their *atmosphere*, so that its central dogmas stir up shocked feelings and produce both a wish to be 'in the know' and a wish to seize opportunities of self-advantage. The work of the poets who are influenced will therefore display a good many mistakes, variations, and contradictions. Hence, supposing additional information about the exact nature of Freud's theories came to light in the future, far from providing authorities on the twentieth century with the confirmation they expected, it would only seem to contradict the theory of my mere 'writer, one of those people not to be taken seriously'.[1]

There remains the fourth objection—that, the rhetoric of the troubadours being highly elaborate, it is difficult to see how a confused mixture of Manichaean and Neo-Platonist doctrines operating upon a background of Celt-iberian traditions could have given rise to it. This objection I have so far dealt with only indirectly and by passing allusion. It deserves a chapter to itself.

9

Arab Mystical Poetry

It happens that as early as the ninth century there occurred an equally 'unlikely' fusion of Iranian Manichaeism, Neo-Platonism, and Mohammedanism in Arabia, and the fusion was reflected in a religious poetry employing erotic metaphors that are strikingly akin to those of courtly rhetoric. In the twelfth century the chief writers of this kind of poetry were al Hallaj, al Gazali, and Suhrawardi of Aleppo. All three were troubadours of supreme Love, of the Veiled Idea, which they treated as beloved object but also as symbol of a longing for the divine.

Suhrawardi, who died in 1191, supposed Plato—whom he knew at second-hand from Plotinus, Proclus, and the Athenian school—to be a successor of Zoroaster. Indeed, his Neo-Platonism displays marked Persian mythical features. In particular, the doctrines about an antithetical relation of the World of Light and the

---

[1] *Eppur si muove!* He would nevertheless be right, and the recognized authorities on the twentieth century in his day wrong.

World of Darkness which he borrowed from the Zend-Avesta were those that had inspired Manes and that became the root of the Catharist faith. These doctrines—exactly as happened later with those of the Cathars—were transmuted into a chivalrous love rhetoric, the nature of which is indicated by the titles of two mystical treatises, *The Lovers' Familiar* and *The Romance of the Seven Beauties*. Moreover, at the time these and other similar treatises appeared there arose in a section of Islam a theological controversy of the same kind as occurred a little later in the medieval world of the West. It is true that in the Mohammedan world the controversy was made more intricate by a denial that man is able to *love* God (as the evangelical summary of the Law commands him). According to Mohammedanism, a finite creature can only love what is finite. In order therefore to express that love of the divine which they believed themselves to be experiencing, Arab mystics of the twelfth century had to resort to symbols having a secret meaning.[1] But, apart from this peculiarity—not without parallel in the situation of courtly rhetoric—the problems set up by the poetry of the Near East and by that of the West are identical.

Orthodox Mohammedanism was no more able than Roman Catholicism to allow that there is in man an element which in being cultivated will bring about the fusion of individual souls with the Divinity. But it was precisely this potential union of Creator and creature that was being implied in the eroticoreligious *language* of Arab mystic poetry. The symbolism employed by the poets caused them accordingly to be accused of holding a disguised Manichaeism, and the charge cost al Hallaj and Shurawardi their lives.[2] There is something poignant in the discovery that the grounds of the controversy are those which reappear in the case of the troubadours, and, later on—as we shall see—in, *mutatis mutandis*, the case of the great Western mystics from Meister Eckhart to John of the Cross.

A brief account of the 'courtly' themes that figure in poetic expositions of Arab mysticism will show how thoroughly the parallel holds both as regards inspiration and expression. Suhra-

[1] Thus praise of wine—wine being forbidden by the Prophet—became symbolical of the divine intoxication of love.

[2] According to Louis Massignon, *Passion de al Hallaj*, p. 161, the chief charge brought against him was in these terms: 'To adore God from love alone is the crime of the Manichaeans. . . . These adore God with a *physical* love, through the magnetic attraction of iron to iron, and their particles of light are impelled like a magnet back towards the focus of light whence they came.'

wardi speaks of lovers as being *Brethren of the Truth*. This was a name given to all mystic lovers who were at one with their beloved in a mutual idealization[1] and who came to form a community analogous to the Catharist Church of Love. Mystics of the illuminative school of Suhrawardi were inspired by Persian Manichaeism, and recently discovered documents relating to this faith contain a fable about a lovely maiden who awaits the true believer on the far side of the Bridge of Sinvat. When he appears she says to him: 'I am thyself!' According to certain interpreters of troubadour mysticism, the Lady of Thoughts is no other than the spiritual and angelical part of man—his true *self*. This may help towards a fuller understanding of what I have called 'the narcissism of passion'.[2]

The Lovers' Familiar is built upon an allegory of 'The Castle of the Soul' which has various floors and compartments. In one compartment there is a feminine being called The Veiled Idea. She possesses secrets that will assuage, and it is she who can impart magic.[3] Other allegorical characters in the Castle include Beauty, Desire and Dread, the Well-Informed, the Tester, the Well-Known—all of whom recall the *Roman de la Rose*. The same chivalric symbolism is found in *The Romance of the Seven Beauties*, the treatise in which Nizami of Ganja describes the adventures of seven maidens attired in the colours of the planets and who are visited by a knight-king. The Castle of the Soul became a favourite symbol for Ruysbroek and Saint Teresa. In a poem by the 'Lovers' Sultan', Omar Ibn al Faridh—to take one among dozens of instances—the author describes the terrible passion holding him in thrall:

> My fellow-citizens, surprised at seeing me a slave, said: 'Why is this youth mad?'
> And what can they say of me except that I am concerned with Nu'm?
> Indeed, yes, I am concerned with Nu'm.
> When Nu'm gratifies me with a glance, I mind not if Su'da is unkind.

Nu'm is a conventional name for a man's beloved, and here it means 'God'. The troubadours also gave to their Lady of Thoughts a conventional name or *senhal*; and authorities today

---

[1] Henry Corbin, Introduction to *The Lovers' Familiar*.

[1] Book I, Chapter 8, in connexion with Tristan.

[3] The Celtic Essylt was also a magician, 'an object of contemplation and a mystic vision'.

have vainly striven to discover who are the historical persons such names refer to.

Both the *salutation* and the *salute* that the initiated wish to give on approaching the Sage, but that the latter considerately gives first,[1] are a constant poetic theme of the troubadours, and later of Dante, and eventually of Petrarch. All these poets attach extreme importance to the 'salute' given by the Lady, and their doing so is easily understood if we bear in mind the two senses of *salutare*—namely, 'to greet' and 'to save'.

Arab mystics all insist that the *secret* of divine Love must be kept. They constantly complain of prying persons (*râgib* or *wâchi*) who want to find out about the mysteries, but not to take part in them with a whole-hearted faith. To somebody's hasty question: 'What is Sufi-ism?' al Hallaj replies: 'Do not turn on Us; see our finger which has already been stained with the blood of lovers.' Moreover, the prying are suspected of evil intentions: it is they who give lovers away to the orthodox authorities. Likewise in most of the Provençal poems there are characters described as *losengiers*—backbiters, careless gossips, spies—upon whom the troubadours heap invective. Our learned commentators nowadays have been rather hard put to it to explain these inconvenient *losengiers*, and have sought to dispose of the problem thus presented by alleging that in the twelfth century lovers must set great store by keeping their affairs secret (whereby no doubt they differed from lovers in other periods!).

Then also the eulogy of a death due to love is the leit-motiv of Arab mystic poesy. Ibn al Faridh wrote:

The repose of love is a weariness; its onset, a sickness; its end, death.
For me, however, death through love is life; I give thanks to my Belovèd that she has held it out to me.
Whoever does not die of his love is unable to live by it.

This is the very cry of Western mysticism, *but also* it is that of Provençal poesy. Saint Teresa's ejaculatory prayer was 'I die of not being able to die!' Al Hallaj wrote: 'In killing me you shall make me live, because for me to die is to live and to live is but to die.' Life is indeed the terrestrial day of beings in a contingent world, in the whirl of matter; but death is the Night of Illumina-

[1] Suhrawardi, *The Rustling of Gabriel's Wing*.

tion, the vanishing of illusory forms, the Soul's union with the Beloved, a communion with Absolute Being. Hence, for Arab mystics, it is Moses who symbolizes the greatest of Lovers, because in having declared on Sinai his wish *to see* God he is held to have expressed a wish for death. And it is easy to understand that the final stage of the illuminative way taken by Suhrawardi and Al Hallaj had to be religious martyrdom at the summit of *ioy d'amor*.

'Al Hallaj went to execution laughing. I said to him: "Master, why this?" He replied: "Such is the coquetry of beauty as she draws her lovers to her."'

Finally, it has been ascertained that so-called Platonic love was in honour among the members of a tribe enjoying a great prestige in the Arab world, the tribe of the Banu Ohdri whose members died of love owing to their persistent exaltation of chaste desire, in accordance with the words of the Koran: 'He who loves, who abstains from all that is forbidden, who holds his love secret, and who dies of his secret, he dies a martyr.' 'Ohdri love' became all the way into Andalusia the name of that which was going to become Courtly Love, first in the south of France, and then in the north of that country, in readiness for *Tristan*. . . .

Can it be established that Arab poesy actually influenced *cortezia*? Renan wrote in 1863: 'An abyss separates the form and spirit of Romance poetry from the form and spirit of Arab poetry.' Another scholar, Dozy, his contemporary, declares that Arab influence upon the troubadours has not been established 'and it will not be'. Today his peremptory tone makes us smile. (How often has someone written that an abyss separates Cathars and troubadours and that my contention would never be established . . .!) From Baghdad to Andalusia Arab poetry is one, one in language and one thanks to continuous exchanges. Andalusia was contiguous to the Spanish dominions, whose dynasties were mingled with those of Languedoc and Poitou. By now the blooming of Andalusian lyricism in the tenth and eleventh centuries has become well known. The detailed prosody of the *zadjal* is that adopted by the first troubadour, William of Poitiers, in five of the eleven poems by him that have come down to us. To try to establish Andalusian influence upon the courtly poems is no longer needful.[1] And I could fill pages with passages from Arabs

[1] Cf. the work of the American, A. R. Nykl, his translation of *The Dove's Necklace* by Ibn Hazm—an exposition of Arab courtly love—and his general

and Provençals about which our great specialists of 'the abyss which separates' would possibly fail to guess whether they were penned north or south of the Pyrenees. The matter is settled. But now here is what I am concerned with.

There occurred during the twelfth century in Languedoc and in the Limousin one of the most extraordinary spiritual confluences of history. On the one hand, a strong Manichaean religious current, which had taken its rise in Persia, flowed through Asia Minor and the Balkans as far as Italy and France, bearing the esoteric doctrines of Maria Sophia and of love for the Form of Light. On the other hand, a highly refined rhetoric, with its set forms, themes, and characters, its ambiguities invariably recurring in the same places, and indeed its symbolism, pushes out from Irak and the Sufis, who were inclined alike to Platonism and Manichaeism, and reaches Arabic Spain, then, leaping over the Pyrenees, it comes in the south of France upon a society that seems to have but awaited its arrival in order to *state* what it had not dared and had not been able to avow either in the clerical tongue or in the common vernacular. Courtly lyrical poetry was the offspring of that encounter.

Thus it was that from the final confluence of the 'heresies' of the spirit and those of desire, which had both come from the one East along either shore of the Civilizing Sea, there was born the great western model of the language of passion-love.

survey, *Hispano-Arabic Poetry and Its Relations with the Old Provençal Troubadours* (Baltimore, 1946). V. also the writings of Louis Massignon, Henry Pérès, Emile Dermenghem, Menendez Pidal, Karl Appel, etc.

IO

A General View of Courtliness

Returning after a long interval to the problems raised in the preceding pages, I feel the need of bringing together at this point a number of fresh considerations. I should like the reader to decide whether they invalidate or, on the contrary, enlarge—in order the better to substantiate—my original contentions (by which I stand), that between *cortezia* and the religious atmosphere of Catharism there was a deeply embedded bond.

It will very likely have been noticed that above I confined myself to *analogies* in order to suggest the possibility of relations between a form of mysticism, a religious notion, or simply a view of man, and a determinate lyrical form. I referred to the connexion between Sufi-ism and the courtly poems of the Arabs; I suggested how a century or more hence the Freudian influence on the school of *Surréalisme* in this present century might be disputed. As originally put forward, my contentions roused some vigorous criticism without invariably being fully grasped.[1] The criticism, plus the numerous discoveries made in the last fifteen years by authorities on courtly love, Catharism, and Manichaeism, as well, possibly, as the experiences I myself have had and my own researches—all that brings me today to a conception of *cortezia*

[1] It should be pointed out that the most virulent attempts made in print to confute me were directed far less against my contentions than against the single theory mentioned in Chapter 7 of this Book II—the theory of Rahn, Aroux, and Péladan, that the poems of the troubadours were a kind of secret language of Catharism. To dispose of that really excessive simplification it is enough to re-read Chapters 8 and 9. I feel that my critics are rather to be held responsible for it than I myself, although I did fall into some incautious statements. It is these, unfortunately, that most helped to ensure the success of the book with a public that read it hurriedly; something, however, not altogether unprecedented.

hardly less 'historical' than the one I sketched above, but far more psychological. I pointed to one *factual* relation (places and dates that are identical whatever we think) between Cathars and troubadours. I ventured to say that this relation cannot be ignored, and that the absence of any connexion between the two sets of people would be more astonishing than no matter what theory—'serious' or 'frivolous'—of the nature of the connexion. But I took care not to go into the actual detail of the 'influence', as many historians go for whom the real is only established by means of written records. I shall now venture a little further, but in my own direction and not in theirs. I put forward no textual and 'scientific' solution of the problem, based on documents, which would mean that, in the words of Karl Jaspers, 'the question no longer pauses there where it runs into mystery but goes on stupidly to lose its point by extracting a reply'. I should like instead to penetrate more deeply into the *problematical* character of Courtly Love, while at the same time treating it as definitely as possible, and to do this because I think the task vital for the West of the present day, and also for the moral and religious conduct of us all.

So I am going to set out a few facts as though they were traps. I shall avoid indicating any causal connexion, and shall refrain from expressing any conclusions that might be taken out of their context, keyless chords upon which hasty critics and readers might otherwise fasten in order to exclaim: 'Proofs!' or 'How true!'

1. *The Psychical Revolution of the Twelfth Century.*

A neo-Manichaean heresy, come from the Near East through Armenia and Bogomil Bulgaria—that of the Goodmen or Cathars, ascetics who condemned marriage but who founded a Church of Love in opposition to the Church of Rome[1]—swiftly spread over France from Rheims, and from the north of Italy pushed into Spain, and then spread all over Europe. Simultaneously other heterodox movements agitated people and clergy. They were movements which sought to counter ambitious prelates and the holy pomps of the Church by means of a refined spiritualism, and they resulted in some cases in the formulation more or less deliberately of premature naturalistic and even materialistic doctrines. Their excesses might be said to illustrate in advance Pascal's well-

[1] As the word AMOR is opposed to ROMA. The heretics held it against the Catholic Church that they had *inverted* the very name of God, which is Love.

known saying that he who wants to play the angel behaves like a beast. But really those excesses betrayed the revolutionary character of the problems which the age threw up and its profound *inordinatio*, of which the most holy saints and the most learned doctors underwent and suffered the passion at least as much as they succeeded in transmuting it into theological virtues and truths. At the level of theological speculation, Saint Bernard of Clairvaux and Abélard were the poles of this drama in the Church. But outside the Church and in its margins, among the common people to whom such disputes appeared *remote and incomprehensible*, there were increasing oscillations. From Henry of Lausanne and Peter of Bruys to Amaury of Bène and the Ortliebian Brothers in Strasbourg, all condemned marriage. Incidentally, marriage had just been forbidden to priests by the monkish Pope Gregory VII. Against this, many of the heretical preachers professed that, as man is divine, nothing done with his body—the devil's booty—can affect the salvation of his soul. 'No sin above the navel', one Dualist bishop declared in order to excuse the licence which several sects either fostered or put up with.

An entirely new kind of poetry sprang up in the South of France, the birthplace of Catharism. It extolled the Lady of Thoughts, the Platonic Idea of a feminine principle, and the encouragement of Love contrary to marriage, and at the same time of chastity.

Saint Bernard of Clairvaux undertook a campaign against Catharism, founded an orthodox ascetic order to match that of the Goodmen or Perfect, and then set up in opposition to *cortezia* the first really effectual form of emotional mysticism in the West—that of the Divine Love.

Many commentaries on the Song of Songs were written for the nuns of the earliest convents for women, from the Abbey of Fontevrault—so near the home of the first troubadour, Count William of Poitiers—to as far as the Paraclete of Héloïse. This epithalamian mysticism is to be found in Bernard of Clairvaux, Hugh of Saint Victor, and Abélard himself.

Héloïse and Abélard first experienced themselves and then described abundantly in courtly poems and in letters the first great novel of passion-love in our history.

Geoffrey Rudel died in the arms of the Countess of Tripoli, the 'faraway princess' whom he had loved without ever having seen. And Joachim of Floris predicted the coming incarnation of the Holy Ghost in a woman.

A General View of Courtliness

All that occurred either in reality, or else in an imagination that informed reality, in the places and at the time in which the legend and the myth of mortal passion were joined—in the *Romance of Tristan*.

In order to counter this powerful and almost universal rise of Love and of the cult of Idealized Woman, the Church and clergy were bound to set up a belief and a worship which met the same profound desire, as this sprang up out of the communal spirit of the time. While the Church had to fall in with that desire, the Church had also to 'convert' it and lead it into the strong stream of orthodoxy.[1] Hence the repeated attempts from the beginning of the twelfth century onwards to institute a worship of the Virgin. It is from that time that Mary has generally received the title of *Regina coeli*, and it is as a queen that from that time art has depicted her. *For the Lady of Thoughts of cortezia there was substituted Our Lady*. The monastic orders which were then being founded were retorts to the orders of chivalry. A monk was 'a Knight of Mary'. In 1140, at Lyons, the canons set up a Feast of the Immaculate Conception of Our Lady. Saint Bernard of Clairvaux vainly protested in a famous letter against 'this new feast of which the custom of the Church knows nothing, which reason does not approve, and that tradition does not authorize . . . and which introduces Novelty, the sister of Superstition and the daughter of Inconstancy'. And Saint Thomas Aquinas, a hundred years later, vainly wrote in as forthright a fashion as possible, 'If Mary had been conceived without sin, she would not have needed to be redeemed by Jesus Christ.' The worship of the Virgin responded to a vital necessity for the Church while under threat and pressure. When several centuries later the Papacy sanctioned that worship, the latter, without waiting for the seal of dogma, had already triumphed in all the arts.

Finally, there is another trait which cannot be attached *laterally* to the others. It is in the twelfth century that there is attested in Europe a radical change in the game of chess which had originated in India. Instead of the four kings which had dominated the game in its first form, a Lady (or Queen) was made to take precedence

---

[1] Which did not prevent the Church of Rome, in the person of Pope Innocent III, who dreamed of 'the empire of the world' and could not stand the defection of Northern Italy and Languedoc, from launching in 1209 a Crusade against the Cathars—the first genocide or systematic massacre of a people recorded by our 'Christian' western history.

over all other pieces, save the King, and the latter was actually reduced to the smallest possibility of real action, even though he remained the final stake and the consecrated figure.

2. Oedipus and the Gods.

Freud calls Oedipan the complex set up in the unconscious by the aggressiveness of the son against the father, who obstructs love of the mother, and by the sentiment of guilt which ensues. The weight of patriarchal authority compels the son to conform socially and morally; the weight of the interdict bound up with the mother (i.e. with the feminine principle) inhibits love; all that has to do with woman remains 'impure'. This complex of Oedipan sentiments is all the more compelling where the social structure is the more solid, the father's power the more assured, and the god from whom the father has received his authority is the more reverenced. But what happens in a society where the union principle is relaxed, the economic power in the hands of the father is divided, and the divine power itself is broken up, either into a plurality of gods, as in Greece, or into a god and goddess couple as in Egypt, or finally, as in Manichaeism, into a beneficent God (who is pure spirit) and a demiurge (who rules matter and the flesh)? The compulsion which created the Oedipus complex weakens proportionately. Hatred of the father is concentrated upon the demiurge and his handiwork: matter, flesh, procreative sexuality—the while a purified sentiment of adoration may be formed for the Spirit-God. At the same time love of woman is partially released. It can be avowed in the form of a worship for the divine archetype of woman, *on condition that this Mother-Goddess remains a virgin*, and thus escapes from the interdict which is maintained as regards a woman in the flesh. Mystical union with this feminine divinity is then tantamount to participation in the legitimate power of the luminous God, a 'divinization', or literally a liberating enthusiasm, which unifies a being and 'consoles' it.

3. An Illustration.

There occurred in France in the twelfth century a marked relaxation of the patriarchal and feudal bond. Property was divided equally among all sons, by a proceeding called *pariage*. Suzerains lost authority. There was a kind of advance Renaissance of individualism. The country was invaded by a dualist religion. Finally, there was that powerful rise of the cult of Love of which I have just recalled the evidences. We are thus confronted with an actualization (or epiphany in history) of the possibility which we imagined in the sub-section above on Oedipus.

If we try to portray to ourselves the psychical and ethical situation in which a man would have been in those days, we notice first of all that he was, willy-nilly, involved in the struggle which deeply divided society, and the powers, families, and even individuals within themselves—the struggle between Heresy, which was present everywhere,[1] and Roman orthodoxy, which had been badly battered. On the Catharist side, marriage and sexuality were condemned without remission by the Perfect or *Consoled*, but were allowed in the case of mere Believers—who were the immense majority of heretics. On the Catholic side, marriage was a sacrament and yet in fact based on material and social considerations; it was imposed on the parties regardless of their feelings. Meanwhile, the relaxation of authority and of the powers allowed, as we have seen, for a fresh possibility of letting woman in, though under cover of an idealization and even of a divinization of the feminine principle. This served but to emphasize the contradiction between the two ideals (themselves in conflict!) and the reality of experience. The natural psyche and natural sensuality both writhed amid the converging attacks, the antithetical condemnations, the restraints both theoretical and practical, and the freedoms that were being very obscurely foreseen in their fascinating novelty. . . .

It was at the heart of such an inextricable situation, and as though resulting from the many confusions which that situation was bound to produce, that there appeared *cortezia*, a literary 'religion' of chaste Love, of idealized woman and her particular 'piety', *joy d'amor*, its detailed rites, the rhetoric of the troubadours, its morals of homage and service, its 'theology' and theological disputes, it initiates, the troubadours, and its Believers—the vast public, both cultivated and not, that listened to them and ensured their social fame all over Europe. Thereupon we behold this religion of ennobling love extolled by *the same men* who persisted in holding sexuality for 'ugly' and 'low'; and often *the same* poet is found to have been both an enthusiastic adorer of the Lady whom he extols and exalts and a scorner of woman

---

[1] Cf. above the words quoted from Raimon V, Count of Toulouse, page 84.

whom he disparages; only recall the lines of Marcabru or of Rambaut of Orange quoted above.[1]

Curiously enough, the troubadours in whom this dichotomy is to be observed did not complain of it! It looks as though they had found the secret of reconciling the irreconcilable in the course of living. They seem both to reflect and to be *overcoming* the division of consciousness (in turn productive of a bad conscience) in the vast mass of a society divided, as we have seen, not only between flesh and spirit, but also between heresy and orthodoxy, and in the very heart of the Heresy, between the exigencies of the Perfect and the actual life of the Believers. . . . Thereupon let me quote one of the most sensitive modern interpreters of *cortezia*, René Nelli. He writes:

'Nearly all the ladies of the Carcassès, of the Toulousain, of the Foix, and of the Albi region, were Believers, and were aware— although married—that marriage was condemned by their Church. Many troubadours were undoubtedly Cathars, or at least were pretty fully aware of the current of ideas that had been in the air for two hundred years. In any case, they sang their lays for castle ladies, *whose bad consciences had to be pacified by song*, and who exacted from them less the illusion of a sincere love than a *spiritual antipode* to marriage, a state into which they had been forced.'

The same author adds that in his opinion, 'there can be no question of taking the chastity thus simulated as being either a real habit or a reflection of manners'; it has to be taken simply as 'a *religious* (and therefore ceremonious) tribute rendered by imperfection to perfection'—that is to say, by the troubadours and by unsettled Believers to the morality of the Perfect.

But what after all (some present-day sceptic will say) can be the concrete meaning of the chastity extolled by jongleurs? And how account for the swift success of an alleged morality which was yet so ambiguous in Languedoc, in North Italy, Rhenish Germany, the whole of Europe, where after all 'religious' passions and theology did not occupy the best part of life, and had surely not suppressed every kind of *natural* impulsion? Since Rousseau the moderns have indeed supposed that there exists a kind of normal nature upon which the pseudo-problems of culture and religion came to be super-added. . . . This touching illusion may assist them in 'living', but not in the understanding of their

[1] Book II, Chapter 8, pp. 96 and 98.

lives. For all, the whole lot of us, lead our lives of civilized people quite without suspecting that those lives are being led amid a strictly insensate confusion of religions never completely dead, and seldom altogether understood and practised; of moral teachings which once upon a time were mutually exclusive but now are superimposed upon one another, or else combined in the background of our elementary behaviour; of unsuspected complexes which, because unsuspected, are the more active; and of instincts inherited less from some animal nature than from customs entirely forgotten, customs which have turned into mental furrows or scars, that are unconscious, and, on that account, easily confused with instinct. They were once upon a time either cruel artifices, sacred rites or magical gestures, or again profound disciplines elaborated by some kind of mysticism remote alike in time and space.

4. A Technique of 'Chastity'.

Beginning in the sixth century there spread rapidly over the whole of India—both among Hindus and among Buddhists— a religious school or 'fashion' the influence of which went on growing for centuries.

'From a formal standpoint, Tantrism looks like a new and triumphal manifestation of shaktism. The secret force (*Shakti*) which animates the Cosmos and sustains the gods (among whom come first Siva and Buddha) . . . is strongly personified; it is the Goddess, Wife and Mother. . . . Creative dynamism falls to the Goddess . . . worship is concentrated upon this cosmic feminine principle; meditation takes account of her 'powers', and Shakti makes deliverance possible. . . . In certain Tantric sects woman herself becomes a sacred object, an incarnation of the Mother. The religious apotheosis of woman was in fact common to every mystical current in the Indian Middle Ages. . . . Tantrism is *par excellence a technique*, even though it is fundamentally a metaphysic and a form of mysticism. . . . Meditation "wakens" certain occult forces, which slumber within every man, and these, once awakened, transform the human body into a mystical body.'[1] The object of the Tantric Yoga ceremonial, with its control of breathing, repetition of *mantras* or holy forms of words, and its meditation on *mandalas* or images containing symbols of the world

[1] Mircea Eliade, *Techniques du Yoga*, pp. 176 to 191.

The Religious Origins

and of the gods—was to transcend the human state. Buddhist Tantrism had close analogies in Hindu Hathayoga, a technique for the control of the body and of vital energy. Certain postures (*mūdras*) described in Hathayoga were intended 'to use as a means of divinization and hence of integration, final unification, the human function *par excellence*, that which determines indeed the incessant cycles of births and deaths—sexual function.'[1]

Thus speaks Siva:[2] 'For my devout followers, I am going to describe the gesture of Lightning (*vajroli mūdra*) which destroys the Darkness of the world and should be treated as the secret of secrets.' The details in the text allude to a technique of the sexual act without consummation, for 'he who keeps (or takes back) his seed into his body, what can he have to fear of death?' as it is said in one Upanishad. In Tantrism, *maithuna* (or ceremonial sexual union) was treated as a Yogi exercise. But most of the texts in which it is described 'are written in a language intentionally secret and obscure, with double meanings, in which a state of consciousness is referred to in erotic terms'[3]—or quite as well the other way round. This is carried so far as to make the reader 'never certain whether *maithuna* is a real act or simply an allegory' At all events, the object is the 'supremely great happiness . . . the joy of annihilation of the self'. And this 'erotic beatitude', obtained by the stoppage not of pleasure but of its physical effect, was resorted to as an immediate experience for entering into the Nirvanic state. The texts point out that 'otherwise the devout person becomes the prey of the sad Karmic law, like any voluptuary'.

What about woman in all that? She remained the *object* of a form of worship. Regarded as 'sole source of joy and rest, the woman lover synthesizes the whole of feminine nature: she is mother, sister, wife, daughter. . . , she is the way to salvation'.[4] Thus Tantrism included the 'novelty' of 'attempting the transsubstantiation of the human body with the aid of an act which, in every form of asceticism, symbolizes the state *par excellence* of sin and death—i.e. the sexual act'.[5] But this act was invariably

---

[1] Op. cit., p. 199.

[2] *Siva Samhita*, 4, 78–102. Cf. Alain Daniélou, *Yoga, The Method of Reintegration* (1949), pp. 45 seq.

[3] Mircea Eliade, op. cit., pp. 205 seq. Sometimes there are 'as many as five equivalent meanings for one term'.

[4] L. de la Vallée-Poussin, *Bouddhisme, études et matériaux* (1898).

[5] Eliade, op. cit., pp. 210 and 212.

described as that of man. Woman remained passive, impersonal, pure principle, without features and without name.

One late mystical school of Tantrism, *Sahajiyā*, 'expands the erotic ritual to astonishing proportions. . . . Great importance is given to every kind of "love" and the ritual of *maithuna* is made the goal of a long and difficult ascetic apprenticeship. . . . During a first period of four months a neophyte has to *serve* a "devout woman" like a servant, sleeping in the same room with her, and then at her feet. During a further four months, while continuing to wait on her as before, he sleeps in the same bed and on the left side. During a third period of four months he sleeps on the right side. Then the couple have to sleep together embraced. And so on. Such preliminaries are intended to ensure the "autonomization" of sensual pleasure, which is considered to be the sole human experience that can bring about Nirvanic beatitude and the subjection of the senses—in short, a seminal stoppage.'[1] Similar practices are prescribed in Taoism, but with the intent of prolonging youth and life by economizing the vital principle rather than with the purpose of winning spiritual freedom by the deification of the body. Tantric 'chastity' thus consisted of making love without actually making it, of seeking mystical exaltation and beatitude through a *She* who had to be 'served' in a humiliating posture, but with the preservation of that self-mastery from which a lapse might result in an act of procreation such as would cause the fall of the *Cavaliere servente* or lover back into the fatal reality of Karma.

5. *The Joy of Love.*

In undeniable contrast to these mystical texts and this abstruse psycho-physiological technique, I now quote some lays of 'light southern troubadours', either amateurs and great lords or else needy jongleurs, whom authorities on the Romance languages unanimously term pure 'makers of rhetoric'.[2] '*Of love I know that it gives great joy to him who observes its laws*', says the earliest known troubadour, William, sixth Count of Poitiers and ninth Duke of Aquitaine, who died in 1127. Thus the Laws of Love were already

---

[1] Ibid.

[2] I apologize for quoting only *fragments* of lays, only words of song! often poorly translated and shorn through this double betrayal of any strictly poetic rhythmic beauty. It should be clearly understood that I put forward no more than stripped meanings.

as settled as a ritual by the beginning of the twelfth century. They were Moderation, Service, Prowess, Long Expectation, Chastity, Secrecy and Pity, and those virtues led to Joy, which was the sign and guarantee of *Vray Amor* or True Love.

Here are Moderation and Patience: '*Of courtliness may boast he who knows how to be moderate. . . . The welfare of lovers consists in Joy, Patience, and Moderation. . . . I approve that my Lady should long make me wait and that I should not have from her what she promised me*' (Marcabru). Here is Service of the Lady: '*Take my life in homage, Beauty of hard pity, so long as you grant to me that by you I shall tend to heaven!*' (Uc de Saint Circ). '*Each day I grow better and am purified, for I serve and reverence the most suave lady in the world*' (Arnaut Daniel). (Likewise the Arab troubadour, Ibn Dâvoud, wrote: 'Submission to the beloved lady is the natural mark of a courtly man.') Here is Chastity: '*He who is disposed to love with sensual love goes to war with himself, for a fool after he has emptied his purse cuts a poor figure!*' (Marcabru). '*Hearken! Its voice* (i.e. the voice of Love) *will seem gentle as the song of the lyre if only you cut off its tail*' (Marcabru).[1] Chastity was held to have the power to deliver from the tyranny of desire by carrying (courtly) Desire to the extreme: '*By excess of desire, I think I shall remove her from me, if nothing is to be lost by dint of loving well*' (Arnaut Daniel). (Likewise, Ibn Dâvoud extolled chastity for its power of 'perpetuating desire').

It is at the height of (true) love and of its 'joy' that Geoffrey Rudel feels the most 'remote from guilty love' and from its 'anguish'. He goes further in liberation: the physical presence of the beloved was soon to become indifferent to him: '*I have a lady friend, but I do not know who she is, for never, by my faith! have I seen her . . . and I love her well. . . . No joy is so pleasing to me as the possession of that distant love.*' *Joy d'Amor* was held not only to liberate a desire under the domination of Moderation and Prowess, but also to be a Fountain of Youth. '*I want to retain (my Lady) in order to refresh my heart and renew my body, so well that I cannot age. . . . He will live a hundred years who succeeds in possessing the joy of his love*' (William of Poitiers).

I have quoted only poets of the first or second generation of troubadours (c. 1120 to 1180). In the thirteenth century those of the last generation made explicit what it was their models had

[1] Note by Professor Jeanroy: 'That is to say, if you succeed in suppressing the consequences.'

celebrated in song. '*It is no longer courtly love if it is materialized or if the Lady yields as reward*', wrote Daude of Prades, although, however, he did not shrink from giving details of the erotic gestures which a lover might venture upon with his Lady. And Guiraut of Calanson:

'*In the palace where she (the Lady) sits are five doors; he who can open the first two easily goes through the three others, but it is difficult for him to come out of them; he lives in the midst of joy, he who is able to remain. Access is by four very sweet degrees, but enters there no churl or lout; such folk are lodged in the outskirts, which occupy more than half of the world.*'

Guiraut Riquier, who is sometimes referred to as the last of the troubadours, made the following commentary on those lines: 'The five doors are Desire, Prayer, Service, Kissing, and Doing, whereby Love perishes. The four degrees are honouring, dissimulating, serving well, and waiting patiently.'[1] As for False Love, it was roundly turned upon by Marcabru and his successors and in terms which can be thought to enlighten us indirectly regarding the nature of true love or at least regarding certain aspects of it. And first of all, Marcabru says, '*it joins hands with the Devil, he who hatches False Love*'. (And indeed is not the Devil the father of material creation and of procreation, in the Catharist view?) The foes of True Love are 'murderers, traitors, simonists, enchanters, voluptuaries, usurers . . . deceiving husbands, false judges and false witnesses, false priests, false abbots, false women recluses and false men recluses'.[2] They are going to be destroyed, 'subjected to every ruin', and tormented in hell.

---

[1] Cf. above (p. 117) the description of Service according to the *Sahajiyā* school. Guiraut Riquier's interpretation is correct. That can be verified by reading this sentence by Aelius Donatus (fourth century) in his Commentary on Terence: *Quinque lineae sunt amoris, scilicet, visus, allocutio, tactus, osculum, coitus.* It should be noted that Desire corresponds to *visus*—the notorious first gaze which inflames—and Service to *tactus*. The theme of the five lines of love can be traced right through the Latin poetry of the Middle Ages down to the Renaissance, where it reappears in Clément Marot and Ronsard. The variations are very slight. But in 1510 Jean Lemaire de Belges wrote in his *Illustrations de Gaule*: 'The noble poets say that five lines there are in loves . . . gazing, speaking, touching, kissing, and the last which is the most desired, and towards which all the others tend for their final resolution—it is that which out of decency is called the gift of mercy (reward).' The contrast with courtly love is plain. And no less is the meaning given to *mercy*, which a number of authors assimilate for their part to grace in the writings of the troubadours.

[2] The Catharists condemned war and every kind of murder, legal or other.

'*Noble Love has promised that it would be thus, there would be the lamentation of the despairing.*

'*Ah! noble Love, source of goodness, by whom the whole world is lit up, I cry unto thee pity. From these moaning clamourings defend me, for fear I may be detained over there (in hell); in every place I look upon myself as thy prisoner and, fortified and cheered by thee on all things, I hope that thou wilt be my guide.*'

Finally, in opposition to those troubadours who no doubt took too much advantage of the ambiguities provided for by the 'service' of courtly love, Cercamon did not hesitate to dot the i's and cross the t's as he wrote: 'Such troubadours, in mixing up truth and falsehood, corrupt lovers, women, and married couples. They tell you that Love goes sideways, and that that is why husbands grow jealous and ladies are in suspense. . . . These false suitors cause a great number to abandon Merit and drive Youth away from them.'

Whatever 'material' reality or absence of reality corresponded in those days to such details of language, there is no disputing the existence of Courtly Rhetoric and its system of virtues, sins, laudations, and interdicts. It is easily read about. That rhetoric went on to enable the romance writers of the North—those who produced the Arthurian cycle, about the Grail and about Tristan—to describe actions and dramas, and not merely to make song about what may still be thought, on the part of the troubadours of the South, to have been a pure sentimental phantasmagoria.

6. *Apology to Historians.*

I do not believe that 'scientific' history so called can be a criterion of the realities which interest me in this book. Let it be affirmed on its behalf that such and such a connexion cannot be established in 'the present state of our knowledge'—that is to say, remains unbelievable till further notice. I am in search of a meaning and hence of illustrative and illuminating analogies. And I do not in the least claim to be confirming any theory whatever in calling the reader's attention to certain 'facts' which 'serious science' now holds to have been 'established' I merely think that those fact are of a kind to feed the imagination. Here are two such 'facts' to muse upon.

In the place of *false* judges, *false* priests, *false* recluses, and of *deceiving* husbands, the Inquisitors of the following century could be counted upon to have read simply 'judges', 'priests', 'recluses', and 'husbands'!

The *Tantra Pancha* is a collection of Buddhist and Tantric tales which was translated from Sanscrit in the sixth century by a doctor of Chosroes I, king of Persia. From that country it progressed swiftly in the direction of Europe, thanks to a series of translations in Syriac, Arabic, Latin, Spanish, etc. In the seventeenth century it was read by La Fontaine in French. It had then been translated from the Persian and the Persian was based upon an old Arabic version. The periplus, *The Romance of Balaam and Jehoshaphat*, is even more astonishing. In its present form it is a story of the spiritual evolution which leads Jehoshaphat, an Indian prince, to discover and embrace Christianity, the mysteries of which are made known to him by the Goodman, Balaam. The version which has come down in Provencal from the fourteenth century, while orthodox in main outline, bears indisputable traces of Manichaeism. According to the French neo-Catharist school,[1] the twelfth-century heretics were acquainted with a version which had not been amended by the Catholics and which was nearer to the original. Whether or not that suggestion comes one of these days to be verified, the Manichaean origin of the romance is attested by fragments of its original wording in eighth-century Uigur, which were discovered in Eastern Turkestan. It is possible to trace the transformation of the Hindu names 'Baghavan' and 'Boddisattva' (Buddha) into 'Balaam' and 'Jehoshaphat' via the Arabic forms of 'Balawhar va Budhâsaf' or 'Yudhâsaf.'

There are innumerable instances of the relations that subsisted between the East and the medieval West. I have selected these two, for which there is incontrovertible evidence, because they refute the modern prejudice according to which any communication held to have occurred between Tantrism or Buddhist Manichaeism and the heresies of the South of France must seem 'highly fantastic and improbable'.

7. *Instead of Definite Conclusions.*

Courtly Love resembles adolescent love when this is yet chaste and hence all the more consuming. It also resembles the love celebrated by Arab poets, who were mostly homosexual, as were a number of the troubadours. Its terms of expression have been taken up and used by nearly every great mystic in the West. It seems to us to have declined at times down to sophisticated fiddle-faddle in the style of the small medieval courts. It can be entirely

---

[1] Déodat Roché, René Nelli, etc.

imaginary, and many people insist that it was nothing but a verbal tourney. But it can also be a vehicle of the detailed though ambiguous realities of an erotico-mystical discipline for which the recipes were in India, China, and the Near East. All that seems to me likely. It may all be 'true' in the various senses of the word—simultaneously and in different ways. It all helps to a better understanding of courtly love, even if courtly love is something that nothing rational will explain.

In concluding the kind of counter-inquiry which I have been carrying out, and taking into account the most sensible objections brought against my *minimum theory* by members of a variety of schools, I am brought back to a kind of spiral that rises over my earliest observations. Courtly love came into existence in the twelfth century during a complete revolution of the western *psyche*. It sprang up out of the same movement which forced upwards into the half light of our human consciousness, and into lyrical expression by the human spirit, the Feminine Principle of *Shakti*, the worship of Woman, of the Mother, and of the Virgin. It shared in the epiphany of the *Anima* which, to my mind, marked the reappearance in Western man of a symbolical East. What makes it intelligible to us today are its historical signs or marks—its literally congenital connexion with the Heresy of the Cathars, and both its surreptitious opposition and its overt opposition to the Christian conception of marriage. But it would leave us now indifferent had it not, after many avatars (the procession of which I am about to narrate), preserved in our own lives an intimate and ever renewed virulence.

I I

From Courtly Love to Arthurian Romance

If now from the South of France we move to the North, we find that in the Arthurian romances—*Tristan*, *Lancelot* and the whole cycle—courtly love, and its rhetoric with many meanings, were transferred from song to narrative. It has been said that the first courtly novel was born from the contact of alien legends with the notion of courtesy. The alien legends in question were the ancient Celtic sacred mysteries (of which, as it happens, writers such as Béroul and Chrestien de Troyes were not more than half aware), mingled with bits of Greek mythology. How far the literatures of Southern and of Northern France were independent of one another has been the subject of prolonged controversy. Today it seems to be agreed that the poets of the Romanic South communicated their style and doctrine of love to the 'story-tellers' of the Round Table cycle. And the course of the transmission may be traced in historical documents.

Eleanor of Aquitaine left her Court of Love—in the South of France, the region of the *langue d'oc*—in order to marry Louis the Seventh, who was king of France from 1137 to 1180; and then, in 1152, she married Henry, who two years later became king of England.[1] At each removal she took her troubadours with her. It is thanks to her and to them, among others, that the Anglo-Norman *trouvères* became possessed of the rules and secret of courtly love. Chrestien de Troyes says that both the matter and spirit of his romances were obtained from Countess Marie of Champagne, Eleanor's daughter. Chrestien wrote a Tristan romance, the MSS. of which have been lost. Béroul was a Norman, Thomas an Englishman. And, reciprocally, the Tristan

[1] Her son, Richard Coeur de Lion, the friend of the Gascon troubadours and himself a troubadour, was excommunicated by Rome.

legend became known over a considerable part of Southern France. So rapid an interaction can be accounted for by the existence of a former connexion between the South of before the Cathars and the Gaelic and Britannic Celts. It was noted earlier that the religion of the druids—whence filids and bards derived their traditions—taught a dualistic view of the universe and made Woman into a symbol of the divine. Now, the Christian heresy of the Perfect drew certain features of its mythology from its Celt-iberian background. It was only natural that in the hands of the poets of the North this mythology should have been invested with darker and more tragic colours. Taranis, god of the stormy sky, takes the place of Lug, god of the sunlit sky. And although the courtly doctrine picked up and revived former aboriginal traditions, it was nevertheless something that the trouvères had learned, not something they had grown up in. That is why they often misinterpret it.

For that matter, it is extremely difficult to bring out the causes or to estimate the precise bearing of their misunderstandings. Are they due to a defective initiation? Was the tradition imperfect? Or was there a heretical tendency within the Heresy itself, a more or less sincere attempt to get back to orthodoxy?[1] Or was it simply that there had been a 'profanation' of courtly subject-matter which the trouvères seized upon none too scrupulously and directed to other ends than those of the troubadours? Pending some thorough research into the matter, let me point out that a number of the Britannic romances turn out to be more 'Christian' and others to be more 'barbarian' than the poems of the troubadours, and yet indisputably it is by those poems that all of them were inspired. We do not know if Chrestien de Troyes thoroughly grasped the rules of love which he was taught by Marie of Champagne. We do not know to what extent he *wished* to make his romances secret chronicles of the Church of Love,[2] or mere allegories of courtly morality and mysticism (as I now incline to believe). It is easy to see why there is an absence of written evidence here. Many interests must have joined forces to prevent the Heresy from being spread, and the Heresy on its side wished to remain esoteric. Obviously, however, Chrestien de Troyes distorts the meaning of the myths he recounts. In the Lancelot romance, which dates from about 1225, symbolism and allegory

[1] Particularly in the case of Chrestien de Troyes.
[2] As has been supposed by Otto Rahn, Péladan, and Eugène Aroux.

are obviously both present, however incongruous are the eluci-
dations with which the author follows his account of each episode.
One elucidation, however, deserves to be mentioned, because,
notwithstanding the author's unawareness of what he was saying,
its Catharist origin is clearly discernible. Lancelot, while wandering in the forest, reaches a place where the road forks. He hesitates
between going left or right. Then, in spite of the warning given
on a cross which appears in front of him, he goes to the left.
Before long a knight in white armour rides up, throws him off his
horse, and takes away his crown. The crestfallen Lancelot then
meets a priest, to whom he makes confession. 'I shall tell you the
meaning of what has befallen you,' the priest says. 'The road to
the right which you ignored at the fork was that of earthly
chivalry, in which you have long triumphed; the road to the left
was that of heavenly chivalry, which allows no killing of men or
overcoming of champions by force of arms: it is the realm of
spiritual things. And you bore with you on this road the crown of
pride. That is why the knight overthrew you so easily; for he
represented the very sin you had committed.'[1]

After that literary historians are at liberty to talk about 'incredible adventures', 'easily contrived marvels', 'touching in-
genuousness', 'primitive freshness', and so on. A little more penetration would lead us to see, on the contrary, that the real bar-
barism is displayed in our contemporary notion of the novel,
which we are quite content to take as a faked photograph of
events without significance, whereas Arthurian romance was
knit by an intimate *coherence* of which we no longer possess so
much as an inkling. Actually, in these wonderful adventures
nothing whatever is without its meaning; everything is symbol or
delicate allegory; and only the ignorant stop short at the apparent
puerility of the tale, this puerility being intended of course to
conceal the underlying meaning from the superficial glances of
the *uninformed.*

[1] In another passage, the knights, having taken Holy Communion, give one
another the Kiss of Peace, according to the Eastern rite, which the Cathars
appear to have taken over.—Finally, M. Anitchkov has shown that the bridge
which the Knights of the Grail have to cross is really the Sinvat Bridge of Manichaean mythology, a bridge thrown across an infernal river, and one that alone
the *elect* are able to cross. 'There is cause for describing the creative group of the
Britannic material as Manichaeizing', Anitchov writes (*Joachim de Flore*, p.
291), after having insisted on the Catharist influences apparent in all those
romances.

But even if the trouvères were inferior to the troubadours in mystical wisdom, their romances do not consist merely of *errors*. They dealt with a new theme, that of physical love, the theme of the fault. The writings of Chrestien de Troyes are not only love poems, as has so often been said; they are also genuine *novels*. For, unlike the Provençal poems, they take the trouble to describe the betrayals of love, instead of merely expressing the passionate surge in its mystical purity. The starting-point of both *Lancelot* and *Tristan* is a sin against courtly love—the physical possession of a real woman, and hence a 'profanation' of love. It is owing to this initial fault on his part that Lancelot fails to find the Grail, and is humiliated countless times while wandering along the celestial way. He has chosen the earthly road, he has betrayed mystic Love, he is not one of the 'Pure'. Alone the 'Pure'—true 'savages' such as Bohort, Perceval, and Galahad—can be granted initiation. Clearly the account of his wanderings and of the penalties he suffers required the narrative form, not that of mere song. In *Tristan* the initial fault is painfully redeemed by the long penance which the lovers undergo. That is why the tale ends 'well' from the standpoint of Catharist mysticism—that is to say, why it culminates in a double self-inflicted death.[1] Thus there are reasons of a spiritual nature to account for the elaboration of a new literary style—the style of the novel—which was to become truly literary, however, only later on, when it became detached from the myth—by then provisionally exhausted—at the beginning of the seventeenth century.

[1] In an analysis of the 'erotic magic' of the Grail cycle (in *Lumière du Graal* (1951), a collection of twenty studies by various authors), René Nelli puts forward some observations which may usefully be set beside Chapter 10 of this Book II. He writes: 'This erotic magic was inspired first of all by a belief that the female body displayed by its mere presence certain supernatural powers, the same that were attributed to the Grail. [The Grail rejuvenated those who contemplated it.] . . . It was also due to faith in an occult force which resulted from a repressed carnal transport. . . . Pure love was understood to be one that remains pure in perilous circumstances, though these be provoked, and that applies the energy of this Desire to higher ends than copulation. Pure love allowed every carnal contrivance save 'the act'. . . . Retained love was indeed the internal motor of the Quest, which bore all the characteristics of being an initiation into a Femininity not to be seized by the carnal senses.' The author seems to have penetrated the 'Tantric' quality of Courtly Love, more truly, I think, as it is manifested in the Arthurian Cycle than it is in the poems of the troubadours.

12

From Celtic Myths to Arthurian Romance

ristan must seem the most thoroughly courtly of Arthurian romances because the epic element—the battles and schemings—is reduced to a minimum and the tragic development of the religious doctrine alone determines the strong and elemental progress of the tale. But *Tristan* is also the most 'Arthurian' of courtly romances, because it incorporates religious and mythological components that are plainly of Celtic origin to a much greater extent than do the romances of the Round Table, and in a way that renders these elements sharply identifiable.

Hubert very truly says about Gaelic literature, that 'it contains matter derived from the religion of the Ancient Britons as by a miracle; for it arose in a Christian country that had been first Romanized and then colonized by the Irish'.[1] Nevertheless, the miracle is attested by a large number of the incidents exploited by Béroul and Thomas, incidents that it has only become possible to account for thanks to the most recent archaeological discoveries about the Celts. Actually, the religious matter has such vigorous poetic power that its survival is easy enough to understand, even in a world which had lost the druidical faith and forgotten the meaning of the druidical mysteries.

The cycle of Irish legends contains many tales about a journey which the hero undertakes to the country of the dead. This hero —Bran, Cuchulinn, or Oisin—'*is attracted by a mysterious beauty*'; '*he sets sail in a magic ship*'; and he lands in a wonderful country. 'In the end he wearies of this land, and wants to return home. It is in order to die.'[2] This evidently is the source of the wounded Tristan's first aimless sea journey which results in his finding the magic balm. Other situations in the Tristan romance have fairly

[1] H. Hubert, *Les Celtes*, II, p. 286. [2] Hubert, op. cit., II, p. 298.

close prototypes in the stories of the Irish cycle. For example, in the tragic idyll of *Diarmaid and Grainne* the two lovers flee to the forest, where the husband pursues them. In *Baile and Ailinn* the lovers arrange to meet in a deserted spot, where death has preceded them and prevents their coming together; 'for it had been predicted by the druids that they would never meet in life, but that they would meet after death, and then never be parted again.'

It would be easy to note further similarities. But the resemblance between certain features of behaviour is even more striking. It will be remembered that Tristan is an orphan and that he is brought up in the castle of his uncle, King Mark. Now it frequently happened among the Celts in the most remote times that children were entrusted 'to the care of a qualified person in some great house, a house of men'. They were taught there by a druid, and were thus sheltered from women. 'This institution, which is commonly given the Anglo-Norman name of "fosterage", was retained in Celtic countries: we find children being entrusted to foster-parents, of whose family they became members, as is shown by the fact that a certain number acquired the family name of their foster-father. These foster-fathers were sought either among members of the mother's family or among druids..'[1] In the same way, Tristan, who is brought up by Mark, his maternal uncle, becomes by fosterage the king's 'son'.[2] The Celtic custom of a ritual gift, of exchanging ostentatory gifts with efforts to go one better (*potlatch*), figures also in *Tristan* and in the Romances of the Round Table. Many episodes begin with a 'blank' promise made by the king to some damsel who has asked him for a gift, without saying of what. As a rule, the damsel wants some highly dangerous mission undertaken. 'Tournaments', Hubert says,[3] 'certainly formed part of this vast system of competition and of going one better.' Further, it is well known that Celtic youths, on reaching puberty—that is, at the time they left the house of men—had to accomplish some feat—the killing of a stranger or some prowess of the chase—in order to win the right to marry. The battle with the Morholt in *Tristan* is the exact reproduction of that

[1] Hubert, op. cit., II, pp. 243–44.
[2] Psycho-analysts will not fail to look upon the unhappy affair of Tristan and Iseult as the consequence of an Oedipus complex. But foster-fathers sometimes had as many as fifty legal sons—so that the link was rather weak—and also, as many documents testify, incest was permitted among the Celts.
[3] Op. cit., II, p. 234.

custom, although in the Romance there is no allusion to its sacred origin. All this renders Hubert's theory plausible—that Celtic mythology was transmitted to the courtly cycle, not through any properly religious channels, but by a more profane cult of heroes and of prowess, which had gradually replaced the gods and their worship in popular legend.

'Gaston Paris noted with acumen that the romance of Tristan and Iseult gives forth a peculiar note which is not heard again in medieval literature, and he accounted for this by the Celtic origin of the poems. It is through Tristan and through Arthur that the most limpid and precious part of the Celtic genius was incorporated in the European spirit.'

Thus Hubert.[1] The 'peculiar note' which Bédier has admirably reproduced in his modern transcription of the legend so unmistakably finds the path to our hearts that we can *isolate* the non-Celtic, and therefore courtly, element which was responsible in the twelfth century for the production of the myth. What differentiates an Irish legend from the legend told by Béroul and Thomas is that in the former what brings disaster is an entirely external *fate*, whereas in the latter it is a secret but unerring *wish* on the part of the two mystic lovers. In Celtic legends action and resolution are determined by an *epic* element, in courtly romances by an *internal tragedy*. Then also Celtic love—in spite of the religious sublimation of Woman by the druids—is above all sensual love.[2] The fact that in some legends this love is secretly at war with orthodox religious love, and is thus compelled to express itself in esoteric symbols, helps us to see how it came about that the Britannic background was so easily absorbed into the symbolism of the courtly romance. But the analogy remains theoretical, although it has doubtless encouraged the modern tendency to confuse Tristan's passion with mere sensuality.

A couple of quotations from Thomas, the most self-conscious of the authors of the five early versions of the legend, will be enough to show how original the courtly myth is. The cohesive principle which courtly mysticism gave to the religious, sociological or epic elements that had been inherited from the old Britan-

[1] Op. cit., II, p. 336.
[2] This is evidenced, for example, by *Tannhäuser*. The *Tannhäuser* of the sixteenth century is a late German adaptation of Hiberno-Scottish legends; it owes nothing whatever to courtly influence. The Montsalvat of the Chaste is replaced by the Venusberg!

nic background is expressed and *expounded* in a language astonishingly modern. The principle is that suffering considered as an *askesis* has to be loved—suffering is indeed the 'beloved pain' of the troubadours. Tristan, on the night of his marriage to Iseult of the White Hand, faces the most cruel of struggles within himself, for he cannot decide to possess his wife.

'Ysolt as Blanches Mains he desired for her beauty and for her name Ysolt: for the beauty alone that was in her, he had not desired her if she had not the name Ysolt, nor for the name without the beauty. . . . Tristram would fain have vengeance; yet *for his malady he seeketh such vengeance as will double his torment.*'[1]
By the very fact that Iseult of the White Hand is now his wife, he must not and cannot any longer desire her.

'An the good that he hath were not his, he had not despised it in his heart: but that which it behoveth him to have, he may not heartily love. If he might not have that he hath, he had longed to win it: he would think to find it better than his own: and *for this cause he may not love his own.* . . . This befalleth many men: when they have some travail and anguish and great pain and distress, *such things they do to escape and deliver and avenge them as thereof cometh great harm*: often they do of purpose things whereof they endure sorrow. I have seen it betide unto many that when they may not have their desire or thing that they love, they strive unto their utmost power: of their distress they do such deeds whereby oft-times they double their grief. . . . Whosoever doth that he desireth not to do because that he may not have some good thing, doth his will despite his desire.'[2] [*Encontre désir fait volier*, are Thomas's own words.]

A Celtic background of religious legends—which, as it happens, were at a very remote period common to both the Iberian South and its *langue d'oc* and to the Irish and Britannic North; customs of feudal chivalry; semblances of Christian orthodoxy; a sometimes very compliant sensuality; and, finally, the individual fancy of each of the poets—there, when all is said and done, are the materials thanks to which the heretical doctrine of Love (which was profoundly dualist in spirit, and probably Catharist in its immediate origin) underwent its transmutations. In this way was the Tristan myth born. I am far from intending to analyse the

[1] *The Romance of Tristan and Ysolt by Thomas of Britain*, translated by Roger Sherman Loomis (New York, 1931). M. de Rougemont's italics.
[2] Ibid. M. de Rougemont's italics.

metamorphosis; it eludes us doubly, in being poetic and in being mystical. But we now know whence the myth came and whither it must lead. And perhaps we have gained an inkling—although this is something that could not be put into words—of how the myth may be enacted in an individual human life or embodied in a piece of imaginative literature.

13

From Arthurian Romance to Wagner, via Gottfried of Strasbourg

The first time *the Myth was created anew*, out of a mind exceptionally conscious of the theological implications, was in the version by Gottfried of Strasbourg about the beginning of the thirteenth century. Gottfried was a clerk who read French—he often quotes lines from Thomas—and who was strongly moved by the controversies which had raged between Bernard of Clairvaux and the Cathars, and had also involved Abélard, the School of Chartres, and several heretics who came dangerously close to the Abbot of Cluny's 'mysticism of the heart'.

A theologian and a poet, and well aware of the significance of his preferences, Gottfried sets forth far better than his models the strictly religious importance of the Dualist Myth of Tristan. But also, and for the same reason, he discloses better than all the others a fundamental element in the Myth—a sensual fret and a 'humanistic' pride that makes up for the fret. There is fret in it, because it depicts the sexual instinct being resented as a cruel fate and as a tyranny; there is pride, because the tyranny is imagined to become a divinizing force—setting man up against God—once it is decided to yield to it. (The paradox heralds Nietzsche's *amor fati*.) Whereas Béroul limits the action of the philtre to three years, and

Thomas makes the 'herb wine' symbolize the intoxication of love, Gottfried treats it as the seal of destiny—the sign of a blind force external to the persons concerned, and as an expression, too, of the goddess Minne's will. That goddess, I ought to say, is a reviviscence of the Grandmother and comes out of mankind's most remote religions. But no sooner is the philtre drunk than it lifts its victims outside all moral bounds into a realm which can only be divine. Thus by the philtre those who drink it are both shackled to sexuality—a law of life—and compelled to go beyond it, thanks to a liberating *hubris* which lifts them over the mortal threshold of duality and of personal differentiation. This second paradox is essentially Manichaean, and it may be said to subtend Gottfried's immense poem.

Gottfried copies Thomas, but also makes what he likes of him. He alters, and in altering causes the reader to sit up and attend; for what he alters are three decisive moments of the action.

(*a*) He somewhat ferociously throws into relief the unmistakably blasphemous nature of the episode of the Judgement by red-hot iron;

(*b*) For the Forest of Morrois he substitutes a 'Grotto of Love' —the *Minnegrotte*—thanks to which he is able to compare the architecture of a Christian church with that of a temple.

(*c*) He decides that, instead of being nominal, the marriage of Tristan to Iseult of the White Hand shall be consummated.

His long unfinished poem—about 19,000 lines have come down to us, but the death of the lovers, though heralded, was never narrated—is alike more religious and more sensual than Béroul's and Thomas's. Above all, he declares and expounds what the Britons show without explanation and apparently without on their own part any astonishment. He thus develops and discloses the extent to which *Catharism* is latent in the anonymous legend.[1]

---

[1] On this subject two large volumes published in 1953 should be consulted: Gottfried Weber, *Tristan und die Krise des Hochmittelalterlichen Weltbildes um 1200.* This infinitely detailed work (with exhausting repetitions) by a learned German philologist contains an abundance of 'scientific proofs' of each point touched upon in the present chapter. I found no need of them in writing the first edition of my book, but certainly they do no harm! Over hundreds of pages Gottfried's religious convictions are compared with the doctrines of Augustine, Bernard, Hugh of Saint Victor, and Abélard, and the comparisons bring out strikingly how deeply Gottfried was a Cathar and how anti-Catholic (in a manner that, to my mind, foreshadows the Renaissance rather than Luther).

From Arthurian Romance to Wagner, via Gottfried

(*a*) The Judgement of God was a barbarian custom, but the Church recognized it in the twelfth century and had indeed just subjected to it some women in Cologne and Strasbourg who were legitimately accused of Catharism. The ordeal consisted in grasping with the bare hand a red-hot iron bar. Only liars and perjurers were burned. As I recalled above,[1] Iseult asks to be subjected to this judgement when she is accused of betraying King Mark. She invites the judgement out of excessive pride and in a spirit of defiance. She swears that no man has ever held her in his arms except the king, unless—and here she laughs—she ought to count a poor pilgrim who has just carried her ashore from a boat; and the poor pilgrim is Tristan in disguise. The ordeal is a success. Gottfried says:[2]

'It was thus manifest and proved that the most virtuous Christ swings to every wind like a weathercock and takes any fold like a mere cloth. . . . He lends himself, and can be adapted, to anything, according to the heart of each, in behalf of sincerity as in behalf of cheating. . . . He is ever what it is wanted he should be.'

The allusion to the 'heart' is unmistakably directed at Bernard of Clairvaux, whose writings were so familiar to the poet as in many places to be imitated by him in their dialectical accounts of suffering, desire, and ecstasy, with, however, inversion of the lessons to be drawn. For the poet, the final ecstasy does not lead into the daylight of God, but into the nocturnal darkness of passion; not to a human being's salvation but to his dissolution. The passage cited above expresses a virulent resentment at orthodox doctrines which 'make Christ take any fold like a mere cloth' and cause Him to sanction posteriorly everything that, in the eyes of Gottfried himself and of the heretics of his day, the 'pure' Gospel and the Dualist Gnosis condemned—the world as manifested, the flesh in general, and in the world the social order of the time—feudal, clerical, and martial—and within that order, marriage.

(*b*) The *Minnegrotte* is pictured as a church, the poet displaying a genuine understanding of liturgical symbolism and of the beginnings of Gothic architecture. But for an altar there is substituted a bed. The bed is consecrated to the goddess Minne as the Catholic altar to Christ, and on the bed the courtly sacrament takes place: the two lovers 'communicate' in passion. Instead of the eucharistic miracle, instead of the transubstantiation of the material kinds and the divinization of him who receives these, flesh commingles

---

[1] Book I, Chapter 4, above. [2] Lines 15733–15747.

The Religious Origins

with spirit in transcendental unity. Lovers, and not believers, are made divine by the 'consummation' of the substance of Love. Whether this is spiritual or physical is left deliberately uncertain, and the uncertainty is, I feel, profoundly significant. And Love is opposed to the fervour of the Cluniacs in the same terms as Eros to Agape; and, I must add, is incompatible with that other sacrament which orthodoxy has 'perverted' in adapting it to social and material ends—the sacrament of marriage joining two bodies even where there is no love between them, a sacrament which the Cathars never stopped attacking as *iurata fornicatio*. Moreover, it seems possible to identify in this episode of the *Minnegrotte* the dialectic which the great mystics were to resort to from the thirteenth to the seventeenth centuries. The three ways—purgative, illuminative, and unitive—are very plainly prefigured here, though inflected or inverted by Gottfried's dualist and even Gnostic convictions.[1]

(c) In being consummated, Tristan's marriage to the second Iseult establishes a parallel (which Thomas avoids) with the loveless marriage of Iseult the Fair to King Mark. Both are stigmatized as due to temporal and physiological necessity, as being part of *the exile of souls* held captive in their imprisoning bodies. Thomas voices with full Manichaean virulence the judgement of courtly moral teaching, which he regards as above the judgement of the Church and of his time, the Church and the time being both guilty in his eyes as in the eyes of all Cathars. But his pronouncement sets in a queer light the erotico-eucharistic 'consummation' that he narrates as taking place in the *Minnegrotte*. In a Catharist view of the world, to make love without loving in accordance with courtliness (in this instance, courtliness is *Minne*), and to yield to a purely physical sensuality, is the supreme and original sin. To love with pure passion, even without physical contact—the sword laid between a couple's bodies and the theme of partings—is the supreme virtue, and the true way to divinization. Between those two extremes, which the Myth illustrates against the psychical and religious background of the twelfth century, every kind of confusion about love is made more than possible—inevitable. We

[1] Regarding Gottfried's Gnosticism, he seems to have believed, like the Carpocratians, that the *purgatio* of tyrannical instinct is only to be obtained by yielding to the instinct in the first place, with the intention, however, of attaining to the illuminative ecstasy that will bring about essential (though not epithalamian) union.

are still in the thick of the consequences now in the twentieth century; otherwise this book would be aimless. But it is possible to stick up landmarks.

Very obviously Gottfried of Strasbourg makes use of the 'matter of Britain' as he likes, and turns the myth of Love-for-death into a Catharist legend with a freedom which may have cost him his life (we do not yet know whether it did or not). But it is equally plain that the framework of the tale, its plot and predominant topics, favoured the poet's intention in a way which should be termed really *congenital*. The myth of Tristan betrays itself, as much in its essence, its innermost structure, its progression and form, as in its teaching, to be fundamentally heretical and dualistic. Chance has no place here, nor is there occasion for any such suspension of judgement as some of our learned friends seem wont to mistake for 'science'.

Tristan is far more profoundly and indisputably Manichaean than the *Divine Comedy* is Thomist.

Nevertheless, Gottfried made the legend *explicit* in a new fashion that is big with consequences. He prefigured that betrayal of genius which Wagner effected six and a half centuries later. Even if we did not know that Wagner's source was Gottfried's poem, a textual comparison of the two works would make it obvious. The short, hurried, antithetical, and breathless lines of the second act of the opera are almost a pastiche of Gottfried.[1] The famous duet in which Tristan and Isolde mingle their names, deny their names, sing of surpassing the separate self, and time, space, and earthly calamity, is taken almost literally from different passages of the poem.[2] But what Wagner resurrected by means of music is, far more than the form, the philosophic and religious content of Gottfried's poem. The created world is the Devil's. Everything within his empire is under the sway of necessity: human bodies are doomed to experience desire, and the love philtre symbolizes the ineluctable tyranny which that means. Man is not free. He is determined by the Devil. But if he accepts his calamitous destiny *up to the death* which will free him from his body, he may attain to

---

[1] And it looks as though Gottfried first imitated Abélard's *sic et non*. The famous love affair between the Doctor and the Nun constantly haunted the author of the most theological version of *Tristan*.

[2] Here is just one instance. Cf. Gottfried, lines 18352 to 18357: '*Tristan und Isot, ir und ich . . . niwan ein Tristan und ein Isot*'; and Wagner, Act II, 2, and all the last part of the scene: '*nicht mehr Tristan . . . nicht mehr Isolde!*'

that fusion of two selves who will thereupon have ceased *to suffer* love and will enter upon Supreme Joy. What Wagner took from Gottfried is all that the Britons did not wish to say or did not know how to say, and were content to expound by means of narrated actions—the religious and heretical nostalgia for an escape out of this wicked world, the condemnation and simultaneous divinization of sensuality, the strivings of the soul to escape from the fundamental *inordinatio* of the period, and from the tragic contradiction between Good—which must be Love—and the Evil that is victorious over Good in the created world. In short, Wagner took from Gottfried his fundamental dualism. And that is how it is that his work still acts upon us, more insidiously and with greater fascination for our sensibility than Joseph Bédier's aesthetic restoration.

14

What has been Ascertained so Far

Allowing for the change of key which was effected in the poetic language of courtly love when this language passed from the South of the troubadours to the less civilized North of the trouvères, we can now realize that all our peregrinations finally lead to the masterpieces of Béroul, Thomas, and Gottfried of Strasbourg. The religions of Antiquity, some of the mystic systems of the Near East; the heresy thanks to which they were revived in the Languedoc, the reaction against that heresy in the Western mind and in feudal custom—all that resonates in a muffled way right through the myth. We have thus been brought back to the *Romance of Tristan*, having ascertained why it was necessarily written at a particular time, the very time in which certain particular heretical traditions intersected, as it were, cer-

What has been Ascertained so Far

tain particular institutions whereby those traditions stood condemned savagely; for that was the moment when the heretical traditions were compelled to find expression in equivocal symbols and to take on the form of a myth.

Taking these convergences in the aggregate, it becomes possible to say that *the passionate love which the myth celebrates actually became in the twelfth century—the moment when first it began to be cultivated—a religion in the full sense of the word, and in particular a Christian heresy historically determined.* Whereupon it may be inferred (a) that the passion which novels and films have now popularized is nothing else than *a lawless invasion and flowing back* into our lives of a spiritual heresy the key to which we have lost; and (b) that underlying the modern breakdown of marriage is nothing less than a struggle between two religious traditions, or, in other words, a *decision* which almost always we reach unconsciously, in complete ignorance of the causes, ends, and perils involved, and for the sake of a morality which, although still alive, we no longer know how to justify.

Moreover, passion and the passion myth are active in many other ways than that in which our private lives are affected.

Orthodox mysticism in Europe has been another passion, and its metaphorical language is at times curiously akin to that of courtly love.

Considered chronologically, the great body of European *literature* expresses nothing other than an increasing secularization of the myth, or—as I would rather say—successive 'profanations' of its content and form.

Finally, *war* in Europe, and every one of the formal modes of conducting it down to about 1914, kept pace with the transformations of the myth, largely owing to their chivalric origin, and perhaps for other reasons as well.

Such are the matters to be dealt with in the Books that follow.

Book III

PASSION AND MYSTICISM

I

How the Problem Stands

Attempts to account for mysticism have often consisted of saying that it is a deflexion of human love; which is but to say that it is a form of sexuality. My examination of the *Romance of Tristan* and of its historical sources has led me to reverse the relation. In this particular case it is fatal passion which has to be identified as a form of mysticism, more or less conscious and definite. That is, of course, no warrant for generalization; but at least it calls for the restatement of a problem which nineteenth-century materialism had thought itself qualified to settle to the detriment of mysticism. Very likely the problem is not one open to being solved simply and finally. But how it stands does require to be made clear.

Whether passion is being treated as a form of mysticism, or vice versa, the two are assumed to be in *some* relation. Possibly, however, the nature of language is what leads us to discern such connexions. It has long been recognized that the metaphors of love and mysticism are akin. But the closest similarities in vocabulary do not necessarily argue any likeness between the things that the words refer to. Thus up to a point we may be the victims of a verbal illusion—of a kind of protracted punning. Nevertheless, here is a problem that has to be faced. Let me indicate why.

In the first place, if passion involved no more than physiological factors the Tristan myth would be unintelligible. Sexual instincts are manifested as a hunger, and this hunger, like that for food, tends to obtain satisfaction at any cost. The more ravenous, the more indiscriminate it becomes. But the passion of the myth is compelled by its very nature to reject satisfaction. The more

141

intense, the more it recoils from being assuaged. This passion, therefore, is not a hunger, but a kind of drug which produces intoxication. It has recently been asserted that every drug-addict is a mystic unawares. But there can be no drugging, physical or moral, except by the effect of some *foreign* agent, which instinct, left to itself, would get rid of as quickly as possible. Animals do not get intoxicated.[1]

In the second place, and conversely, mysticism does not seem able by itself to account for passion. As soon as we suppose that it does, we see that this involves explaining why the most striking metaphors employed in mystical writing are drawn from the language of sexual love, and not, for example, from the vocabulary of breathing or nutrition; why what it has *invariably* been attempted to equate with mysticism should be sexual instincts, and this long before the advent of Freud and his school.

Such is the dilemma in which we are landed: if we try to treat passionate love as a mere matter of sex, it is evident that we then do not know what we are talking about. If conversely we seek to connect this love with anything *alien* to sex it will have queer results, as Schopenhauer might have said. Let us treat the problem as it is propounded by the myth, and as it must have appeared in the twelfth century. An actual instance—especially as it is a piece of literature produced *before* there arose the great wave of orthodox mysticism—supplies the best starting-point for an inquiry into how the 'very queer results' arise.

---

[1] There is, it is true, *formica sanguinea*, an insect which keeps in its nest a parasite exuding a delicious sweat, and the presence of the parasite ends by upsetting everything. This ant's pathological habit has been compared to dipsomania. So long as ants remain speechless, any theory is possible.

2

'Tristan' as the Account of a Mystical Experience

As we have seen, the *Romance of Tristan* is in many respects a first 'profanation' of courtly mysticism and of the doctrines which had inspired it—Neo-Platonism, Manichaeism, and Sufi-ism. The mythopoeic process was only too successful, either because Béroul and Thomas, or their forerunner, did not fathom at all points the unalloyed teaching of courtesy, or else because they were carried away by the ardour of narrative construction (in the modern and literary sense of the term), and wished to meet the inclinations of their audience, which consisted of people less civilized than were the inhabitants of the South. For what distinguishes the Romance is that its plot turns upon a *transgression* of the rules of courtly love, since the whole dramatic story proceeds from there having been adulterous intercourse. That is how it is a novel in the modern sense, not merely a poem. Yet, taking them together, and bearing in mind what provides the internal motive power of the action, most of the situations mark stages in a mystical career. There are 'moments' in the pure tradition of the Cathars, and others can be connected with mystical experience in general as regards details which are identical among orthodox and heterodox alike, and also among the pagans—Persians, Arabs, and even Buddhists. It will not do therefore to suppose that we are dealing with some commonplace novel about adultery. Tristan is unfaithful to heresy, the mystic virtue of the Pure, which was a *virtue* also for the authors of the legend. The fault lies not in his being in love, but in his fulfilment of his love.

To compare two forms of mystical experience is a delicate and perilous task, and all the more so here for the fact that one of them is distorted by an epic superstructure. Nevertheless, let me suggest a rough parallel between what happens to Tristan and a properly mystical experience. If I lead a reader to rash inferences, I can repair the damage later. After being wounded in overcoming the Morholt, Tristan has himself put on board a boat with neither sail nor oar. He has only his sword and his harp. The boat is cast adrift, so that he may go in quest of the soothing balm which shall rid his blood of its poison. This is the very model of a yielding up to the influence of the supernatural at the beginning of a mystical experience. This is how a soul, fatally wounded by sin, renounces rational and visible aids, and courts an unknown grace. Modern poetry supplies many accounts of this desperate but eloquent setting out at a venture, which, although then but a rudimentary form of the mystic quest, allows no ignoring of the lyre and symbolic sword—symbolic of a challenge to established society. Few no doubt of our latter-day poets have experienced a 'fatal love'. For some, the quest dwindles into a pleasant cruise from which they return with a manuscript ready for the press. Others distil a drug productive of picturesque visions. Nearly all give the secret away.

But Tristan has met love. At first he failed to recognize it. When King Mark—established authority—despatches him to bring back the faraway princess, he does not suspect that the mission is going to seal his own fate. Then occurs the irremediable mistake of drinking the *love-potion*. In analysing the content of the myth, I pointed out that, in being predestined, the error is tantamount to an alibi. The lovers insist that they have been in no way to blame for anything they have done, as their passion cannot be acknowledged either to society (which looks upon it as criminal) or to themselves (since it condemns them to die). That is the psychological aspect of their experience. But there is a religious aspect also. The irrevocable drinking of the potion, which appears at the time to be due to chance, but which looks afterwards as if everything had conspired to bring it about, symbolizes a soul's *election* by omnipotent Love, its being unexpectedly seized by its vocation as if in its own despite. Thereupon, with the drinking of the potion, Tristan (as Gottfried of Strasbourg says of Tristan's father) 'entered upon another life'. To quote Gottfried further: 'His senses were as though delivered from all natural curbs, and his life was being consumed.' The words perfectly confirm what I have described as passion in opposition to what is natural love.

In the ordinary way this first and crucial summons should open the way to fasting and self-mortification, and lead to an *endura*. But Tristan, carried away by the violent effect of the first revelation which may sometimes inflame the blood, transgresses the rule of the Pure. He obtains his symbolical kiss by force, and profanes it. Thereupon the powers of evil are let loose.

> Sigh, ah sigh, wind so wild!
> Sigh, ah sigh now, my child!
> O Irish maid, thou wayward, winsome maid!

Thereupon a lifetime of penance is going to be required in order to wipe out the sacrilege. But the fundamental misfortune of this love is not only that the sin must be redeemed. The *askesis* of self-redemption must also, and above all, deliver a man from having been born into this world of darkness and lead him to the state of final and fortunate detachment in which he can undergo the deliberate death of the Perfect. Tristan's penance therefore has a meaning entirely different from Christian repentance. And although there are times in the Romance when orthodoxy and heresy seem to get singularly mixed, such indications leave one in no doubt regarding the predominant intention, an intention made unmistakable at the last by the death of the two lovers in sombre splendour. Every episode, moreover, points to this intention; for example, that of the 'harsh life' led by Tristan and Iseult in the Forest of Morrois. In the *Roman en prose*, 'We have lost the world, and the world us', Iseult laments; and Tristan answers: 'If the whole world were now with us, I should see but you alone.' This must indeed be an *endura*. The retreat in the forest symbolizes a period of fasting and self-mortification such as we know that the Cathars underwent in order that their faculties might be all absorbed in the exclusive contemplation of love.

A profound characteristic of passion—and also of mysticism in general—may be discerned here. Later Novalis, a mystic devoted to Night and to a secret Light, wrote: 'The lover is alone with all that he loves.' For that matter, among many possible interpretations, it can be held that his maxim states a purely psychological piece of observation—that passion is by no means the fuller life which it seems to be in the dreams of adolescence, but is on the contrary a kind of naked and denuding intensity; verily, a bitter destitution, the *impoverishment* of a mind being emptied of all diversity, an obsession of the imagination by a single image. In the face of the assertion of its power, the world dissolves; 'the others' cease to be present; and there are no longer either neighbours or duties, or binding ties, or earth or sky; one is alone with all that one loves. 'We have lost the world and the world us.' Such is ecstasy, a flight inward from all created things. How can we avoid calling to mind those 'deserts' of the Dark Night described by Saint John of the Cross! 'Put things far away, lover! My road is flight!' And several centuries before Novalis Saint Teresa of Avila declared that a soul when in ecstasy should feel 'as though there were only God and itself in the world'.

Are we entitled to compare religious geniuses of the first rank with a poem in which the mystical element is quite rudimentary? Admittedly, to do so would be blasphemy of a kind if the Romance were concerned with no more than a passion of sensual love. But everything points to our being on the *via mystica* of the Perfect. The difference from orthodox mysticism lies in the content of the spiritual states and the goal of those states, not in their form.[1] I shall return to this presently.

In the meanwhile, here is a further point of comparison. Spanish mystics have a well-known habit of insisting on an account of what they *suffer*. Saint John of the Cross says in *La Noche oscura*:[2]

[1] Gottfried of Strasbourg's *Tristan* contains the following passage:

> It is not without reason
> That this hollow
> Has been put away in a wilderness.
> It means
> That the place of love
> Lies not in beaten ways
> Nor about our human dwellings.
> Love haunts the deserts.
> The road that leads to its retreat
> Is a hard and toilsome road.

Should it still be doubted what kind of love is being referred to, let me say that Gottfried admits having wandered in the desert himself, but without meeting the reward of his pains (he means that he has not become one of the Perfect).

> I have known the hollow
> When only eleven years old.
> But to Cornwall have I never been.

How could physical love be intended here? The last line shows clearly that the 'hollow' is purely symbolical, since it may exist elsewhere than in Cornwall. Possibly 'Cornwall' stands for a temple or grotto of the heretics.

[2] Saint John of the Cross, *Complete Works*, translated by E. Allison Peers (London, 1934), I, p. 407. *The Dark Night of the Soul*, II, v.

'So brilliant and pure is the light of contemplation that when this Divine light assails the soul, in order to expel its impurity, the soul feels itself to be so impure and miserable that it believes God to be against it, and thinks that it has set itself up against God. This causes it so much grief and pain (because it now believes that God has cast it away) that one of the greatest trials which Job felt when God sent him this experience, was as follows, when he said: "Why hast thou set me opposite to thee, and I am become burdensome to myself?"'

The saint does not refer to bodily or moral pains arising from the mortification of senses and will, but to the soul suffering separation and rejection while its love is most ardent. A hundred pages could be quoted in which there recurs the same lament of the soul about feeling deserted by the divine and being overwhelmingly anguished; about 'the sense of a deep void . . . of a cruel death to the three kinds of goods that may assuage the soul—temporal, natural, and spiritual goods'; and about 'the feeling of rejection which counts among the sternest ordeals of the state of purification'.

Tristan is but an adulterated and sometimes ambiguous expression of courtly mysticism. In interpreting some of those situations in the Romance which seem most thoroughly 'mystical', it is wise, if we do not wish to go seriously astray, to set out from human love and by way of sublimation—not in the opposite direction, from divine Love to metaphors, as we need to do when dealing with the great orthodox mystics. Bearing this in mind, we may trace in the myth more than one aspect of the sufferings undergone in mystical experience. It will be recalled how the troubadour laments:

> Heaven! How doth it thus befall?
> The farther off I am the more I long for her.

And, indeed, never does love thrill Tristan so wildly as when he is parted from his 'lady'. This can be accounted for by elementary psychology, but the point here is that it represents the anguish undergone in a purifying *askesis*. We have seen that in the Romance the repeated *partings* of the lovers answer to an altogether internal necessity of their passion. Iseult is a woman beloved, but she is also more than this: she is symbol of luminous Love. When Tristan wanders far away from her, his love for her waxes, and the more he loves her the more he is afflicted. But, of course, by

now we are aware that the real purpose of the partings is to produce suffering. This brings us back to mysticism from the other
end, so to speak. The more Tristan loves, the more he wants to be
parted from the beloved. This means that the more he loves, the
more he wants to be rejected by love. So strongly does he want to
be rejected that he comes to doubt Iseult's 'love' for him, treats
her like an adversary, and commits himself to a 'blank' marriage
with the other Iseult—the other 'faith', the other Church, whose
communion he has to decline!

Only in one passage of the Romance does orthodoxy for a
moment have the better part. When the effect of the love-potion
has at last worn off, Tristan and Iseult go to visit the hermit Ogrin
in his cell. This results in a meeting between one who endures for
the sake of his God and the lovers who endure for the sake of
another Love. It is then that they repent—for the first and last
time. Iseult is to go back to her legal husband—heresy is to return
to the bosom of the Church. But as the king draws near with his
escort of barons, the lovers exchange a ring of everlasting fidelity and secrecy. Submission is but simulated. And presently in
demanding the ordeal of the red-hot iron the queen is seeking to
avenge herself upon the king's God, whom this ordeal dupes twice.

However external and a matter of form these correspondences
may be, they cannot fairly be dismissed as mere coincidences. But
if the forms are the same, it remains to be seen in what respect the
matter differs and how the matter can ever have come to be
treated as identical in both cases. It might all be regarded as a gross
confusion of Creator and creature, in the Romance; a case,
according to the text-books, of the famous 'divinization of
woman'. Supposing Iseult had been merely a beautiful woman—
as subsequent centuries were to think—the mystic similitudes
which I have set forth would belong to the order of language,
and specially to metaphor. I shall not try to deny that aspect of the
question. It will have consideration. But I believe that there is a
good deal more. For if there were not, then the whole religious
background of the legend would have to be either denied or
neglected, notwithstanding the historical evidence. As regards the
meaning of the myth, we should be brought back to o, and the
Romance would not be a courtly novel; or else, again, courtly
love would cease to be what it actually was, and would set itself to
resemble what our men of learning imagine it was. That is as good
as to say that we can understand nothing about nothing. Once

again, the matter in question is the *passion* of love, and not love purely profane and natural. What, it seems to me, lies at the heart of the antithesis between the two forms of mysticism is that the Romance deals, not merely with profane and natural love, but with *passionate* love. Orthodox mysticism brings about a 'spiritual marriage' of God and the individual soul already in this life, whereas the heretical looks to union and complete fusion, and this only after the demise of the body. In the eyes of the Cathars, this world was past all possible redemption, and their belief implied in theory that profane love is absolute misfortune, an impossible and blamable attachment to an imperfect creature. In the eyes of the Christian, on the other hand, divine love is a misfortune also, since man in his fallen state is unable to love God fully in return, but it is a misfortune which nevertheless creates man anew, and which, far from being antagonistic to profane love, results in making this love holy through marriage. Accordingly, the mystic lovers in the Romance are compelled to pursue the *intensity* of passion, not its fortunate appeasement. The keener their passion, and the more it can detach them from created things, the more readily do they feel that they are on the way to attaining the death in *endura* which they desire. But by Christian mystics, on the contrary, the reality of the mystical state is subjected to the test of the deeds and works that issue from it.[1] At least, such has been the constant intention of those mystics who concentrated their prayers upon the truly incarnated Christ. The Perfect, however, did not believe in the Incarnation, and could not be aware of the *return* of the soul to a life renewed. 'I die of not being able to die,' Saint Teresa says; but she means that she is not able to die to the old life enough to become alive in the new, and thus to obey without anguish.

I see nothing in *Tristan* to recall the 'rejection of gifts' which is spoken of by Eckhart and Saint John of the Cross. The lovers now and then complain of their passion and curse the fatal potion which has been the cause of their terrible sufferings. '*Amor par force les demeine.*' But ultimately it is complete passion that they accept like a *last* revelation in death. So with their attitude to creatures. They are not going to *meet* them again after having

[1] Saint Teresa says: 'In order to please God, and in order to receive great benefits from Him, these benefits must—such is His will—pass *through the hands* of holy mankind in whom, as He Himself has said, He finds His satisfaction.' Meister Eckhart did not see this, but cf. Chapter 3 below.

passed through their passion and its *askesis*. They are unaware of that movement of *return to the world* so characteristic of Christianity. Saint John of the Cross also has experienced perfect detachment. 'When the passions are mortified, the soul receives no more nourishment from creatures; and in that way is filled with obscurity, and is deprived of the objects which the passions were presenting to it.' (*Noche oscura, III*.) (The passage can certainly bear comparison with that admirable cry by Bernart of Ventadour: 'She has taken my heart, she has taken my self, she has taken from me the world, and then she has eluded me, leaving me with only my desire and my parched heart.') Beyond that state, Saint John of the Cross experienced complete viduity, in which not only the world and his neighbour, and love with its object, but even the *desire* of love, seem to escape at the height of the exaltation. 'Empty of all covetousness, nothing impels upward and nothing draws downward.' (*Maxims*.) The troubadour Arnaut Daniel also refers to the 'excess of desire' which takes away 'all desire'. But the theopathic state does not lead Saint John of the Cross to condemn creatures. Meister Eckhart—who is, perhaps mistakenly, held to be a Platonist—has the ability to say in magnificent terms that the pure soul is the place of redemption for creatures who have lost their nature through sin. 'All creatures pass from their life to their being. All creatures bear themselves into my reason so as to be within me reasonable. I alone, I bring all creatures to God.' That is the movement which is lacking theoretically in any kind of mysticism based on the luminous Eros.

Where the two forms of mysticism differ most is as regards *humility*. And there again the key to the antithesis lies in the mystery of the Incarnation. The Romance is steeped in the Celtic atmosphere of knightly *pride*. The high deeds which Tristan performs are inspired by a desire to be valiant. Like all passionate people, he foolhardily revels in the sense of power which comes over him in moments of peril. Hence ultimately he grows to want danger for its own sake, to want to experience passion for a never-ending passion, and to desire an irrevocable death. At this extreme, prowess appears as the material sign of a process of *divinization*. True mystics, on the contrary, are the very essence of prudence, rigour, and clear-sighted obedience. If 'death is my gain', it is because 'Christ is my life' and because Christ was incarnated—that is, came down to us. That is why a Christian does not fall into the delusion of supposing that death for the sake of love can transfigure him; instead he accepts the limitations of his terrestrial vocation. 'Nothing impels him upward, nothing draws him downward', Saint John of the Cross said, and this *'because he places himself at the centre of his humility'*.

3

Curious but Inevitable Transpositions

The whole of European poetry has come out of courtly love and out of the Arthurian romances derived from this love. That is why our poetry employs a pseudo-mystical vocabulary, from which, quite unaware of what they are doing, persons in love still draw today their most commonplace metaphors. Yet even as the romantic myth had made use of a stock of imagery, names, and situations taken out of the accumulations left by Celtic religion—that is to say, a religion already dead—so our literature and our passions now ignorantly and pervertedly employ a terminology which mysticism alone invested with a valid meaning.

More than once the ambiguous character of the myth has caused us to hesitate in the presence of this or that episode. Was it a case of profane love—according to the letter of the Romance —or of a symbol of the luminous Eros, or even a symbol of the Church of Love? It is thus understandable that a reader unaware of the mysteries should almost unavoidably be brought in consequence to transpose into profane life all these too carefully veiled allegories. The process is easily imagined. Saint Augustine wrote this prayer: 'And behold, thou wert within me, and I out of myself, when I made search for thee!' He was addressing God, eternal love. But suppose that a troubadour—one of the Geoffrey Rudels —should have expressed the same prayer while pretending to address it to his Lady. The lover, accustomed to mystical metaphors, which he interprets with their profane meaning, is tempted to see in the same phrase an expression of the passion which he loves: the passion that is tasted and savoured for its own sake, in a kind of indifference to its living and external object. So we saw above that Tristan does not love Iseult in her reality but to the extent that she revives *in him* the delightful cautery of desire. Passionate love tends to grow like the exaltation of a kind of narcissism.

Once the mysteries had been forgotten, it was inevitable that readers of the Romance should interpret its too skilful allegories as applying to profane life. The modern mind has supposed that the transposition thus effected—after the twelfth century—could serve as a *primary datum*. It has supposed that it could 'explain' the higher by the lower—unalloyed mysticism by human passion. And so it founded a new 'science', which was based on the study of language in general and on the similarity of metaphors in particular. But where did the metaphors originate? In a kind of mysticism which, as I have shown, was disguised, persecuted, and then forgotten. So thoroughly was it forgotten as heresy and so completely did it pass into everyday use through poetry that the Christian mystics took up its metaphors as if these had been *natural*. And we today have done likewise, and so have our men of learning. *The 'science' is therefore valid on condition the signs are changed in every one of its statements.* For instance, where the science speaks of mysticism as having resulted from a sublimation of instinct, it is enough to change the direction of the relation stated, and to write: The 'instinct' in question is the result of the profanation of an early form of mysticism.

But the modern mind is so reluctant to accept this conversion that I had better go further into the mechanism of the transpositions, and even recognize the validity of some of the current objections. For after all has not mysticism, it will be said, been open in at least one tendency, to every kind of confusion? Was it not first the mystics who took advantage of the language of the pagan Eros?

4

Orthodox Mystics and the Language of
Passion

The central event in the world from the standpoint of every
kind of religious life that is Christian in content and in
form must be the Incarnation. To shift however little
from this centre involves the double peril of humanism and idealism. The Catharist heresy idealized the whole of the Gospel, and
treated love in all its forms as a leap out of the created world. The
craving for this flight into the divine—or enthusiasm—and for
this ultimately impracticable transgression of human limitations,
was bound to find expression, and thereby to betray itself fatally,
through the magnification in divine terms of sexual love. Conversely, the most 'Christocentric' mystics have had a propensity
to address God in the language of human feeling—the language of
sexual attraction, of hunger and thirst, and of the will. This is a
magnification in human terms of the love of God.

In this way we become aware of the two great streams into
which all mysticism divides. They are seldom met with pure in a
particular work. Even in writings the most truly representative of
one or the other, both may nearly always be discerned, if only as
temptation coincides in a believer with the will to obedience.
Historically speaking, it is not very easy to isolate either. But
theologically the position is clear. The first stream is that of
unitive mysticism, which aims at a complete *fusion* of the soul with
the divine. The second stream may be called *epithalamian mysticism*,
which aims at the *marriage* of a soul to God, and which therefore
implicitly maintains an essential distinction between creature and
Creator.

It will make for clearness, while avoiding an excessive simplification, if I take a few individual examples—the only examples

worth while in this domain.[1] We thereby shall obtain some insight into the cause of the curious fact *that the misuse of the language of love by religious writers must be linked, from a historical standpoint, with the orthodox stream.*

The first example I take from Rudolf Otto, who in his book *West-Östliche Mystik*[2] first compares the founder of German mysticism in the fourteenth century, Meister Eckhart, with the Hindu mystic Sankara, and then contrasts them. The interesting thing for my present purpose is that Otto distinguishes East and West by calling these two forms of mysticism respectively eros and agape, rather in the way I have done above.[3] Sankara, according to Otto, rejects the world and condemns it beyond appeal. *Nirvana*, Sankara said, cannot accept *sansara*, which is life in its diversity and infinite flux. Eckhart, on the contrary, discerns the presence of God in every creature, so that through the soul of a believer all creatures 'pass from their existence into their being'. It has been possible for Otto to carry out his comparison, because in the Middle Ages in Europe there existed a mystical tradition akin to Sankara's. It was, Otto says,[4]

'a mysticism of exaggerated emotion where the "I" and the "Thou" flow together in a unity of intoxicated feeling. Eckhart knows nothing of such emotional orgies or such a "pathological" love (as Kant calls it). For him love is not erōs but the Christian virtue of agápē, strong as death but no paroxysm, inward but of deep humility, at once active in willing and doing as Kant's "practical" love.

'Here Eckhart differs completely from Plotinus, though he is always represented as his pupil. Plotinus also is the publisher of a mystical love, but his love is throughout not Christian agápē, but the Greek erōs, which is enjoyment, and enjoyment of a sensual and supersensual beauty arising from an aesthetic experience almost unknown to Eckhart. In its finest sublimation it still bears within it something of the erōs of Plato's Symposium: that great

[1] For indeed generalizations are nowhere more misleading than in connexion with the mystics. In *St. Jean de la Croix et l'expérience mystique* (Paris, 2nd ed., 1931), Jean Baruzi admirably remarks on page 613 that if we attempted to take a general view of the various forms of mysticism known to us, 'the mystical experience would seem homogeneous only in so far as it is commonplace and in so far as we failed to apprehend its nature.'

[2] Gotha, 1929.   [3] Book II, Chapter 4.

[4] *Mysticism East and West*, translated by Bertha L. Bracey and Richenda C. Payne (New York and London, 1932), p. 212.

Orthodox Mystics and the Language of Passion

Daemon, which is purified into a divine passion out of the ardor of procreation, yet even then still retains a sublimated element of the original passion.'

For Eckhart, the true mystic way is not that which ascends from an emotional state in order to reach supreme union at the summit of a love ecstasy. 'Minne einigt nicht', he writes, 'Sie einigt wohl an einem Werk, nicht an einem Wesen.'[1]

'Rather the "at-one-ment" [i.e. union] [Otto continues] is itself the condition and the first ground of the possibility of true agápē. Nor has his agápē anything in common with the Platonic or Plotinian erōs, but it is the pure Christian emotion in its elemental chastity and simplicity without exaggeration or admixture.'[2]

And from this union results 'confidence, faith, surrender, service'.

Indeed, I myself feel that it is a communion rather than a union; for, as Eckhart expresses it elsewhere,[3] when 'the soul escapes from its nature, its being and its life, and is born into the Divinity, no distinction remains but this: the Divinity is still God, and the soul is still a soul'. The spiritual act of love is initial, not final. A Christian holds that to die to self is the beginning of a more real life here below, not the ruin of the world. Moreover, Otto quotes a further passage from Eckhart which does not refer to union, but to an equality of the soul with God. 'Und diese Gleichheit aus dem Einen in das Eine mit dem Einen ist Quelle und Ursprung der aufblühenden glühenden Liebe.'[4] Otto finds this passage to confirm how for Eckhart 'the proper expression of the feeling of at-one-ness is not a mystical *pleasure*, but agápē, a love of a kind which neither Plotinus nor Sankara mentions or knows.'[5]

It would thus seem that Otto succeeds in plainly defining two *poles* of universal mysticism, and that the East (Sankara, Plato, Plotinus) differs from the West (here typified by Eckhart) in the very way I have been saying that Catharist mysticism is to be

[1] 'Love does not unify; it unites all right in act, never to an essence.'
[2] Op cit., p. 213.
[3] At the end of the sermon, *Nisi granum frumenti*. It must be admitted that there is an elusive ambiguity about Eckhart's use of the word 'union' (*Einung*), and yet it would seem clear enough from the passage I quote here that Otto is right and that he believed in no essential fusion.
[4] And this identity out of the One into the One with the One is fount and source of a flowering glowing love.'   [5] Op. cit., p. 214.

distinguished from the Christian doctrine of love. But Eckhart, it must be recognized, did not dwell in the odour of sanctity. The Avignon pope, John XXII, in a bull issued in 1329, went the length of condemning several of his theses. Among these the tenth is stated in the bull to read as follows:

'We become completely changed into God and are converted into Him even as the bread is changed into the body of Christ in the sacrament: I am thus changed into Him because He Himself makes me become His. Unity and not similitude. By the living God, it is true that there is then no longer any distinction.' As extracted from Eckhart's writings, this thesis seems expressly to contradict Otto's interpretation. It puts Meister Eckhart in the Eastern camp, making out that his mysticism aspires after an *essential* union and so is heretical.

One certainty is that Meister Eckhart is the dialectician *par excellence* and that it is only too easy to extract from his writings the most contradictory truths. Of his work it has proved possible to say that 'negation and affirmation together form the truth. One is not true without the other, and one is inconceivable except in relation to the other. Affirmation and negation are inseparable, being but two aspects of one truth.'[1] It is no less significant to notice that Flemish mystics vigorously attacked Eckhart's writings on those very heads regarding which he seems to Otto to have been orthodox—essential union and the neglect of works. Every one must stand to the East of somebody else, and Meister Eckhart evidently represented the heresy I am calling 'eastern' in the opinion of Ruysbroek. Ruysbroek, in his *Book of the Twelve Beguines*, refers to Eckhart—who had been his own master—and to Eckhart's faithful disciples as 'those false prophets' who 'imagine that they partake of God by their nature'. 'These persons who want to be not only God's equals, but God Himself, are more wicked and diabolical than Lucifer and his satellites.' And again:'They will neither learn, nor know, nor will, nor love, nor thank, nor extol, nor desire, nor possess. . . . That is what they call the perfect poverty of the spirit. . . . But those who are born of the Holy Ghost and sing his praises, practise every virtue. They know and love; they seek; they find. . . .' In short, they act.

It is evident that Ruysbroek accuses Eckhart of Quietism. He puts forward against him a kind of activism of love. He himself did not believe that all distinction between the soul and God can

[1] B. Groethuysen in *Hermes* (Paris, July, 1937).

be abolished. The soul cannot train itself to partake of the Divine, but only to resemble God. It can behold God in the *mirror* of a spirit that has been entirely purified. 'We contemplate what we are and are what we contemplate; for our essence, without losing any of its proper personality, is united to the divine truth which respects the distinction.' And again, 'The abyss separating us from God is one', he says, 'which we perceive in the secret places of the self. It is essential distance.'

This brings me to the point I wish to set forth. If the soul is able to achieve essential union with God, then the soul's love of God is a happy love. It may be expected to display no need of the vocabulary of passion, and this is indeed what history shows. 'I fancy', the Abbé Paquier writes,[1] 'that the Eckhartian mystics never resort to the language of human love.' On the contrary, if it is believed, in accordance with Christian orthodoxy, that the soul cannot achieve essential union with God, the soul's love of God becomes, in the strictest sense, an *unhappy mutual love*. It may then be expected to express itself in passionate language, in the vocabulary of the Catharist heresy as this has become 'profaned' by literature and been taken over by human passions. For the rhetoric of the Heresy is the best fitted to describe and communicate the altogether ineffable nature of the emotion experienced. Here again the documentary evidence supports and makes clear the apparent paradoxes of my outline. It is Ruysbroek who, with his doctrine of an essential distinction, introduces into the writings of the mystics of the North the 'epithalamian' vocabulary.

'Here then the irresistible desire has come [he says]. To compel oneself continually to seize what cannot be seized. . . . And the object of this desire can be neither given up nor seized.[2] To give it up is unbearable, to retain it impossible. Silence itself lacks the strength to grasp it in its hands.'
Ruysbroek pours into his glowing style all the metaphors of passionate love. He speaks of being submerged in love, of swooning away, of embraces and of hurricanes of eagerness, of the fire of

---

[1] Cit. apud Baruzi, *St. Jean de la Croix*, p. 642. The absence of 'epithalamian' expressions may possibly serve as a criterion for deciding whether or not a given mystic believed in essential union, and in that case Abbé Paquier's remark goes against Otto's contention: we are led to put Eckhart among the heretics. Obviously I am simplifying matters, but the question is one worth examining closely.

[2] One of the troubadours says: 'Love neither forsakes me nor can it well take me.'

love that burns the soul day and night, of orgies of love, over-flowing delights, of being intoxicated with love, and of love's bruisings. 'He has drunk up my spirit and my heart', Ruysbroek causes one of his beguines to say in referring to Christ. 'I have become lost in his mouth', another says. And a third declares: 'Oh, to drink in the glances of love and to be engulfed in them intoxicated!'

In the thirteenth century the Franciscan mystics supply a no less striking instance of the use of courtly terminology. Saint Francis himself, it is well known, learned French in his youth, and delighted in French tales of chivalry. He dreamed of becoming 'the finest knight in the world', or, in his own words, 'a great baron adored by all the world'. It will be remembered that he began his ministry by removing his clothes in the presence of the bishop and of a great crowd assembled in the main square of Assisi. When he was quite naked, he said to his richly attired father that henceforth his only father would be God. The bishop threw his cloak over Francis, who fled into the countryside declaiming verses in French in a loud voice. He felt that the utter destitution of his body had made it the humble servant of his soul. Thereupon there was nothing to hamper his ascent towards the Supreme Good. Remembering the French romances he had read, Francis made Poverty his 'Lady', and deemed it an honour to be her 'knight'.

The Franciscan wandering knights spread over Italy as the troubadours had spread over the South of France. They were to be met with on the roads and in market places, and from village to castle. The poems of Jacopone da Todi—'God's jongleur'—the lauds of his imitators, the letters of Saint Catherine of Siena, the Book of the Blessed Angela di Foligno, and the many tales of the Fioretti,[1] show that the rhetoric of the troubadours and of the courtly romances was the direct inspiration of the Franciscan poetic impulse, which in turn deeply influenced the mystical voca-bulary of subsequent centuries.

'Remember, O creature, that thy nature partaketh of the angels. Dost thou tarry in this mud, and thou shalt have to stay for ever in darkness.'

So one of the lauds attributed to Jacopone da Todi and his

---

[1] Saint Francis called Friar Giles 'a paladin of the Round Table', and the saint's *miracles*—such as the conversion of the Gubbio wolf—occurred in the same circumstances as did the feats of *prowess* of the wandering knights.

followers; and the suggestion in this passage that men are in some way angels disturbingly recalls the doctrine of the Cathars. Other lauds, while obviously more Catholic in their inspiration, are for that reason only the more 'erotic' and 'courtly' in phraseology. For example:

'My heart melteth like ice on fire when I straitly embrace my Lord, and cry: "The love of Love consumeth me, I am united with Love, intoxicated by love."

'In flames I burn and languish, crying: "In living I die, and in dying I live. Yet do I not love, but am athirst for love; I hunger to be united with Love."'[1]

5

Courtly Rhetoric in Spanish Mysticism

If now we turn to the writings of the great Spanish mystics of the sixteenth century, Saint Teresa and Saint John of the Cross, we find them employing the whole rhetoric of courtly love, even its most delicate shades of expression. Here are the chief topics common alike to the troubadours and to these orthodox mystics:

'To die of not being able to die.'[2]
The 'sweet cautery'.
'Love's dart' that wounds but does not kill.
The 'salute' of love.
Passion that sets one apart from the world and other beings.
Passion that renders every other kind of love colourless.

[1] From *Ciascun amante*, described as 'a dance of mystic love'.
[2] This famous exclamation of Saint Teresa's was inspired by the Franciscan Angela di Foligno, who said: 'I die of a desire to die!'

To complain of an ill that is yet prized more than every joy
and worldly good.

To deplore that words should betray an 'ineffable' emotion
which nevertheless demands to be avowed.

Love as a purifying emotion that drives away all vile
thoughts.

The substitution of the will of love for the real will.

The 'struggle of love' in which it is needful to be defeated.

The symbolism of 'castles' as havens of love.

The symbolism of the 'mirror' for imperfect love reflecting
perfecting love.

The 'stolen heart', the 'ravished understanding', the 'rape of
love'.

Love treated as an ultimate 'understanding' (*conoscenza* in
Provençal).

All this kind of thing has led the materialistic psychologist—from
Voltaire to Freud—to declare with odd assurance, and purely on
verbal grounds, that mystics are the victims of a sexual aberration.
And, as is well known, the views put forth by the learned in the
nineteenth century have now become the prepossessions of the
vulgar. However, not only is the materialistic attitude to mysticism clearly more indicative of an obsession in those who cling
to it than enlightening about mysticism itself, but also it is an
attitude based upon an error at once historical and psychological.
For (*a*) the language of passion, as the mystics employ it, has not
been to begin with the language of the senses and of nature,
but the rhetoric of a kind of *askesis* exemplified by the twelfth-
century heresy of Southern France; and (*b*) geniuses such as Saint
John of the Cross and Saint Teresa must have been more alive
than any one else to the perils of 'spiritual luxuriousness' (the
expression is Saint John's), and both speak of it so freely that in
their case the usual suspicion of an 'inhibition' must be meaningless.

These two points deserve to be elaborated. In the first place, it
needs to be insisted that the language of the mystics is not open to
being confused with the profound nature of the experiences they
underwent. J. Baruzi writes of Saint Teresa that 'the source of
many of her images has been traced, but it is not so easy to find
the origins of the psychological language in which she undoubtedly
most truly expressed her nature'. All mystics, and Saint Teresa as

much as any of them, complain of a want of new words (*nuevas palabras*) with which to praise the works of God as they experience these in spirit. Their silence is *truer* than their speech. The only thing I wish to do here is to consider the *inherited material* of their literary vocabulary.

To confine myself to an instance which is at one and the same time the most celebrated, the best known, and that which has most strikingly misled the authorities, the fact is that Saint Teresa constantly employs and even refines upon courtly rhetoric. Is this a matter of literary influence? Of some underground heretical connexion? Or even of an independent recreation which might be partly accounted for on the lines of remarks made in the preceding chapter? 'How can we tell', Baruzi says, 'whether some of the images which John of the Cross takes from the Song of Songs were extracted directly from the Biblical poem or were not at the same time images which he rediscovered and, so to speak, verified for himself, because they expressed a newly experienced delight?'[1] These are questions which I do not believe any one is equipped to settle. The best informed specialists hesitate over attributing to very famous—and, as it happens, orthodox—mystics, such as Ruysbroek or Saint Teresa, the originating of the actual terminology used by Saint John of the Cross. As regards Saint Teresa, however, we may trace unmistakable sources. The fondness shown by the mystics for the romances of chivalry has often been pointed out. Saint Teresa in her girlhood doted upon them.[2] It seems even that she once thought of writing a romance herself in collaboration with her brother Rodriguez. It is also well known that the religious writings which were her intellectual nourishment were all the work of authors strongly imbued with courtly and chivalric rhetoric. M. Gaston Etchegoyen says:[3]

'The noble language of *Amadis of Gaul*, its erotic metaphors, and its subtle refinements, are found also in Francisco de Ossuna and Bernardino de Laredo [writers whom Saint Teresa made her master] as well as in the *Exclamaciones* and the *Castillo interior*.

'In Spain the authors of romances of chivalry display the same realism as those of treatises on mysticism, sacrificing a sense of the marvellous in favour of a more familiar and moving intimacy, as they tend to treat the human and the divine on one plane,

[1] Op. cit., p. 343.   [2] Vide her *Vida*, cap. II.
[3] *L'Amour divin: essai sur les sources de sainte Thérèse* (Paris, 1923), Part IV.

161

either by *contemplating the divine from a secular standpoint or by giving the human a divine interpretation.*

'Above all, courtly and divine love encourage one another to a like heroic notion of moral obligation, of action, and of faith. Amadis of Gaul and Saint Teresa could both have taken for their motto: "To love in order to act." [Although courtly love, in its pristine purity, loved in order to suffer, in order 'to endure'.]

'A fusion of divine and courtly love was effected, not in the feeble extravagances of the romances of mystic chivalry, but by the twelfth-century troubadours of Provence. The most fecund material in their doctrine, and in their symbolism and terminology, was taken over by mysticism in the thirteenth century, thanks to St. Francis of Assisi.

'Considering St. Teresa alone, we see that the romances of chivalry had a psychological influence upon her, and also a literary influence which is chiefly evident in the warlike symbolism of the *Castillo interior.*'

What an extraordinary return and incorporation of heresy by means of a rhetoric devised by heretics for use against the Church, and which the Church, thanks to the saints, eventually wrested from them! Let me summarize the stages of the process. The heresy of the Perfect is brought down from Eros to Venus and is carried the length of kinship with a poetry of love apparently altogether secular; the confusions that this involves flatter natural desires, so that little by little the heresy vanishes from before the eyes of the worldly whom the deceptive charms of art have taken in, and they treat the language as simply poetry. Finally, first a hundred and then another three hundred years later, nobody remembers that the garment was ever meant to cover anything but nature, and Christian mysticism comes along in order to make it into a cloak for Agape!

The partiality of the Christian mystics for the terminology of passion has generally been interpreted psychologically according to the materialistic superstition.[1] Everything possible—and indeed rather more than everything possible—has been attributed to a 'deflexion' of sexual instinct. On the whole, the nineteenth century never felt greater self-satisfaction than when equating the superior with the inferior, the mental with the material, and the significant with the insignificant. It called this 'explaining'. There is no need to demonstrate that most of the time it was merely

[1] Cf. the writings of Max Nordau, Krafft-Ebing, Murisier, Leuba, Freud, etc.

casting its critical sense to the winds. But I may remark that its propensity in this direction may well testify to some deep *resentment* of poetry and indeed of all creative—and hence venturesome—activity of the mind.

But it is desirable to insist further, that for men of the sixteenth century erotic language was more innocent than it is in our eyes. We are the neurosis victims, heirs of a bourgeois form of Puritanism that has come down to us from a disbelieving nineteenth century. Saint John of the Cross, who described in a remarkable page of psychological penetration the moves of a flesh attracted by the beginnings of mystic exaltation (*Noche oscura*, I, v. 3), exaggerates no more than he dissimulates the relative gravity of such incidents. To recite at this point the formulas of 'sublimation' and 'inhibition' is simply to refuse to understand what one is talking about. Where is the inhibition, where the censorship, in Saint Teresa's writing to a religious who has complained of experiencing an emotion of the senses each time he enters upon prayer, 'I find that this is indifferent to prayer, and that it is best to pay no attention whatever to it.' So, Saint John of the Cross, replying to one of his brothers, who could not communicate without experiencing sexual emotion, and who, accordingly, had been commanded not to communicate more than once a year, advises him not to be upset about it, to receive the sacrament each week, whatever happens—and the brother is cured, because he no longer fears excessively. If we are required to say anything further about psycho-analysis, let us not fail to notice that Saint John of the Cross plays here the part of a doctor, not that of a neurotic.

'It will perhaps seem to you [writes Saint Teresa] that some of the things to be met with in the Song of Songs might have been put differently. Considering our grossness, I should not be surprised if that came to your mind. I have even heard some persons told that they should avoid hearing them. O God! how great is our wretchedness! It befalls us as it befalls those venomous animals which change into poison everything they eat.'

From the formal comparison of the *writings* of Eckhart with those of Ruysbroek, Saint Teresa and Saint John of the Cross, we may now infer that metaphors borrowed from current language by the mystics have a character in close relation to their doctrine of union or to their faith in the Incarnation. Ruysbroek, Saint Teresa, and Saint John of the Cross are very distinctly

'Christocentric'. Everything in their minds sets out from the drama of the division which sin opened between man and his Creator; all ends in moments of active communion in Grace, and that is what they call 'marriage'—the communion of the elect soul with Christ the Church's bridegroom. But the way of the *parted* man is passion—and passion is everywhere in their writings, whereas it is absent from those of Eckhart.

That is why orthodox mysticism—the kind least suspect of equivocal partiality—was led *by the very object of its faith* to use, and at times to abuse, the language of passionate love. A use and an abuse into which modern psychology was bound to read meanings agreeable to its doctrine, but meanings that seem to me to be controverted by history.

6

A Note on Metaphor

However, the matter may be carried further. It is possible to say: 'Let us grant that the language of passion was derived from a courtly literature, itself produced in the atmosphere of a certain heresy. Did not this heresy in turn arise out of sublimated physiological proclivities?' *Historically*, the question has nothing to go on; and yet theoretically the objection is possible and even inevitable. But to ask if 'mind' or 'matter' is the ultimate *cause* of phenomena involving both is like asking: 'Which came first, the hen or the egg?' For example, we are quite unable to tell whether the language of mysticism resulted from a materialization of the spiritual—in which event the latter would be a first cause—or on the contrary from a sublimation of physiological phenomena—in which case these phenomena must underlie what is being expressed. But one thing is certain: we are

A Note on Metaphor

confronted with two factors which never exist singly. That should content everybody, although in fact it contents no one.

Metaphor, indeed, affords another instance of that eagerness of the contemporary mind to settle a question in favour of whatever is lower. We speak of a *bitter* taste, and also of a *bitter* pain. This everybody is ready to explain by saying that to speak of a bitter pain is to use a metaphor and to give the epithet a figurative sense. The *real* meaning of the word 'bitter' is made a physical sensation, which is thus held to have preceded any mental one. Very possibly, but actually we do not know. It is impossible for anybody who thinks that the physical came first to give *reasons* for his opinion. Nobody has found out that the 'material' meaning of every word has actually preceded the 'mental' meaning. The opinion that it has is merely based on a presumption—that the physical is *more true and more real* than the mental, and hence that the physical is at the foundation of all things and is the principle of all *explanation*.

The mechanics of this presumption have been set forth and criticized by Dr. Minkowski and Arnaud Dandieu[1] both pertinently and with subtlety. According to these writers, literal and figurative meanings cannot be subordinated to one another, because both express in their respective departments an indivisible reality, which is more profound than, and also anterior to, either its sensorial or mental aspects. How could we otherwise explain that one and the same word serves to denote such diverse things? Actually, a pain may be no less bitter than the taste of salt, and what we denote by the same word in each case is a way of being affected—whether by the senses or by thought—in the wholeness of our existence. Likewise with our metaphors of love. People nowadays do not hesitate to argue as follows: '*Love* means to me sexual attraction. Saint Teresa everlastingly talks of love. Ergo, she was not only a mystic, but an erotomaniac unawares.' But we have seen that Saint Teresa was unaware of nothing, and that, on the contrary, 'passionate' lovers may be mystics unawares. The arguments cancel out. We know nothing of primal origins. What we have been able to distinguish is the interplay of the two factors in historical evolution. Let me sum it up again, for clarity.

Our language of passion comes down to us from the rhetoric of

[1] E. Minkowski, *Vers une Cosmologie* (Paris, 1936), chapter on metaphor, and Arnaud Dandieu and R. Aron, *La Révolution nécessaire* (Paris, 1931), chapter on Marcel Proust.

the troubadours. It was a supremely ambiguous rhetoric. Its symbols of sexual attraction were the product of Manichaean dogmatics. But little by little, as it was gradually separated from the religion in which it originated, it passed into manners, and became part of the common language. Now, a mystic who wishes to describe his ineffable experiences is compelled to resort to metaphor. He takes his metaphors wherever he comes upon them, and as they already are, although he can, of course, inflect their meaning. Beginning with the twelfth century, the current metaphors became those of courtly rhetoric. If the mystics adopted them unhesitatingly, it was not in the least that they were 'sublimating' sensual passions; they used them, because the habitual form of of expressing such passions—which had themselves been given substance by another kind of mysticism—suited the expression of the spiritual love which they were experiencing. The form of expression was the more appropriate to describing the 'unhappy' relations which a soul entertained with its God, that the form had been the more thoroughly humanized, i.e. was detached from the heresy. For the heresy had assumed the possibility of union between God and soul, which implied divine felicity and the unhappiness of every human love; whereas orthodoxy assumes that union is impossible, which implies divine unhappiness and renders human love possible within its own limits. It follows that what is the language of human passion according to the heresy corresponds to the language of divine passion according to orthodoxy. There has thus been a continuous interaction, and it is altogether arbitrary to isolate this or that moment and set it up in the guise of a primary *datum*.

7

The Mystic Deliverance

The time has come for us to be arbitrary in this way and to decide the question in favour of the mental—that is to say, in favour of the primacy of mind. Whether arbitrary *ante* or *post rem*—and in this case there is no real difference—the decision can nevertheless be justified by arguments. In the first place, it seems to me that the language of passion can be accounted for on the view that mind comes before matter because it expresses, not the triumph of nature over mind,[1] but an encroachment of mind over instinct. 'There is love whenever desire is so great as to go beyond the confines of natural love', the troubadour Guido Calvacanti declared in the thirteenth century; and it is in his transcending the confines of instinct that man is set up as mind. This is alone what enables human beings to speak. For language offers the possibility of lying *as much as* the possibility of stating what is. Animals cannot lie; they are unable to state what instinct does not supply; they cannot go beyond necessity or beyond satisfaction. But passion—the love of love—is, on the contrary, an urge going beyond instinct and thereby it *gives* instinct *the lie*. In such circumstances the lie can only be uttered by mind.[2]

Secondly, if Saint John of the Cross, and even Ruysbroek and Saint Francis, obviously appeared later than the moment at which passionate love flowered into consciousness, this moment is in turn later than the pseudo-Christian mysticism of the Cathars.

[1] As is implied in such an everyday expression as 'blinded by passion' or 'madly in love'.

[2] How deeply are statement and lying bound together in passionate love! Indeed, the will to expression, the will to self-description, as if in order to obtain a more intense self-enjoyment, is typical of all passion. And it also implies the conviction that other people must fail to understand, and that if they question or accuse us they must be lied to for the sake of preserving the very essence of passion.

Passion and Mysticism

And, thirdly, it has probably been a mistake to suppose that the proposition, 'Every erotomaniac is a mystic unawares', can be countered by the statement, 'Or the other way round.' The *epigoni* of the great mystics may sometimes seem to us as if they had been erotomaniacs unawares.[1] Nevertheless, erotomania is unquestionably a kind of drugged state, and everything goes to show that Eckhart, Ruysbroek, Teresa, and John of the Cross were the exact opposite of any drug-taker. For a drug-taker is the victim not of his passion but of the material means which he employs in order to obtain his transports. Although a drug-taker's passion may have originated in a conscious or unconscious desire to escape from an intolerable terrestrial confinement, it remains that he is first and foremost the slave of his drug. Psychologically speaking, he is a fallen being, whose senses are deadened, whose mind has become clouded, and who ends up in idiocy. But the great mystics, on the contrary, urge the need of pushing beyond the trance stage and of reaching a clarity of mind ever purer and more daring, and even of verifying the high gifts of grace by means of their repercussions *in everyday life*. Saint Teresa deemed good only those visions that impelled her to act better and to love more. Above all, the great mystics are agreed in seeing at the summit of their ascent the attainment of a sovereign freedom of the soul. Saint John of the Cross and Meister Eckhart say in different words the same thing: a mystic should strive after attaining a state in which he is able 'to forgo his gift' and to desire it no longer for its own sake. In spiritual marriage, according to John of the Cross, a soul comes to love God without any longer *feeling* its love. It might seem as if this were a state of perfect indifference; actually, it is the perfect state of hard-won poise and of immediately active understanding. On the far side of trances and *askesis*, the mystic experience culminates in a state of the most thorough 'disintoxication' of the soul and of the utmost self-possession. And only then does *marriage* become possible, meaning as it must, not the enjoyment of eros, but the fecundity of agape.

Thus ultimately orthodox mysticism stands forth as the highest way of purgation and as the most effective discipline for transcending passionate love, even when in a sublimated form. The

[1] Especially the female *epigoni*, such as Marguerite Marie Alacoque in the seventeenth century, who so vividly describes the nuptial bed and what takes place in it!

168

cycle of Christian *askesis* leads the soul back to happy obedience, to acceptance of creature limitations, albeit with a spirit renewed and a freedom regained.

8

The Twilight of Passionate Love

It is the dogma of the Incarnation that radically distinguishes orthodox mysticism from heretical. It is that dogma which gives an altogether different meaning to the word 'love' in the two cases.

The Catharist heretics set up Darkness against Light, as is done in the Gospel according to Saint John. But the Word of Light did not, in their view, put on the form of Darkness; it was not 'made flesh'. They did not want the perfect Light to communicate itself to us through life. (They did not believe in the humanity of Christ.) They wanted to go straight to Love by means of love, and from Darkness into Light without transition. Thus were they bound to founder, as Icarus foundered. (He who would go to God without passing through Christ is going to the Devil, said Luther energetically.) They felt that Darkness is a mystery of the Light, the final secret of which Light alone knows.[1] But they did not know that Darkness is the Anger of God—called forth by our rebellion—and not the work of an obscure demiurge. (Such at least is the biblical doctrine.) Refusing to be taught by the Light in this life and by means of 'matter', misunderstanding an Agape that sanctifies creatures, and so ignorant of the true nature of what they held to be sin, they ran the risk of being irremediably lost in sin precisely when they thought they were escaping from it.

---

[1] Karl Jaspers has magnificently expressed the final assumption of Darkness by the Light in his *Philosophie*.

And hence it came about that there was a fatal confusion between the divinizing Eros and that Eros which is the captive of instinct. Hence it came about that the 'enthusiastic' passion, the *joy d'amor* of the troubadours, was fated to issue in unhappy human passion. This impossible love left in men's hearts an unforgettable cautery, a truly devouring ardour, a thirst which death alone could quench: they suffered 'the torture of love' and set themselves to loving it for its own sake.

The passion of the Perfect called for a divinizing death. The thirst which it put into men's hearts when they were without faith, but had been overwhelmed by the fiery poetry, drove them to seek in death no more than the supreme thrill. And likewise, the love of the Lady became, as soon as it was no longer a symbol of union with uncreated Light, the symbol of an impossible union with woman; retaining from its mystical origin an indefinable divine element, falsely transcendent, an illusion of the liberating glory of which suffering remained the sign! Thus occurred a tragic reversal. To surpass oneself to the extent of union with the transcendent, when the goal is no longer the Light, and while ignorant of the 'way', is to cast oneself down into Darkness. The surpassing thereupon is no more than an exaltation of narcissism. It is intended to achieve not *liberation* from the senses, but a painful *intensity* of sentiment. Intoxication by the spirit.

The history of passionate love in all great literature from the thirteenth century down to our own day is the history of the descent of the courtly myth into 'profane' life, the account of the more and more desperate attempts of Eros to take the place of mystical transcendence by means of emotional intensity. But magniloquent or plaintive, the tropes of its passionate discourse and the hues of its rhetoric can never attain to more than the glow of a resurgent twilight and the promise of a phantom bliss.

Book IV

THE MYTH IN LITERATURE

I

Of the Influence of Literature on Conduct

It will now be seen what sin is and how sin proceeds. It is when human will turns from God in order to be a will unto itself, that it arouses its own ardour and burns with its own affection, an ardour which is proper to it and has nothing in common with the ardour that is divine.—JAKOB BOEHME.

In a general way it is difficult *to check* the actual influence of the arts upon the everyday life of a period. Does music refine manners? And what may be the effect of painting? Architecture, it is true, produces dwellings, but the fact does not constitute its character as art. So with this or that philosophy. Very different, however, is the situation of a literature which may be shown historically to have bestowed its vocabulary upon passion. If literature can boast of having affected the manners of Europe, it is certainly due to our myth. More accurately, it is due to the rhetoric of the myth, as inherited from Provençal love. There is no need to attribute to sounds and words any magical power over our conduct. The adoption of certain linguistic conventions naturally involves and fosters the rise of the latent feelings most apt to be expressed in this way. That is the sense in which it may be said, following La Rochefoucauld, that few people would fall in love had they never heard of love.

Passion and expression are not really separable. Passion comes to birth in that powerful impetus of the mind which also brings language into existence. So soon as passion goes beyond instinct and becomes truly itself, it tends to self-description, either in order to justify or intensify its being, or else simply in order to keep *going*. In this sphere, tracing the process is easy. The emotions first experienced by an upper class and then through imitation by the masses are literary creations in the sense that a given rhetoric is the sufficient condition for them to be *avowed* and hence for them to be made conscious. In the absence of this rhetoric, the emotions would no doubt still exist, but accidentally, lacking recognition, and they would be treated as unmentionable and contraband peculiarities. But it has invariably happened that the putting into circulation of a new rhetoric caused neglected potentialities of the heart suddenly to become profusely actualized. The publication of *Werther*, for example, led to a wave of suicides. Rousseau made the whole of the French court take to drinking milk. Chateaubriand's *René* filled several generations with melancholy. This is because in order to admire nature unadorned, to adopt a certain gloomy mien, or even to commit suicide, it is necessary to be able 'to explain', either to oneself or to others, what one is feeling. The more a man is given to sentiment, the more likely is he to be wordy and to speak well. Likewise, the more passionate a man is, the more likely is he to reinvent the tropes of the rhetoric, to rediscover their *necessity*, and to shape himself spontaneously according to the notion of the 'sublime' which these tropes have indelibly impressed upon us.

That is why it will be easy enough to mark the stages of the transformation undergone by the courtly myth in the *morals* of the peoples of Europe. It can be taken for granted that, except of course for certain delays and simplifications, these stages have kept pace with the *literary* transformations to which over the same lapse of time the myth was being subjected. In describing the sweep of classical mysticism, I was able to note the moment at which the myth was incorporated. The sweep was an ascending one, and led to a release through a snapping of the spell. Literature, on the contrary, is the way downward to manners. Hence it is the popularization of the myth—or better still, its 'profanation'[1]—that I am now going to survey.

[1] This word I am invariably using in the two senses of 'sacrilege' and of 'secularization'.

2

The Two Roses

The best starting-point is supplied by the *Roman de la Rose*, written between 1237 and 1280, about a century after Béroul and Thomas had produced their versions of *Tristan*. The Albigensian crusade had devastated the courtly civilization of Languedoc and scattered the last of the troubadours. What happened to the tradition of Love? It seems clear that as early as the middle third of the century the heretics—now being hunted by the Church and dispersed all over Europe—forsook giving literary expression to their 'religion'. Likewise Catharism was henceforth to be buried in the deep and dumb layers of the people, whose social life precluded noble ceremonial, so that the magnificent symbols of the great age of feudalism were no longer available. The apparent silence, however, did not halt its progress. The Church of Love was reproduced in countless sects more or less secret and more or less revolutionary, and their close similarity of feature testifies to a common origin and to a tradition faithfully preserved. In fact, all these sects denied the dogma of the Trinity—at least in its orthodox form; all evinced a high-flown spirituality; all professed a doctrine of 'radiant joy'; all were anti-clerical, cultivated poverty and vegetarianism, and displayed an egalitarian spirit, extending in some instances to complete communism. Presently these same features were being displayed all together among the Brethren of the Free Spirit and the Rhenish Ortliebians—who were perhaps in touch with the Waldenses, neighbours of the Cathars—and not only among the Waldenses themselves, but also among the disciples of Joachim of Floris, among the beguines and beghards of the Low Countries, the English Lollards, the Moravian Brethren (if not among the Hussites); and, further, among the heretics of the Reformed Churches—Schwenckfeldt, Weigel, the Anabaptists and the

175

Mennonites. Luther, Calvin, and Zwingli fought these dissenters with the same violence that Rome had employed against its own sectarians. But they could not and did not wish to wipe them out entirely. Nowadays Mennonite communities in which Russian strains have mingled—Dukhobors and Khlystis—exist as far afield as Canada and Paraguay. Their notion of love has not changed.

But before the middle of the fourteenth century courtly literature had turned into simply a means of expression—a rhetoric. This rhetoric tended automatically *to idealize* the profane objects it dealt with. As soon as this tendency made itself felt, it excited, as it was bound to do, a so-called 'realistic' reaction. The double movement finds its illustrious witness in the *Roman de la Rose*, which was written in two parts, each by a different author. The first part, produced in about 1237, was the work of Guillaume de Lorris; the second part, by Jean de Meung, was finished before 1280.

The Rose of Guillaume de Lorris is love of the ideal woman, by now a real woman and yet inaccessible in her garden frosted over with allegories. Danger, Male-Bouche, and Shame defend Bel Accueil from the boldness of suitors. The *obstacle* to the union of love is figured by a necessity that is now moral and no longer in the least religious. The lover has to deserve his reward, not by any mystical *askesis*, but by a refinement of mind. Jean de Meung, on the other hand, looks upon the Rose as no more than sensual pleasure. A most outspoken realism supersedes Lorris's fiddle-faddle; Platonism gives place to an apology of sensual enjoyment, and emotional fervour to cynicism. The Rose is won by main force. Nature triumphs over Mind; and reason over passion.

Each of the two parts of the Romance had its own progeny. Lorris led to Dante—who perhaps translated him—and on to Petrarch and much further, down to the allegorical novels of the seventeenth century and to *La Nouvelle Héloïse* in the eighteenth. From Jean de Meung the ancient tradition, according to which passion is to be rejected as 'a sickness of the soul', was transmitted to the lower levels of French literature—to *gauloiserie* and the schools of broad Gallic jokes, to controversial rationalism, and to a curiously exacerbated misogyny, naturalism, and man's reduction to sex. All this has simply been pagan man's normal way of defending himself against the myth of unhappy love. Perhaps in effect his attitude has not been so very different from the realistic Christian vision. That, however, is a matter to which I shall return.

3

Sicily, Italy, Beatrice, and Symbols

In about the year 1200 Rambaut de Vaqueiras, a troubadour of
Languedoc, exchanged some verses with the powerful Mar-
chese Alberto Malaspina. It would seem clear that at this time
similar exchanges—call them 'literary' if you like—kept the
South of France in touch with Lombardy and Venetia. Once
again, the map of the influence exerted by the troubadours coincides with the map of heresy. A little later the Franciscan movement
arose out of a like conjunction of the 'spiritualists'—this time,
inside the Church—and the poets. Meanwhile, around Palermo,
where Frederick the Second held court, there blossomed the so-
called Sicilian School. To what extent this courtly poesy of the
South was inspired by the troubadours is still obscure. Only one
Provençal poet is known to have appeared at the Sicilian court,
and Frederick was a persecutor of heresy. It may also be wondered
how far the Sicilians still had 'intelligence of Love'. Was all they
had preserved of the *trobar clus* simply the trick of baffling the
reader? There is a temptation to think so, in view of the way
Dante and his friend Cavalcanti attacked their master, Guittone
d'Arezzo, and mocked his disciples, calling them 'sectarians of
ignorance, blind men claiming to distinguish colours, geese
striving to rival eagles'.

When Dante comes upon Bonagiunta da Lucca in Purgatory
he takes the opportunity of expounding the *dolce stil nuovo*. This
was the artful and caressing style in which the Northern School
had reacted against the influence of such indefatigable imitators as
Bonagiunta. It was novel, but at the same time a return to sound
tradition. Its striking feature was its *conscious* renovation of the
symbolical vocabulary of the troubadours. The style into which
the Sicilians had fallen was a dubiously allegorical one. In treating
the Lady as a real woman, they addressed her with a conventional

and frigid amorousness. Dante, Cavalcanti, and still others, favoured more spontaneity, more of the ardour of a wooer; but they were nevertheless aware that the Lady was entirely symbolical. Indeed, they were not only aware of it; they said so—and this was their novelty. For such was the paradoxical secret of courtly love; stilted and inanimate when addressed to woman, it became all ardent sincerity as soon as it was directed to the Wisdom of Love. Dante is never more passionate than when Philosophy is the theme of his song, unless it is when Philosophy has turned into Holy Science. This sincerity was an unmistakable legacy of the troubadours; and quite the opposite of what somebody today would imagine. In the *Convivio* Dante speaks of it as a secret needing to be veiled in 'a lovely deceit'. This the Cathars had well understood. But it should be borne in mind that they never said so.

It is because Dante and his friends felt that they must *define* their art that, better than any one else, these Italian poets enable us to pierce the real mystery of the troubadours; rather in the way the seven colours of the spectrum can be distinguished at dusk whereas in broad day they form but a single luminousness the very strength of which precludes analysis. It is at this stage of poetry that the themes mingled by the *trobar* in the artless transparency of his symbolism become evident. Jacopo da Lentino, last of the Sicilians, utters the following plaint:

'Oft doth my heat die, and more cruelly than by a natural death, for your sake, Lady, whom it desires and loves more than self. . . .

'I have within me a fire that I feel will never be put out. . . . How is it that this fire consumeth me not?'
Dante too says:[1]

'Love, that discourseth to me in my mind yearningly of my lady, moveth many a time such things with me anent her that my intellect loses its way among them.

'His discourse soundeth so sweetly that the soul that heareth him and feeleth, must cry: "Oh me! that I have not power to tell that which I hear of my lady."'
And the symbolical meaning of the Lady can no longer be in doubt when Guido Guinicelli refers to her as the source of 'our faith':

'There goeth she along the road, so filled with nobility and grace that she puts down the pride of him to whom she giveth

---

[1] Canzone III.

greeting, and, be he not already of our faith, she doth bring him to it.'

Dante, moreover, can have been no blasphemer when in the *Vita nuova*[1] he penned that verse with its sublime beginning, '*Angelo chiama in divino intelletto*';

'An angel crieth in its divine intelligence and saith: "Lord, in the world a marvel is displayed in act, emanating from a soul that shineth after as here on high. Heaven, that hath no other lack than to possess her, craveth her of its Lord and every saint entreateth the grace." Pity alone defendeth our cause; for God speaketh, intending my lady: "Beloved mine, now suffer in peace that your hope be, so long as it pleaseth me, there where is one who looketh to losing her and who in Hell shall say to the damned: 'I have beheld the hope of the blessed.'"'

Can he have been referring to Beatrice as a woman? Is it her presence as such that the saints entreat and that is the hope of the blessed? Or is she the Holy Ghost in the act of upholding His Church with the charity of Christ—Pity—till every soul shall have been able to attain to the New Life?[2] What must seem like blasphemy here below is that the ambiguity is still maintained. That is how there arose a discussion between Orlandi and Cavalcanti about the meaning of their words. 'Is this Love life or death?' the first boldly inquired. 'The power of love often produceth death. . . . There is love whenever desire is so great as to go beyond the confines of natural love. . . . As it is not due to quality, it perpetually reflects its own effect. It is not a pleasure, but a contemplation.' There can be no doubt about it. Love is mystic passion. But the part played by natural love in the heavenly prospect still needed to be made clear. This was done by Davanzati, when, in a little fable written towards the end of the thirteenth century, he described the real nature of the Love he praises and insisted that it is perilous to stop short at the terrestrial forms which are merely its image. He says:

'As a tigress assuageth her cruel pangs by gazing into a mirror wherein seemingly is the image of the whelps she hath been seeking—thanks to this pleasure the hunter is forgotten, and she

---

[1] XIX, pp. 34–47, in Dent's edition.

[2] Beatrice certainly existed, and Dante certainly loved her. Hence here we have a *sublimation*, the opposite of what happened in the case of the troubadours. Beatrice becomes in turn Philosophy, Wisdom, and the Holy Science that shows the way into Paradise and makes intelligible its mysteries.

tarrieth there, and goeth not in pursuit—so he whom love hath penetrated draws in life from beholding his lady, for 'tis thus he doth assuage his heavy affliction. . . . But the lady hath not a kind heart; the day passeth and his hopes are unfulfilled.'

Here, unmistakably, the Lady with the unkind heart is a woman who turns Love to her own advantage. In a moral bestiary belonging to the same period I find the same fable with this ending:

'I trow this beast is ourselves. Her whelps whereof a hunter hath despoiled her are our virtues; and the hunter is the Devil, who maketh us to see that which is not. 'Tis thus that many have perished because they put off going after the Lord.'

The moment was approaching when poets would yield to the spell of the mirror and of profaned rhetoric. Petrarch allowed himself to be snared by 'that which is not', but the image of his Laura, who, as he later lamented, detained him over long from 'going after the Lord'.

4

Petrarch, the Converted Rhetor

Chè mortal cosa amar con tanta fede,
Quanta a Dio sol per debito conviensi.

'Everybody—even the man on some small rock washed by the sea—is aware that the world has witnessed one superlative lover and that this lover was Petrarch. Best of all, it is true. . . . What do we mean by a man *simply* in love? This is nothing of the kind. Petrarch was in love extraordinarily, blazingly, like a very sun.'[1]

That is the astonishing thing about Petrarch, that in his describing his memorable passion the symbols of the troubadours were quickened for the first time by an entirely pagan breath! Pagan, and not in the least heretical! Petrarch stands at the antipodes not

[1] C. A. Cingria, *Pétrarque* (Lausanne, 1932).

only of Dante, but also of the rhetors whom Dante attacked. The 'secret' I spoke of just now had evaporated. It was no longer effective. The language of Love had at length become the rhetoric of the human heart. For reasons given above (Book III), this 'radical profanation' was bound to produce the kind of poetry most suited to serve orthodox mysticism, and it was indeed from this poetry that the mystics in due course drew their finest metaphors. The temptation was irresistible, and a few examples—chosen almost haphazard—will show why.

Here is Petrarch's sonnet on the first anniversary of his love for Laura:

> And still I bless the day, the hour, the place,[1]
> When first so high mine eyes I dared to rear;
> And say, 'Fond heart, thy gratitude declare,
> That then thou had'st the privilege to gaze.
> 'Twas she inspired the tender thought of love
> Which points to heaven, and teaches to despise
> The earthly vanities that others prize:[2]
> She gave the soul's light grace, which to the skies
> Bids thee straight onward in the right path move;
> Whence bouy'd by hope e'en now I soar to worlds
>   above.'

Where Petrarch excels is in taking Tristan's harp[3] and in plucking from it the wail of the 'exquisite anguish', the cherished ill, the delight that is consuming him.

> O vivid lustre! of power absolute
> O'er all my being—source of that delight
> By which consumed I sink, a willing prey.[4]

> Oh breathing death! yet ill I joy to feel![5]
> Unsanction'd thus to rule, oh! whence thy art?

[1] Sonetto XIII. Translations by Francis Wrangham.

[2] Saint Teresa says: 'These graces are accompanied, so far as the mind is concerned, by a complete detachment from creatures. One then feels far more of a stranger to worldly affairs.'

[3] He was acquainted with the Romance and quotes it a number of times. For example, in the *Trionfo d'amore*, he says:

> Here be the erring knights in ancient scrolls,
> Lancelot, Tristram, and the vulgar souls
> That wait on these.

[4] Canzone LXXII. Translation by Lady Dacre.

[5] Saint Teresa says: 'It is a martyrdom at once exquisite and cruel.'

. . . . . .

> Without a helm, upon a swelling sea,
> I feel my fragile bark the wind's poor sport.[1]

We have already met with this bark—on board which, like Tristan, Petrarch has taken his harp with him—and we have also met the 'sway' which he laments while aware that he has willed it fatalistically.

> And thus my martyrdom no limit knows,
> A thousand deaths and lives each day I feel.[2]

Elsewhere he speaks of Laura as his 'beloved enemy', and his lament recalls that of Tristan when giving up Iseult so that she may return to her husband.

> O cruel absence! why
> Didst thou remove me from the menaced woes?[3]

For when Laura is near her eyes

> inflaming with a light divine
> So burn my heart, I dare no more repine.[4]

But here again woman, whether absent or present, is never but the *occasion* for a torment he cherishes above all else:

> I know to follow while I flee my fire:
> I freeze when present; absent, my desire
> Is hot.[5]

All romantic love is summed up in this last line. And how much better does Petrarch dissect the nature of the melancholy than it ever was to be by its most self-conscious victims when in due course it became the *mal du siècle*!

'Often am I assailed by other passions [he says elsewhere],[6] but their assaults are short and passing. At times, however, this ill

---

[1] Sonetto CXXXII. Translation by Susan Wollaston.

[2] Sonetto CLXIV. Translation by R. G. Macgregor. Saint Teresa says: 'The soul . . . would fain have its anguish never end.' Again: 'Once the soul is put to this torture, it would fain pass thus the whole of the life remaining to it.'

[3] Sonetto CCLIV. Translation by R. G. Macgregor.

[4] *Trionfo d'amore*. Translation by Anna Hume. Saint John of the Cross says: 'O sweet cautery!' And cf. his meditation on this line in *The Living Flame of Love*.   [5] Idem.

[6] *Secretum meum (De Contemptu mundi)*.

invades me with an obstinacy that grips and torments me for days and nights on end. The ordeal affords me no ray of light nor tremor of life; it is an infernal night and a cruel death. And yet—here is what may well be called the height of woe!—I feed on these particular pains and sufferings with a kind of delight so poignant that if I am snatched away from them it is against my will.'[1]

And Saint Augustine, with whom on this occasion Petrarch supposes himself to be having a dialogue, is made to reply:

'Thou knowest full well what ails thee. Presently thou shalt learn its cause. Tell me: Why art thou so sad. Is it really the way of things in the world? A bodily pain? Some unjust stroke of fortune?' Petrarch says: 'Nothing in particular of the kind.'

He was experiencing in advance of the age of romanticism what Chateaubriand, in a memorable phrase, called 'the vagueness of the passions'. And here is the summons to death:

> Loose me from forth my darksome prison here,
> That to so glorious life the passage bars.[2]

The 'infernal night' has been changed into Day; the 'cruel death' into a new Life. And in order that passion shall not lack a touch of the sublime, here also is divinization. Petrarch asks how he can possibly go on living while parted from his lady.

> Love's answer soon the truth forgotten shows—
> 'This high pure privilege true lovers claim,
> Who from mere human feelings franchised are.'[3]

Then there was his famous ascent of Mount Ventoux, which gave him much food for thought. And above all there was the Black Death, which ravaged Europe in 1348, and reminded him that his 'human qualities' bound him to a pitiful state of being. In the *Song of the Great Plague*—a matchless masterpiece of self-examination—he says:

---

[1] Saint Teresa says: 'From this desire which fills the whole soul as in a flash, there arises a pain uplifting the soul above itself and above all created things. The soul but yearns to die in this solitude. If it is then addressed, and although it may strive with all its strength to give answer, its efforts are defeated. Try as it may, it cannot snatch itself out of this solitude.'

[2] Sonetto LXXII. Translation by Lady Dacre.

[3] Sonetto XV. Translation by R. G. Macgregor. Saint Teresa says: 'How great the sway of a soul uplifted by God Himself to this height, from which it surveys all things but is bound by none!'

Ceaseless I think, and in each wasting thought[1]
So strong a pity for myself appears
That often it has brought
My harass'd heart to new yet natural tears;
Seeing each day my end of life draw nigh,
Instant in pray'r, I ask of God the wings
With which the spirit springs,
Freed from its mortal coil, to bliss on high;
But nothing to this hour, pray'r, tear, or sigh,
Whatever man could do, my hopes sustain.

'Take up at length, wisely take up your part:
Tear ev'ry root of pleasure from your heart,
Which ne'er can make it blest.'

Too long has he pinned his hopes to 'the false and fugitive sweetness' of an idealized love.

For o'er my heart from time to time I feel
A subtle scorn, a lively anguish steal,
Whence ev'ry hidden thought,
Where all may see, upon my brow is writ.
For with such faith on mortal things to dote,
As unto God alone is just and fit,
Disgraces worst the prize who covets most.

But how shall he tear out of his heart this blaspheming love, this demented desire?

Passion, whose strength I now from habit feel
So great that it would dare with death itself to deal.

The very self-awareness betrayed in such a cry—a cry giving away the ultimate secret of the courtly myth—is the sign that a man has been touched by grace. What can tear out the vain hope is a single-minded faith in forgiveness. And at last converted expectation discovers that to which it is really looking:

'It lifts you now to hope more blest and sweet,
Uplooking to that heaven around your head,
Immortal, glorious spread.
If but a glance, a brief word, an old song,
Had here such power to charm.
Your eager passion, glad of its own harm,
How far 'twill then exceed if now the joy so strong.'

[1] Canzone CCLXIV. Translation by R. G. Macgregor.

5

The Inverted Ideal of 'Gauloiserie'

To impose a style on the life of the passions—that dream of the whole of the pagan Middle Ages tormented by Christian law—such is the secret wish that was to give rise to the myth. But inevitably the faith 'unto God alone just and fit' was confused with doting on 'mortal things'. And it was this confusion, not orthodox doctrine, which set up the tragic antithesis between body and soul. The poesy of *cortezia* had received its inspiration from the Eastern (monasticism hails from the East) and heretical disposition to asceticism shown by the Perfect. Clearly, then, it is this that little by little, by means of a literature of idealization, infected the ruling class of medieval society. There was bound to be a reaction in the direction of 'realism'; and, as it happens, this reaction was strongest in the middle class. Its beginnings are visible quite early in the twelfth century, in the very hey-day of courtly love. The glorification of wanton indulgence was carried to the same extreme as the glorification of chastity. *Fabliau* contended with poem; shamelessness with idealism. The *Débat de l'âme et du corps*, which belongs to this period, is the first witness to a struggle that the doctrine of Christian marriage was supposed to resolve. A soul just parted from its body assails its erstwhile companion with bitter reproaches, alleging that if it is condemned to damnation the body is to blame. But the body retorts with a *tu quoque* (which has some justification!). So, keeping up their belated recriminations, the two go forward together into everlasting torment.

It was the growing resentment by the body displayed here that inspired the *fabliaux*, and they met with tremendous success—their readers frequently being the same persons who enjoyed reading idealizing romances. The fabliaux were ribald anecdotes hawked about all over medieval Europe and retold with countless variations. They heralded the comic novel, which in turn heralded the novel of manners, which heralded the controversial naturalism of much of the fiction of the nineteenth century. But it does not seem to me that these successive literary styles were engendered in a direct line. More closely than with its predecessors, each step in the movement towards a fiction that should be 'true to life' was connected with a corresponding step in the movement towards a refined artificiality; and hence progression was impelled by a reaction. Charles Sorel was the product of *L'Astrée*,[1] not of the fabliaux; Marivaux's novel *Marianne*[2] was the product of Marivaux's own comedies, not of Sorel; and Zola, the product of the decay of romanticism as much as, if not much more than, of Balzac—who, in Zola's day, passed for a realist.

To return to the thirteenth century, perhaps we have not hitherto sufficiently understood how the sensuous and often pornographic style of the fabliaux betrays an *absence of realism* identical, when all is said and done, with that of the idealizing courtly epics. I believe that *gauloiserie*—I mean, the ribaldry and salaciousness of the fabliaux—expresses an attitude which is simply the inversion of Petrarch's. A passage from Huizinga[3] should make this clear.

'French authors like to oppose "l'esprit gaulois" to the conventions of courtly love, as the natural conception and expression opposed to the artificial. Now the former is no less a fiction than the latter. Erotic thought never acquires literary value save by some process of transfiguration of complex and painful reality into illusionary forms. The whole genre of *Les Cent Nouvelles Nouvelles* and the loose song, with its wilful neglect of all the natural and social complications of love, with its indulgence towards the lies and egotism of sexual life, and its vision of a never-ending lust, implies, no less than the screwed-up system of courtly love, an attempt to substitute for reality the dream of a happier life. It is once more the aspiration towards the life sublime, but

---

[1] *L'Astrée* is a pastoral romance by Honoré d'Urfé, the first parts of which appeared in 1610 and the last part—posthumously—in 1627. M. de Rougemont's point here is shown in the fact that Charles Sorel (1597–1674) wrote a novel of adventure, *Histoire comique de Francion* (1622), with the deliberate object of destroying the vogue of the pastoral romance in France at that time, and that, on finding that *L'Astrée* was still extremely popular, he went on to publish a mock pastoral entitled *Le Berger extravagant* (1627).—Translator.

[2] Published from 1731 to 1741.

[3] *The Waning of the Middle Ages*, op. cit., p. 99.

this time viewed from the animal side. It is an ideal all the same, even though it be that of unchastity.'

This underlying connexion between *gauloiserie* and an over-refined treatment of love is brought to the surface in a thirteenth-century satire called *L'Évangile des femmes*—a sequence of quatrains, the first three lines of each extolling woman in the courtly manner and the last being brutally depreciatory. Another indication of the connexion is the fact that if chivalry made a mock of marriage from above, *gauloiserie* was undermining it from below. The procedure adopted by the latter is well indicated in the *Dit de Chiceface*. Chiceface is a fabulous monster who feeds only on women who keep their marriage vows and he is terribly emaciated. But his comrade Bigorne, whose diet consists exclusively of submissive husbands, is the very barrel of a fellow.

There should also be noted the attitude taken up by the clergy while these two opposite but interrelated tendencies—both begotten by the myth—were making their way in literature. It was Canon Petrarch who gave the example. His later poems are devoted to eulogy of the Virgin—Our Lady in contrast to 'my' Lady—but with no forsaking on that account of the customary vocabulary of courtly poesy.[1] Dante may be said to have avenged the troubadours aforetime by putting the 'Knights of Mary' in hell. These knights were Italian monks who were also known as 'Jolly Knights', because, although they had enlisted under the leadership of a saint, they led dissolute lives.

---

[1] According to A. Jeanroy, op. cit., II, p. 130, no poem devoted solely to the Virgin is known to exist earlier than the second third of the thirteenth century.

6

The Later History of Chivalry down to
Cervantes

The influence exercised by Arthurian romance throughout
the thirteenth, fourteenth, and fifteenth centuries is attested
by hundreds of texts. It was an influence that spread over
the same area as that of the troubadours—that is to say, over the
whole of Europe. The German *Minnesänger* were nurtured on
Catharist legends; and for that matter all they did was to adapt the
tales of Chrestien de Troyes from the French. The Romance of
Tristan was translated into every language of the West. Malory's
prose version in the *Morte Darthur* dates from the end of the
fifteenth century. Dante looked on the epic and romantic cycle
of Northern France as a model for all narrative prose, and Bru-
netto Latini included in his *Rhetoric* a portrait of the ideal woman
which had been extracted from *Tristan*. Countless imitations were
produced as far afield as Norway, Russia, Hungary, and the
Hispanic lands; and the most instructive examples of these in the
fifteenth and sixteenth centuries are the tales of *Amadis* in Portuguese, in Spanish, and finally in French.

It is remarkable, but doubtless not surprising, that the authors
of some of these imitations were brought to rediscover the original meaning of the mystical legends, although, owing either
to caution or to lack of penetration, they only made use of a
thoroughly Catholic mythology—something, as we have seen,
that could hardly be in harmony with the original intention. In
1554 there was published in Spain a book by Hyeronimo de
Sempere entitled flamboyantly *Libro de Cavalleria celestial del pié
de la rosa fragrante*. In this Christ is given the guise of the Lion
Knight; Satan, of the Serpent Knight; John the Baptist, of the
Desert Knight; and the Apostles are turned into the twelve

Knights of the Round Table. Manichaeistic esoterism, ever latent in Arthurian romance, reappears as a filigree within such symbols.

Cervantes does not name the numerous romances of 'heavenly chivalry' which were being found thrilling in his day.[1] In *Don Quixote* he is concerned merely to discredit romances of secular adventure. This neglect on his part remains puzzling. It tells in favour of the theory that he was aware of the true meaning of courtly literature, and mocked his contemporaries with a sense of desperation for clinging to an illusion of which they had lost the key. On this theory, the character Don Quixote was ridiculous only because he wished to undergo an *askesis* for which he had not received initiation and to follow a way of life for which the times were altogether out of joint. The Roman Church had triumphed. The best thing was to be on the winning side, together with the decent and realistic Sancho Panza.

7

'Romeo and Juliet', and then Milton

Yet Rome had not triumphed everywhere. In one island her power was still disputed—the island home of the last of the bards. In Cornwall and in Scotland the traditions of the bards were still alive when James Macpherson published in 1765 his so-called *Works of Ossian*.[2] In Ireland they survive to this day. I must forgo touching upon the problem of the extent to which English literature, both popular and learned, is connected

[1] I have already mentioned the influence of this literature on Saint Teresa and on the Spanish mystics in general.

[2] Although Morven and Selma, it has been established, are names Macpherson himself invented, Ossianic ballads really did exist in Scotland in the eighteenth century.—Translator.

with this background of Celtic legend. But it is significant to find at the end of the seventeenth century a sound scholar such as Robert Kirk, the theologian and humanist, writing a treatise on sprites which bears no trace of either scepticism or irony.

We know almost nothing about Shakespeare—but he has left us *A Midsummer Night's Dream*. It has been alleged that he was a Roman Catholic—but *Romeo and Juliet* is the one courtly tragedy, as well as the most magnificent resuscitation of the myth that the world was to be given till Wagner wrote and composed his *Tristan*. So long as the life and even the identity of Shakespeare remain matters of speculation, it is futile to inquire whether or not he was privy to the secret traditions of the troubadours. But it may be noted that Verona was a main centre of Catharism in Italy. According to the monk, Ranieri Saccone—for seventeen years a heretic—Verona contained nearly five hundred Perfect, not to mention the far more numerous Believers. It is quite likely that the legends of those days preserved some memory of the violent struggles between Patarenes and orthodox that the city had been the scene of.

In the margin of the religious disputes of the sixteenth century, which caused the ancient heresies to be wrapped in an ever greater darkness, the tragedy of the *Veronese Lovers* tears aside the veil for an instant and leaves in our eyes the negative record of a flash, 'the black Sun of Melancholy'. Sprung up out of the depths of a spirit avid of transfiguring torments, out of the abysmal night in which the lightning flash of love plays now and then on features motionless and fascinating—that *our own self* of horror and divinity to which the most splendid poems of Europe are addressed —resurrected all of a sudden in its full stature, as though stunned by its provocative youth and drunk with rhetoric, on the threshold of the Mantuan tomb here once again the myth stands forth in the glow of a torch which is being held aloft by Romeo.

Juliet rests, put to sleep by the potion. The son of Montague enters, and he speaks.

> How oft when men are at the point of death,
> Haue they beene merrie? Which their Keepers call
> A lightning before death. Oh how may I
> Call this a lightning? O my Loue, my Wife,
> Death that hath suckt the honey of thy breath,

Hath had no power yet vpon thy Beautie.
Thou art not conquer'd; Beauties ensigne yet
Is Crymson in thy lips, and in thy cheekes,
And Deaths pale flaggs not aduanced there.

           . . . Ah deare Juliet:
Why art thou yet so faire? I will belieue,
Shall I belieue? that vnsubstantiall death is amorous?
And that the leane abhorred Monster keepes
Thee here in darke to be his Paramour?
For feare of that, I still will stay with thee,
And neuer from this Pallace of dym night
Depart againe: heere, here will I remaine,
With Wormes that are thy Chambermaides: O here
Will I set up my euerlasting rest:
And shake the yoke of inauspicious starres
From this world-wearied flesh: Eyes looke your last,
Armes take your last embrace: And lips, O you
The doores of breath, seale with a righteous kisse
A dateless bargaine to ingrossing death:
Come bitter conduct, come vnsauoury guide,
Thou desperate Pilot, now at once run on
The dashing Rocks, thy Sea-sick wearie Barke:
Here's to my Loue.   *(Drinks.)*
        O true Appothecary:
Thy drugs are quicke. Thus with a kisse I die.

Death's *consolamentum* has sealed the one kind of marriage that
Eros was ever able to wish for. Once more there comes a profane
'dawn', and once more the world goes on again. Restored to his
strict reign, the Prince declares:

A glooming peace this morning with it brings. . . .
Go hence, to haue more talke of these sad things.

There is no doubt that Milton, although a Puritan, underwent
the influence of Cabalistic doctrines, and anything less 'spiritual-
izing' it is impossible to imagine. But does not the revolt of the

Puritans against the monarchy and the bishops who had turned
worldly remind us of the rebellion of the Pure against feudalism
and the clergy?

Two poems that Milton wrote in youth—*L'Allegro* and *Il
Penseroso*—describe the antagonism of Light and Darkness, and
the necessary choice which at that time he had not yet made.
(Indeed, he never did choose, or at least chose with such reservations as to leave it impossible to determine more closely than
he wished in which direction.) Even before embracing the cause
of the Puritans, Milton, searching for an epic theme, had sometimes turned over in his mind the Celtic legend of Arthur and the
Knights of the Round Table. In *Il Peneroso*, after he has hailed
black Melancholy, he turns to the 'sad Virgin' and bids her the
soul of Orpheus to sing, or else to call up him that left half-told
the story of Canace's husband,

> That own'd the vertuous Ring and Glass,

and also 'great bards' who

> In sage and solemn tunes have sung,
> Of Turneys and of Trophies hung;
> Of Forests, and inchantments drear,
> Where more is meant than meets the ear.

Milton, when preparing his *History of Britain*, studied the Arthurian
chronicle and its legends. In *De Doctrina christiana* he attacked—to
quote a recent French commentator[1]—'the creative power of
God, and also the dogmas of the Trinity and the Incarnation; and
he repudiated traditional theological definitions which could not
be supported from the Bible'. Even if we set aside this last feature,
which, after all, links Milton with the Reformation, is this not the
one and same heresy that everywhere and at all times appears as
the mainspring of the grand lyrical poetry of passion?

As for Milton's 'materialism', it does not contradict a 'courtly'
doctrine of love as much as might be supposed. Between a monism
assimilating mind to matter, or vice versa, and a dualism which
condemns matter in the name of mind, there is a gap which the
history of Gnostic and Manichaean sects shows to be not unbridge-
able, especially on the ethical plane. Idealism and materialism have
important presuppositions in common. Extreme licentiousness

[1] Floris Delattre, *Milton* (Introduction to *L'Allegro*, to *Il Penseroso*, and to
Samson Agonistes) (1937).

sometimes goes hand in hand with an extreme and fanatical chastity. And Milton's negation of death leads him into infer- ences similar to those expressed by the Cathars. Like them, Milton thinks that a good will issues from intellectual principles, and that a good will can purge us of evil desires—of sensual leanings, the major sin. And Fludd, his master in occultism, taught that light is the divine substance.

It remains that Milton's theories are more 'rational' and are open to a more practical social application than those of the here- tics of Southern France. (He looks on marriage, for example, as 'a remedy for incontinence'.) Hence these theories did not foster such excessive confusions of the carnal with the spiritual as had previously not failed to occur among Neo-Manichaean sects.

8

'L'Astrée', or from the Mystical to the Psychological

The history of what happened to the myth in the Romance in the seventeenth century can, alas! be summed up in a sentence. Its mystical element was degraded into pure psychology. The Romance was given over to an excessively refined literature. Honoré d'Urfé, La Calprenède, Gomberville, and Georges de Scudéry, together with his sister Madeleine, had none of them the remotest notion of the esoteric meaning of the chivalry of legend. The symbolical nature of the subjects that they dealt with afresh merely induced them to write interminable novels à clef. Polexandre is Louis XIII, Cyrus is the Great Condé, Diane is Maria of Medecis, and so on. The incidents remained the 'annoyances' that love meets with, but the obstacle to the satis- faction of love was no longer the secret and metaphysical wish for death of *Tristan*; it became that fad of the ruling class, a point of honour. It is the heroine who is the more cunning in the invention of excuses for parting. She delights too in terrifying her chivalrous suitor; and in Gomberville's novel Polexandre roams like one possessed over the five continents to make amends for whatever may have been the cause of a single angry glance from his mistress. In the end he is still uncertain whether this 'queen of the unattainable Island' is not going to have him beheaded. But, as a rule, the tales finish up with a wedding. Foreseen on the first page, the wedding is delayed till the ten thousandth when the author is a star performer in his line. The happy ending was first introduced in the allegorical novel of the seventeenth century. The genuine courtly romance culminated in death; it dissolved into an elevation outside the world. Now there was a general desire that everything should be tidied up; society had to be in the right, and hence the endings of novels became a return to something essentially alien to romance—happiness.

In *L'Astrée* the great tragic themes of the myth reappear as no more than melancholy echoes. No doubt there are the twelve laws of Love, ingeniously contrived partings, a eulogy of chastity, and even challenges to a death of release. But the stark and elemental interactions of *Tristan* have dwindled into mere coquetting, and the struggle between Night and Day has become but the play of twilight. No longer does the drawn sword lie between the two lovers; instead Céladon places there a gilt globe tied with his shepherdess's favour. And here is something that sums up all the rest. In the fifth and final volume, the despairing Céladon summons death, and Astrée, on her side, also feels that there is only one way out. Together they go to the Fountain of Truth, which is guarded by lions and unicorns, and ask for an end to be put to their ills. According to the oracle, the spell put upon the fountain will only be broken at the death of the most constant lover and of the most constant mistress. (Incidentally, this recalls the way the lovers in *Tristan* seek forgiveness on the score that the effects of the love-potion have been beyond their control.) Céladon takes his courage in both hands and advances. But thereupon, *mirabile dictu*! the lions and unicorns set to devouring one another, the sky grows dark, thunder roars, and the Genie of Love appears in order to make known that after all the spell is broken. Astrée and Céladon have fainted—a metaphorical death—and are carried to the dwelling of the druid Adamas, where they revive; and presently they get married.

'L'Astrée', or from the Mystical to the Psychological

It is customary to declare the prodigious success of *L'Astrée* unaccountable. And yet its charms are not unequal to those of our recent French novels of fancy and enchantment. And the psychology of French writers has not ceased to delight in allegorical elegance; witness Jean Giraudoux. La Fontaine doted on *L'Astrée*, and declared it 'exquisite'. Its scene is laid on the banks of the little river Lignon, north of Saint Etienne, and Rousseau went there specially from Lyons in order to seek out the shade of Diane and Silvandre. It is true that the two characters were entirely unknown to the landlady at his inn. She told him that the neighbourhood possessed excellent blacksmiths, and that its wrought iron work was deservedly reputed. 'The good woman', he notes with disappointment, 'must have taken me for a locksmith's apprentice.'

Actually, I feel quite capable of undertaking the eulogy of *L'Astrée*. From the standpoint of literary *art*, it is an achievement of capital importance. Never have the resources of a more highly accomplished rhetoric been harmonized to such a degree. One cannot imagine a novel being better written; or more severely regulated in its progress by the laws of an unerring aesthetic. The use of 'constant characters' —shepherd, shepherdess, fickle youth, coquette, bold lover, and so on—guarantees exactitude, and I may even say, veracity, to the interplay of emotion. Here it is art and not 'life' that directs matters. We are in the presence of a creation of the mind, and not of a confusion of cloudy reflections, of more or less damaging admissions, and undeserved bits of luck (as novels are today). In a word *L'Astrée* is a real *œuvre*. It presupposes the mastery of one's craft and twenty-five years of attentive effort. The literary snobbery that made it a success was more enlightened than ours.

But also the fact that the book has such finish allows us to put a plain question: What is the actual success of literary effort worth? If we recall the primitive myth, every theme of which *L'Astrée* takes up afresh, it strikes us that in Urfé's book the tragic is degraded to emotion, and fate into a piece of fictional machinery. All is turned into moralizing and aiming to please. Are we to suppose that the most admirable literature, by reason of its very impeccability, is simply a *by-product* of the mystic systems that bring forms and myths into existence? And that in order to flower and to be fulfilled in a work of art, literature would seem to require the provisional drying up of the deep springs that have

195

watered it? Is it not for that reason that literature, however strongly it may indulge the passions of the heart, offers practically no resistance to attacks from a realistic mind and from what is called civic sense—as appears in our own day? Whereas mystic systems and religions draw an added vigour from the confutations and mockery that may be strewn in their path?

A decree of the semi-official Boileau—his short *Dialogue sur les héros de roman*—was enough to condemn to silence and neglect —even in our text-books today—both the fiction of spells and enchantments engendered by *L'Astrée* and its parasite, the comic novel.[1] Only one more flame, a flame tenuous and pure, was going to be lit—Madame de Lafayette's *La Princesse de Clèves*. In this novel of unhappy love, death is given the mild form of a voluntary parting, and in place of chivalry we have virtue, a virtue which sides in the end with the world.

9

Corneille, or Giving Battle to the Myth

It was in the French classical drama—and therefore at the heart of an intolerant order—that passion most strikingly scored its revenge. Corneille's *La Place royale* is a distinctly unkind play. Alidor, in love with Angélique as she with him, 'is disturbed by a love that attaches him too closely', and so he tries to arrange that his mistress shall fall into the arms of his friend Cléandre. Whence it is commonly imagined that Corneille was the first writer to represent passion being controlled, if not by morality, at least by reason. This would mean that he was the first writer to escape from the domination of the myth, and the matter is accordingly worth examining. Here is how Alidor complains in Act I:

[1] Sorel's *Berger extravagant* [mentioned above, p. 186, note.—Translator] repeats in the key of burlesque, alias 'realism', all the artificial situations of *L'Astrée*. Likewise Scarron's *Roman comique* (1662), etc.

'Tis surfeit of her love oppresses me like doom.
Did she grow cool a moment, I should escape my gloom.
Some touch of jealousy, one look of irritation—
At once I could subdue my mad infatuation.
But she is without fault, and more perfect than she
Is the attachment fond that she displays to me.
By such intentions sweet is all she does impelled
That I'm o'erwhelmed with favours till my peace lies felled.

There is no need to go on. These opening lines are enough to rouse our suspicions. What! Happiness he declares to be fatal to his peace, and were only Angélique unfaithful to him that would cure him of his love! This Alidor must be a queer monster! Let us say rather that what he is trying his best to conceal is all too obvious. He too is a lover who yearns to burn! But his yearning he can only admit by asserting its opposite; for he appears on the stage of history at a period when a yearning for misfortune has become difficult to avow. 'I blush to suffer grievous ills that I lament', he declares presently. Thus shame is what inspires his deceit. Actually, he suffers from the absence of any *obstacle* between the too fond Angélique and himself. The game he wants to play is short of a King Mark. He is in the situation of Tristan and Iseult at the end of their three years in the Forest, when Tristan was able to renew the obstacle by restoring the queen to her husband. Alidor has to invent a rival. Thwarted in the gratification of his yearning by the lack of anything that can part him from Angélique, but ashamed to admit how that lack causes him to suffer, he thinks of deploring that he should be fettered *too closely* by her fidelity, when actually he despairs of being fettered closely enough. In proclaiming a need to be free he expresses a deep-seated wish to be in such a position as no longer to want any freedom whatever. This is the position in which he would be the moment Angélique gave the least sign of escaping from him. But he is artful, as the following passage from the play shows:

CLÉANDRE. Was ever lover glowing with an ardour such
     As to complain that he was being lov'd too much?

ALIDOR.   What! Can you then suppose I am so commonplace
     That vulgar feelings I'd contentedly embrace?

His manner is haughty; let us be on our guard. It is a sign that he is about to indulge in more deceit. He continues:

'Tis mad to be the slave of what has us in thrall,
And mad to feed with love what's not at beck and call.
I hate its forcing me; hence firmly I'm intending
To keep my expectations on my will depending.
Free of ardour's bondage, 'tis my ambition bold
That as I please I'll warm, and as I please grow cold.

The passage may erroneously be regarded as typical of Corneille: will-power triumphs over passion. But even if we were unaware of the existence of the myth, the remainder of the comedy would show us that Alidor's real desire is exactly the opposite of what he thus haughtily contends that it is. ''Tis mad to be the slave of what has us in thrall' really means: 'It is only worth while becoming the slave of what holds us completely in thrall—what, in eluding us, causes our ardour to glow ever more intensely— for that is what would truly *please* us.' The last six words, 'and as I please grow cold', are simply a piece of rhetorical artifice intended to persuade the reader, or Cléandre, or Corneille himself, that freedom is desired, whereas what is wished for is obviously 'ardour'—and no subservient ardour either.

Let me repeat that it is easy to be taken in. Corneille does his best to ensure that we shall be. In the dedication of the play to some unidentified person, he says:

'It is from you I have learned that a decent man's love should always spring up at the bidding of his will; that love should never be where it might also not be; that if nevertheless this happens, it is a tyranny the yoke of which must be thrown off; and, lastly, that a person beloved is under far greater obligation to our love when this results from our choice and her qualities than when it arises from a blind attraction and is compelled by some inherent disposition we are unable to fight against. . . . Nothing is a gift unless it might also be withheld from us.'

This is good, and well put. But do not let us overlook that to refuse obedience to inexorable compulsion and to give only with the freedom that makes a gift worth while were two things inculated by courtly love as fundamental; they were made requisite in one of the *leys d'amor*. Moreover, there was an ulterior motive in requiring them; it was believed that they would tell against marriage. In spite of themselves, Alidor and the Angélique, whose fidelity he deplores, are in a situation equivalent to the married state; and he wants to escape from this situation, not owing to

love of freedom, as he alleges, but owing to love of passion. He
says:

> Whatever be the cost, my chains must be struck off,
> For fear that union could my self-control corrode,
> And turn a love by force into a love I owed.

This is most faithfully the language of courtly love. But we must
note a curious contradiction. To begin with, Alidor declares that
he wants peace; but now he expresses a fear of marriage on the
ground that peace is precisely what it would bring to him.

> Let me give her offence and thus stir up her hate.
> As long as o'er her heart my sway I have retained
> Desir'd recovery can never be attained.

His desire of recovery—let us read: 'desire to be on fire and therefore a fear of recovery—is satisfied in Act V. Later on, in an
Examination of the play, Corneille recognizes this, at the same
time as he necessarily simulates surprise at it.

'This fondness for peace [he writes] does not prevent Alidor
from showing in the fifth act that he is still passionately attached
to this mistress, notwithstanding his having resolved to be rid of
her, and notwithstanding the betrayals he has inflicted upon her,
*so that it seems as if he only begins to love her once he has given her
cause to hate him.*'

Here is a clean breast of the matter. But from the purely psycho-
gical aspect in which Corneille views it, he is bound to overlook
the significance of the *myth* that directs Alidor's behaviour, and
in the end he decides very feebly that Alidor is simply guilty of a
logical fallacy. 'This displays', he says, 'an unevenness of conduct
that is vicious.'

Corneille's blindness regarding his real intention should not
astonish us, even though this intention is so perfectly carried out.
The centre of the myth of unhappy love is, as we have seen, a
passion that cannot be admitted. Corneille's originality lies in
having sought to attack and deny this passion by which he was
sustained, and to attack and deny the myth that he reinvented in
his two most splendid tragedies, *Polyeucte* and *Le Cid*. He wished
to preserve at least the *principle* of freedom—that is, the principle
of the human person—without however sacrificing to it the
delightful and tormenting effects of the irresistible 'love-potion'
—here metaphorical. Better still, he made the wish to be free a

highly effective instrument of the passion which it claimed to cure. Hence the unparalleled tension of these 'dramas of duty', as those incapable of liking them will ever go on calling them.

10

Racine, or the Myth Unloosed

In relation to the myth, the antithesis in which Racine and Corneille are usually placed amounts to this—that Racine sets out from the assumption that the love-potion divests those who have drunk it of every shred of responsibility—'C'est Vénus tout entière à sa proye attachée'[1]—whereas Corneille insists on treating the potion as 'a tyranny the yoke of which must be thrown off'. That is how it happens that there is a voluptuous harmony in the one and a dialectical tension in the other, the former allowing himself to be carried along by the stream, the latter battling against it even as it sweeps him along (or the better to feel himself being swept along).

An *invitus invitam*[2] being the subject of *Bérénice*, this play may be described as a plot from Antiquity being interpreted by a 'modern' who bears in mind the courtly notion of unhappy returned love. The *invitus invitam* thus becomes the very expression of the myth. But Racine, in his early plays, accommodates the scope of the myth to the proportions of an excessively 'allowable' psychology.

[1] *Phèdre*, Act I, iii. The heroine is avowing her passion for her stepson, and describes herself as the personification of Venus intently ravening her prey.

[2] 'Titus, who passionately loved Berenice, and even, so it was supposed, had promised to marry her, sent her away from Rome, *against her will and against his own*, soon after he had succeeded to the purple of the empire.'—Suetonius, as adapted by Racine in the preface to *Bérénice*.

Racine, or the Myth Unloosed

'I have not [he says] gone so far as to make Berenice kill herself, as Dido did, because Berenice and Titus had not given one another the ultimate pledges which Dido exchanged with Aeneas, and hence unlike Dido she was under no obligation to renounce life.'

Obviously the 'plea' being opposed here to the passion of Darkness is artificial and weak.

'A tragedy [Racine continues] need not necessarily include bloodshed and death; it is enough that the action should be lofty, the characters heroic, and *the passions excited in it*, and that pervading the whole there should be that majestic sadness wherein all the enjoyment of tragedy resides.'

But the 'majestic sadness' referred to is only half the myth—its diurnal aspect and its moral reflection in our lives as finite creatures. There is lacking the nocturnal aspect and its mystic flowering in the infinite life of Darkness. There is lacking what might symmetrically be called 'that majestic delight wherein all the pain of Romance resides'. For in order to reach this other aspect, or even to become aware of it, he would have had to go as far as death, the death he deems unnecessary. Contrary to received opinion, the much extolled classical sense of decency involves a metaphysical impoverishment which engenders confusions of incalculable effect. For, after all, let Racine's 'sadness' be as 'majestic' as you please, inasmuch as it is self-confined and implies neither a beyond nor any reversal of plot into joy, and inasmuch, further, as it is accepted for what it is in the world of day and nevertheless is called 'enjoyment', I do not see how it can ever be more than a *morosa delectatio*.

No doubt we are entitled to dispute the ultimate truth of the mystical (Manichaean) belief at the root of the passion myth. None the less, it must be admitted that the belief endows the drama and the ordeals of the lovers with a grandiose justification. If the lovers are infatuated with obstacle and with their consequent anguish, that is because the obstacle is death in disguise and because death is the pledge of their transfiguration, of the moment in which what has hitherto been Darkness will be revealed as absolute Light. But Racine, in failing to go the length of death, constrains both us and himself to savour an essentially dubious sadness. The Eros of *cortezia* claimed to release men from the life of matter by way of death; and Christian Agape aims at sanctifying life itself. But Racine, in being content to represent

201

'passions excited' and to produce the 'sadness' in which he invites us to find an indefinite 'enjoyment', betrays a rather morbid acceptance of the defeat of mind and of the resignation of the senses. At this stage Racine's work is already hinting that his surrender to the *mal du siècle*—that is to say, to the secularization of passion—can only lead him into Jansenism; for Jansenism is the kind of morose mortification—self-punishment, Freud calls it—most appropriate to the romantic temperament. But his conversion could never have occurred had it not been for a crisis in which he himself became aware of the true character of his frenzy. *Phèdre* marks not only a decisive moment in the poet's life, but also one in the transformations which the myth underwent in the course of European history.

I I

'Phèdre', or 'Punishing' the Myth

The death-theme is omitted from *Bérénice* by the operation of a moral 'censorship' of unmistakably Christian origin. At this stage Racine neither can be, nor does he wish to be, entirely clear-sighted. For then he would be compelled to reject that which he dares cherish only in his innermost heart without admitting to himself that he is cherishing it. But the shock of a passion which he conceived for some woman—very likely, the actress Champmeslé—together with the first stirrings of a real faith, drove him—as if in his own despite and more wholeheartedly than he had foreseen—to the limits of avowal.

In *Phèdre* death gets its own back. Yes, Racine was now aware that it is necessary for a tragedy to include bloodshed and death if it is about passionate love. However, he did not want death to be a transfiguration. He was now siding with day, and death could be no more than the penalty for his previous protracted indulgence. Passion, his own passion, is what he punishes when consigning the daughter of Minos to death, and passion is also his victim. Under cover of the ancient story, Racine penalizes himself twice over. First, by making the obstruction incest—that is to say, an impediment there is no admitting any wish to overcome. Public inclination—to which Racine was invariably very attentive—continued to side with Tristan against King Mark, with the seducer against the deceived husband; but it could never have sided with an incestuous couple. Secondly, Racine penalizes himself at second-hand by refusing to allow that Hippolytus shall return Phaedra's passion. *Phèdre* was written for Marie Champmeslé, who played the queen; and Hippolytus is Racine—Racine as he now wished himself to be: insensitive to the fatal spell. Identifying Phaedra with the woman he loved, he scored over the object of his passion, and convinced himself that this passion was to be condemned *beyond appeal*.

But, as I have said, Racine at the time he wrote *Phèdre* was in the thick of a crisis and still undecided regarding its resolution. Hence the profound duplicity of the play. The moral law, the law of day which Racine wished to obey henceforth, compelled him to make the young prince insensitive to Phaedra's love. Her love is therefore termed 'incestuous', although she is only Hippolytus's step-mother. At the same time, the old Adam, the natural Racine, sought to evade this rigorous law, which, in banning incest, makes passion impossible. He did so by causing Hippolytus to be in love with Aricia; for she, as will be seen, is Phaedra in disguise. It is a highly subtle device.

'As regards the character of Hippolytus [Racine writes in the preface to *Phèdre*], I had noticed in the Ancients that Euripides was reproached with having represented him as a philosopher free of all imperfection: so that the death of this young prince aroused far more indignation than pity. I thought I ought to give him some frailty *which should render him a little guilty towards his father*, without however depriving him of any of that magnanimity thanks to which he spares Phaedra's honour, and allows himself to be oppressed without accusing her. *I call "frailty" the passion that he feels against his will for Aricia, who is daughter and sister of his father's mortal enemies.*'

So Aricia in the play is 'the love forbidden by the Father'—a veiled substitute for incestuous love.[1] Pyscho-analysis has recently made us familiar with more cunning subterfuges! But it is not incest, it is passion, that interests and involves Racine. The other means he hit upon of referring to it in voluptuous terms, even while submitting to its being condemned, was that of the unimpeachable argument of the love-potion. Here, as in the myth, 'Destiny' is made to relieve both the author and those who love of all responsibility.

> The gods, dear prince, if once your hour is come,
> Care little for the reasons that should guide us.[2]

These are not gods that Corneille would have worshipped! Nor would he have allowed that gods can be deceived, nor that a fault can be laid at their door.

> The gods will bear me witness,
> Who have within my veins kindled this fire.[3]

And here is the waiting-woman Oenone who speaks to Phaedra in the same strain as the waiting-woman Brengain speaks to Isolde:

> You love. We cannot conquer destiny.
> You were drawn on as by a fatal charm.[4]

I spoke of 'duplicity', but this is so thoroughly essential to the play, producing as it does the very crisis from which the play issues, that to blame the author would be foolish. *Phèdre* had to be. The myth had to be brought up into the light. There had to be this painful upthrust on the part of the yearning for death as it first sought its self-release by means of an impossible avowal, then held back, and finally attained to self-confession in the very moment of renunciation—keeping pace with the motion of the queen on three occasions.[5] All this had to be, in order that passionate love might finally succumb to the Norm of Light. For in

[1] Hippolytus, referring to Aricia in Act I, asks:

> Shall I espouse
> Her rights against my sire, rashly provoke
> His wrath?

The translations are by R. B. Boswell (1890).
[2] *Phèdre*, Act I, i.   [3] Act II, v.   [4] Act IV, vi.
[5] The confession to the Nurse in Act I; that in Act II to Hippolytus: 'Hé bien, connoy donc Phèdre et toute sa fureur!'; and the avowal made to Theseus in Act V.

Phèdre terrestrial day, for the first time since the rise of the myth in the twelfth century, triumphs over the death of the woman lover, thus reversing the whole of the interaction in both *Tristan* and *Romeo and Juliet*.

> Death from mine eyes veiling the light of heav'n,
> Restores its purity that they defiled.
>
> She dies, my Lord!
>
> > Would that the memory
> Of her disgraceful deed could perish with her![1]

In spite of everything, in spite even of this last touch that Racine made into a piece of deceit, I believe he must have been sincere when in the preface to *Phèdre* he wrote:

'This I can vouch for, that I never wrote a tragedy in which virtue was more plainly exhibited than it is here. The least faults are severely *punished*. The mere notion of a crime is regarded with as much horror as crime itself. *The frailties of love are treated as real weaknesses.* Passions are brought before the eye only in order to show how much disorder they cause.'

This is far removed from the intention of 'exciting passions' in order to gratify a desire for 'majestic sadness'. It is within sight of Port Royal.

Racine, like Petrarch, belonged to the race of troubadours who betray Love for love. Nearly all of them ended up in religion. But let us notice: a religion of retreat—perhaps as a final insult to intolerable day.

[1] Act V, vii.

12

Eclipse of the Myth

In spite of Corneille and in spite of Racine up to *Phèdre*, the end of the French seventeenth century suffered from, or rather benefited by—whichever you like—a first eclipse of the myth alike in manners and in philosophy. The ordering—not to say, the drilling—of feudal society by the King-State involved somewhat far-reaching changes in emotional relations and in customs. Marriage became once again the basic institution, and reached a point of stability at which it was with difficulty to be made to remain in subsequent centuries, and which in previous centuries had not been known. An 'alliance' between two families was negotiated with as much formality as one by diplomatists. If the parties happened to have a real or fancied inclination for one another, this merely added an element of exquisite perfection and of agreeable luxury to the arrangement—an ultimate touch of whimsicality amounting almost to insolence. (In the eighteenth century it quickly came to be considered bad taste.) Suitability of rank and a matching of 'qualities' were the perfect standards of a satisfactory marriage, curiously like the custom of China. Indeed, it was in the 'rational' seventeenth century that European manners became severed from religious beliefs, even as Confucius considers they should be, and, although the change apparently attracted no notice, were made to conform to the current laws of reason, and hence to ignore the Christian absolute. No longer the unforeseeable effects of grace, but 'worth', decided that there should be a union, and it was 'worth' alone which rendered 'agreeable' a prospective partner whose pros and cons had been ingeniously weighed. Such was the triumph of Jesuitic morality. Emotion was imprisoned in the showy contrivances of the classical baroque. For that matter, the analytic treatment of passion by such writers as Descartes, its conversion to clearly distinct psychological categories and to rational hierarchies of qualities, worthiness, and faculties, must of necessity have brought about the dissolution of the myth and the arrest of its original impetus. For the sway of the myth is not asserted but there where precisely all moral categories vanish—beyond Good and Evil, in *transports*, and in the transgression of the sphere within which morality is valid.

The case of Spinoza would deserve a chapter to itself, but his influence on manners only made itself felt two centuries after him, when the *Sturm und Drang* philosophers had translated him into German for the benefit of poets, and these had translated him into metaphors for the benefit of an emotional middle class. The ultimate result was to produce chatter about the divinity of countryside impressions on a Sunday. Spinoza defines love as 'joy accompanied by the idea of an external cause'.[1] The definition is accurate in a single instance, the only instance this mystic considers —when the external cause is a God with whom our soul may identify itself.[2] But Spinoza disregards the existence of *obstruction*. Actually, our human passions are always connected with antagonistic passions, our love with hate, and our pleasures with our pains. Between joy and its external cause there is invariably some gap and some obstruction—society, sin, virtue, the body, the separate self. Hence arises the ardour of passion. And hence it is that the wish for complete union is indissolubly linked with a wish for the death that brings release. It is because passion cannot exist without pain that passion makes our ruin seem desirable to us. When the Portuguese nun Mariana Alcaforado wrote to the man who had seduced her, she said: 'I give thanks to you from my innermost heart for the despair into which you have cast me; I despise the peace in which I lived before knowing you. Adieu! Love me, then, for ever, and go on making me suffer the cruellest torments!' Towards the end of the eighteenth century, another woman, Julie de Lespinasse wrote: 'I love you as one ought to love—with despair!'

[1] *Ethics*, Book III, def. 6.
[2] This supports what was said earlier in connexion with Eckhart. Unitive mysticism is unaware of divine *passion*.

But till the advent of Rousseau the eighteenth century in France was indeed a period of total eclipse for the dark Sun of Melancholy. The 'points' and 'worthiness' which the rakes of the Regency and of the reign of Louis the Fifteenth considered 'civil' were no longer in any sense moral, but intellectual and physical. When the distinction between mind and body took the place of the separation of mind from believing soul, the result was to divide a human being into intelligence and sex. Actually, with every obstruction removed, passion was without impetus. And it became the fashion to talk of *passionnettes* or little passions. The god of Love was no longer an adamant destiny but a cheeky child. Hardly anything was forbidden. Of the natural obstruction of modesty enough was retained for the needs of the rhetoric of desire, but no longer even enough for the needs of that of love. 'A fine virtue', Madame d'Epinay said, 'that has to be attached with pins!' (I fancy that those pins were not mentioned by chance: 'Love *points* you', the rhetoric said. A little later blood was going to flow under the Terror; but we are for the moment only at 'war in lace cuffs'.)

Yet this century of sensuality was not that of sensual health, if it was thought to cure it of the myth. 'The women of our time do not love with the heart; they love with the head', said Abbé Galiani. 'An old blind *débauchée* of wit', wrote Horace Walpole in a letter, and thereby gave perhaps the best description of feminine Don-Juanism. For it is woman who dreamed of Don Juan, and although there were Richelieus and Casanovas to incarnate the dream I am less sure of their reality than of that of the desire which created them. That desire was well viewed by the Goncourt Brothers in their classical book on woman in the eighteenth century. 'Instead of giving her the satisfactions of sensual love and settling her down to voluptuousness, love fills her with anxieties, drives her from one trial to another, from one attempt to another, shaking in front of her as she goes step by step into shame the temptation of spiritual corruptions, a *falsehood about ideals*, the elusive caprice of dreams of debauchery.'

'A falsehood about ideals' sums up indeed whatever cynical reaction the myth may have given rise to. I have mentioned more than one example. The eighteenth century was too polished to allow *gauloiserie*: it replaced that by an *affectation* of voluptuous facility. In the sally that all love amounts to no more than the touching of two skins I see less the affirmation of an inhuman materialism than a proof of the secret persistence of the myth in the hearts of the men of the eighteenth century. A modicum of amorous illusion and diffused idealism had to subsist for Chamfort to have considered it *piquant* to note down the maxim and to have published it. It could still astonish. It was no more—and was destined never to become more—than an inverted idealism.

13

Don Juan and the Marquis de Sade

If we shut our eyes after gazing at a white statue we shall have the image of a black. In the same way, the eclipse of the myth conjured up the exact opposite of Tristan. If Don Juan, historically speaking, is no invention of the eighteenth century, the period nevertheless played in relation to this character the very part assigned in Manichaean doctrine to Lucifer as regards Creation. The period gave shape to Tirso de Molina's (Don Juan) *Tenorio*, and endowed the hero of that play with two thoroughly typical features—*noirceur* and *rascality*. Nothing could be more directly the reverse of the twin virtues of chivalrous love—candour and courtesy!

The way in which the mystical character of Don Juan stirs the emotions of woman and fascinates the minds of some men is to be accounted for, I fancy, by his *infinitely contradictory* nature. Don Juan is at one and the same time sheer spontaneity of instinct and sheer mind aflutter over the sea of possibility. He is constant inconstancy, and also the constant quest of the one woman whom desire in its untiring self-deception is never able to find. He is the insolent avidity of a youth renewed at every fresh encounter, and he is also the hidden weakness of an inability to possess, because devoid of enough *being* ever *to have*. Let me be content with taking the dramatic Don Juan as an inverted reflection of Tristan, and in Mozart's *Don Giovanni* rather than in Molière's *Don Juan*; for the latter, in my opinion, is by far the less significant.[1]

The contrast occurs first in the external demeanour and movement of the two characters. Don Giovanni seems always to be riding the high horse, and always to be poised in readiness to leap forward again whenever he chances to have halted in his progress. But Tristan walks on to the stage with the somnambulistic deliberation of one hypnotized by some object of wonderful and inexhaustible value. The former possessed a thousand and three women,[2] the latter only one. But it is the man of many who is poor, whereas in a single being infinitely possessed there is concentrated the wide world. Tristan can forgo the world—because he loves! But Don Giovanni, although incessantly loved, is never able to love in return. Hence his anxiety and his agitated wanderings. Don Giovanni seeks in the act of love a voluptuous profanation. By remaining chaste, Tristan wishes to achieve a divinizing 'prowess'. Don Giovanni's line is rape, and no sooner has he scored than he surrenders the field and flees. But the rule of courtly love made of rape the crime of crimes, a felony for which there is no remission; and of homage a pledge unto death. Don Giovanni, however, likes crime for its own sake, and in that way subjects himself to the morality which he transgresses. In order to enjoy abusing it, he has the greatest need of its existence. Tristan, instead, considers that he is freed from the play of rules, from sins and virtues, having been granted the grace of a virtue which transcends both the world and the Law. In sum, the antithesis is as follows—Don Giovanni is the demon of unalloyed immanence, a prisoner of worldly appearances, and the martyr of a more and more deceptive and despicable sensation, whereas Tristan is the prisoner of a realm lying beyond night and day and the martyr of a *rapture* which is tranformed at death into unalloyed bliss. It may also be noted that if, when the Commander holds out his hand in the last act, Don Giovanni jokes, laughs loudly, and provokes death, he thereby redeems in a supreme act of defiance the base deeds that would have dishonoured a true knight; but Tristan, sad

[1] It may be mentioned incidentally that at its original production in the seventeenth century Molière's play had no success.
[2] In Spain alone, and plus 1,062 in other countries!—Translator.

and brave, never surrenders his pride till luminous death is at hand.

I see the two to have only one feature in common. Both appear sword in hand.

From about the time Louis the Fourteenth died in 1715 till Louis the Sixteenth ascended the throne in 1774, Don Juan reigned over the dreams of a French aristocracy that had gradually fallen from feudal heroism. The Duke of Richelieu and the Duke of Lauzun on the topmost social rungs, Bezenval and Casanova at the level of the rascally adventurer—such were the paragons who took the place of the ideal destroyed in the preceding century. The repression of the myth by an all-embracing irony and the applauded triumph of 'felons' soon excited some curious reactions. Amid so much pliancy, so much intellectual and sensual refinement, so much satiation, one most profound human need was left ungratified—the need of suffering. If the body social encourages this need, it grows enfeebled, as is shown by the waning of the Middle Ages; but if the body social remains unconscious of this need or imagines that the need can be ridiculed, it quickly dries up and grows enervated. Thereupon the mind proceeds to invent in the guise of acts of cruelty the sufferings it has forbidden the heart to undergo. Kindness is a stranger to those who have not suffered: their fancies lose all vital touch and all capacity for being in sympathy. Woman in the eyes of men of the eighteenth century was merely 'an object'. At one extreme there had been the ideal woman, the unalloyed symbol of a Love drawing love away beyond visible forms; at the other there was now woman as a mere means to pleasure, the more or less agreeable instrument of a sensation which kept men self-isolated.

I distinguish in the contradition between Don Juan and Tristan, in the intolerable tension of a mind that experiences this contradiction for itself, because susceptible to sensuality and desirous of the courtly idea, the basis for the writings of the Marquis de Sade and the very motives of his rebellion. Sade admired the poetry of Petrarch, as he remarks in his *Crimes de l'amour*. The admiration had been traditional in his family ever since his direct ancestor, Hugues de Sade, married Petrarch's lady, Laure de

Noves.[1] Petrarch seems to have been simply unaware of the existence of either desire or bodies; unaware of the reality of 'an object'. Sade, a product of the eighteenth century, was only too conscious of its monotonous tyranny. What Petrarch ignored was the physical obstruction upon which a lover has to get his own back. Yet the object is only too unmistakably there: it is the means to pleasure, and pleasure is a doom. How be released from it except by excess, since all excess issues from the mind! Nothing could be more icily rational than the countless 'voluptuous' inventions of the Marquis's rage. Where pleasure is, there must suffering be; and suffering is the sign of a redemption. We are purified by evil; let us sin then to the utmost so as to destroy it by subjecting it to tortures which will nevertheless afford us some pleasure, and this will be part of our *askesis*! A dialectical frenzy seized Sade. Only murder can restore freedom, and it must be the murder of the beloved, inasmuch as loving is what fetters us. Only one's love can be really killed, for one's love alone is *sovereign*. The crime of an impure love will redeem purity.

With this key in hand, let us now consider a passage from *La Philosophie du boudoir*, in which Dolmancé puts forward a moral defence of murder.

'What! [he says] An ambitious *sovereign* shall be able to destroy as he likes and without scruple the foes that hamper the execution of his schemes for achieving greatness! *Cruel, arbitrary and imperious laws* shall likewise murder in every century millions of human beings! And yet weak and unfortunate private persons such as ourselves shall not be allowed to sacrifice a single being to our *revenge* or to our caprice? Could anything be more barbarous or more ridiculously queer? And should we not, *under cover of the most profound mystery, avenge* ourselves *abundantly* for this absurdity?' [Italics mine.]

Had the Marquis de Sade been asked what were the inner motives of his weird moral professions, no doubt he would have taken refuge in a cold-blooded prolixity. But every one of his arguments is transparent. They all mean the exact opposite of what they say literally.[2] His glorification of sex is a continual and deliberate

---

[1] Abbé de Sade, the Marquis's uncle, is the author of *Remarques sur les premiers poètes français et les troubadours*, and of three (anonymous) volumes of Memoirs of Petrarch.

[2] 'Sade wrote *Juliette ou les Malheurs de la vertu* (1791), and then *Justine ou les Prospérités du vice*. It is the exact opposite (and therefore, according to

profanation of the profaned eighteenth-century morality. It is the act of an atheist taking 'the negative way' (because he despairs of unloosing his bonds), and therefore challenging love to manifest itself by killing the criminal.[1] For only thus could release be obtained—according to the faith of the troubadours.

14

La Nouvelle Héloïse

B rought up in the Genevan countryside, Rousseau escaped the influence of urban Don Juanism; but he was unable to steer clear of a literature to which his temperament responded very deeply. This literature may be called Petrarchism. Strictly speaking, Rousseau's novel is not a resuscitation of the

---

psycho-analysis, the exact opposite of this opposite, and so on) of *Remedies for One and the Other Fortune* by Petrarch,' C. A. Cingria remarks in his *Pétrarque*.

[1] The above analysis of the sadistic crime has been strikingly supported in two remarkable studies by Pierre Klossowski: 'Le Mal et la Négation d'autrui dans la philosophie de D. A. F. de Sade' (*Recherches philosophiques* (Paris), IV, 1934–5) and 'Temps et agressivité' (ibid., V, 1935–36). The author considers that Sade looked upon evil as the only element in nature. In *La Nouvelle Justine* there occurs this passage: 'Yes, I hold nature in abhorrence; and this is because I am only too well aware that I detest it. Apprised of its horrible secrets, I have taken a kind of pleasure in copying its dark wickedness.' Hence the sadistic desire to obtain release from the tyranny of sex through excesses of debauchery.

Another truly Manichaean attack on Creation is as follows: 'The life principle in every being is no other than the death principle. We take in both at one and the same time and nourish them within us.' But if life and created nature are but dark wickedness and cruelty, it becomes necessary to obtain release from them by exceeding this cruelty and wickedness. And there is but the alternative to be cruel either to ourselves or to others. Sade chose others. He preferred to be a criminal rather than a victim. Hence the Sadistic conscience is the antithesis of the romantic conscience. The romantic—Petrarch—punishes himself in order to preserve the beloved, whereas Sade sought to kill the beloved.

primitive Tristan myth. It lacks the savage violence of the legend, and, still more markedly, the esoteric background. What Rousseau resuscitated was the spiritual state originally brought into existence by imitators of the troubadours through their 'secularization' of a doctrine that they were aware of only as a profane rhetoric. This spiritual state is *acedia*—the happy melancholy cultivated by Petrarch, the Vaucluse hermit. The analytic summaries added by a zealous editor to the third edition of the novel contain situations such as the *leys de cortezia* allowed for. Rousseau puts the *Canzoniere* into prose, and makes them rather middle-class in the process.[1] Honoré d'Urfé had turned courtesy into a profane casuistry. Rousseau made of it a kind of refined pietism. Here again the deterioration is obvious.

The Héloïse who lived in the twelfth century[2] and whose letters to Abélard have been preserved, is far closer to Iseult, Juliet, and Mlle de Lespinasse than to Julie d'Étanges, the heroine of Rousseau's novel. And, in spite of his magnificent name, there is nothing either mystical or chivalrous about Saint-Preux, the hero. Moreover, although the novel ends with death, it is only after passion has been renounced; and the death of Julie is Christian—as far as Rousseau is able to make it so. In a letter to his publisher, by the way, he insists at length on his own Protestantism and that of his characters; but without impugning his sincerity, it may be suspected that his 'Calvinism' concentrated on the Supreme

---

[1] A quotation here, an allusion there, show that Rousseau was well acquainted with Petrarch, the real inventor of a feeling for nature and of the poetry of solitude.

[2] Let me repeat that the famous love of Abélard and Héloïse is the *first historical example* of the kind of passion dealt with in these pages. In the Latin *Funerary Hymn* for Héloïse—composed perhaps by herself—the woman lover beseeches as follows:

> Relieve me of my cross,
> Lead me to the light,
> And give my soul release!

Whereupon the chorus of nuns sings:

> Let them have respite from their labour,
> And from their painful love!
> Union for those who dwell in heaven they besought,
> Even now are they in sanctuary with the Saviour.

Abélard returned this passion rather poorly. But his extremely heretical theology is akin on essential matters to the spiritual doctrine of the Cathars. And in his *Lamentations* he gives voice to the same loud cry as romanticism and Tristan: *Amoris impulsio, culpae iustificatio.*

Being as easily as it seemed to overlook Christ. All this does not prevent me from confessing a very lively liking for the style of the novel. In this respect, indeed, *La Nouvelle Héloïse* is the only novel comparable to *L'Astrée*. Its clear-sighted psychology, too, there are serious grounds for admiring. Moral 'Rousseauism' is being hastily judged when we attribute to the author the beliefs of his characters. If Rousseau was the first to describe such errors, it was because he had suffered from them more than most people and was the more strongly resolved to get away from them. But the moral of the story is commonly overlooked, and the tone, the emotional content, and a certain complaisance such as the romantic style fosters, are all that we notice. Evidently Rousseau was no more taken in by the 'religion' of love than Petrarch had been at the end of his life. Once Julie is married and she analyses the past common to her lover and herself,[1] there could not be a piece of closer reasoning, albeit feminine, than she employs in tracking down the deliberate confusion of Eros with Agape.

'Virtue is so essential to our hearts that when once true virtue has been forsaken we fashion another to our own liking, and hold to it perhaps the more strongly for having chosen it ourselves.'

Yet there is good reason for believing that the atmosphere of *La Nouvelle Héloïse*, so fresh to the eighteenth century, had a power of contagion which the moral of the story was quite unable to weaken. And it is in this contagious power that the myth unquestionably reappears—enfeebled, ashamed, and embarrassed, but, thanks to an indefinable funereal shudder, recognizable enough through the veil of virtuous tears. Hardly has Saint-Preux had his 'expectations' fulfilled than[2] he begins gloomily to doubt.

'No [he says], it is not those transports that I most regret. Ah, no! Take away if you must those intoxicating favours for which I would lay down my life a thousand times, but *give me back everything else, all that has a thousand times obliterated them*. Give me back that close union of soul. . . . Julie, please tell me: can it be that previously I did not love you, or is it that I now love you no longer? What a doubt!'

The ambiguity of his sigh frightens him, and yet he goes on to admit with a kind of vexation which he barely conceals, 'My feelings for you have become more calm, it is true, but also more affectionate, and, moreover, of a different kind. . . . The sweetness

[1] Part III, Letter XVIII.   [2] Part I, Letter LV·

of friendship moderates the frenzy of love.' The Tristan part of him comes to life once he has been guilty of the 'fault' of possessing the beloved, and it would readily forgo the 'calm sweetness' he speaks of. He too has wanted to burn, and to keep his desire unsatisfied. He too is going to invent fresh and altogether gratuitious *obstructions*—excuses for parting and situations voluptuously hopeless. That is why there is the insistence—painful and, coming at this moment, somewhat overdone, I feel—on the plebeian origins of Saint-Preux, which are held to exclude all possibility of a legal union. That is why, too, social prejudice is assimilated to the exigencies of a virtue declared to be religious *ad hoc*. But the unavowable motives of the confusion are readily discernible. In the twelfth century chastity was ordained by courtly love; now chastity has become a middle-class custom. But, whether one or the other is being deferred to, what is really at work is the myth. In the letter already quoted, where Julie recalls the trials they have had together, she also describes as a 'holy ardour' the chaste love that ravished them—notwithstanding that as such it was already open to being condemned—but 'a crime', 'horrors', 'corruption', are the names she gives to this same love when she considers that stage of it which began with the gift of her physical self. Clearly, the fault they care about is the infringement of *cortezia*, not the infringement of the middle-class virtue which they all too often invoke. I might go on: the exegesis of *Tristan* could easily be repeated for *La Nouvelle Héloïse*. In both, obstruction produces the same interaction. There is, however, this decisive difference: Rousseau ends with marriage—that is to say, with the triumph of the world as sanctified by Christianity—whereas the legend glorified in death the complete dissolution of terrestrial ties.

15

German Romanticism

The state of mind of the lovers in *La Nouvelle Héloïse* is sentimental, not mystical.[1] Yet it was by taking this state of mind as a starting-point that romanticism set out to recover a primitive mysticism with which it was unacquainted, but the sacred and fatal power of which it grew aware of in flashes.

I have traced the gradual degradation of the myth as it passed from Thomas's *Tristan* via Petrarch and *L'Astrée* down to French classical tragedy. Little by little it was made humane and broken up into components less and less mysterious. Finally Racine felled it, thought not before he had suffered a most grievous wound in the course of his struggles with the dark angel. Then Don Juan sprang on the stage, and from Molière to Mozart the myth underwent a major eclipse. But with the appearance of Rousseau's novel, which was produced on the margin, so to speak, of the eighteenth century, we are launched upon a new journey, a journey over the same road, but in the opposite direction. Via *Werther*—a retort to the *Héloïse*, which, in ending far more badly, is closer to the original model—we come to Jean Paul, Hölderlin, and Novalis. Amid the commotion of the French Revolution, the Terror, and the ensuing European wars, it became possible to make certain admissions and a certain kind of suffering was enabled to proclaim its true nature. For the first time, the worship of Darkness and of Death rose up into the field of lyric *awareness* . Hardly had Napoleon been overcome than Europe was invaded by a more insidious tyranny, which lasted till the day Wagner caused the

[1] It may be Rousseau's fault, or more likely that of the poetical movement known as Symbolism, but nowadays many ladies imagine that 'mystical' means 'sentimental'—stained glass, blue shadows, arpeggios, mental somnolence, sensual reverie!

myth all at once to stand forth to its full height and charged with its full virulence. Music alone could utter the unutterable, and music forced the final secret of *Tristan*.

It is not my intention to enumerate the countless manifestations of the myth in European literature, chiefly in recent times. I wish only to mark the stages of its alterations, and to resolve some merely apparent contradictions. There is no need to bring forward every piece of evidence for the statement that without exception all the German romantics revived the courtly theme, the theme of unhappy mutual love.[1] Even if the quotation of a few selected passages, which I shall leave to speak for themselves, looks like special pleading—because agreeing so perfectly with my account of the myth—these passages will prove more eloquent than any commentary.

Here is a letter to Hölderlin from his Diotima:

'Last evening I reflected for a long time about passion. No doubt *the passion of supreme love is never fulfilled here below*! Be sure to understand my feeling: to seek *this* satisfaction would be madness. *To die together*! (But silence! That seems like over-excitement, and yet it is so true!) Such is the only fulfilment. But we have sacred duties in this lower world. We are left with nothing but the most perfect confidence in one another and faith in that all-powerful divinity of Love which, though invisible, will go on guiding us for ever and will for ever strengthen our union.'[2]

I quote from the private diary of Novalis:

'It occurred to me while seated on the tomb [of his betrothed] that my death could provide mankind with an ensample of everlasting fidelity, and in a way establish that it is possible to love as I have loved. . . .

'When pain is being shunned, that is a sign that one no longer wants to love. Whoever loves must everlastingly remain aware of the surrounding void, and keep the wound open. May God grant that I shall preserve this pain which is exquisitely dear to me. . . .

'Our vows were not exchanged for this world.'

---

[1] In 1808 A. W. von Schlegel began a modernized version of *Tristan*. Many others—among them Rückert (1788–1866), Immermann (1796–1840), Platen (1796–1835)—followed suit with poems or poetic dramas. Platen's poem begins: 'He whose eyes have once beheld beauty is already marked out for death.'

[2] Italics in the original.

And here are some of the maxims of Novalis:

'All passions end like a tragedy. Whatever is finite ends in death. All poetry has a tragic element.

'A union formed even unto death is a marriage bestowing on each a companion for Night. It is in death that love is sweetest. Death appears to one still alive as a nuptial night, the heart of sweet mysteries.

'The intoxication of the senses may be related to love as sleep is to life. It is not the better part, and a man of strength must always prefer waking to sleeping.'

The following two passages strike a truly Manichaean note:

'We must keep God and Nature apart. God has nothing to do with Nature: He is its goal, the substance in which it must eventually be harmonized.

'We are spirits that have come out of God; we are divine seed. One day we shall become even as our Father Himself.'[1]

Hymnen an die Nacht renew the theme of the 'Dawn' poems of the troubadours. Dark Eros beseeches that morning shall not be born again:

'May thy spiritual fire devour my body; may I be closely united with thee in an ethereal embrace, and then may our nuptial night endure for ever and ever.'

And there might be quoted all those works of Tieck's in which love is termed 'a sickness of desire, a divine apathy.'[2] To extol a death undergone deliberately for the sake of love and in order to be absorbed into the divine—such was the deep religious purpose of the new Albigensian heresy called German romanticism. Death is the ideal goal of 'lofty men' in Jean Paul's *Die unsichtbare Loge*. In Novalis death blends with love. Kleist made of it 'the one fulfilment' possible for 'a supreme passionate love' to which the body would not lend itself. But poets were not alone in succumbing to the appeal of a nocturnal other world; a philosopher such as Schubert speculated on the *Nachteseite* of existence. Fichte himself defines a love in-essence-impossible—the true love that

[1] The painter Otto Runge had a Manichaean view of the world also. In a vast undertaking which he projected, 'The Four Seasons', he intended to depict the four seasons of the spirit—Morning, infinite illumination of the universe; Day, infinite form of the created; Evening, infinite negation of existence at the beginning of the universe; Night, infinite depths of the knowledge of God, the Absolute Existence.

[2] Tieck in *Sternbald* tells the story of the troubadour Geoffrey Rudel, and in *Phantasus* and elsewhere dwells at length on the characteristics of courtly love.

rejects any object whatever in order that it may launch into the infinite. He says it is 'a desire for something altogether *unknown*, the existence of which is disclosed solely by the need of it, by a discomfort, and by a void that is in search of whatever will fill it, but that remains unaware of whence fulfilment may come'. Hoffman voices an identical view when he names this *unknown* something 'poetry'.

'And now [he says] there shoots up, like a pure celestial flame giving out warmth and light but not burning, all the ineffable felicity of the higher life, born in the innermost recesses of the soul. The spirit puts out a thousand feelers, every one vibrating with desire. It weaves its net around *her* who has appeared, and she is his . . . *and she is never his*, for the thirst of his aspiration is ever slakeless.'

In German romanticism the Western mind set out again on the venture previously undertaken by the unitive mystics; it adopted the old heresy of passion and sought to achieve the ideal transgression of all limitations and the negation of the world through extreme desire. On every side the scattered components of the myth reappeared and came together ready for Wagner, who, in fashioning them into a final synthesis, was the one and only poet who dared exhibit the myth for what it is. We should not be surprised to find that the first poem inspired by recollection of the Cathars and Catharist mysticism is the work of a most thoroughgoing romantic—Lenau's epic *Die Albigenser*. The following lines from this poem form a kind of profession of faith of that 'new religion' dreamed of by Novalis and his friends:

> The age of Christ, now screened from us by God,
> This age also will pass.
> The New Alliance will be broken;
> And then our God we shall behold as Spirit:
> There shall be celebrated the Alliance Everlasting.
> *Spirit is God!* That almighty cry will go resounding
> Like joyful thunder through the springtime night!

16

The Myth Withdraws into the Human Breast

The intimate rhythm of German romanticism, the diastole and systole of its heart, are enthusiasm and metaphysical melancholy. It is the abysmal dialectic of the Manichaean heresy and the perpetual reversal of day into Darkness and of night into Light. The same impulse which bears a soul towards the light and divine unity, is, when considered from the standpoint of this world, no more than an impulse towards death and essential separation. Such is the tragical character of transcendental Irony, the perpetual motion of romanticism, the passion that ruins without respite all the objects which it is able to conceive and which it desires—nature, the beloved, the self—all that is not uncreated Unity and dissolution beyond return. But the enthusiasm is real; it is the *endieusement* of the troubadours, the *endiosada* of the Spanish mystics, *joy d'amor* in the dionysiac delirium. Out of it spurt perpetually, at the supreme point of elevation, extravagant fantasies. There is romantic gaiety as there is being moved and melted: moments of relaxation between two contradictory transports, returns to the world.

It is such a moment of queer joy, born of metaphysical irony, that French romanticism lacks. In this romanticism the data are the same, but the rhythm is less ample and the mind goes too swiftly to the point. France, during the Revolution and Empire, had no energy to spare for speculation in the realms of the spirit: it had no 'new religion', no romantic philosophers,[1] little or no metaphysics and little or no fancy—that superabundance of a mind uplifted by its own drama. French romanticism failed to get beyond the sphere of individual psychology. It thus gained in lucidity, and hence, within its narrower purview, was brought more swiftly than the Germans to mournful conclusions.

[1] Not till a century later did one appear—Bergson, the disciple of Schelling.

The Myth in Literature

Certainly André Chénier is being a true romantic as he describes

L'enthousiasme errant, fils de la pâle Nuit.

And Chateaubriand's famous invocation, 'Arise swiftly, longed-for tempests, that are to bear René away into the expanses of another life!' is an unalloyed chant of the passion of Darkness. But there was no mystic dawn on the spiritual horizon, nor true joy of love at the summit of those transports. The self was never transcended. It recoiled from the final illusion of a cosmic release. It fell back, disenchanted, upon the analysis of its own sadness and clear-sighted ineffectuality. French romanticism was over-ripened; it was disillusioned, and—I am tempted to say—too exact. By the side of it, Jean Paul and Novalis cut callow figures. The attraction of death among the Germans stimulates the sweetness of being alive; perhaps this is because a German is more simple and more strongly assured of the reality of another world. A French romantic has been the poorer for remaining an eloquent sceptic, and on account of his fear of seeming ingenuous and of the prolific vulgarity in which the most truly German poets deliberately revel notwithstanding their nostalgia![1] Chateaubriand's René amuses himself one day by dropping willow leaves one by one into a stream and endowing with an idea each leaf that the stream carries away. He watches intently for the accidents of which his leaves are in danger. The reader feels he is reading some German poet, and expects that the world's treasure will presently be exhibited. But swiftly the eighteenth-century Frenchman grows aware of how he is behaving and thinks its ridiculous. 'So this is the depth of puerility to which man's magnificent mind can sink!' The 'magnificent mind' therefore ends up with an epigram: 'And yet is it true that many a man will bind his fate to things of such small worth as my willow leaves.' (The remainder of the admirable paragraph will repay reading down to the famous invocation, 'Arise, longed-for tempests! Come, Auster!'[2])

---

[1] Cf. the portrait in Novalis's diary of Sophie von Kühn, his former betrothed, who died at sixteen. He recalls her favourite dishes and notes that she liked wine. A Frenchman shrugs his shoulders at such childishness.

[2] In connexion with Chateaubriand's invocation, the Song of Songs says: 'Awake, O north wind; and come, thou south; blow upon my garden, that spices thereof may flow out'; and Cantico XXVI by Saint John of the Cross runs:

Come, South Wind, that awakenest love,
Blow through my garden,
And let its odours flow.

To the unintentional rationalists that the French romantics
to the atheists who did not manage to believe in their most
soling fancies, love could not long be 'the ineffable felicity o
superior life' that E. T. A. Hoffmann called it; but rather
'taciturn and ever threatened' love that is the subject of Alfre
Vigny's most splendid verse. The absence of a naïve interes
the quotidian forms of life facilitated detachment of mind and
abstract purification of sentiment. Beings and things—their p
texts—once pierced by a disillusioned gaze, were quickly
longer genuine obstacles. And the myth, deprived of its extern
shapes, became what it is in essence—a voluptuous destruction
the self by the self. 'We have learned better without having ex
perienced enjoyment', René says; 'there are still desires an
men have no more illusions. . . . Men live with a full heart in a
empty world.' Thereupon woman herself ceased to be the indispensable symbol of the nostalgia of passion. In Sénancour's *Obermann* the 'obstacle' is entirely within; it consists of the duality
of a self unable to achieve either vindication or dissolution, unable
to attain either self-possession or possession by another.

We knew that Tristan did not love Iseult for herself, but only
on account of the love of Love of which her beauty gave him the
image. He, however, did not know this, and his passion was naïve
and strong. René, and Obermann still more, are unable even to
believe in the image; they have grasped that the drama takes
place inside them, between the intolerable laws of finite terrestrial
existence and the desire after a transgression of our limits, fatal
but divinizing.

Few, however, were the French romantics who attained to
this bold, arid, and exact self-knowledge, which is closer to negative mysticism than might be supposed. Most of them reverted in
time to the illusions of human love, without being able to recapture the vigourous simplicity of the myth. They refined amazingly
on the traditional 'pretexts' for the parting of lovers: from *Le Lys
dans la vallée*—the most ingenuous—to *Adolphe*—the most fully
conscious—the 'pretext' is sometimes marriage and honour, or
soical duty, or virtue, or the lover's melancholic secret or some
religious scruple, or, lastly, avowed narcissism. The myth became
progressively more thoroughly internal, while the obstacle invoked crumbled and dissolved in sceptical criticism, and while
moral rules degenerated and all vestiges of a 'sacred' element
vanished from social life.

17

Stendhal, or the Fiasco of the Sublime

A man of the eighteenth century who had received the mark of romanticism, and moving, moreover, in a highly sceptical world, Stendhal provides the perfect example for an analysis of the profanation of the myth.

Here was a man whom the need of passion tormented; he had discovered in his 'soul'—that is to say, in a yearning after the sublime—the void spoken of by Fichte, the insatiable call of the unknown, of the Unknown Woman that alone will fill this void. To love passionately would be indeed to live! He imagined quite sincerely that his longing was physical (and trotted out his own little materialistic explanation of it). Had he been told that what he felt was but the impress of the myth upon his mind, a habit inherited from European culture, and in particular from literature, he would have roared with laughter; for he was convinced that mysticism and religion were dead. But he had to admit that his desire for passion, that even passion itself in the world he lived in, were frowned upon alike by reason and by the prevailing scepticism. Hence the need he experienced of justifying that need. Hence his famous treatise, *De l'Amour* (1822). The opening words of the preface betray that it is a controversial work.

'Although dealing with love, this little book is not a novel, and above all contains none of the distractions of a novel. It is simply an accurate and scientific treatise on a type of madness which is very rare in France.'[1]

And to this madness Stendhal gives the name of 'passion-love'.

He declares that there are four kinds of love—passion-love, sympathy-love, sensual love, and vanity-love. It is only the first which finds grace in his eyes. He accounts for it by means of the crystallization theory. 'I call "crystallization" that process of the

---

[1] Translation by Vyvyan Holland (London, 1928).

mind which discovers fresh perfections in its beloved object at every turn of events.' Thus in the salt mines of Hallein, near Salzburg, if a bough stripped of its leaves is dropped into the depths of a disused working, it is picked out two or three months later 'with a vast number of spangled shifting, glittering diamonds'. On this theory, falling in love is to endow a woman with perfections she does not in the least possess. And why do we do this? Because we need to love, and because the only thing that can be loved is beauty. In more simple language, crystallization is the process by which a man idealizes the woman he loves.

I believe it was Ortega y Gasset[1] who first pointed out that this famous theory makes passionate love a mere *error*. 'Not that passion is held to err often,' Ortega adds, 'but that it is deemed to be in itself an error. . . . Stendhal's case is pretty obvious: he did not truly love, and, above all, he never was truly loved.' Tristan loved, Don Juan was loved; but a man who had nothing in common with the former except nostalgia and nothing in common with the latter except inconstancy was led to describe love as 'a soul-sickness'—in the pure tradition of Antiquity, except for his saying that in being afflicted with this sickness he felt happy. Thus, in *De l'Amour*, Stendhal is a doctor studying in his own person the symptoms and progress of a malady he does not consider likely to be fatal. The whole difference between his 'crystallization' and the idealization of *cortezia* lies in this—that Stendhal is aware that there must be a de-crystallization, the return to a state in which the beloved will be viewed as she actually is. In his conviction, the antidote to the love-potion is inconstancy. Tragedy is being turned into farce.

One feature of his book strikes me: the description is admirably vivacious, accurate, and at times profound, but it is completely pessimistic, inasmuch as he is dealing with an error and is disconsolate when freed from it. Whence comes a pessimism incompatible with the view of life which he has elaborated for himself? That is the question he never asks himself. He notes, it is true:

'Pleasure does not leave half the impression that pain does, and in the second place, apart from this drawback in the amount of emotion produced, *sympathy* is only excited about half as much by a picture of happiness as it is by one of misfortune.'
And again:
'A soul made for passion feels in the first place that this happy

[1] *Uber die Liebe*, op. cit.

life [marriage] *irks him*, and perhaps, also, that it only gives him commonplace ideas.'

A little further on he says:

'There are very few moral afflictions in life that are not rendered precious by the *emotion* which they excite.'

That is something true. We like pain, and happiness does rather bore us. You find it quite natural? And yet a Hindu or a Chinese is astonished. A resurrected citizen of classical Greece would be none the less so. How have we acquired this odd like and dislike? Are they not contrary to nature? Once again Stendhal does not ask, not being in a position to answer. As a crude materialist—the crude are the best: they are the most straightforward—he boldly suppresses the whole problem, thanks to his theory of crystallization, his theory of an error. In his opinion, passion is to be accounted for by an error propitious to desire. 'This phenomenon', he says, 'arises from the promptings of Nature which urge us to enjoy ourselves and which drive the blood to the head.' There you are! A man's faculties become clouded, and they set to 'crystallizing'. But it is not explained how instinct decides to commit the error requisite for this crafty process—I mean, instinct alone, left to itself.

Like Ortega y Gasset, I think that Stendhal's explanation is inaccurate in the first place as regards the facts. There is one love which, far from going astray, is alone able to recognize in the beloved his or her real though hidden virtues. Secondly, his solution seems of the verbal type. For to say that passion is an error— as it may be sometimes—does not explain how the error arises. Neither instinct nor nature is in the habit of going wrong in that way. If an error occurs, it must be due to the mind. The truth is that Stendhal fell victim to a spiritual experience that went beyond what his materialistic beliefs could cope with. Yet he was a contented victim; and that is why he did not push his inquiry further. His book *De l'Amour* really bears witness to the dread which invaded his self-analytic mind in the presence of the myth —not that he actually wished for release from this myth, but that he had lost the clue to understanding it.

However, it must not be supposed that Stendhal in the course of his inquiry did not more than once 'get hot'. He devotes two long

chapters to love in Provence in the twelfth century, and he repro-
duces in an appendix the rules of courtly love.[1] 'A singular civilization', he says. And then he ponders for a bit. It looks as if he must
suspect something. But no. 'I could quote', he goes on, 'twenty
anecdotes to show the prevalence in the Provence of that time
of *an amiable and witty gallantry between the two sexes conducted on
strict principles of justice. . . .*' And in the next chapter he of course
does not fail to quote all twenty anecdotes.

18

Wagner, or Completion

Now fades the world with all its glamours
Life in holiest loving, ne'er more to awaken,
Truest, deepest soul's desire.

The man who put that into *Tristan und Isolde* knew that passion
is something more than an error. He understood that it is one of
the fundamental decisions open to a human being, a choice exercised in favour of Death if Death is release from a world under the
sway of evil. But the boldness shown in *Tristan und Isolde* is of a
kind that is only put up with owing to a complete misunderstanding, a misunderstanding which, in being built up and maintained by a sort of social consensus, is tantamount to a blindness
at once obstinate and unconscious. The assertion has so often been
made by qualified persons that in the end the world has come to
believe that Wagner is dealing with sensual desire. In the face of
all the flagrant evidence to the contrary which the opera affords,
the belief is significant. It indicates the *social necessity* of myths, of
deceits which society puts forth in self-defence out of a wish to
preserve the established forms of its organization, even while the

[1] François Raynouard (1761–1836) and Claude Fauriel (1772–1844) had
recently brought about a revival of medieval studies in France.

The Myth in Literature

individuals of whom it consists surrender semi-consciously (and under cover of withstanding them) to the passions that threaten its ruin.

In writing *Tristan*, Wagner transgressed the taboo. He *said* everything—admitted everything, not only in the words of his poem, but still more in the notes of his score. He sang of the Darkness of the dissolution of forms and beings, of the release of desire, of desire become anathema, and of the tremendously plaintive and blessed twilit glory of the spirit after it has been rescued at the price of a fatal wound inflicted on the body. But the malevolent content of the message had to be denied in order to be admitted. At all costs the content had to be travestied, and given some tolerable interpretation according to common sense. The overwhelming mystery of Darkness and of the destruction of our bodies was declared to be the 'sublimation' of a poor secret of broad day—the attraction of the sexes, the purely animal law which the body obeys; what society needs in order to procreate and to consolidate itself, what the middle class needs in order to feel life. That this was done so quickly does not testify to any exceptional social vitality; rather the operation was facilitated by the frivolousness of the ordinary theatre-going public, by its clumsy sentimentality, and—frankly—its wonderful ability not to hear what is being sung. Hence Wagner's *Tristan* can be revived with impunity before audiences who feel stirred in complete security, so strong is the widespread certainty that *nobody will credit its message.*

The drama opens with a monumental evocation of the powers that rule the world of day—the hate and pride, and the barbarous and sometimes even criminal violence, of feudal honour. Isolde wishes to avenge the affront she has suffered. The potion she gives to Tristan is intended to bring about his death, but a death disallowed by Love, a death in accordance with the laws of day and of revenge—brutal, accidental, and devoid of mystical significance. The highest Minne, however, causes Brengain to make a mistake that can preserve Love. For the death-potion she substitutes the drink of initiation. Hence the one embrace which conjoins Tristan and Isolde as soon as they have drunk is the solitary kiss of the Catharist sacrament, the *consolamentum* of the Pure! From that moment the laws of day, hate, honour, and revenge, lose all power over their hearts. The initiated pair enter the nocturnal world of ecstatic release. And day, coming back with the

228

royal procession and its discordant flourish of trumpets, is unable to recapture them. At the end of the ordeal which it compels them to undergo—this is their passion—they have already foreseen the *other* death, the death that will alone fulfil their love.

The second act is the passion song of souls imprisoned in material forms. When every obstacle has been overcome, and the lovers are alone together in the dark, carnal desire still stands between them. They are together, and yet they are two. The 'und' of *Tristan und Isolde* is there to indicate their duality as creatures. Here music alone can convey the certitude and substance of their twin nostalgia for one-ness; music alone can harmonize the plaint of the two voices, and make of it a single plaint in which there is already being sounded the reality of an ineffable other world of expectation. That is why the leitmotiv of the love duet is already that of death.

Once again day returns. The treacherous Melot[1] wounds Tristan. But by now passion has triumphed. It wrests away the apparent victory of day. The wound through which life flows out is passion's pledge of a supreme recovery—that recovery of which the dying Isolde sings once she has cast herself upon Tristan's corpse in an ecstasy of the 'highest bliss of being'.

Initiation, passion, fatal fulfilment—the three mystic moments to which Wagner, with a genius for simplification, saw that he could reduce the three acts of the drama, express the profound significance of the myth, a significance kept out of sight even in the medieval legends by a host of epic and picturesque detail. Nevertheless, the art form adopted by Wagner renews the possibility of 'misunderstanding'. The story of Tristan *had* now to be in the form of an opera for two reasons connected with the very essence of the myth. Even as the sin of the first man, and of each man, brings time into the world; and even as the transgression of the rules of chaste love by the legendary lovers turned the poetic lay of the troubadours into a novel[2]—so the powers of day, when brought forward in the first act, introduce struggle and duration, the elements of drama. But a play does not allow everything to be stated, for the religion of passion is 'in essence lyrical'. Hence *music* alone is equal to conveying the transcendental interaction,

---

[1] Melot is the informer, a character constantly figuring in courtly poems. The troubadours called him the *losengier*.

[2] Cf. Book II, Chapter 11, p. 123. A novel is a poem which no longer expresses a moment, but duration.

the wildly contradictory and contrapuntal character of the passion of Darkness, which is the summons to uncreated Light. European music has been defined as the emotional harmony of opposites—in musical terminology, counterpoint. It is the expression of a painful duality, which, although permanent at the level of life, vanishes in the luminous grace beyond physical death. Now, a play completed by music is an opera. Hence it is not by chance that both the Tristan myth and the Don Juan myth have received full expression only in operatic form. If Mozart and Wagner have produced the masterpieces of musical drama, it is thanks to a previous affinity that links this form of artistic expression with the subject each of them took. Music alone speaks worthily of tragedy, of whom she is mother and daughter.

However, in the case of *Tristan* the plastic share in a stage production comes to raise a new obstruction to the direct apprehending of the myth. Actors, the costumes they wear, and the scenery,[1] all keep attention focused on reality, demand the presence of 'day', and fatally contradict the profound significance of the action. So long as our eyes are fixed on the stage, we are at the mercy of terrestrial shapes—and ridiculous at that. There, all too visibly before us, are a fat woman and a mighty warrior who are both being a prey to the anguish of desire. But let us shut our eyes, and at once the play is illuminated. The orchestra describes broadly the extent of an entirely internal tragedy. The melodies in their distressing morbidity disclose a world in which carnal desire has become no more than an ultimate and impure apathy of souls in process of curing themselves of life. Only the sorrowful lighting of the third act—the yellowish obsession of the fevered—is able to give to my *eyes* the profound sense that the lovers are being exiled into ecstasy. Because artificial and over-crude, this lighting successfully heralds the extinction of day and shows that dawn has already become no more than a dusk vainly intensified.

Another critical commonplace—incidentally quite at variance with the one according to which *Tristan* is a glorification of

[1] Especially the realistic scenery which producers insist on using—the decoration of the tent aboard ship in Act I, the painted ivy on the walls of the castle in Act II. This is precisely where extremely simple, abstract, metapyhsical, dreamlike, scenery is called for, and not Tristan's interminable gesticulations while breathless on his couch and Isolde hampered by her veils. [Note of 1954: The new scenic production of *Tristan* at Bayreuth, which is the work of Wieland Wagner, fulfils the hope which I expressed in the first version of this book. It is now possible to sit through the second act with one's eyes open.]

sensual desire—is about Schopenhauer's alleged influence over Wagner. Whatever Nietzsche and even Wagner himself may have thought, it seems to me that this influence is greatly exaggerated. A composer of Wagner's calibre does not put 'ideas' to music. No doubt he obtained out of Schopenhauer some phrases which he used in his poem, and an intellectual coherence that justified his giving the action certain internal movements—that is all, and it is not of great interest. About the *askesis*, the negation of the created world, the identification of sexual attraction with a will-to-live that clouds the understanding—all the mystical element that has rashly been called Buddhist, Wagner did not need to be taught. It is because he carried it pulsating within his own breast that he was the first to discover the evidence of it in the symbols of the Minnesänger, in the Manichaean legend of Parzival, and underlying the Christian imagery of the Holy Grail—that sacred stone of Persians and Cathars, that cup used by Gwyon,[1] the Celtic divinity.

That Wagner restored the mislaid significance of the legend in all its virulence is no contention I am trying to get accepted; it is what the words and music of the opera amply make evident. It is through this opera that the myth was completed. But such an 'end' bears two contradictory meanings—like most terms in the vocabulary of existence, since they are used of beings in a position to act, not of inanimate things. 'Completion' means that a being, a myth, or a work has been fully expressed; it also means death. Hence, once 'completed' by Wagner, the myth had lived. *Vixit* Tristan!

And there began the era of its phantoms.

[1] Gwyon (whence 'guyon' meaning 'guide' in Old French) means the Führer who has in his custody the secrets of initiation with a divinizing voice.

19

The Myth is Popularized

The myth took *the way of poetry*.
Edgar Allan Poe begot Baudelaire, who begot *Symbolisme*, which begot mandragora, disembodied women, *jeunes Parques*, hardly feminized appearances of 'leakages'—as one speaks of leakages of water—fissures in reality, flights into dreams. The tradition became enfeebled, intellectualized, sophisticated. The way was decidedly too narrow for a man to enter upon it whole-heartedly, and in fact taking this way was delegated to some detached human *faculties*.

The myth also took *the way of the novel*.
But this way soon opened on to a crowded main road, such as people stroll along on Sundays to watch the fine big cars go by and to complain of the speeding. Balzac's *Le Lys dans la vallée*, Constant's *Adolphe*, Fromentin's *Dominique*, Flaubert's *Madame Bovary*, Zola's *Thérèse Raquin*, André Gide's *La Porte étroite*, Proust's *Un Amour de Swann*, are successive French steps in psychological dissociation, in the degradation of the external 'obstacle', and in the conscious admission (which, because conscious, is alien to romance) that this is in its nature exclusively intimate and subjective—a nature religious in the case of Gide, quasi-physiological in that of Proust. Parallel to these steps are D'Annunzio's *Trionfo della Morte*—admirable as a commentary on Wagner —Tolstoy's *Anna Karenina*, and most of the great Victorian novels, especially *Tess of the D'Urbervilles* and *Jude the Obscure*; and in our own time the Platonistic novels of Charles Morgan.

But, following Wagner, masterpieces became less significant of the descent of the myth into manners than have been mass-produced novels, popular stage successes, and, above all, films. The real tragic element in our period has been diffused in mediocrity. Thereupon to be truly serious implies an understanding, and the rejection or acceptance, of what moves or stirs the masses— an understanding of the broad anonymous rivers that sweep detached individuals along with a force the mind still finds it repugnant to gauge. The process whereby our literature, whether middle-class or 'proletarian', has come to consist mainly of novels, and of love stories at that, corresponds precisely to an invasion of the contemporary mind by the now completely profaned content of the myth. The myth, indeed, must cease to be the real thing once its sacred framework is removed and the mystic secret which it both divulged and veiled is vulgarized and popularized. The *claim to passion* put forward by the romantics thereupon becomes a vague yearning after affluent surroundings and exotic adventures, such as a low grade of melodramatic novel can satisfy symbolically. That this no longer has any kind of valid meaning is evident as soon as we realize how impossible it is for the readers of these novels to imagine a mystic reality, an *askesis*, or any effort on the part of the mind to throw off its sensual fetters; and yet courtly passion had no other purpose, its language no other key. Purpose and key have been lost and forgotten; and passion, although the need of it still disturbs us, is now a mere sickness of instinct, seldom fatal, usually poisonous and depressing, and quite as degraded and degrading in comparison with the Tristan myth as the consequences of dipsomania, for example, must be in comparison with the divine intoxication described in the poetry of the Arab mystics.

The drama has been more instructive. During the Second Empire the French middle class made a last attempt to accommodate within its social framework the lawless workings of the passion. For the passion survived any form of mysticism, thanks ambiguously to romanticism. Heredity—or whatever went by the name—transmitted the attenuated virus of the love-potion; literary culture kept alive, at least in a portion of youth, the want of a nostalgic cautery; and all this made up a complex which was taken to be 'nature' itself, although it represented only a psychological, and perhaps only a physiological, remainder. The attempt to normalize passion for the middle class, by recreating a form of conventional expression which would be acceptable to the social order, was shown in the French drama from Alexandre Dumas to Henry Bataille. The 'eternal triangle', which served as a model for most French playwrights down to 1914, simple reduces the

The Myth in Literature

Tristan myth to proportions suitable for modern society. King Mark is become the Cuckold; Tristan, the junior lead or gigolo; and Iseult, the idle, dissatisfied wife who reads novels. Here again two moralities confront one another. The felon barons of the legend are now the supporters of the established order. They defend middle-class marriage, the laws of inheritance, convention, and a settled state of affairs. They side with the husband, and are therefore slightly ridiculous. But it is the other morality which invariably triumphs—even though at the price of a pistol shot. This is romantic morality, holding the claims of love to be indefeasible and implying the superiority from a 'spiritual' standpoint of mistress over wife. As for the love-potion, an alibi for responsibility, it is now romantically called 'irresistible passion', and the supporters of the established order wisely lump belief in it with whatever they contemptuously refer to as a 'literary' attitude. Eventually even, it was no longer attempted to dispute that the distillation of the old love-potion obtains encouragement from its victims. Proust, for example, devotes hundreds of pages to a minute analysis of the way this encouragement operates and of the unconscious stratagems to which it resorts.[1]

I have called all this recent literature middle class. Indeed, because its trend is invariably against the middle class, it has had the effect of contributing to the stability of the established order. Literature is thus employed—unconsciously, of course—to ensure that the subversive desires of the individual mind shall be volatilized in sensual reverie. It is true that the morality of marriage comes off rather badly, but that does not matter, since the middle class is well aware that the institution is no longer grounded in morality or religion, but rests upon financial foundations—prospects of inheritance, dowries, the social position of each party, business connexions, and so on.

There is thus a wish *to enjoy* the myth as *cheaply* as possible; and this wish is expressed with complete artlessness in sentimental films.

Art has seldom worked in a more artificial and rhetorical convention than it did in American film studios during the early nineteen-twenties. It was then that the happy ending had its heyday. Every plot had to lead up to a final lingering kiss against a background of roses or rich hangings. The convention was faithful to the myth in the last stage of the latter's downfall. It allowed

[1] See in particular *Un Amour de Swann*.

234

the complete fusion of two contradictory wishes—the wish that nothing shall be settled and the wish that everything shall be settled, the one romantic, the other middle-class. The profound satisfaction which spectators unfailingly find in a happy ending must be due precisely to its resolving the contradiction of their double wishfulness. For there can be no love story unless love meets with opposition. There is accordingly an abundance of obstructions to the fulfilment of love, and it does not matter how far-fetched they are, because the wish for romanticism renders the spectator impervious to the straining of his credibility. For an hour or two, accordingly, the story can rebound, and we be full of heartfelt suspense, which is what we want. But the obstruction of love must ultimately mean death and a renunciation of terrestrial goods. This we no longer want once we have grown aware of what it is. A plot-maker has therefore to devise the suppression of any obstacle at some point earlier than death, and the result is the ending which novels and films commonly have. Yet the ending must also possess a 'poetical' atmosphere that will conceal the bump back into everyday life, and that will also, as compensation for the way romanticism has been disappointed, fill the middle-class citizen and his wife with a sense of relief. Hence in the modern drama, in the popular novel, and in the films which incessantly resort to the triangular plot, the tragic idealism of the primitive myth has turned into a rather vulgar nostalgia, the idealization of tame desires; and, moreover, these desires are being redirected towards worldly enjoyments, which means that in relation to courtly love they are being completely inverted.

The *religion* of the troubadours lent itself to a very cunning indulgence of *instinct*, instinct being excited by the very insistence on denying it. The equivocal character of the mystical phraseology of heresy thereupon brought into being as early as the thirteenth century a profane rhetoric of passion. And it is the spread of this phraseology in the novel (and in the drama) that in the course of the last hundred years has caused instinct to become the real basis of a rhetoric, the tropes of which now give it a semblance of ideality.

20

The Glorification of Instinct

As the Rose of Guillaume de Lorris was countered by Jean de Meung's, and as Petrarch's crystalline rhetoric was countered by Boccaccio's sensual phantasmagoria, so romanticism has brought about in our day a revolt that its leaders would like to think 'primitive'. The object of idealization is no longer feeling, but instinct. I have in mind a school of Anglo-American novelists in revolt against middle-class Puritanism—a school including D. H. Lawrence, Erskine Caldwell, and their disciples or imitators. These writers seem to be saying in effect:

'We have had enough of being made to suffer for ideas, for ideals, for idealized and perverted little hypocrisies which no longer take anybody in. You made woman into a kind of divinity —coquettish, cruel, and vampiric. Your fatal women, your adulterous women, and your women made arid by virtue, have emptied life of all delight for us. We shall get our own back on them. Woman is first and foremost a female. We are going to make her drag herself to the domineering male on her belly.[1] Instead of singing of courtesy, we shall praise the cunning of animal desire, the complete obsession of the mind by sex. And our vast bestial innocence will rid us of your liking for sin, which is but a disease of the procreative instinct. What you call morality is what makes us nasty, gloomy, and shameful. What you call dirt can purify us. Your taboos are sacrileges on the real divinity, which is Life. And life is instinct released from mind, a great solar power that crushes and magnifies the prolific man, the magnificent unleashed bully.'

One of these prophets has even gone the length of saying: 'I want to be as vital as a cow.'

[1] There is an incident of this kind in Caldwell's *Tobacco Road*.

Possibly this new mystic doctrine of 'Life' has inspired some fine literary work, but it also has a political aspect. In curiously identical guise, it is met with at the origin of a movement no longer needing to be either examined or convicted. This movement has called itself National Socialism, Fascism, or Communism, according to the doctrinal and economic excuses it has employed in order to seize power. It denies the next world, not so as to suppress the gods, but so as to use their thunder by deifying the here-below. To be divested of moral personality and merged again in the cosmic flux of instinct remains a *theoretical* aspiration for the bards of solar primitiveness; but the *practice* cannot mislead us for a moment. There are no magnificent bullies, only bullies. The idea of beauty, which Lawrence supposed was still firmly operative, is the legacy of a bankrupt period: it is a debt nobody *there* is prepared to honour. The totalitarian ruling caste is not going to consider itself accountable to a Platonic 'spirit' that it looks upon as being to blame for all the trouble and as having already paid for this with its life. So much is quite obvious.

It is no less obvious that when under pretence of destroying whatever is artificial—idealizing rhetoric, the mystical ethics of 'perfection'—people seek to swamp themselves in the primitive flood of instinct, in whatever is primeval, formless, and foul, they may imagine they are recapturing real life, but actually they are letting themselves be swept away by a torrent of *waste-matter* pouring from the distintegration of the ancient culture and its myths. Moreover, there is nothing truly primitive about men today. The existence of what the current jargon calls heredity, and the Church original sin, means that we have irrevocably lost all direct touch with our origins. To plunge down below our moral rules is, therefore, not to abolish their restraints; it is to yield to an insanity from which wild animals would recoil. The mistake lies in supposing that 'the real thing', the longing for which has now become an obsession, is there to be found. It is not lying in wait for us on the far side of a surrender to enervated instinct and resentful flesh. It is not hidden, but lost. The only way to recover it is by building it up afresh, thanks to an effort that shall go against passion—that is to say, by some action, a putting in order, a purification, that will bring us back to the sober mean. Truly to act in this respect is not to escape out of a world deemed diabolical; it is not to kill this hampering body. But neither is it to fire a revolver at spirit on the ground that spirit has deceived us.[1] To act is indeed to accept the conditions we have been given in the conflict between the spirit and the flesh; it is to strive to surmount the two antagonistic powers, not through their destruction, but by uniting them. Let the spirit come to the aid of the flesh and so recover the support of the flesh, and let the flesh submit to the spirit and thus recover peace. There lies the way.

The Eros of death and the Eros of life—each conjures up the other, and each has no true end or ending but the other, which it has been striving to destroy! And so everlastingly till all life and all spirit shall have been consumed. Such is the pursuit undertaken by the man who mistakes himself for a god. It is the last of the motions of passion, and the exasperation of this motion we call war.

21

The Spread of Passion into Every Sphere

The *social function* of the sacred myth of courtly love in the twelfth century was to order and purify the lawless forces of passion. Its transcendental mysticism secretly directed the yearnings of distressed mankind to the next world, and concentrated them there. No doubt it was a heresy, but a peaceful one, and in some respects productive of a civilizing stability. But its being opposed to the propagation of the species and to war was enough to cause society to persecute it. It was the Roman Church that carried fire and the sword to the provinces which had been won for the Heresy. In destroying the material shape of this religion, the Church doomed it to spread in a form more dubious

[1] A Nazi officer is reported to have said: 'Every time I hear the word "Geist" [spirit] I slip the safety-catch of my revolver.'

and perhaps more dangerous. Tracked down, repressed, and disorganized, heresy soon underwent a thousand distortions. The disorders which it had encouraged in spite of itself, the glorification of human love that was the inversion of its doctrine, its language both essentially and opportunely equivocal, and also open to every kind of abuse—all this was bound to defy the judges of the Inquisition, and then to invade the European mind even where still orthodox, and finally, by a kind of irony, to bestow its passionate rhetoric upon the mysticism of the highest saints.

When myths lose their esoteric character and their sacred purpose they take literary form. The courtly myth was peculiarly fitted to do this, since the only way of stating it had been in terms of human love, which were given a mystical sense. Once this mystical sense had vanished, there remained a rhetoric which could express our natural instincts, but not without distorting them imperceptibly in the direction of another world; and this other world, in growing more and more mysterious, answered the need of idealization which the human mind had acquired from a mystical understanding first condemned, then lost. This was the opportunity of European literature, and this alone will account for the sway which literature has exercised from that moment all the way down to our own time, first over the upper classes alone, later over the masses as well—a sway unique in the history of civilizations.

Nevertheless, when the dark forces had been deprived of their sacred element, the classical style sought to impose *an art form* upon these obscure powers deprived of their sacred form. Romanticism supervened to attack these ritualistic vestiges. Hence, at the end of the eighteenth century, there occurred the magnification of all that the Tristan myth, and later its literary substitutes, had been intended *to contain*. The middle-class nineteenth century witnessed the spread into the profane mind of a 'death instinct' which had long been repressed in the unconscious, or else directed at its source into the channels of an aristocratic art. And when the framework of society burst—under a pressure exerted from quite another quarter—the content of the myth poured out over everyday life. We were unable to understand this diluted elevation of love. We supposed it to be a new springtime of instinct, a revival of the dionysiac forces which a so-called Christianity had persecuted. The whole of modern literature took up the hymn of 'liberation'. Why, then, did literature strike such a melancholy note? How is it that the novel—which for the first thirty years of this century outdistanced all other literary forms—has resulted in no more than a shifting and slippery analysis of human doubts and human emptiness? There can be no doubt that by 1930 the novel had run dry of all its sap, and could only recover an ephemeral virulence by putting itself at the service of partisan mystic systems. Does this mean the end of romanticism?

The spectacle afforded by contemporary manners does not allow that to be inferred. The present breakdown of middle-class marriage is a delayed triumph—perverted, if you like, but nevertheless a triumph—for a profaned passion. But far outside marriage and the realm of sex properly so called, the content of the myth together with its phantoms have now invaded other spheres. Politics, the class war, national feeling—everything nowadays is an excuse for 'passion' and is already being magnified into this or that 'mystic doctrine'. The reason for this is that we have grown incapable of giving up anything for the sake of something better, incapable of regulating our desires, of understanding their character and object, and of keeping their vagaries within bounds. We can no longer express ourselves figuratively.

The last surviving formalities of love were swept away by the war of 1914, and I would emphasize the symbolical fact that we have stopped making formal declarations of love at the very time we have allowed wars to begin without any declaration either. We are returning to the age of abduction and rape, though minus the ritual that has surrounded such violence in Polynesia. The gradual profanation of the myth, its conversion into rhetoric, and in turn the dissolving of the rhetoric together with the thorough popularization of its content, can be traced step by step in a sphere at first sight entirely alien to what we have been examining—in the gradual transformation of European warfare and its methods.

Book V

LOVE AND WAR

I

How They Are Similar

From desire to death via *passion*—such has been the road taken by European romanticism; and we are all taking this road to the extent that we accept—unconsciously, of course —a whole set of manners and customs for which the symbols were devised in courtly mysticism. And, as I have said, passion means suffering. Therefore, inasmuch as our notion of love enfolds our notion of woman, it is linked with a theory of the *fruitfulness of suffering* which encourages or obscurely justifies in the recesses of the Western mind a liking for war.

This peculiar connexion between a certain view of woman and the European conception of war has had profound consequences for morality, education, and politics. In order to deal with the subject in a manner commensurate to its importance, it would be necessary, not only to have a thorough grasp of the matters so far touched upon in these pages, but also to have thoroughly mastered military theory, and to be acquainted with what psychological research has collected in the course of the last half-century or so regarding 'the fighting instinct' and its relation to the sexual instinct. But in this field an examination of *formal modes* is no less instructive than an inquiry into *causes*, and it is certainly less deceptive. There is no need, for example, to invoke Freudian theories in order to see that the war instinct and eroticism are fundamentally allied: it is so perfectly *obvious* from the common figurative use of language. Let me then consider some similarities in the practice of the *arts* of love and war from the twelfth century down to the present day. I must not be taken, however, to be presupposing that the transformation of the myth has necessarily been prior to the transformation of warfare, or vice versa.

2

The Warlike Language of Love

Already in Antiquity poets used warlike metaphors in order to describe the effects of natural love. The god of love is an archer who shoots *fatal arrows*. Women *surrenders* to man, and he *conquers* her because he is the better warrior. The Trojan War was fought for the possession of a woman. And one of the oldest novels we possess—Heliodorus's *Theagenes and Chariclea*, written in the third century—already refers to the '*battles* of love' and to the 'delightful *defeat*' suffered by the man who '*falls under the unerring shafts*' of Eros. Plutarch makes it clear that the sexual morals of the Lacedaemonians were determined by their military requirements. The eugenics of Lycurgus, and his detailed laws concerning the relations of husband and wife, had no other aim than to ensure the aggressive vigour of the soldiery.

All this confirms the natural—that is to say, the physiological—connexion between the sexual and fighting instincts. But it would be idle to seek any kinship between the *tactics* of the Ancients and their notion of love. The two fields remained under quite distinct rules, and offered no ground for comparison. But this has not been true in Western Europe since the twelfth and thirteenth centuries. The language of love was then enriched with phrases and expressions which had unmistakably been borrowed from the art of giving battle and from contemporary military tactics. It is no longer a question of the more or less dim awareness of a common origin, but truly of a close similarity of detail. A lover *besieged* his lady. He delivered *amorous assaults* on her virtue. He *pressed her closely*. He *pursued* her. He sought to *overcome* the final *defences* of her modesty, and *to take them by surprise*. In the end the lady *surrendered to his mercy*. And thereupon, by a curious inversion typical enough of courtesy, he became the lady's *prisoner* as well as her *conqueror*. He became a *vassal* of this *suzerain*, in accordance with the laws of feudal warfare, as if it had been he

244

who suffered defeat.[1] It only remained for him to give proofs of his *valour*. So much for polite language. But slang, both military and civil, was rich in words and phrases which were rendered even more significant by their coarseness. And when firearms came into use, they gave rise to countless jokes of *double entendre*. Writers, indeed, delighted to take advantage of the resemblance, for it provided them with an inexhaustible rhetorical topic.

'O, all too fortunate captain [Brantôme writes],[2] who at the front and in the towns hath fought and killed so many men who were the foes of God! And O, more and more fortunate still, you who hath fought and overcome in many other assaults and bouts such a lovely Lady under the banners of your bed!'

It is not surprising that, once such metaphors had become *commonplace*, mystical writers should have employed them and transposed them—in the way I have described earlier[3]—to the key of divine love. Francisco de Ossuna—who was steeped in courtly rhetoric and was one of Saint Teresa's favourite authors—writes in his *Ley de Amor*:

'Do not believe that the battle of love is like other fights in which the clamour and fury of an appalling war prevail on either side; for love fights only by means of caresses and threatens only with tender words. Its arrows and blows are gifts and blessings. Its encounter is a most effective promise. Sighs make up its artillery. Its taking possession is an embrace. Its slaughter consists of giving one's life for the beloved.'

It was shown earlier that courtly rhetoric began by expressing the *struggle* between Day and Night. The part played by *Death* is of capital importance: it marked the defeat of the world and the victory of the life of light. Love and death were connected by *askesis*, as instinct connects desire and war. But neither the religious origin nor the physiological kinship of the fighting and procreative instincts was enough to determine the *exact* use of warlike phrases in European erotic literature. What does account for everything is that there existed in the Middle Ages a rule actually applicable to the arts of both love and war—the rule called chivalry.

[1] The German for 'defeat' is *Niederlage*, which literally means 'in the position of being on the ground, of lying under'. The French, in saying 'avoir le dessous' for 'having the worst of it', also invoke the sense of 'under'. The *Roman de la Rose*, it may be noted at the same time, uses the symbol of a besieged tower and speaks of 'securing allies in the stronghold'.

[1] *Rodomontades espagnoles.*   [1] Book III, above.

3

Chivalry: a Rule of Love and War

'To formalize love', according to J. Huizinga,[1] 'is the supreme realization of the aspiration to the life beautiful.' He is describing the ideals of medieval society.

'To formalize love [he says again] is a social necessity, a need that is the more imperious as life is more ferocious. Love has to be elevated to the level of a rite. The overflowing violence of passion demands it. Only by constructing a system of forms and rules for the vehement emotions can barbarity be escaped. The brutality and the licence of the lower classes were always fervently, but never very efficiently, repressed by the Church. The aristocracy would feel less dependent on religious admonition, because they had a piece of culture of their own from which to draw their standards of conduct, namely, courtesy.'

I need not recall that courtesy not only owed nothing to the Church, but went against ecclesiastical morality. This in itself should be enough to bring about the revision of many opinions about the spiritual unity of the Middle Ages! But if courtly morality did not succeed in transforming the private behaviour of the upper classes, who continued 'astonishingly rough', at least it played the part of an ideal that made externals very handsome. It triumphed in literature, and succeeded, moreover, in impressing itself upon the most violent reality of the period—I mean, war. At no other time has an *ars amandi* given birth to an *ars bellandi*.

It is not only in the detailed rules of personal combat that the effect of the ideal of chivalry was evident, but also in the fighting of battles, and even in politics. Military formality came to be treated as if it had a kind of religious validity. Men often allowed

[1] *The Waning of the Middle Ages*, op. cit., p. 96. I cannot speak too highly of this admirable work.

Chivalry: A Rule of Love and War

themselves to be killed in order not to infringe absurd rules. Froissart asserts that the 'Knights of the Star had to swear never to fly more than four acres from the battlefield, through which rule soon afterwards more than ninety of them lost their lives'.[1] Likewise, the requirements of strategy might be sacrificed to aesthetics or courtly honour.

'Some days before the battle of Agincourt [Huizinga says][2] the king of England, on his way to meet the French army, one evening passed by mistake by the village which the foragers of his army had fixed upon as night quarters. . . . The king, "as the chief guardian of the very laudable ceremonies of honour", had just published an order, according to which knights, while reconnoitring, had to take off their coat-armour, because their honour would not suffer knights to retreat, when accoutred for battle. Now, the king himself had put on his coat-armour, and so, having passed it by, he could not return to the village mentioned. He therefore passed the night in the place he had reached, and also made the vanguard advance accordingly.'

There are countless instances where a futile carnage resulted from the attempt to fulfil at great peril vows of an overweening arrogance. Indeed, danger was what knights courted for its own sake, even as on other occasions they showed themselves prompt with excuses for not keeping their word. Courtly casuistry furnished excellent excuses of this kind. It not only ruled morality and law, but also regulated ceremonial, tournaments, hunting, and especially love. Honoré Bonet's *L'Arbre des batailles* is a treatise on the laws of war, which discusses with the help of biblical texts and articles of canon law such questions as: 'If in the course of the fighting a knight loses a piece of armour he has borrowed, does he have to make it good?' 'Is it allowable to fight a battle on a holy day?' 'Is it better to fight after a meal or fasting?' 'In what circumstances is it legitimate for a prisoner of war to escape?'

As for the political aims inspired by the notion of chivalry, they were chiefly—again according to Huizinga—to fight for a universal peace which a union of kings was expected to preserve once it has been won, and to conquer Jerusalem and expel the Turks. Both these aims were chimerical, and nothing shows better how the courtly ideal was in flat contradiction with the 'stern reality' of the age. It represented a pole of attraction for thwarted spiritual aspirations. It was a form of romantic escape

[1] *Ibid.*, p. 86. [2] Ibid., pp. 86–87.

at the same time as a brake applied to instinct. The detailed formality of war was devised to check the violent impulses of feudal blood, even as the cult of chastity among the troubadours was intended to check the erotic excitement of the twelfth century. 'Two attitudes to life were formed, so to speak, side by side in the medieval mind—one, pious and ascetic, attracted all moral sentiment; the other, spurred on by a sensuality given over to the devil, went to the opposite extreme. According as one or the other was in the ascendant, there arose a saint or a sinner; but on the whole they balanced one another, though not without now and then a wide swing of the scales.'

4

Tournaments, or the Myth in Action

There was, however, one place where the erotic and fighting instincts were in almost perfect harmony with the ideal courtly rule. This was the strictly circumscribed area of the lists where tournaments were held. There the frenzy of the blood had full play, even though it was under the aegis of a sacred ceremonial and subject to symbolical restraints. A tournament was the sporting equivalent of the mythical function of *Tristan*, as this function has been defined in these pages. Passion was to be expressed with all its strength, but also to be veiled religiously so that it might be acceptable to social opinion. A tournament was a physical representation of the myth.

'Literature did not suffice [Huizinga says][1] for the almost insatiable needs of the romantic imagination of the age. Some more active form of expression was required. Dramatic art might have supplied it, but the medieval drama in the real sense of the word treated love matters only exceptionally; sacred subjects were its

[1] Ibid., pp. 68–69.

Tournaments, or the Myth in Action

substance. There was, however, another form of representation, namely, noble sports, tourneys, and jousts. Sportive struggles always and everywhere contain a strong dramatic element and an erotic element. In the medieval tournament these two elements had so much got the upper hand, that its character of a contest of force and courage had been almost obliterated by its romantic purport. With its bizarre accoutrements and pompous staging, its poetical illusion and pathos, it filled the place of the drama of a later age.'[1]

Nothing seems to me better able to place us in the dreamlike atmosphere of the *Romance of Tristan* than the accounts of tourneys in Chastellain's chronicles and the memoirs of Olivier de La Marche, both men having been historiographers of the gorgeous and chivalric Duchy of Burgundy in the fifteenth century. They succeed in uniting love and death in an artificial and symbolical landscape pervaded by a lofty sadness.

'The hero who serves for love, this is [to quote Huizinga again][2] the primary and invariable motif from which erotic fantasy will always start. It is a sensuality transformed into the craving for self-sacrifice, into the desire of the male . . . to suffer and to bleed for his lady-love. The expression and the satisfaction of desire, from having both seemed unattainable, were transmuted into something loftier—a heroic action undertaken for the sake of love. Death thereupon became the only alternative to the fulfilment of desire, and in any event release seemed assured.'

The ceremonial of the tournaments drew its inspiration from the romances of the Round Table. A Passage of Arms of the fifteenth century is based on a fictitious chivalrous adventure connected with an artificial scene called 'The Fountain of Tears'.

'A fountain is expressly constructed, and beside it a pavilion, where during a whole year a lady is to reside (in effigy, be it understood), holding a unicorn which bears three shields. The first day of each month knights come to touch the shields, and in this way to pledge themselves for a combat of which the "Chapters" of the Passage of Arms lay down the rules. They will

[1] The dramatic function of tournaments may possibly have been one source of modern tragedy. For this tragedy came into being at the very moment tournaments went out of fashion, in a time when their warlike, sporting, and theatrical components were breaking up. In that case, tragedy might be regarded as an 'action' deprived of the *physical* danger implicit in a tournament, but on that account giving all the greater satisfaction to a need of sentimental and spiritual emotion.   [2] Ibid., p. 67.

find horses in readiness, for the shields have to be touched on horseback. . . .

'The knight should be unknown. He is called "le blanc chevalier", "le chevalier mesconnu", or he wears the crest of Lancelot or Palamedes. The shields of the Fount of Tears are white, violet, and black, and overspread with white tears.'[1]

The erotic factor in tournaments is also shown by the custom according to which a knight carried—like Lancelot—the veil or a fragment of the dress of his lady, and sometimes after the lists handed this to her stained with his blood.

'The Church was openly hostile to tournaments; it repeatedly prohibited them, and there is no doubt that the fear of the passionate character of this noble game, and of the abuses resulting from it, had a great share in this hostility.'[2]

However, when tournaments reached the height of their vogue, it was a sign that chivalry had begun to decline. At the beginning of the fifteenth century—about the time of the Battle of Agincourt—new brutalities drove it into literature, entertainments, and symbolical games. The fifteenth century witnessed the appearance of the foot-soldier; and less than a hundred years later the lanzknechts introduced from the East the use of the drum. 'Its hypnotic and discordant beat symbolized the transition from chivalry to the modern art of war. It was a step in the mechanization of warfare.' And finally chivalry was killed by the invention of artillery. 'There is an irony of fate in the fact that Jacques de Lalaing, prototype of the Hainault pattern knight of the fifteenth century, should have been killed by a cannon ball.'

Yet the formalities of war and of courtly love had given European customs an impress that did not fade till the present century. The notion of personal valour and of the warlike feats represented by the duel and by prowess (the single-handed combat between two leaders); the notion of regulating the conduct of battles according to a quasi-sacred etiquette; the view that military life must be ascetic (long fasts before the ordeal of battle), rules for settling who should be the victor (he, for example, who *spent the night* on the battlefield), and finally the close parallel between erotic and military symbolism—all that never ceased to determine the modes of making war throughout the ensuing ages. So that any alteration in military tactics may be looked upon as related to an alteration in the notions of love, or vice versa.

[1] Ibid., p. 72.   [2] Ibid., p. 71.

5

Cannon and Condottieri

'I taly had at no time enjoyed a state of such compleat prosperity and repose as in the year 1490; and some time before and after. The people also had taken advantage of this halcyon season, and been busied in cultivating all their lands, as well as mountains and vallies; and being under no foreign influence, but governed by their own princes. Italy not only abounded with inhabitants and riches, but grew renowned for the grandeur and magnificence of her sovereigns, for the splendor of many noble and beautiful cities; for the seat and majesty of religion, and for a number of great men of distinguished abilities in the administration of public affairs, and of excellent accomplishments in all the sciences and in every noble art. She had also no small share of military glory according to the knowledge and practice of arms in those days.'[1]

The military glory had been obtained by *condottieri*. Professional soldiers in the service of princes and popes, the *condottieri* were much less given to making war than to ensuring that war did not take a toll of lives. They were not only adventurers, but skilled diplomatists and astute traders. They knew the price of a soldier. The essence of their tactical practice was to make prisoners and to disorganize the enemy's forces. Sometimes—and this was their supreme achievement—they succeeded in defeating the foe in a truly overwhelming manner: they robbed him of all his strength by buying up his entire army. Only when this was not possible did they have to fight. But, according to Machiavelli, in those days there was nothing dangerous about a battle.

'Fighting invariably takes place on horseback, the soldiers being protected by arms and assured of preserving their lives if taken

[1] Francesco Guicciardini, *Storia d'Italia*; translation by Austin Parke Goddard, 1763.

prisoner. . . . The lives of the defeated are nearly always spared. They do not remain prisoners for long, and their release is obtained very easily. A town may rebel a score of times; it is never destroyed. The inhabitants retain the whole of their property; all they have to fear is that they will be made to pay a levy.'

In its own field—then deemed inferior—this art of war was the expression of a culture admirably humane, of a profound 'civilization', the opposite of a 'militarization'. In Burckhardt's phrase, the State had become a work of art. War itself had grown civilized, to the full extent that such a paradoxical statement can be true. Duels between commanders were in honour, and were enough to bring a campaign to a close. For that matter, these duels were no longer a submission to the 'judgement of God', but the triumph of one personality over another. The use of fire-arms was deplored as being incompatible with human dignity; and the condottiere Paolo Vitelli put out the eyes and cut off the hands of some *schioppettieri* of the enemy, who had been captured, because it seemed to him infamous that a gallant and perhaps noble knight should have been wounded by a common, despised foot-soldier. Love had undertone a similar alteration.

Burckhardt lays stress[1] on the way in which marriages were arranged without fuss, with short engagements, and how a husband's claim on his wife's fidelity was never asserted as strictly as in northern climes. Women of the upper class were as well educated as the men, and enjoyed full moral equality, at a time when exactly the opposite was the case in France and the Empire. And if war had turned into diplomacy in the highest quarters and had become venal in practice, the same was true of love. Courtesans could play a leading part in social life, very much as the hetaerae of Ancient Greece had done. The most famous among them were remarkable for being highly cultivated; they wrote and recited verse, played musical instruments, and were excellent conversationalists. This paganizing of the life of sex marked a considerable decline in the influence of *cortezia* and a depreciation of the tragic myth. The Platonism in vogue at the small ducal courts, and so well described by Cardinal Bembo and by Baldassare Castiglione (in the dialogues of his *Libro del Cortegiano*), was really, in a refined and thoroughly hedonistic form, a liking for social functions. It was then that 'courtesy' acquired its

[1] J. Burckhardt, *The Civilization of Italy in the Renaissance* (London and Vienna, 1937).

modern meaning of politeness and good breeding. The view that life was evil had become a thing of the past. And 'the death instinct' had apparently been neutralized.

It was upon this happy, immoral, and entirely peace-loving[1] Italy that the French troops of Charles the Eighth presently descended. The roar of *thirty-six brass cannon* spread panic through the peninsula as if this roar had been the signal of the end of the world. Charles brought with him into Italy, Guicciardini says, 'the seeds of innumerable calamities, horrible events, and changes in all scenes of affairs. For from this passage derived their origin not only changes of states, but also new fashions, new and bloody ways of making war, and diseases unknown till those days.' The peace and concord that had hitherto prevailed in the land were so upset that it was afterwards impossible to restore order and quiet. Not that the Italians had been unaware of the use of artillery, but they despised all these new engines, as I have already mentioned, and as is shown by Ariosto's invective on fire-arms. The French, Guicciardini continues,

'... brought a much handier engine made of brass called *cannon*, which they charged with heavy iron balls. ... They were planted against the walls of a town with such speed, the space between the shots was so little, and the balls flew so quick, and were impelled with such force, that as much execution was done in a few hours as formerly in Italy in the like number of days. These rather diabolical than human instruments were used not only in sieges, but also in the field.'

Another thing that terrified the Italians was that whereas in the militia of the *condottieri* 'many of their men at arms, being a mixture of peasants, people in low life, and subjects of different potentates, ... they were generally persons that had neither natural nor acquired parts to enable them to act gallantly', the French forces appeared in the form of a *national* army.

'The men at arms were almost all subjects of France, and not of the mean sort, but gentlemen and noblemen.' The officers 'lay under no temptation to go into another service either to gratify ambition or avarice.'

---

[1] It is only fair to recall that killing was very common. But murder remained an individual affair. In the present militarized world, on the other hand, the individual is deprived of this means of venting his passions, it having become the prerogative of the community. Cf. the passage quoted from the Marquis de Sade, above, p. 212.

It was seen that there must now be great slaughter, and indeed at the Battle of Rapallo, which practically opened the campaign, '. . . there were killed, in fighting and in the pursuit, above a hundred men; doubtless a great slaughter, if we consider the manner of fighting in Italy in those days.'

And this was no more than a beginning! Burckhardt says that the devastation wrought by the French seemed trifling in comparison with what was done a little later by the Spaniards, 'in whom perhaps a strain of non-western blood, or perhaps familiarity with the sights provided by the Inquisition, let loose diabolical instincts'. Artillery and the massacre of civilians! Modern warfare had come into being. Little by little this warfare was going to transform the inspired and magnificent knights into troops disciplined and uniform. The transformation was going to result in our own day in abolishing every vestige of the passion for making war, as gradually men serving machines became themselves machines and felt neither anger nor pity while performing a few automatic movements intended to deal death at a distance.

6

Classic Warfare

In the seventeenth and eighteenth centuries the main effort of the men of war was directed to controlling the mechanical monster in order that as many as possible of the humane features of warfare might be preserved. It was not possible to give up technical inventions—artillery and fortifications. But at least the *rules* of tactics and strategy could be so multiplied as to allow the intellect and the 'valour' of the commanders to retain a semblance of supremacy among the factors entering into the struggle. Chivalry stood for an attempt to endow instinct with a kind of correct deportment. Warfare in the classical age of Western

Europe was conducted with great formality because there was a wish to preserve and renew this correct deportment, notwithstanding the advent of inhuman factors. Following the desolation left by the Thirty Years' War, there was a desire to keep expenditure within bounds—men cost dear!—and to avoid alarming a population so thoroughly as to render recruitment impossible.

Vauban turned siege into a kind of mental operation carried out in stages, and these stages, it has been well said, were rather like the five acts of a French classical tragedy.

'It is at this period that war did indeed become the equivalent of a game of chess. When, following a series of complex manoeuvres, one of the two adversaries had lost or won several pawns—towns or fortresses—there came the great battle. Standing on some hilltop, from which he could survey the whole field, the entire chessboard, a marshal skilfully caused his splendid regiments to advance or retreat. Check and mate, the loser put his pawns away: the regiments marched off to winter quarters, and everybody went about his business pending the next game or campaign.'[1]

It may be inferred that every time war has recovered the aspect of a *game*, this was because society wished to reintroduce the passion myth into its culture—that is to say, wished to confine a lawless force within a framework and give it a ritual form of manifesting itself. This is what actually happened in the seventeenth century, as may be seen from the chapters on *L'Astrée* and on French classical tragedy in Book IV, above.

'Here matter was being made mental, so as to determine the behaviour of the fighters, who, after all, are living and thinking beings.' So wrote Foch about war in the eighteenth century.[2] It is a curious remark, but it is based on a passage in Von der Goltz, which is worth quoting:

'The mistake made by generals who can only follow rules is that they look upon the aim of war as being to carry out neatly organized manoeuvres and not to wipe out the forces of the enemy. The military world has invariably fallen into this mistake whenever it has neglected the natural trend of things and the

---

[1] J. Boulenger, *Le Grand siècle* (Paris, 1915).

[2] Ferdinand Foch, *Les Principes de la guerre* (Paris, 1929). This is a new edition. The first appeared in 1903, and was translated by Hilaire Belloc under the title, *The Principles of War* (London, 1918).

influence of the heart on human resolution, and has abandoned the plain and simple notion underlying the laws of war—*that matter must be made mental.*'

The statement is typical of the attitude of mind that made its appearance with the French Revolution—at a time, that is to say, when collective *instincts* and catastrophic *passions* were being let loose. The two modern strategists I have quoted do in fact blame the generals of Louis the Fourteenth and Louis the Fifteenth, of Queen Anne and Frederick the Great, for having sought to carry on war at the price of getting as few men killed as possible. Yet this was the supreme achievement of a civilization whose whole aim was the regulation and ordering of Nature, matter, and the determinism of both, according to the laws of human reason and of personal benefit. It may have been an illusory aim, but without it no civilization and no culture are possible. Racine, too, as I have recalled, was at one time of the opinion that it is possible to construct a tragedy without using crime as the chief ingredient.

The classical age may be summed up in its refusal to see any nobility in disaster. It recognized, not only that war and passion were inevitable evils, but also that they were desired. Nevertheless, it placed the greatness of man in his ability to limit their effect and to make them serve other ends; I may even say—in his ability to subordinate them to the civilian art of diplomacy. Louis the Fourteenth was wont to engage in war over legal and personal questions unconnected with national honour. The War of the Spanish Succession was a quarrel between a husband and his father-in-law over the payment of a stipulated dowry. And in this same age marriage was negotiated upon similar considerations —reciprocal advantages, suitable social rank, landed estates or financial substance. Passion no longer played any part in it whatsoever.

As far as that goes, love itself was about to become a matter of tactics. It was to lose its dramatic halo.

7

Fighting in Lace Cuffs

The eighteenth century affords the best illustration of the resemblance between love and war, as a few indications are enough to show. Don Juan succeeded to Tristan; perverse sensuality to fatal passion. And at the same time war was 'profaned': in place of Judgements of God and in place of sacred chivalry, ascetic, bloody, and barded with iron, there arose a crafty diplomacy and an army commanded by courtiers in lace cuffs, who, since they were libertines, did not intend to jeopardize the refinements of life.

The epic legends, and likewise the romances of the Round Table, abound in accounts of incredible slaughter. A knight depended for his fame on the number of enemies he had transfixed, the number of heads he had cut off. If possible, he had to cleave a man in two at a single stroke of his sword. The ferocious exaggerations in these tales show plainly enough what actually excited the passion of men and women in the Middle Ages. Glory be to blood! But in the eighteenth century it was considered a famous feat to have reduced an invested town at the price of only three dead on both sides. A skilled art was in honour. Marshal de Saxe wrote: 'I do not favour battles, particularly at the beginning of a war. I am sure a good general can make war *all his life* and not be compelled to fight one.' If, after all, there had to be hand-to-hand fighting, it was not in anything less than a pitched battle or a proper siege; and the tradition of chivalry in its wildest and most lofty aspect recovered a last moment of prestige. Behold the great Condé in his plumed hat prancing up and down among the enemy's troops, like the true hero of *L'Astrée* that he was!

Love and War

And what supreme civility in the face of death at Fontenoy![1]

But it was John Law, the Scot who was commissioner-general of finance in France during the minority of Louis the Fifteenth, who achieved the complete 'profanation' of war and of its sacred passion. He was in favour of reverting to the methods of the *condottieri*, although no doubt unaware that these had forestalled him.

'Victory [he wrote][2] always falls to the side having the last crown. France keeps up an army costing 100 millions a year, which means two milliards every twenty years. We are not at war for more than five out of these twenty years, and this war, moreover, puts us back at least one milliard. It thus costs us three milliards in order to make war for five years. Lasting success being uncertain, what is the consequence? That with plenty of luck, we may expect to destroy 150,000 of the enemy by fire, sword, flood, famine, fatigue, and disease. Thus the destruction, either directly or indirectly, of one German soldier costs us 20,000 livres, to say nothing of the losses suffered by our own population, losses which are only repaired at the end of twenty-five years. Instead of all this costly, clumsy, and dangerous paraphernalia, would it not be much better to save money by buying up the enemy's army whenever occasion arose? An Englishman has reckoned that a man is worth £480. That is a topmost figure, and they are not all so dear, as everybody knows; but at least we should save half our cash and the whole of our population, for in return for our money we should get an extra man, whereas under the present system we lose the man we had without being able to employ the other whom we destroy at such cost.'

The Goncourt Brothers have admirably discerned the fundamental identity of what occurred in love and war during the eighteenth century, This is how they describe the 'tactics' of the roués of the period:

'It is this warfare and this game of love that perhaps disclose the most profound characteristics of the century, its most hidden devices, and—quite unexpected in the French temperament—something like a genius for duplicity. What nameless great diplomatists and great politicians, more ingenious than Cardinal

---

[1] When the head of the English column was fifty paces from the French lines, the officers on either side saluted, and Lord Hay, a captain of the Guards, called out: 'Tell your men to fire!' But, 'No, sir, you shall have the honour,' replied the Comte d'Auteroche. The first volley mowed down the French. —Translator.

[2] *Œuvres* (Paris, 1934).

Dubois, more insinuating than Cardinal Bernis, were numbered among the little group of men who made the seduction of a woman the centre of their thoughts and the main business of their lives! . . . What schemings worthy of a novelist or strategist did they not engage in! Not one of them ever undertook a woman without having first made what is called a *plan*, without having given the night to walking up and down and studying the stronghold. . . . And the attack once launched, they remained to the end the same astounding actors, very like the books of the period, in which no single emotion is not given as either feigned or dissimulated. "Neglect nothing", was the motto of one of them.'[1]

The motto would have been appropriate to a general, but it was one unfortunately which leaders like Soubise[2] never forgot except on the battlefield.

8

Revolutionary War

Between Rousseau and German romanticism—that is to say, between the first reawakening of the myth and the fullness of its tempestuous maturity—there occurred the French Revolution and the campaigns of Bonaparte. Into war there returned catastrophic passion.

From a strictly military standpoint, what novelty was contributed by the Revolution? 'An outburst of passion never before equalled', is the answer given by Foch. According to him, the

---

[1] E. and J. de Goncourt, *Les Femmes au XVIIIe siècle* (Paris, 1864).

[2] Frederick the Great defeated Soubise at Rossbach in Saxony in 1757. This gave rise to a popular song in Paris, the first verse being:

> Soubise dit, la lanterne à la main,
> J'ai beau chercher; où diable est mon armée?
> Elle était pourtant là, hier matin,
> Me l'a-t-on prise, ou l'aurais-je égarée?
> —Translator.

heresy of the old school had been to seek to make war into an *exact science* when it is really *a terrible and passionate drama*. Everybody knows, of course, that an explosion of sentimentality preceded and accompanied the Revolution, an event passionate far more than—in the strict sense of the word—political. With the murder of the king—a deed which in a primitive society would have had a sacred and ritualistic significance—the violence that had long been pinned down by the classical formality of warfare became once again something at once horrifying and alluring. It was the cult and blood-spilling mystery that gave rise to a new form of community—the Nation. *And a Nation requires that passion shall be translated to the level of the people as a whole.* Actually, it is easier to feel that this happened then than to give an account of it. Every passion, it may be objected, presupposes the existence of *two* beings, and it is therefore difficult to see, if passion was taken over by a Nation, to whom the Nation then addressed itself. Let us remember, however, that the passion of love is at bottom narcissism, the lover's self-magnification, far more than it is a relation with the beloved. Tristan wanted the branding of love more than he wanted the possession of Iseult. For he believed that the intense and devouring flame of passion would make him divine; and, as Wagner grasped, the equal of the world.

> Eyes with joy are blinded . . .
> I myself am the world.

Passion requires that the *self* shall become greater than all things, as solitary and powerful as God. Without knowing it, passion also requires that beyond its apotheosis death shall indeed be the end of all things.

And nationalist ardour too is a self-elevation, a narcissistic love on the part of the collective Self. No doubt, its relation with others is seldom averred to be love; nearly always hate is what first appears, and what is proclaimed. But hate of the other is likewise always present in the transports of passionate love. There has thus occurred no more than a shift of emphasis. And what does national passion require? The elevation of collective might can only lead to the following dilemma: either the triumph of imperialism—of the ambition to become the equal of the whole world—or the people next door strongly object, and there ensues war. Now it is to be noticed that a nation undergoing the early surges of its passion seldom recoils from war, even if that war must be hopeless. A nation thus unconsciously expresses a readiness to court the risk of death, and even to meet death, rather than surrender its passion. 'Liberty or death', the Jacobins yelled, at a time when the forces of the enemy seemed to be twenty times as strong as their own, and when therefore 'liberty' and 'death' were words very near to having one and the same meaning.

Thus Nation and War are connected as Love and Death are connected. And from this point onwards nationalism has been the predominant factor in war. 'Whoever writes upon strategy and tactics should confine himself to expounding a *national* strategy and tactics, for these alone can be of use to the nation for whom he writes.' Thus General von der Goltz, a follower of Clausewitz. And Clausewitz constantly asserted that the Prussian theory of war must be based on the experience gained in the French Revolutionary and Napoleonic campaigns. The Battle of Valmy was a victory of passion over 'exact science'. It was to the cry of 'Long live the Nation!' that the Sans-culottes repulsed an allied army still bent on conducting operations on 'classic' lines. It will be recalled that Goethe, after witnessing the battle, said: 'On this field and on this day a new era begins in the history of the world.' To this famous pronouncement Foch adds:

'Truly enough a new era had begun, the era of national wars that are fought *under no restraints whatever*, because a nation throws all its resources into the struggle, because the aim of these wars is not to safeguard some dynastic claim, but to defeat or propagate philosophical ideas and intangible advantages, because these wars are staked upon feelings and passions, elemental forces never enlisted before.'

There is a certain parallel between the love affairs of Bonaparte and then Napoleon on the one hand, and, on the other, his campaigns in Italy and Austria. One kind of battle such as he engaged in corresponds to his conquest of Josephine—a bold stroke delivered by the weaker adversary, who hurls the whole of his forces against one decisive spot, and bluffs. Another kind of battle corresponds to his dynastic marriage with the Archduchess Marie Louise—and this was a big affair destined to find a place in the text-books: Wagram, for example, where military science, having assumed rhetorical proportions, was combined with an overwhelming and violent element of surprise. Possibly the defeat at Waterloo was due to an excessive parade of military science, possibly to the fact that by then national-revolutionary dash was exhausted. Certainly, at any rate, Napoleon was the first to take the passion factor into account each time he gave battle. That is why a general whom he had just defeated in Italy was heard to exclaim: 'It is incredible how this fellow Bonaparte ignores the most elementary rules of war!'

9

National War

Beginning with the French Revolution, 'the hearts of the soldiery' became part of the armoury of battle, and, as Foch puts it, war grew 'fierce and tragic'. This does not mean that it thereupon became possible for any individual soldier to decide a war, provided he was sufficiently heroic; only that the collective emotions came into play—what one may dare call the passionate might of the Nation. The romantic poets had a notable share in the wars of emancipation which Prussia fought against Napoleon. And the essentially passionate philosophies of thinkers like Fichte and Hegel were the earliest reinforcements of German nationalism. That is why the wars of the nineteenth century became more and more bloody. It was no longer rival interests that came into conflict, but antagonistic 'religions'. And, unlike interests, religions do not compromise; instead they exact a heroic death. At all times religious wars have been by far the most violent.

And yet, although this is true as regards the first three-quarters of the century, and above all of the period from 1848 to 1870, following the latter date national passions were provisionally appeased, and for forty years they gave place to capitalistic and commercial enterprise. Violence was still resorted to in the name of the Nation, but material advantages were undoubtedly what ruled. Foch insists on this very well in his *Principes de la guerre*.

'War [he says] became national in the first instance for the sake of winning and securing the independence of peoples—that of the French in 1792–93, of the Spaniards in 1804–14, of the

Russians in 1812, of the Germans in 1813, and of Europe in 1814. At this stage it produced those glorious and powerful displays of popular passion known as Valmy, Saragossa, Tarancon, Moscow, and Leipzig.

'War then went on being national for the sake of winning *unity of races* or *nationality*. This is what the Italians and the Prussians claimed to be fighting for in 1866 and 1870. In its name also the king of Prussia, after he had become German emperor, put forward a title to the German provinces of Austria.

'But if war is still national today [1903], it is for the sake of securing economic benefits and profitable trade agreements.

'After having been the violent means whereby peoples wrested a place in the world for themselves which made them into nations, war has become the means to which they still resort in order to enrich themselves.'

'Trade follows the flag.' The colonial era was the last period of 'peace' that Europe can be said to have deserved. I have already pointed out[1] that in manners and in literature this era was characterized by a final attempt to mythologize passion. The reaction does not bear comparison with chivalry (although its social purpose was the same), because it was adapted to the present scale of society. What now inspired convention and the formality of our behaviour was no longer any spiritual principle, but calculations of private advantage, which cannot supply the community with a stout armature. The very Nation being invoked had lost its romantic prestige: the flag protected the interests of the State, not the passions or honour of the best elements in the body social. And the office of the State was now no more than the honorific one of a board of directors; it made war in behalf of banks, as in the case of the conquest of Madagascar. In short, colonial warfare was but an extension of capitalistic competition in a form that laid a heavier burden on the country at large though not on the great business firms.

Towards the end of the nineteenth century love[2] among the

[1] Book IV, Chapter 19, above.
[2] I mean that abstract and striking thing, unreal but significant, the *average of typical expressions* of love in a given period—as unreal and as significant whether ugly or beautiful, whether at the end of the nineteenth century or during the famous century of Louis the Fourteenth, whether vicious or virtuous. There are signs which are not a particular period itself—every period contains some of everything—but which belong to one period rather than to another. That is all I mean.

middle classes had become a most curious medley of nervous sentimentality and of regard for dividends and dowries, as it still is today in matrimonial advertisements. Pure sex, if it happened to intrude, could only cloud these petty schemings and mass-produced 'noble sentiments', in the same way as a drop of water clouds absinthe. War likewise had become a compound into which entered, on the one hand, the working up of popular opinion—what was the *Revanche* for 1870–71 but a piece of national sentimentality?—on the other hand, the ambitions of business-men and financiers. The true warlike element had to provide for itself surreptitiously. War was growing middle-class. Blood was getting commercialized. Army men already seemed anomalous to the realists, and to women and idle gapers a kind of thrilling survival.[1] Yet it was being generally supposed that the tremendous potential of frenzy and slaughter which had been piled up in Europe as a result of the cultivation of passion for centuries could be disposed of without incurring havoc. The war of 1914 was a most impressive consequence of this disregard for the myth.

IO

Total War

With the Battle of Verdun in 1916, which the Germans called the *Materialschlacht* or Battle of War Material, it must seem that the resemblance instituted by chivalry between the *modes* of love and war came to an end. No doubt it had always been the concrete aim of war to overcome the enemy's resistance by destroying his armed might.[2] But the nation it

[1] The attitude was that of democracies on the occasions when they grow excited over a royal wedding.
[2] To force a woman's resistance by seducing her is peace; to do so by violating her is war.

was sought to defeat was not thereby destroyed: all that collapsed were its defences. Victory was determined by pitched battles against a professional army, the investing of fortresses, the capture of a commander—in short, by a system of exact rules the application of which was in consequence an art. And the victor triumphed over what was *alive*, a country or a people, either of which could be an object of desire. The whole face of war was thus changed with the introduction of the material and inhuman methods employed at Verdun.

For as soon as war, from having been merely military, becomes a 'total war', the destruction of armed resistance means the wiping out of the whole live might of the enemy—the workmen incorporated in factories, the mothers who are begetting future soldiers; in short, the whole of the 'means of production', things and persons lumped together. War is no longer the rape, but the murder, of the hostile and coveted object of desire. Verdun, moreover, was but the preamble of this new kind of war; for there the process was confined to the methodical destruction of a million *soldiers*, and no civilians. But it was a *Kriegspiel* that allowed the final touches to be put to an instrument which is now able to operate on a far wider scale—against areas such as London, Paris, or Berlin; that is to say, not against cannon-fodder, but against the flesh and blood manufacturing the cannon—an instrument of obviously much more far-reaching effect.

The technique of dealing death from afar has no equivalent in any imaginable code of love. Total war eludes both man and instinct; it turns upon passion, its begetter. And it is this, not the scale of the massacres, that is new in the history of the world.

This suggests three remarks.

War arose *in the country*, and in connexion with fighting it has been customary down to the present time to speak of *campaigns* and of *fields*. But since 1914 we have witnessed the *urbanization* of war. The first Great War provided a large portion of the peasant masses of Europe with their introduction to mechanical civilization. It was a kind of conducted tour of a World Exhibition of death-dealing arts and industries, with daily demonstrations upon live subjects.

The effect of this general enlistment of the mechanized means of destruction was *to neutralize the actual passion for war* in the hearts of fighting men. The assuaging of violence in bloodshed gave place to mass brutality, and rival hordes were hurled at one another. not by the impulse of passionate frenzy, but in obedience to the calculating brains of engineers. Henceforth, man was no more than the servant of matter; he himself became a material, and one that is more effective the less human it is in its individual reflexes. In this way, notwithstanding the drug-effect of propaganda, victory came to depend ultimately on the laws of mechanics rather than on the forecasts of psychology. The fighting instinct was thwarted. From 1914 to 1919 the explosion of sex which had usually accompanied huge armed struggles could only occur among civilians at the rear. In war, despite efforts in official quarters and on the part of certain popular writers and photographers to spread a high-flown sentimentality, a soldier's coming on leave was now simply the onrush of a male obsessed by an enforced continence that had lasted too long. Countless doctors and soldiers testified to the way in which a war of material was accompanied by a 'sex disaster'.[1] A widespread impotence—or at least its premonitory symptoms, chronic onanism and homosexuality—was the result vouched for by statistics of a sojourn of four years in the trenches. That is how it came about that presently for the first time there was a general revolt of soldiers against war,[2] because war, from being an outlet for the passions, had become a kind of vast castration of Europe.

Total war thus implied the discarding of *every accepted mode* of fighting. Beginning with 1920, all the 'diplomatic fuss' of ultimatums and 'declarations' of war ceased to have currency. Hostilities were no longer brought solemnly to a close by the signing of treaties. The arbitrary distinction between open and fortified towns, civilians and soldiers, authorized and unauthorized means of destruction, all disappeared. It follows that the defeat of a country could no longer be symbolical or metaphorical—that is, be confined to certain agreed *signs*—but had actually to be its death. Here again we see that once the notion of rules is discarded, war can no longer be an act of rape between nations; it must be a sadistic crime, the possession of a dead victim, and hence in fact a

[1] Cf. *Sittengeschichte des Weltkriegs* (two vols., Vienna and Leipzig, 1930), the results of an inquiry by the late Magnus Hirschfeld and twelve other German doctors.

[2] The modern lanzknecht, realizing that this total war is the negation of the passion for war, embarked upon absurd adventures, which he sought precisely because they were absurd and inhuman. Cf. notably the novels of Ernst Jünger (*A Chronicle from the Trench Warfare of 1918* (London, 1930), etc.) and of Ernst von Salomon.

non-possession. It can no longer exhibit a normal sexual instinct, or even the passion that employs and transcends this instinct, but only that—as we have seen—irresistible perversion of passion, the 'castration complex'.

II

The Transplanting of Passion into Politics

Games require to be played on an enclosed ground. When the field of war, from being such a ground—the lists decorated with symbols—became a bombardment sector, passion was ousted from it. And passion thereupon sought and found other means of expression. Moreover, it was driven to do so by as much as anything the weakening of private and moral powers of resistance and by the altered nature of war. On the one hand, manners in democratic countries have grown so flexible as not to tend any longer to set up absolute *obstructions* such as intensify passion. On the other hand, the totalitarian system of breaking in the young tended to banish from private life every kind of internal tragic experience and ambiguous emotion. Lawlessness in manners and authoritarian hygienics operated to roughly the same effect. The human need of passion was thwarted, whether hereditary or acquired through culture; its intimate and personal impulses were enfeebled by such regimentation.

Love between the wars became a curious medley of anxious intellectualism—a number of novels in the twenties depicted dread and the middle-class defiance of restrictions—and of materialism—what Germans called the *neue Sachlichkeit*. It was clearly recognized that romantic passion could no longer obtain the ingredients necessary to sustaining its myth, could no longer select means of resistance in the midst of an atmosphere charged with tempestuous and secret devotion. A pathological fear of

Love and War

falling in love in a simple, straightforward manner and of suffering 'deceptions of the heart', together with a feverish hankering
after 'experiences', formed the 'climate' of the chief novels in
vogue. The unambiguous significance of this was that *the individual
relations of the sexes had ceased to be the most appropriate theatre for
passion to occur in*. Passion, it seemed, was being detached from its
concomitant. We entered upon a period of wandering *libidos* in
quest of new spheres of activity. The first to offer itself was that
of politics.

The mass-politics practised since 1917 are simply an extension
of total war by other means, if I may be allowed to convert
Clausewitz's definition of war as 'diplomacy carried on by other
means'. The political use made of the term 'front' at once shows
this. Moreover, a Totalitarian State is but the state of war being
prolonged and renewed, and then made permanent, in a nation.
But if total war abolished the merest possibility of passion, politics
transferred individual passions to the level of the Collective Being.
Everything that a totalitarian education withheld from individuals
was heaped upon the personified Nation. It is the Nation (or the
Party) that had passions. It is the Nation (or the Party) that took
over the whole interplay of exciting obstructions, *askesis*, and the
rush made unwittingly towards a heroic and therefore divinizing
death. Whereas within and at the bottom personal problems were
now sterilized, externally and on top the passionate potential was
being intensified daily. Eugenics took control of the morality that
concerns the citizens of a State, and eugenics are a rational negation
of any kind of private 'experience'. Yet this only served to increase the tension of the whole, personified in the Nation. The
Nation-State said to the Germans: 'Beget children!'—and that
was a negation of passion. But it also said to its neighbours: 'There
are too many of us within our frontiers. I must therefore have
more territory!'—and this was a new passion. Hence all the tensions abolished at the bottom were heaped on the top. Unmistakably, when rival wills to power confront one another—and
there were already *several* Totalitarian States!—they are bound to
clash passionately. Each becomes for some other an *obstruction*.
The real, tacit, and inevitable aim of the totalitarian elevation
was therefore war, and war means *death*. Furthermore, as happened with passionate love, not only was this aim vigorously
denied by those concerned, but also it actually was unconscious.
Nobody dared to say, 'I want war', any more than in passionate

The Transplanting of Passion into Politics

love the lovers said: 'We want death.' Nevertheless, everything being done hastened the attainment of this aim. And everything that was being excited could only find its true significance in war.

There is abundant evidence of this novel resemblance between politics and passion. The restraints which the State imposes in the name of the nation's greatness result in a collective *askesis*. The umbrageous susceptibility of Totalitarian Nations is the equivalent of a knight's honour. And, moreover, let me stress one striking feature. The masses respond to the dictator in a particular country *in the same way* as the women of that country respond to the tactics of suitors.

I wrote in 1938:

'Hitler's success with the German masses may seem surprising, but a non-German would be quite as much astonished by the kind of behaviour that pleases German women. The Latins woo a woman by turning her head with flattering talk, and it is likewise with a flood of flattering talk that French politicians woo their voters. Hitler is more rough and ready. He expresses anger and grievances in the same breath. He does not persuade; he casts a spell. Conjuring up destiny, he asserts that this destiny is himself. He thus releases the masses from responsibility for their conduct, and hence he rids them of any oppressive sense of moral guilt. The crowd surrenders to the dread saviour, and hails him as its liberator in the very moment he paralyses and possesses it. We should note that the popular term in Germany for getting married is *freien*, a verb which means literally "to free'. Hitler is presumably only too well aware of this.

'"There is [he writes][1] something so thoroughly feminine about the attitude and reactions of the great majority of the common people that its opinions and conduct are the result of feeling far more than of pure cogitation. The masses are not very susceptible to abstract ideas. On the other hand, they are easily gripped by an appeal to emotion. . . . In all ages the force that has launched the most violent revolutions has not been the announcement of some scientific idea which seized the crowd, but a fanaticism that stimulated it and an actual hysteria which infected it with wild enthusiasm."

'Yes, this has been so "in all ages". But the novelty today is that this passionate influence over the masses described by Hitler

[1] *Mein Kampf.*

269

is accompanied by a rationalizing influence over individuals. Furthermore, this influence is not obtained by some agitator, but by the Leader who incarnates the Nation. That is why the transference of passion from private to public life has resulted in an unprecedented concentration of power. It will need a superhuman Wagner to orchestrate the stupendous catastrophe of passion become totalitarian.'

We are brought to the verge of a conclusion that I was far from foreseeing when I began this book. The gradual transformation which the European myth of passion underwent proves to have taken the same course alike in the history of methods of warfare and in the history of literature. And in both cases the transformation culminated in an aspect which receives too little notice—I mean, the dissolution of the *formal modes* instituted by chivalry. In literature 'throwbacks' occur, but in the realm of war every change is irreversible; and it is in this realm that the need of providing a fresh solution first became evident. The answer of the twelfth century was courtly chivalry, with its romantic morality and myths. The answer of the seventeenth century is symbolized in French classical tragedy. The answer of the eighteenth was Don Juan's cynicism and rationalist irony. But romanticism was no answer, unless—and this is possible—its eloquent surrender to the nocturnal forces of the myth is regarded as an ultimate attempt to enfeeble the myth by deliberate excess. However that may be, the defence was hardly proportionate to the peril simultaneously let loose. The anti-vital forces long dammed up by the myth then overflowed into the most various spheres, so that there followed a dissociation—using the word in the exact sense of a 'severance of the bonds that hold society together'.

And yet I feel that to allow all passion to be absorbed by the Nation can prove no more than an emergency measure. The menace may be held off for the time being, but it is also being made to weigh permanently upon the very lives of those peoples who have thus been formed into solid masses. No doubt the Totalitarian State is a newly devised *formal mode*, but one too vast, too rigid, and too geometrical for the complex lives of human beings, however militarized, to be successfully shaped and organized within its framework. Police measures do not constitute a culture, or slogans a morality. Between the artificial framework of great States and the everyday life of men and women, the gap is too wide, so that restlessness and uncertainty are greater than ever. Nothing is *really* settled.

It is possible that we shall have total atomic war, spiritual and moral disintegration, and the problem of passion together with the civilization that brought this problem into existence, will vanish in smoke. But it seems to me more likely that the problem will arise again in totalitarian countries even as it has never ceased to exercise us who belong to liberal societies. In the two concluding books of this work, accordingly, I treat the problem as still active. The first of them deals with a conflict in our manners between the myth and the institution of marriage; the second sums up an attitude which I put forward less as a final answer than as what I have chosen for myself.

Book VI

THE MYTH v. MARRIAGE

I

The Breakdown of Marriage

The Middle Ages had two rival moral systems—one upheld by Christianized society; the other the product of heretical courtesy. The first took marriage for granted, and even made it into a sacrament; the second promoted a set of values in the light of which—at any rate theoretically—marriage was a mistake. The attitude of each to adultery clearly indicates their mutual antagonism.

In the eyes of the Church, adultery was at one and the same time a sacrilege, a crime against the natural order, and a crime against the social order. For the sacrament conjoined in one and the same act two faithful souls, two bodies capable of begetting, and two juridical persons. It was therefore a sacrament that made holy the fundamental needs of both the species and the community. Whoever broke the triple undertaking given at the altar did not thereby become 'interesting', but an object of pity or contempt. The Roman Catholic synthesis was intended to harmonize fire and water, as alike in Scripture and in the Fathers it was possible to find thoroughly contradictory theories regarding the holiness of procreation—the law of the species—and regarding the holiness of virginity—the law of the spirit. The Old Testament, for example, deems a numerous progeny the sign of election, whereas Saint Paul says that it is good for a man not to touch a woman, even if he also says that it is better to marry than to burn.

The heresy which was bound up from the beginning with the *cortezia* of the South of France condemned Catholic marriage on

The Myth v. Marriage

each of the three heads just mentioned. It denied that marriage was a *sacrament*, declaring its sacramental character to be established by no single unambiguous text in the Gospel.[1] It declared procreation to be the work of the Prince of Darkness, the Demiurge who, in its view, had created the visible world. It sought to destroy a social order which could countenance and demand war as a manifestation of the collective will to live.[2] But the mainspring of its triple rejection of marriage was in reality a doctrine according to which Love is the divinizing Eros, everlastingly in anxious conflict with the fleshly creature and this creature's enslaving instincts.

Accordingly, the appearance of the *passion* of Love was bound radically to transform the attitude to adultery. Doubtless, unalloyed Catharist doctrine never condoned the fault *per se;* on the contrary, it prescribed chastity. But, as I have pointed out earlier, inextricable misunderstandings were produced by the courtly symbol of love for the Lady, obviously a kind of love incompatible with marriage in the flesh. To an uninitiated reader of the Provençal poems and Arthurian romances, Tristan was no doubt guilty of a fault in committing adultery, but at the same time the fault took on the aspect of *a splendid experience more magnificent than morality*. What for Manichaeans was a dramatic expression of the struggle between faith and the world thereupon became for such a reader an ambiguous and searing 'poesy'. And this poesy was seemingly altogether secular. Its seductive power was intensified by the reader's own ignorance of the mystical significance of its symbols, for he supposed these to point merely to some *vague* and *pleasing* riddle.

Only thus can we account for the fact that in the twelfth century an adulterer or adulteress suddenly became somebody 'interesting'. King David, in lying with Bath-sheba, was held to have committed a crime and to have made himself into an object of

---

[1] According to Father B. M. Lavaud, the Roman Catholic sacrament is open to being justified by the account of the miracle at Cana ('a mere hypothesis', he says, however), by the passage in which Jesus states that what God has joined man must not put asunder, or, finally, by the conversations between the risen Jesus and his disciples regarding the Kingdom of God, 'which the Evangelists and the Acts mention, but do not describe in detail'. Father Lavaud points to nothing more substantial than these three 'hypotheses' as ground for attributing to the traditional dogma a *biblical* authority. Vide his article in *Études carmélitaines*, April 1938, p. 186.

[2] The Gnostics (e.g. Carpocrates) often asserted that 'crimes are a tribute paid to life'. Cf. Schultz, *Dokumente der Gnosis*, op. cit.

contempt. But when Tristan carries off Iseult, his deed turns into romance, and he makes himself into an object of admiration. What had hitherto been a 'fault' and what could only give rise to edifying remarks on the perils of sin and on remorse now became—in symbol—something mystically virtuous, and later on was degraded (in literature) into a disturbing and alluring entanglement.

I do not want directly to suggest that the present breakdown of marriage is simply the latest aspect of the discord between a medieval heresy and orthodoxy. The heresy, as such, exists no longer; and if orthodoxy does still exist, it must nevertheless be admitted no longer to play a direct part in the lives of our contemporary societies, to the formation of which it contributed so much. In my opinion, the present general demoralization reflects a confused strife in our lives as a result of the co-existence of two *moral* systems, one inherited from religious orthodoxy, but no longer sustained by a living faith; the other derived from a heresy of which the 'in-essence-lyrical' expression has come down to us in a form altogether profaned and therefore distorted. On the one hand, we have today a morality concerned for the species and the general well-being of society, though none the less bearing some impress of religion—what are called middle-class morals. On the other hand, there is a morality spread among us through our literary and artistic atmosphere and general culture—and this produces passionate or romantic morals. The whole of middle-class youth in Europe was brought up to regard marriage with respect; and yet at the same time all young people breathe in from books and periodicals, from stage and screen, and from a thousand daily allusions, a romantic atmosphere in the haze of which passion seems to be the supreme test that one day or other awaits every true man or woman, and it is accepted that nobody has really lived till he or she 'has been through it'. Now, passion and marriage are essentially irreconcilable. Their origins and their ends make them mutually exclusive. Their co-existence in our midst constantly raises insoluble problems, and the strife thereby engendered constitutes a persistent danger for every one of our social safeguards.

In bygone times it fell to the myth to restrain this latent lawlessness, and to fit it symbolically into moral categories. The myth provided an outlet, and operated to the benefit of civilization. But it came about that the myth was abased and profaned together with the formal modes which had furnished its physical embodiment. If it were now to strive to rise into existence again, we know that no powers of *resistance* would be strong enough to serve as its mask and excuse. Every month sees a flood of articles and books about the breakdown of marriage. They are not in the least likely to settle the problem; for only the myth— that is to say, our unawareness—could bring about in behalf of passion a kind of *modus vivendi*. In making us more keenly alive to the problem, these articles and books contribute, on the contrary, to hampering the elaboration of a settlement. They are themselves evidence of the breakdown, and signs also of our inability to repair it with things as they are. For the institution of marriage was founded on three sets of values which subjected it to *compulsions*, and it was precisely in the effect and interaction of these that the myth achieved expression.[1] But today the compulsions have been either relaxed or abandoned.

There were, in the first place, sacred compulsions. Pagan races have invariably made marriage the subject of a ritual, vestiges of which long survived in our own customs. The ritual covered the purchase, abduction, and exorcism of the bride. Nowadays, owing to economic uncertainties, dowries (even on the Continent) have lost importance. The customs derived from nuptial abduction now only live on as rustic practical jokes. In France no longer does a mother call on the parents of the girl whom her son wishes to marry and formally ask for her hand. Nowhere now is a betrothal very often the occasion for a lawyer's presence at a full-dress reception. And few couples feel any 'superstitious' need of having their union 'blessed' by a priest.

There were, in the second place, social compulsions. But today considerations of rank, blood, family interests, and even money, are receding into the background so far as democratic countries are concerned, and hence the mutual choice of a marriage partner tends more and more to depend on individual circumstances. That is why divorce is steadily on the increase. Likewise epithalamial ceremonies have either been greatly simplified or else are dispensed with altogether. Customs of remote and sacred origin such as that of 'the semi-publicity of the nuptial bed'[2] were kept up in the French provinces right into the seventeenth century. The original mystery had been forgotten, but the ritual continued to give weddings their social character and to fit them into the

[1] Cf. Book I, above.   [2] *The Waning of the Middle Ages*, op. cit.

life of the community. But in the eighteenth century the ceremony of 'bedding the bride' had already become nothing more than an occasion for mild and picturesque gallantries. Nowadays the honeymoon, to the extent that it survives and retains any significance, must be held to indicate a wish for escape from habitual social surroundings and an insistence on the private nature of what is called wedded bliss.

There were, finally, religious compulsions. But the modern mind, in so far as it is still able to distinguish between Christianity and sacred and social compulsions, recoils from it with horror. For a religious vow is taken for 'time and eternity', which means that it makes no allowance for temperamental vagaries, alterations of character, and changes in taste and external circumstances, such as every couple must expect to experience. And it is on there being no such ups and downs that modern couples make what they call their 'happiness' depend. I shall return to this presently.

From such a general decay of institutional obstructions a slackening of tension was bound to ensue, so that it is no wonder that there is now a vast confusion. Adultery has become a topic either for delicate psychological analysis or else for facetious jokes. Fidelity in marriage has become slightly ridiculous: it is so conventional. Strictly speaking, the two hostile moral systems are no longer in *conflict* (and hence no myth is any longer possible), but are approaching a state of mutual neutralization, which will be reached when the old values—not transcended, but abased— have finally dissolved.

2

The Modern Notion of Happiness

Now that marriage has ceased to enjoy the safeguards of a system of social compulsions, the only possible basis on which it can rest is individual choice. This means, actually, that the success of any given marriage depends upon an individual notion of the nature of happiness, which at best may be assumed to be identical in the minds of both parties. And yet if in any event it is perplexing enough to define happiness in general, definition becomes impossible when account has to be taken of the contemporary wish to control one's own happiness, or—what doubtless amounts to the same thing—to be able *to experience* the ingredients of one's happiness and to be able to analyse them and roll them over the tongue, so as to give here and there a neat pat of improvement. Your happiness, it is being asserted from the pulpits of magazines, depends on this or on that; and this or that is invariably something that must be *acquired*, usually for cash. The consequence of this propaganda is that we are obsessed by the notion of a facile happiness and at the same time are rendered incapable of being happy. For everything thus suggested introduces us to a world of comparisons in which, until there are men like gods, no happiness can be established. Happiness is indeed a Eurydice, vanishing as soon as gazed upon. It can exist only in *acceptance*, and succumbs as soon as it is laid claim to. For it appertains to being, not to having, as the moralists in all ages have insisted; and our own age brings no new factor to disprove them. Every wish to experience happiness, to have it at one's beck and call—instead of *being* in a *state* of happiness, as though by grace —must instantly produce an intolerable sense of want.

To wish marriage to be based on such 'happiness' implies in men and women today a capacity for boredom which is almost morbid, or else a secret intention not to play fair. Perhaps it is only this intention or hope that can account for the readiness of couples to get married 'without believing in it'. The dream of potential passion acts as a perpetual distraction to paralyse the revulsions of boredom. People are not unaware that passion is a woe, but they imagine that such a woe will be splendid and 'vital' in a way ordinary life cannot be, and more exciting than the 'happy-go-lucky' present. Either a resigned boredom or else passion—this is the dilemma our lives come up against as a result of the contemporary notion of happiness. In any case this notion threatens the ruin of marriage as a social institution that is defined by its stability.

3

'It's Wonderful to be in Love!'

In the twelfth century in Provence love was regarded as a dignity. It not only imparted a titular nobility, but actually ennobled. Troubadours were raised socially to the level of the aristocracy, which treated them as equals. That is perhaps how there has been imposed on us today through the medium of literature the altogether modern and romantic notion that passion is something morally noble, and need know no law and no custom. Whoever loves passionately is supposed to be thereby made one of an exalted section of mankind among whom social barriers cease to exist. A Tzigane may carry off a princess; a mechanic, marry an heiress. Likewise, a beauty queen has some hopes of becoming the wife of an earl or millionaire. This is a modern 'adaptation'—to use a cinematographic term, such as is alone appropriate here[1]—of the theory that love is above the established social order.

[1] German films in the days of Hitlerism freely used the Hollywood plot in which a workman or chauffeur comes 'to deserve' his employer's daughter.

The Myth v. Marriage

The profane passion is something absurd, a kind of drug, a 'sickness of the soul', as the Ancients supposed, everybody is ready to grant, and moralists have said so *ad nauseam*; but in this age of novels and films, when all of us are more or less drugged, nobody will *believe* it, and the distinction is capital. The moderns, men and women of passion, expect irresistible love to produce some revelation either regarding themselves or about life at large. This is a last vestige of the primitive mysticism. From poetry to the piquant anecdote, passion is everywhere treated as an *experience*, something that will alter my life and enrich it with the unexpected, with thrilling chances, and with enjoyment ever more violent and gratifying. The whole of possibility opens before me, a future that assents to desire! I am to enter into it, I shall rise to it, I shall reach it in 'transports'. The reader will say that this is but the everlasting illusion of mankind, the most guileless and—notwithstanding all I have said—the most 'natural'; for it is the illusion of freedom and of living to the full. But really a man becomes free only when he has attained self-mastery, whereas a man of passion seeks instead to be defeated, to lose all self-control, to be beside himself and in ecstasy. And indeed he is being urged on by his nostalgia, the origin and end of which are unknown to him. His illusion of freedom springs from this double ignorance. A man of passion wants to discover his 'type of woman' and to love no other. Gérard de Nerval, in one of his poems, tells of a dream in which a noble Lady appears to him in a landscape of childhood memories.

> She's fair, dark-eyed, and in old-fashioned clothes
> That in another life I may withal
> Have seen before, and now but do recall.

Without question this is a mother-image, and psycho-analysis has shown what tragic impediments that may imply. But to quote a poet is either of no value or of too much. I want to confine myself to the illusion which most people in the present century have been *taught*: what obsesses them far more than a mother-image is 'standardized beauty'. Nowadays—and we are only at the beginning—a man who falls passionately in love with a woman whom he *alone* finds beautiful is supposed to be a prey to nerves. So many years hence he will have to undergo treatment. Admittedly, every generation forms a standardized notion of beauty as a matter of course, even as fashion concentrates at various times on heads, bosoms, hips, or the slim lines of the open-air girl. But nowadays our sheep-like aesthetic tastes exert a greater influence than ever before, and they are being fostered by every possible technical and sometimes political means. A feminine type thus recedes more and more from personal imponderables and is selected in Hollywood or by the State. This influence of standardized beauty is a double one. On the one hand, it preordains who shall be an appropriate object of passion (and to this extent the object is drained of personality); on the other hand, it disqualifies a marriage in which the bride is not like the obsessing star of the moment. In short, the present so-called 'freedom' of passion is a question of advertising power. A man who imagines he is yearning for 'his' type, or a woman for 'hers', is having his or her private wishes determined by fashionable and commercial influences; i.e. by novelty.

4

Marrying Iseult?

Now suppose that, in spite of everything, a man succeeds in plumping for a particular type as his type—a type which will be a cross between what naturally appeals to him and what the cinema has taught him to like. He meets a woman of this type, and identifies her. There she is, the woman of his heart's desire and of his most intimate nostalgia, the Iseult of his dreams![1] And of course she is already married. But let her get a divorce, and she shall be his! Together they will experience 'real

---

[1] The title of a novel by Max Brod, *Die Frau nach der man sich sehnt*—the women we yearn after, of our nostalgia—supplies the best definition of Iseult. Passionate love wants 'the *faraway* princess', whereas Christian love wants 'our *neighbour*'.

life', and the Tristan he nurses like his hidden daemon in his bosom will wax and bloom. As regards the revelation of the myth, that is all that matters. There we have the real 'marriage for love' of our time—with passion as the bride! But thereupon the on-lookers (or the public) display a certain uneasiness. Will the lover with all his desires gratified continue to be in love with his Iseult *once* she has been *wed*? Is a cherished nostalgia still desirable once it has recovered its object? For Iseult is ever a stranger, the very essence of what is strange in woman and of all that is eternally fugitive, vanishing, and almost hostile in a fellow-being, that which indeed incites to pursuit, and rouses in the heart of a man who has fallen a prey to the myth an avidity for possession so much more delightful than possession itself. She is the woman-from-whom-one-is-parted: to possess her is to lose her.

And thereupon begins a new 'passion'. There is a deliberate effort to renew both obstacle and struggle. The woman in my arms I must imagine as other than she is. I give her another guise, I cause her to recede in my dreams, I strive to disturb the emotional tie that is gradually being formed thanks to the smoothness and serenity of our lives. For I must devise fresh obstructions if I am to go on desiring, and if I am to magnify my desire to the dimensions of a conscious and intense passion that shall be infinitely thrilling. And only suffering can make me aware of passion; and that is why I like to suffer and to cause to suffer. When Tristan carries off Iseult to the forest, where there is nothing any longer to obstruct their union, the daemon of passion sets down a drawn sword between their two bodies. Let us descend a few centuries, stepping down at the same time the whole gamut that stretches from the age of religious heroism to the drab confusion in which men and women of our own profane era are struggling: instead of the knight's sword, it is the sly dream of the husband that comes between him and the wife he can only continue to desire by imagining she is his mistress.[1] In countless nauseating novels there is now depicted the kind of husband who fears the flatness and same old jog-trot of married life in which his wife loses her 'allure' because no obstructions come between them. Such husbands are the pathetic victims of a myth the mystical promise of which long ago faded out. In the eyes of Tristan, Iseult was nothing but the symbol of luminous Desire: his other

[1] The recipe was made available as early as Balzac's *Physiologie du mariage* (1828).

world was the divinizing death that was to release him from terrestrial ties. So Iseult had to be the Impossible, for every possible
love recalls us to its bonds, reduces us to those limits of time and
space without which there are no 'creatures'—whereas the one
goal of infinite love is compelled to be the divine: God, our idea
of God, or the deified Self. For a man whom the myth now haunts
without disclosing its secret, there is no other world beyond
passion except another passion, which he must pursue in another
turmoil of appearances each time more fleeting. Originally it was
of the essence of mystic passion to be *without end*, and that is how
this passion became distinct from the throb of carnal desire.
But whereas infinity in the eyes of Tristan was an eternity from
which there could be no return and in which his lacerated spirit
would at last dissolve, men and women today can look to nothing
but the everlasting return of an ardour constantly being thwarted.

Formerly victims of the myth could not throw off its spell
except by escaping out of the finite world. Today a passion calling
itself 'irresistible' (as an alibi for the discharge of responsibility)
cannot even discover how to be *faithful*, since its end is no longer
transcendence. One after the other, it exhausts illusions it has
found all too easy to grasp. Instead of leading to death, it is broken
off by unfaithfulness. How patent the degradation of a Tristan
who has *several* Iseults! But it is not he who should be blamed;
for he is the victim of a social organization in which the obstructions have been cheapened. They break down too soon, before the
undertaking has been completed. A soul that sets out to rise in
opposition to, and above, the world, has incessantly to begin its
ascent afresh. And thereupon a modern Tristan lets himself turn
into the antithetical Don Juan type—the man of successive love
affairs. The categories break down, and the experience itself
ceases to be outstanding. Alone the mythical Don Juan could
evade this consummation. But he knew no Iseult, no unattainable passion, neither past nor future, nor sensual anguish. He
lived always in the present, having no time to love, to wait, or to
remember; and nothing that he desired could resist him, because
he *loved* not what did resist.

To love in the sense of passion-love is the contrary of to live. It is
an impoverishment of one's being, an *askesis* without sequel, an inability to enjoy the present without imagining it as absent, a never-
ending flight from possession. To love with passion-love meant 'to
live' for Tristan; as the true life which he summoned was trans-

figuring death. But we have lost transcendence. Death is but a slow consumption.

It is evident in the light of a knowledge of the original myth that the popular novels and films of the present day are the sign of a decay of the individual person; the sign of a sort of sickness of being. Nearly all the complications to which plots resort do not amount to more than a monotonous arrangement of the contrivances of an enfeebled passion in quest of *secret* obstructions. Passion now only wants somehow to keep going. For instance, there is the psychology of jealousy, a jealousy that has been wished for and that is provoked and surreptitiously encouraged—and not only in 'the other'! A man or woman wants the beloved to be unfaithful in order that he or she may once again go forth in pursuit and once again 'experience' love for its own sake. Rapture is now no more than a sensation, and it leads nowhere. Married people are constantly being thrown back into a realm of comparison, which is the realm of jealousy. Extruding from his or her own self and also from the present as it is given, unable to take the other as he or she is, because that would mean being first of all content with oneself, a man or woman now sees on every side nothing but things to be coveted, qualities that he or she feels the want of, and grounds for comparison that invariably turn against the comparer. It hurts a husband to find that other women seem beautiful in a way his wife is not, even when everybody else insists that hers is the greater beauty. For he does not understand either how to possess or how to enjoy what reality has given him. He has lost the one essential—a sense of constancy. For to be faithful is to have decided to accept another being for his or her own sake, in his or her own limitations and reality, choosing this being not as an excuse for excited elevation or as an 'object of contemplation', but as having a matchless and independent life which requires *active* love.

I am not trying to attack passion here. I confine myself to describing it, well aware that I shall convince not a single victim of the profaned myth. But it was necessary to show briefly by means of a few features *how* this passion leads to a number of psychological fates the effects of which are beyond dispute. It has got to be admitted that *passion wrecks the very notion of marriage at a time when there is being attempted the feat of trying to ground marriage in values elaborated by the morals of passion*. Of course it would be going too far to suggest that a majority of people today are a prey to Tristan's frenzy. Few are capable of the thirst that would cause them to drink the love-potion, and still fewer are being elected to succumb to the archetypal anguish. But they are all, or nearly all, dreaming about it, or else have mused upon it. And however worn and faded the mark of the original myth, it still hugs the secret of the anxiety that is nowadays disturbing married couples. The contemporary mind recoils from nothing so much as from the notion of a limitation deliberately accepted; and nothing pleases this mind more than the mirage of infinite transcendence which the reminiscent impress of the myth keeps up. To try to *grow conscious* of the nature of the situation—that sums up the ambition that inspired the preceding analyses; but I realize that they have taken me to the limits of the displeasing. We are too fond of our illusions to suffer gladly any attempt even to name them.

5

From Lawlessness to Eugenics

Nevertheless, modern marriage, which may be said by antiphrasis to be founded upon the remnants of the myth, amounts to a permanent state of lawlessness, and this must obviously involve perils such as no *social* order can tolerate. I say nothing of the spiritual peril to which the morals of escape engendered by the myth must expose a moral being. The social peril is enough to account for the number of attempts made since the first world war 'to re-establish' marriage.

There were the respectable efforts of the Churches to define the institution afresh, together with the moral duties which it implies.[1] Humanists restated the arguments of Goethe and Engels in favour of marriage. According to the former, marriage is the greatest

[1] The encyclical *Casti connubii* replied to the decisions of the Anglican Lambeth Conference. The oecumenical meetings at Stockholm and Oxford of representatives of all the non-Roman Churches also touched on the problem.

achievement of European culture and the solid foundation of any private life; according to the latter, monogamic unions provide the most sensible relation between the sexes in a society that has been emancipated from the restraints of money and class. Others sought to found a science of conjugal relations. Jung analysed the 'psychological conflict' and the 'neuroses' that lie, in his opinion, at the root of the evil; he hinted that medical psychology could put everything straight. Van de Velde and Hirschfeld suggested that the best course would be to spread a more accurate knowledge of sex.

So many inquiries and so many panaceas indicate how serious the question is, but they have not produced any adequate means of settling it. Curiously enough, too, every one of these learned authors devotes a few lines to extolling passion, or at least to seeming to countenance it. There are obvious reasons for hesitating to offend readers in their most intimate and assured convictions. To do so would seem 'puritanical'. Some of these writers, however, go further, indulging in the paradox that loving passion may crown a union that has been perfectly achieved (according to their recipe). Nobody, so far as I know, has dared to say that love, *as understood nowadays*, is the flat negation of the marriage to which it is claimed that this love can serve as support. The reason is that nobody seems to know exactly what passionate love may be, and neither where it comes from nor whither it may lead. There is indeed a feeling that something is wrong, but writers also fear (quite correctly) that if they attacked passion they would pass for Philistines. So the fundamental problem is passed over with a simulated lightness. 'We must get ourselves read, and win confidence. There is no going against the tide of a whole epoch. Passion has always existed, it therefore always will exist; and we are no Don Quixotes.' No doubt! And yet something *must* be done. Hence the one question confronting the historian and sociologist is: *What mechanism* will be released in order to put matters right—what mechanism or what collective reflex?

Two large-scale experiments furnish one kind of answer, and perhaps point to the solution to which we shall all be brought.

Revolutionary Russia was the scene of a youthful 'outburst' of sex which it is tempting to regard as unprecedented in European annals.[1] As for marriage, theoretically it was swept away

[1] Actually, similar happenings occurred among the youth in so-called bourgeois countries. But in Russia principles of 'emancipation' were advertised; elsewhere the young were content to put these principles into practice.

during the early stages of the Soviets. Nihilist or romantic intel-
lectuals had inspired the young Bolshevist leaders with a doctrine
that found expression in unmarried cohabitation, abortion, and
the desertion of babies—in short, in whatever was imagined to
defy reactionary prejudices mistakenly thought to have been
fostered by bourgeois capitalism. Lenin, in a famous letter to a
woman Bolshevist named Zetkin, describes this collapse of morals,
and protests with all the vigour of a 'professional' revolutionary
—and hence of a Puritan—against the sexual lawlessness which—
using the words in their contemptuous Marxian sense—he termed
'petit bourgeois'. Twenty years later, a 'restoration of morals'
had been achieved, not owing to any sudden revival of virtue nor
thanks to the efforts of some philanthropic society, but as a result
of the deliberate action of a dictatorship fully alive to the conditions requisite for its survival. Stalin's immediate aim was to re-
build the framework of his nation. For in the absence of a framework economic life was in danger of collapse, and 'national
defence' could not be organized without constant appeal to the
passion of the early revolutionaries, and it was precisely this passion that Stalin had determined to get rid of. To lay down new
social foundations, and especially that most stable and most
stabilizing of units: the family, became therefore a vital necessity.
The nature of the mechanism of productivist dictatorship compelled the so-called Socialist State to decree a series of laws against
divorce—which was made more burdensome—and against abortion and the deserting of babies born out of wedlock. The sudden
severity of these laws, the psychological shock which they inflicted, propaganda, and measures enabling the police to keep a
watch on private life, transformed the moral atmosphere of
Russia round about the year 1936.[1] Marriage was instituted again
on strictly utilitarian, collectivist, and eugenic principles; and there
was promoted a spirit in which individual problems tended to
lose all their dignity, legitimacy, and lawless virulence.[2]

In pre-Hitlerite Germany the level of lawlessness to which sex
sank was possibly quite as low as that reached in Russia before

[1] Cf. Hélène Iswolsky, *Femmes soviétiques* (Paris, 1937).

[2] When dealing with the U.S.S.R. the words 'family', 'eugenics', and
'abolition of passion' should all be put in inverted commas. The headlong
drop in the population compelled Stalin to encourage births. But who can be
sure that his plans were carried out? And his motives, I repeat, were not in the
least 'moral'; rather were they military.

Stalin. The gradual decay of social restraints was not accompanied by any outward violence, but on that very account the marriage morals of the young were all the more seriously undermined. At the same time the decline of the passion myth in the fatherland of romanticism involved far more complicated consequences than in France, and they seemed of the greatest variety. The morbid shamelessness of the German post-war years, the *neue Sachlichkeit* promoted by advanced writers and artists, the homosexuality so common in the secret societies that were a prelude to Hitlerism, the sadistic outbursts in the Baltic *Freikorps*, the so-called 'political' crimes committed by leagues of youth, certain forms of nudism, the 'trial betrothals' that became customary among students, the serious manner in which passionate quarrels involving 'threes' or 'fours' were treated—on the model of Friedrich Schlegel's *Lucinde* —all these were so many signs of the sex stampede that followed the weakening of matrimonial restraints and the decline of the myth of fatal love. Already the elements of despair and of private surrender to impulse, which are implicit in any pseudo-legitimization of a strictly individual 'happiness', were rising to the surface.

But Hitler's dictatorship, for the very reason that it claimed to operate for racial and military ends, was bound to address itself at the very outset to repairing this breakdown in the nation's morals. To begin with, the anti-social ideal of 'happiness' and that of 'living dangerously' were countered by the promotion of a collective ideal. '*Gemeinnütz geht vor Eigennütz!*' The general interest comes before that of individuals! Next, by means of every spectacular, didactic, and even religious instrument that it could devise, Hitlerism effected the extraordinary *transference*[1] which resulted in making the one legitimate and possible object of passion the concept of a Nation symbolized in its Führer. First, woman was bereft of her romantic halo and relegated to the position of wife, her only function being to bear and to bring up children till at the age of four or five they could be handed over to the Party. Next, certain steps in eugenics were taken. A 'school of future brides' was opened in order to supply wives to the S.S. (*Schutz-Staffeln*), Nazi protective squads, troops selected as supposedly incarnating the racial ideal. Entrance to this school was confined to girls of fair complexion, of Aryan blood, and at least five feet eight inches in height. Hence, in Germany, a man's 'type of

---

[1] Referred to in Book V, above.

290

woman' was fixed for him, not by the recollections of his unconscious nor by exotic fashions, but by the scientific section of the
Ministry of Propaganda. In 1938 similar schools were set up for
all German women, and attendance at these schools may well have
become compulsory. It was decreed that marriages would henceforth be celebrated 'in the name of the State'. The ultimate aim is
obvious. It was to reach a point at which only eugenic marriages
would be legal, and would be allowed to take place entirely
according to social, racial, and physiological data; they would
not be affected in any way by individual 'taste'. Then scientific
marriage would have fulfilled the dream of Lycurgus: it would
have become a stage in military training.

Stalin's experiment failed, if we can trust the accounts of the
present state of the manners of youth in U.S.S.R. Nazi-ism belongs to the past. Yet the totalitarian temptation is still there. We
are not forbidden to imagine that our democracies will one day
yield to it in the name of some 'science' or sociological hygiene.
The enforced practice of eugenics *may* succeed there where all moral
doctrines had failed, resulting in the effective disappearance of any
'spiritual'—and hence artificial—need of passion. The cycle of
courtly love would be complete. The Europe of passion would be
no more. A new and unforeseeable Europe would be taking its
rise in the laboratory.

6

The Significance of the Breakdown

The better to see our situation, let us look at America—that
other Europe which has been released from both the routine
practices and traditional restraints of the old. No other
known civilization, in the 7,000 years that one civilization has been
succeeding another, has bestowed on the love known as *romance*

anything like the same amount of daily publicity by means of the screen, the hoarding, the letter-press and advertisements in magazines, by means of songs and pictures, and of current morals and of whatever defies them. No other civilization has embarked with anything like the same ingenuous assurance upon the perilous enterprise of making marriage coincide with love thus understood, and of making the first depend upon the second.

During a telephone strike in 1947, the women operators in the county town of White Plains, near New York, received the following call: 'My girl and I want to get married. We're trying to locate a justice of the peace. Is it an emergency?' The women telephone operators decided forthwith that it was. And the newspaper which reported the item headed it: 'Love is Classified as an Emergency.' This commonplace newspaper cutting provides an example of the perfectly natural beliefs of Americans, and that is how it is of interest. It shows that in America the terms 'love' and 'marriage' are practically equivalent; that when one 'loves' one must get married instantly; and, further, that 'love' should normally overcome all obstacles, as is shown every day in films, novels, and comic-strips. In reality, however, let romantic love overcome no matter how many obstacles, and it almost always fails at one. That is the obstacle constituted by time. Now, either marriage is an institution set up to be lasting—or it is meaningless. That is the first secret of the present breakdown, a breakdown of which the extent can be measured simply by reference to divorce statistics, where the United States heads the list of countries. To try to base marriage on a form of love which is unstable by definition is really to benefit the State of Nevada. To insist that no matter what film, even one about the atomic bomb, shall contain a certain amount of the romantic drug—and romantic more than erotic—known as 'love interest', is to give publicity to the germs that are making marriage ill, not to a cure.

Romance feeds on obstacles, short excitations, and partings; marriage, on the contrary, is made up of wont, daily propinquity, growing accustomed to one another. Romance calls for 'the faraway love' of the troubadours; marriage, for love of 'one's neighbour'. Where, then, a couple have married in obedience to a romance, it is natural that the first time a conflict of temperament or of taste becomes manifest the parties should each ask themselves: 'Why did I marry?' And it is no less natural that, obsessed by the universal propaganda in favour of romance, each should seize the first occasion to fall in love with somebody else. And thereupon it is perfectly logical to decide to divorce, so as to obtain from the new love, which demands a fresh marriage, a new promise of happiness—all three words, 'marriage', 'love', 'happiness', being synonyms. Thus, remedying boredom with a passing fever, 'he for the second time, she for the fourth', American men and women go in quest of 'adjustment'. They do not seek it, however, in the old situation, the one guaranteed—'for better, for worse'—by a vow. They seek it, on the contrary, in a fresh 'experience' regarded as such, and affected from the start by the same potentialities of failure as those which preceded it. That is how divorce assumes in the United States a less 'disastrous' character, and is even more 'normal', than in Europe. There where a European regards the rupture of a marriage as producing social disorder and the loss of a capital of joint recollections and experiences, an American has rather the impression that 'he is putting his life straight', and opening up for himself a fresh future. The economy of saving is once again opposed to that of squandering, as the concern to preserve the past is opposed to the concern to make a clean sweep in order to build something tidy, without compromise. But any man opposed to compromise is inconsistent in marrying. And he who would draw a draft on his future is very unwise to mention beforehand that he wishes to be allowed not to honour it; as did the young millionairess who told the newspaper men on the eve of her marriage: 'It's marvellous to be getting married *for the first time!*' A year later, she got divorced.

Whereupon a number of people propose to forbid divorce, or at least to render it very difficult. But it is marriage which, in my opinion, has been made too easy, through the supposition that let there be 'love' and marriage should follow, regardless of outmoded conventions of social and religious station, of upbringing and substance. It is certainly possible to imagine new conditions which candidates for marriage—that true 'co-existence' which should be enduring, peaceable, and mutually educative—should fulfil. It is possible to exact tests or ordeals bearing on whatever gives any human union its best chances of lasting: aims in life, rhythms of life, comparative vocations, characters, and temperaments. If marriage—that is to say, lastingness—is what is wanted, it is natural to ensure its conditions. But such reforms would have little effect in a world which retained, if not true passion, at least the nostalgia of passion that has grown congenital in western man.

The Myth v. Marriage

When marriage was established on social conventions, and hence, from the individual standpoint, on chance, it had at least as much likelihood of success as marriage based on 'love' alone. But the whole of western evolution goes from tribal wisdom to individual risk; it is irreversible, and it must be approved to the extent it tends to make collective and native destiny depend on personal decision.

It is also clear that the present breakdown of marriage, in Europe as in America, results from a plurality of profound or proximate causes, of which the cult of romance is but an instance. (But it was my due to myself to insist on it here.) For the quest for individual happiness to have precedence on social stability, and for respect of psychological evolution to have precedence on the meaning of a vow, is something which can be connected with the romantic complex. But there is more to it, and in other domains, or at other levels of reality, at times social and at other times psychical.

Woman's emancipation—her entrance into the professions and her claim to equality of treatment—is a perceptible factor in the breakdown. The popularization of psychological knowledge is another. Men and women of the twentieth century, even with only a smattering of the existence of Freudian complexes, of the play of repressions and inhibitions, and of the origin of neuroses, are inclined to require more than their ancestors did from marriage and from conjugal life. Those demands will go on growing with the diffusion of the 'human sciences', the early stammerings of which have already in perceptible measure modified the self-awareness of western man. Finally, there are signs of a more profound event—one possibly comparable to that which invaded the collective psyche in the twelfth century, and which I called in Book II the 'Reascent of the Shakti'. The strong revival of Mariology in the Roman Catholic Church with its popular millions; the most recent work of C. G. Jung and his school,[1] on the eternal Sophia, Wisdom, and Mother-Virgin; and also (and really otherwise) the revival of interest in Catharism shown by the *avant-garde* of European literature, and in the elevation of the

[1] Cf. C. G. Jung, *Antwort auf Hiob* (1952), where the author does not hesitate to write that the proclamation in 1950 of the Dogma of the Assumption of the Virgin marks the most important religious event since the Reformation. See also Henry Corbin's study of the Eternal Sophia in *Revue de Culture européenne*, No. 5, 1953.

The Significance of the Breakdown

'Child-Woman', saviour of rational man, or the repeated announcement that the feminine principle is about to get even with patriarchal pretensions[1]—all that allows the premonition of a vast evolution of the modern psyche in prospect, and even though the first principle and the implications of such an evolution are withheld from us, nevertheless an evolution that will possibly provide the future historians of our western society with the key to a breakdown of which we so far see but the superficial, sporadic, and incoherent symptoms.

We can feel how vain any attempt would be at present 'to resolve' the contradictions which so many men and women put up with in marriage. Harmonization or a new equipoise is being worked out, perhaps—invisibly. Its nature keeps it for the present out of range of individual awareness. Any solution that I might be tempted to offer, even if deemed 'it' in the next century, would be stamped today as ineffectual, or, if it could effect anything, would do more harm than good. If I had hit upon it, and had the power to make my contemporaries adopt it, I should carefully refrain from doing so. For a breakdown of this sort is no accident. To try to arrest it as a fever is stopped would be not so much to cure it as to deprive ourselves of any prospect of one day understanding its secret. And it would be at the same time a kind of cheating, either because a solution would mean really no more than an attempt to get back to the former equipoise, and how precarious that was the breakdown itself shows, or else because any solution must cast over the future of the community a theory or precepts reasonable enough in themselves, but the remote effects of which cannot be estimated so long as the general *significance* of the breakdown escapes us.

We shall be better employed in deciphering the message and in patiently decoding the ambiguous tidings which the breakdown brings us concerning ourselves—concerning our secret wishes, the genuine tendency—possibly creative—sometimes betrayed in our rebellions, our ingenuous illusions, and our sins. To seek to repair the breakdown of marriage by means of moral, social, or scientific measures inspired by the sole desire to stop further damage, might very well be to deny arbitrarily to this breakdown

---

[1] Cf. notably, and in addition to the works cited above on Catharism and Courtly Love, such books as *Arcane 17* by André Breton, the lyrical novels of Julien Gracq, the studies by Robert Graves concerning the Great Goddess, and by Adrian Turel on matriarchates.

what seems to be its actual character—namely, that of a quest, as yet carried on blindfold, for *a fresh equipoise* of the married couple —a harmony that will reconcile the invariably simultaneous, contrary, and legitimate demands of the stability and evolution of both the species and the individual, and indeed the needs both of the fulfilment of the person and of the Absolute that alone judges and raises up that person.

Book VII

ACTIVE LOVE, OR KEEPING FAITH

I

We Must Take Our Stand

How futile the intellectual attitude that would describe itself as being against passion! There is no arguing with passion, no reasoning with it; for it does not wish to have reason on its side. To succumb to passion is precisely to rest content with being in the wrong according to the world—in the great, irrevocable wrong of preferring death over life. To attack passionate love successfully would require a spiritual violence more lethal than this love itself. For first and last, at the beginning and the end of passion, there is no 'delusion' about man or about God—and *a fortiori* no moral delusion—but a crucial decision: a man wishes to be his own god.[1] Passion brands the heart the moment the cold-blooded serpent—the complete cynic—has whispered his eternally unfulfilled promise: *Eritis sicut dei*! How artless and innocent the moralist who thought to turn a man from taking this fatal, divinizing road by 'demonstrating' to him that it leads to ruin! By pleading every earthly reason, and offering him the support of all the arts of *living*, when earth is what this man contemns, and life is the fault he regards as needing to be redeemed! Such a man's passion can be overcome only by killing him before he can kill himself, and in some other way than he wishes to die.

As for rendering innocuous the area of culture into which passion has dug its roots, that is a task that the State will probably see to as part of its hygienic policy. But for me, here and now, the problem offers no loophole through relying upon the time to

[1] I confine myself to the limiting case of Tristan. There are cases of passion in Christian marriage, and in passion cases of the married status.

come. If indeed we must assume that nobody can be aware of the nature of his own desires nor plumb the depths of his own most secret inclinations, at least each may survey what he has done and face the consequences of the decisions he has ventured. All I now intend to offer, then, is a statement of the stand I personally have taken—of the choice that I am conscious of having made in my own life. It is no cut-and-dried solution. Probably there is no solution, as I have said above. Even were such a solution possible, it could avail only for me alone: nobody ever decides except for himself. But having written a whole book about passion, I must not shirk *completing* the description with an account of this feature of the subject, thanks to which the book will be lifted, not into some abstract sphere where passion cannot subsist, so that discussing it must be triviality, but into the concrete world where choice determines our lives.

2

A Critique of Marriage

If no argument that I can see is valid against true passion, so likewise it seems to me that reason is equally powerless to justify marriage; I feel indeed that every one of the extremely varied objections that the finest minds have ever urged against it is still *fully* valid. At all times the Philistine's reasons have betrayed a bad conscience beside the romantic's ironies; but in the face of plain veracity these reasons are utterly put to rout. The notorious peaceful fireside only exists at the level of a certain political speechifying, either middle-class or aiming to edify. Tolstoy describes it as 'hell'. And I think he deserves the greater credence. Inasmuch as when taken one by one most human beings of both sexes are either rogues or neurotics, why should they turn into angels the moment they are paired? Push open the first door that offers. The quiet which a wife is supposed to ensure the noble breadwinner, on his returning home at night exhausted and anxious to relax in domestic peace, ranges nine times out of ten from a restless running to and fro of little attentions to an uncontrolled bawling. Were some of the 'peaceful' conversation that enlivens 'the domestic hearth' of a business man or mechanic selected at haphazard and made into a gramophone record, censorship would for once have established a *raison d'être*!

Yes, the romantics are right; and so are the realists; and so are the scholars who declare in the name of their vocation that one must choose between writing books and producing children. *Aut liberi aut libri*, as Nietzsche put it. And Kierkegaard is right over them all, because, first, he extolled passion as being the highest value in the 'aesthetic stage' of life; then rose above passion by extolling marriage as being the highest value in the 'ethical stage' (the 'fullness of time'); and finally condemned marriage as the highest obstruction in the 'religious stage', since marriage fetters us to time where faith requires eternity. What objections can be brought against this man that he himself has not already more accurately stated? Kierkegaard is able to praise both the Philistine and the romantic, and to put them both so thoroughly in the right as to make them ashamed of ever having doubted themselves; but in the end he not only crushes the Philistine who is content to marry a brewer's widow or the young lunatic who is in love with a king's daughter, but also the pious man who has imagined that religion ought to be a happy union—a marriage with his own virtue. For the sinner's love of God is 'essentially unhappy', and this Christian passion is the only truth, a truth from which every one of our human 'duties' (including that of being happy) does but turn us aside. Kierkegaard first denounces the Protestant ministers who objected to celibacy; then Luther and Calvin who were both married; then the Fathers who praised marriage; and finally Saint Paul who suffered marriage. Christ alone lived like a Christian! How refute this extremist? Unbelievers are referred to the arguments of the romantics, which are valid against their secular moralizing; and believers to the arguments of Saint Paul, which are valid against their humanism. What does the Apostle say?

'It is good for a man not to touch a woman. Nevertheless, to avoid fornication, let every man have his own wife, and let every woman have her own husband. The wife hath not power of her own body, but the husband; and likewise also the husband hath not power of his own body, but the wife. Defraud ye not one the other, except it be with consent for a time, that ye may give yourselves to prayer; and come together again, that Satan tempt you not for incontinency. But I speak this by permission, and not of commandment. For it is better to marry than to burn. But as God hath distributed to every man, as the Lord hath called every one, so let him walk. Let every man abide in the same calling wherein he was called. They that use the world be as not abusing it: for the fashion of this world passeth away.'

And here comes the finishing stroke:

'He that is unmarried careth for the things that belong to the Lord, how he may please the Lord: But he that is married careth for the things that are of the world, how he may please his wife.'

Everything to be urged against marriage is true, and therefore should be urged against it, either from the romantic standpoint—if we believe in Iseult—or from the standpoint of the whole-hearted scholar—if we believe in our work—or from the purely spiritual standpoint—if we believe. Hence it is impossible to uphold marriage till we have passed beyond the first two criticisms, and are on the way to the third—that is, till we are keeping steadily before us the inhuman requirement of perfection as a perpetual question, as a goad that can prevent us from again exposing ourselves to human objections.

If I fail to consider the state which is not only beyond marriage but also beyond every human order, the state called the Kingdom of God ('There shall be neither men nor women'), my wisdom and hope are *restricted* to a relative perfection—the poise in imperfection that is marriage. Thereupon, if I cannot reach this poise, all I may do is to rebel against my creature state; yet if I reach this poise too readily, I become the Philistine pilloried by the romantics, or the moral being caught in the toils of society, and I am thereupon denied any understanding of those 'cruel' truths of the spirit spoken of by Nietzsche.

But if I am convinced that the Apostle is right and agree with him, I adopt an open mind towards the imperfect poise of marriage and—happily or unhappily—live in wait of perfection. I realize that it is a *wild* attempt I am making (although at the same time an altogether natural one) to live perfectly in imperfection. But I also realize that this attempt must possess an unshakable truth if it incessantly bears witness to what transcends every kind of consequence, however excellent.

3

Marriage as a Decision

Once we ask ourselves what is involved in choosing a man or a woman *for the rest of one's life*, we see that to choose is to wager. Both in the lower and the middle classes the wiseacres urge young men 'to think it over' before taking the decisive step. They thus foster the delusion that the choice of a wife or husband may be governed by a certain number of accurately weighable pros and cons. This is a crude delusion on the part of common sense. You may try as hard as you like to put all the probabilities at the outset in your own favour—and I am assuming that life allows you the spare time for such nice calculations—but you will never be able to foresee how you are going to develop, still less how the wife or husband you choose is going to, and still less again how the two of you together are going to. The factors involved are too diverse. Suppose you could weigh them as they are now (assuming them to be finite in number) and you were so deeply versed in the conduct of human affairs as to know the values of every one of them and their order, you would still be unable to foresee how a union entered upon with all the *facts* duly weighed was going to shape. Nature is said to have required several hundreds of thousands of years for the selection of those species which now seem to us adapted to their surroundings. And yet we have the presumption to suppose that all of a sudden in the course of a single life we may solve the problem of the adaptation to one another of two highly organized physical and moral beings! For this is what all unsatisfactorily married persons suppose whenever they grow convinced that a second or third trial is going to yield a closer approximation to 'happiness', notwithstanding that everything goes to show that even a hundred thousand trials would not provide the first inchoate and altogether empirical data upon which to build a science of 'happy marriage'. It needs to be recognized frankly that the problem with which we are confronted by the practical necessity of marriage becomes the more hopelessly insoluble the more we strive 'to solve' it in a rational way.

True, I have not stated the case quite fairly; for as a rule everything happens as if the happiness of a married pair actually did depend on a finite number of factors—character, beauty, fortune, social position, and so on. But as soon as individual demands are put forward, these external data lose importance, and it is imponderables that determine our decision.[1] Thereupon it is common sense that turns out to have argued unfairly in recommending that our choice should result from a mature and reasonable submission of the data to impersonal criteria.

But after all the logical fallacy is negligible; what matters is the moral fallacy which the logical implies. When a young engaged couple are encouraged to calculate the probabilities in favour of their happiness, they are being distracted from the truly moral problem. The attempt to minimize or to conceal the fact that, when considered objectively, a choice of this kind is a wager fosters the belief that everything depends on wisdom or on a set of rules, when actually everything depends on a *decision*. And yet, inasmuch as no set of rules can be anything but imperfect and provisional, if we are to be guided by rules we also need some kind of guarantee. But the only possible guarantee would be one supplied by the strength of the decision whereby we commit ourselves during the rest of our lives 'for better, for worse'. And it is precisely to the extent that we persuade ourselves that the matter is above all one of calculation and of weighing up that the decision in itself is made to seem secondary or superfluous. I therefore feel that it would be more appropriate, both to the essential nature of marriage and to the facts for young people to be taught that their choice must always have an arbitrary element, of which they are undertaking to bear the consequences, whether the consequences turn out happy or unhappy. I do not seek to defend acting on 'rash impulse'; to the extent that probabilities can be weighed, it would be stupid not to weigh them. But I insist that

---

[1] The further we get away from the *species* and the nearer we come to the *person*, the more choice becomes particular. And to this endowment of the beloved with a particular personality there may correspond an increasingly specific quality of instinctive behaviour. Such is Dr. Marañón's argument in favour of monogamy.

the guarantee of a union in appearance sensible never lies in this appearance. It must lie in that irrational event, a decision that we venture upon in spite of everything and that lays the foundation of a new life in being a consent to take new chances.

Let me forestall any misunderstanding. 'Irrational' in no way means 'sentimental'. To choose a woman for wife is not to say to Miss So-and-So: 'You are the ideal of my dreams, you more than gratify all my desires, you are the Iseult altogether lovely and desirable—and endowed with a suitable dowry—of whom I want to be the Tristan.' For this would be deceit, and nothing enduring can be founded on deceit. Nobody in the world can gratify me; no sooner were I gratified than I would change! To choose a woman for a wife is to say to Miss So-and-So: 'I want to live with you just as you are.' For this really means: 'It is you I choose *to share* my life with me, and that is the only *evidence* there can be that I love you.' If anybody says, 'Is that all?'—and this is no doubt what many young people will say, having been led by virtue of the myth to expect goodness knows what divine transports—he must have had little experience of solitariness and dread, little experience indeed of solitary dread.

Alone a decision of this kind, irrational but not sentimental, sober but in no way cynical, can serve as the basis for a real fidelity; and I do not say: 'A fidelity that will prove a recipe for "happiness"'; I only say: 'A feasible fidelity, because it is not being wrecked at birth by some necessarily inaccurate calculation.'

4

On Keeping Troth

The morals of marriage are distorted by the way the plighting of a troth is made into a problem when no problem ought to arise till *after* a troth has been plighted and is considered to be absolute. The problematical element in marriage belongs not to *cur* but to *quomodo*, to the 'how' and not to the 'why'. Kierkegaard says: 'Morality does not set out from an ignorance which needs to be changed into knowledge, but from a knowledge that requires to be put into practice.' It is not the nature of the pledge exchanged in marriage that is problematical, but the consequences involved by the pledge. (Likewise, theology is distorted by setting out from the 'problem of God'—exactly as though in unbelief—when the *real* problem is to know how to obey Him.) For a troth does not have to give its reasons, or then it is not a troth, any more than anything else potentially noble and great would be; any more than passion!

The moralists, and also some of the sociologists, have tried to maintain that monogamy is natural, and, moreover, beneficial. The theme is one open to interminable discussion. And it will become highly pertinent the day men behave rationally and in obedience to their own best interests, the day they no longer have passions and cease to prefer error as such, and no longer deserve the disturbing epithet of 'human' in the active sense. Meanwhile, I fancy that men and women as they are now must look upon fidelity as the least natural of virtues, the one most inimical to 'Happiness'. In their eyes and as they put it, faithful marriage can only exist as the result of an 'inhuman' effort. Their fundamental claim, their religion of Life, is diametrically opposed to it. They think fidelity is a discipline dictated (to our spontaneous impulses and desires) by an absurd and cruel prejudice, or else is a prudent abstinence. Or else again they regard it as the consequence of an inability to live to the full; of a spiritless liking for what is comfortable and conventional; of a lack of imagination; of a contemptible timidity; or of a sordid calculation. The habit of people today, their acquired nature, is to make the most of every situation for its own sake, without any longer referring their conduct to what 'judges' and 'measures' the enjoyment which they thereby obtain. Actually, an acquired respect for the social order is the only thing that still upholds the notion of fidelity. But this is not treated as a serious obstruction, and is circumvented in a hundred ways. Listen to the excuses of a husband who deceives his wife. He may say: 'It's of no importance, it doesn't alter our relations, it's merely a passing affair, a lapse without a sequel', or else: 'It's absolutely vital for me, and tremendously more important than all your petty morals and assurances of bourgeois happiness!' Between a cynical attitude and tragic romanticism there is no real contradiction, as I showed earlier.[1] In each case it is a matter of *escaping* from some actual pledge, because a pledge is thought to be a hateful limitation.

Forgoing any rationalist or hedonist form of apology, I propose to speak only of a troth that is observed *by virtue of the absurd* —that is to say, simply because it has been pledged—and by virtue of being an absolute which will uphold husband and wife as persons. Fidelity, it must be admitted, stands emphatically athwart the stream of values nowadays admired by nearly every one. Fidelity is extremely *unconventional*. It contradicts the general belief in the revelatory value of both spontaneity and manifold experiences. It denies that in order to remain lovable a beloved must display the greatest possible *number* of qualities. It denies that its own goal is happiness. It offensively asserts first, that its aim is obedience to a Truth that is believed in, and secondly, that it is the expression of a wish to be constructive. For fidelity is not in the least a sort of conservatism, but rather a construction. An 'absurdity' quite as much as passion, it is to be distinguished from passion by its persistent refusal to submit to its own dream, by its persistent need of acting in behalf of the beloved, by its being persistently in contact with a reality which it seeks to control, not to flee.

I maintain that fidelity thus understood sets up the person. For the person is manifested like something made, in the widest

---

[1] *Gauloiserie* as much as passion having been an escape from reality, a way of idealizing it. Cf. p. 186, above.

sense of making. It is built up as a thing is made, thanks to a making, and in the same conditions as we make things, its first condition being a fidelity to something that before was not, but now is in process of being created. Person, made thing, fidelity—the three terms are neither separable nor separately intelligible. All three presuppose that a stand has been taken, and that we have adopted what is fundamentally the attitude of creators. Hence in the humblest lives the plighting of a troth introduces the opportunity of making and of rising to the plane of the person—on condition, of course, that the pledge has not been for 'reasons' in the giving of which there is a reservation which will allow those reasons to be repudiated some day when they have ceased to appear 'reasonable'! The pledge exchanged in marriage is the very type of a *serious* act, because it is a pledge given once and for all. The irrevocable alone is serious. Every life, even the most disinherited one, has some immediate potentiality of dignity, and it is in an 'absurd' fidelity that this dignity may be attained—in a readiness to say 'No' to dazzling passion, when there is every earthly reason for saying 'Yes'—to say 'No' by virtue of the absurd, by virtue of an old promise, of human unreason, of a reason of faith, of a pledge given to God and underwritten by God. And perhaps later on, afterwards, a man or woman may find that the folly of the accepted sacrifice was the greatest wisdom; and that the happiness he or she has forgone is being restored, even as Isaac was restored to Abraham. But this can only happen if he or she has not expected it. And it may also be that nothing rewards our loss: we are among dimensions where ordinary worldly measures no longer avail. But are we still capable of imagining a dignity and greatness in no way romantic and the opposite of excited ardour? The fidelity of which I am speaking is foolish, and yet our folly is then of the most sober and everyday kind. *A sober folly that rather closely simulates behaving sensibly*; that is neither heroic nor challenging, but a patient and fond application.

However, everything has still not been made plain. Tristan also was faithful. And so is every true passion. (Not to mention the successive fidelities which we display in one after another of our 'affairs' nor the fidelity of all those Tristans who are really Don Juans in slow time.) It remains accordingly to show where the difference lies, and to ascertain why a faithful husband should not simply be the man who has identified his wife with Iseult.

When the lover in the Manichaean legend has undergone the

great ordeals of initiation, he is met, you remember, by a 'dazzling maiden' who welcomes him with the words: 'I am thyself!' So with fidelity in the myth, and Tristan's. Fidelity is then a mystic narcissism—usually unconscious of course, and imagining itself to be true love for *the other*. In analysing the courtly legends, however, we saw that Tristan is not in love with Iseult, but with love itself, and beyond love he is really in love with death—that is, with the only possible release there can be for a self guilty and enslaved. Tristan is true neither to a pledge nor to a symbolical being named Iseult. She is but a lovely pretext, and all the time he is being true to his most profound and secret passion. The myth seizes on 'the death instinct' inseparable from any form of created life, and transfigures it by bestowing upon it an essentially spiritual goal. To destroy oneself, to despise happiness is thereupon a way of salvation and of acceding to a higher life, to 'the highest bliss of being' sung of by the expiring Isolde. It is a fidelity destructive of life, but that also destroys the fault in divinizing the now 'innocent' *self*!

Of this original mystical form, 'passionate troth' has by now preserved no more than the illusion of giving access to a more ardent life. But the power of the illusion betrays that the original religion still obscurely survives—a religion that was prior to our modern 'instinct' and that secretes the intimate riddle of passion at depths which our psychologists are unable to plumb.

'Our vows were not exchanged for this world', Novalis wrote, having in mind his lost love. The words are at once a moving expression of courtly fealty and an *irrevocable* negation of life. But the troth of marriage is, on the contrary, a pledge given for *this* world. Inspired by an unreason 'mystical' (if you like) and, if not hostile, at least indifferent to happiness and the vital instinct, fidelity in marriage requires a re-entry into the real world, whereas courtesy meant only an escape from it. In marriage the loving husband or wife vows fidelity first of all to *the other* at the same time as to his or her true self. And whereas Tristan showed himself constant in a steadfast refusal, in a desire to exclude and deny creation in its diversity and to prevent the world from encroaching upon spirit, the fidelity of the married couple is acceptance of one's fellow-creature, a willingness to take the other as he or she is in his or her intimate particularity. Let me insist that fidelity in marriage cannot be merely that negative attitude so frequently imagined; it must be active. To be content not to deceive one's wife or husband would be an indication of indigence, not one of love. Fidelity demands far more: it wants the good of the beloved, and when it acts in behalf of that good it is creating in its own presence the neighbour. And it is by this roundabout way through the other that the self rises into being a person—beyond its own happiness. Thus as persons a married couple are a mutual creation, and to become persons is the double achievement of 'active love'. What denies both the individual and his natural egotism is what constructs a person. At this point faithfulness in marriage is discovered to be the law of a new life, though not of natural life (that would be polygamy) and not of life for the sake of death (that was Tristan's passion).

The love of Tristan and Iseult was the anguish of being *two*; and its culmination was a headlong fall into the limitless bosom of Night, there where individual shapes, faces, and destinies all vanish: 'Iseult is no more, Tristan no more, and no name can any longer part us!' The other has to cease to be the other, and therefore, to cease to be altogether, in order that he or she shall cease to make me suffer and that there may be only 'I myself am the world!' But married love is the end of anguish, the acceptance of a limited being whom I love because he or she is a summons to be created, and that in order to witness to our alliance this being turns with me towards day.

A life *allied* with mine, for the rest of our lives—that is the miracle of marriage. Another life that wills my good as much as its own, because it is united with mine: and were this not for the rest of our lives, it would be a menace, such as is ever present in the exchanged pleasures of an 'affair'! But few people now seem to be able to distinguish between an obsession which is undergone and a destiny that we shoulder.

Hence it must be shown with the help of a plain example.

To be in love is not necessarily *to love*. To be in love is a state; to love, an act. A state is suffered or undergone; but an act has to be decided upon. Now, the *promise* which marriage means cannot fairly be made to apply to the future of a state in which I am at the moment, but it can and should mortgage the future of conscious acts which I take on—to love, to remain faithful, to bring up my children. That shows how different are the meanings of the word 'to love' in the world of Eros and in the world of Agape. It is seen even better when it is noticed that the God of Scripture *orders* us to love. The first commandment of the Decalogue is:

'Thou shalt love the Lord thy God with all thy heart, with all thy soul, and with all thy mind'; it can only be concerned with acts. It would be altogether absurd to demand of a man a state of sentiment. The imperative, 'Love God and thy neighbour as thyself', creates structures of active relations. The imperative, 'Be in love!' would be devoid of meaning; or, if it could be obeyed, would deprive a man of his freedom.

5

Eros Rescued by Agape

Thereupon charitable love, Christian love—which is Agape —appears at last and risen to its full height. It is the expression of being in action. And it is Eros, passionate love, pagan love, that spread through the European world the poison of an idealistic *askesis*—all that Nietzsche unjustly lays at the door of Christianity. And it is Eros, not Agape, that glorified our death instinct and sought 'to idealize' it. But Agape has got its own back by rescuing Eros. For Agape is incapable of destruction, and does not even wish to destroy what destroys.

'I desire not the death of a sinner, but that he may live.'

The god Eros is the slave of death because he wishes to elevate life above our finite and limited creature state. Hence the same impulse that leads us *to adore* life thrusts us into its negation. There lies the profound woe and despair characterizing Eros, his inexpressible bondage; and in making this bondage evident Agape has delivered Eros from it. Agape is aware that our terrestrial and temporal life is unworthy of adoration and even of being killed, but that it can be accepted in obedience to the Eternal. For, after all, it is here below that our fate is being decided. It is on earth that we must love. In the next world, we shall meet, not divinizing Night, but the forgiveness of our Creator and Judge.

Active Love, or Keeping Faith

This prospect is one that natural man was unable to imagine. He was condemned to put his faith in Eros—to trust in his most powerful desire and to expect release through this desire. Yet Eros could lead him but to death. But a man who believes the revelation of Agape suddenly beholds the circle broken: faith delivers him from natural religion. Now he *may* hope for something; he is aware that there is some other release from sin. And thereupon Eros in turn has been relieved of his fatal office and delivered from his fate. *In ceasing to be a god, he ceases to be a demon.*[1] And he finds his proper place in the provisional economy of Creation and of what is human.

The Pagans could not do otherwise than make Eros into a god; Eros was the most powerful force within them, the most dangerous and the most mysterious, the most deeply bound up with the event of living. All pagan religions deify Desire. All seek to be upheld and saved by Desire, which is thus instantly transformed into the greatest enemy of life, the seduction of Nothingness. But once the Word was made flesh and had spoken to us in human language, we learned the tidings that it is not we who have to deliver ourselves but God Who will deliver us, *God Who loved man first* and came down to him. Salvation is no longer something beyond, and ever a little more out of reach during the interminable ascent of Desire, the consumer of life; it is here below and is attainable through obedience to the Word.

And hence what have we to fear from desire? It loses its absolute hold over us the moment we cease to deify it. This is attested by the display of fidelity in marriage. For the foundation of this fidelity is an initial refusal *on oath* 'to cultivate' the illusions of passion, to render them a secret worship, or to expect from them any mysterious intensification of life. I may also indicate how it is so by consideration of something well known. Christianity has asserted the complete equality of the sexes, and this as plainly as possible. Saint Paul says:

'The wife hath not power of her own body, but the husband; and likewise also the husband hath not power of his own body, but the wife.'

Once she is man's equal, woman cannot be 'man's goal'.[2] Yet at

---

[1] Sin, it has been remarked by R. de Pury, is not Eros, but the sublimation of Eros.

[2] As Novalis supposed, thereby effecting a revival of courtly mysticism and of the old Celtic tradition.

the same time she is spared the bestial abasement that sooner or later must be the price of divinizing a creature. But her equality is not to be understood in the contemporary sense of giving rise to rights. It belongs to the mystery of love. It is but the sign and evidence of the victory of Agape over Eros. For a truly mutual love exacts and creates the equality of those loving one another. God showed His love for man by exacting that man should be holy even as God is holy. And a man gives evidence of his love for a woman by treating her as a completely human person, not as if she were the spirit of the legend—half-goddess, half bacchante, a compound of dreams and sex.

But from these premisses let us proceed to the concrete psychology of married equality. When a man is faithful to one woman, he looks on other women in quite another way, a way unknown to the world of Eros: other women turn into persons instead of being reflections or means. This 'spiritual exercise' develops new powers of judgement, self-possession, and respect.[1] The opposite in this of an erotic man, a steadfast man no longer strives to see a woman as merely an attractive or desirable body, as merely an unintended movement or a fascinating expression; he feels, as soon as tempted, the difficult and serious mystery of an independent, alien existence; he realizes that he has been desiring only an illusory or fleeting aspect of what is actually a complete life, and that perhaps this aspect has been but a projection of his own reverie. Thus temptation recedes disconcerted instead of *making* itself into an obsession; and fidelity is made secure by the clear-sightedness it induces. The sway of the myth is by so much weakened, and although this sway is unlikely ever to be entirely abolished without leaving traces in hearts drugged by images, hearts such as men harbour today, at least it loses its efficacy. The myth no longer determines a person.

In other words, it may be said that fidelity secures itself against unfaithfulness by becoming accustomed not to separate desire from love. For if desire travels swiftly and anywhere, love is slow and difficult; love actually does pledge one for the rest of one's life, and it exacts nothing less than this pledge in order to disclose its real nature. That is why a man who believes in marriage can

---

[1] 'Respect', as I use the word here, means that we recognize in a being the fullness of a person. A person, according to Kant's famous definition ['A person is the subject whose actions are imputable.'—Translator], is what cannot be used by man as an instrument or thing.

no longer believe seriously in 'love at first sight', still less in the 'irresistible' nature of passion. 'Love at first sight' is no doubt a legend that was accredited by Don Juan, as the 'irresistible' nature of passion was earlier accredited by Tristan. Neither the excuse nor the alibi can deceive any one who does not wish to be deceived because he thinks deception will be to his advantage; they are tropes of a romantic rhetoric, and allowable in that form, but only becoming ridiculous if confused with psychological truth.

.My analysis of the myth has made it plain why people *like to believe* in irresistibility, which is an alibi invoked by the guilty. 'I didn't do it, I wasn't there; it was an irresistible power that acted in the stead of my person.' That is the pious lie[1] of a minister of Eros. But what a lot of self-encouragement resides in the word 'irresistible'! As for 'love at first sight', it is supposed to excuse Don Juan's lapses. All literature invites us to accept it as the sign of a very strongly sensual nature. Don Juan, the man of loves at first sight who led a 'tempestuous' life, passes for a kind of super-man or supermale. This is a myth with an indeterminate power, hovering over moral contingencies; but we may be confident that it is a product of *compensatory dreams*—compensating either for an imposed and detested fidelity, or for a masochistic jealousy, or for the beginnings of impotence. Indeed, Don Juan's behaviour is typical enough of one kind of sexual weakness. It is in a state of general weariness, sexually localized, that the body is led to commit these sudden lapses, not unakin to the puns that obsess a weary mind. But when body and mind are normally vigorous the chances of love at first sight must be very slender. It would thus seem that monogamy, in making sexual relations normal, becomes the best assurance of pleasure—that is, of the entirely carnal eros, which is not in the least to be deified.[2]

It may be objected that marriage must then be simply 'the grave of love'. But it is of course the myth once again that suggests this, thanks to its obsession of obstructed love. It would be more accurate to echo Croce and to say that 'marriage is the grave of savage

[1] On the unmistakable connexion between passion and lying, I have insisted, pp. 46–49, and p. 167, above.

[2] I must repeat, however, that arguments of this kind cannot serve as a foundation for the institution of marriage. It is simply a matter of observation that refutes the current fancies which we owe to the Tristan myth and its Donjuanesque negative. But such 'reasons' are altogether ineffective as regards anyone who prefers the myth and wishes to believe in the revelations of passion.

love',[1] and more often the grave of sentimentality. Savage and natural love is manifested in *rape*—the evidence of love among all savage tribes. But rape, like polygamy, is also an indication that men are not yet in a stage to apprehend the presence of an actual person in a woman. This is as much as to say that they do not know how to love. Rape and polygamy deprive a woman of her equality by reducing her to sex. Savage love empties human relations of personality. On the other hand, a man does not control himself owing to lack of 'passion' (meaning 'power of the libido'), but precisely because he loves and, in virtue of his love, will not inflict himself. He refuses to commit an act of violence which would be the denial and destruction of the person. He thus indicates that his dearest wish is for the other's good. His egotism goes round via the other. This, it will be granted, is a notable revolution.

And we may now pass beyond that altogether negative and privative statement of Croce's, and at last define marriage as *the institution in which passion is 'contained', not by morals, but by love.*

6

Paradoxes of the Western Attitude

These few remarks on passion and marriage will have set forth the fundamental antagonism of Eros and Agape—that is to say, the antagonism of the two religions that are struggling for the upper hand in the West. It seems to me that once we are aware of this antagonism, of its historical and psychological origins, and of the spiritual issues involved, we must feel the need of revising a number of our current opinions—in the sphere of morality first and foremost, but in the spheres of

---

[1] Benedetto Croce, *Etica e Politica*.

culture and philosophy as well. As a conclusion to this work, I need doubtless only state the *corrective principle* which my inquiry into passion may be said to establish.

In the eyes of Orientals, the outstanding characteristic of the European attitude is the importance it attaches to passionate forces. They regard this as a heritage of Christianity and as the explanation of our strenuousness. And it is true that the three terms, 'Christianity', 'passion', and 'strenuousness', correspond to the three predominant features of the European psyche, so that such opinions seem self-evident. Yet if the conclusions which I have drawn from my investigation of the courtly myth are accurate, this view of Christian Europe calls for considerable correction.

In the first place, it was not Christianity that caused passion to be cultivated; it was a heresy of Eastern origin. This heresy began by spreading in precisely those regions which Christianity had not yet fully evangelized and where pagan cults still flourished in secret. Passionate love is not Christian love, nor even what has been called 'a Christian by-product', nor 'the change of address of a force which Christianity aroused and directed towards God'.[1] It is rather a by-product of Manichaeism. More accurately, it became a cult through the collaboration of the Manichaean religion with our most ancient religious beliefs and through the struggle that ensued between heresy and Christian orthodoxy. That is a first important correction. Next, it is imperative to point out that our well-known 'Western strenuousness' has two distinct sources. If the term is intended to refer to our war frenzy I have shown that historically this frenzy is connected in the clearest possible manner with passion. Like passion, the taste for war follows on a notion that life should be ardent, a notion which is the mask of a wish for death. It is an inverted strenuousness, and self-destructive. But our strenuousness has another aspect, and one not to be connected with passion for a moment. I mean, our mechanical genius, which is the reflection of a human attitude the exact opposite of passionate: a faith in the value of created things, of matter, and of the action of the mind upon the visible world. Neither passion nor the heretical faith out of which it sprang could have inspired a belief that the control of Nature should be the aim of our lives, inasmuch as originally this control

[1] Leo Ferrero, *Désespoirs*. The problem of passion is admirably defined by this little book in its psychological data.

was held to be a function of the Demiurge, and salvation was held to lie precisely in an escape away from his devilish rule.[1]

We may ask ourselves whether this most striking expression of the restlessness of the European mind has not resulted from a disposition peculiar to our Continent, or whether it is not due to some indirect influence of the Christian ambition defined by the Apostle as the deliverance of the creature from the bondage of corruption—an ambition that may be taken as tending to re-establish the Cosmos under the original rule from which sin has caused it to break away. In Europe the Christian ambition to change the souls and conduct of sinners has given rise to an ambition to transform the human environment (whence comes the myth of revolution) and also the natural environment (whence came the attention bestowed on technics). But supposing Christianity had been established in India or China two thousand years ago, would the results there be by now the same? The answer to this question is irrelevant here. It is enough to note that the Christiano-occidental (or creative) components of European strenuousness have been inspired by a will exactly the opposite of that of passion.

What is misleading, and what indeed has produced an inevitable misunderstanding about our contemporary restlessness, is that war and our mechanical genius have been in collusion. When at the French Revolution war became 'national', it at once needed the assistance of every creative force, and that of mechanical force in particular. Thus did the passion of war become the principal motive power of mechanical research. This has been very obvious since 1915. The truly monstrous combination of the death-dealing and creative forces changed the nature both of war and of our technical genius. Mechanized war got rid of passion, and technics, in becoming lethal, were unfaithful to the ambitions with which they had originated. Europe is possibly going to succumb to the fate it has thus prepared for itself. But obviously it is not Christianity—as so many writers allege—that will be responsible for the disaster. The catastrophic spirit in Europe is not Christian.[2] On the contrary, it is Manichaean. That is what those

[1] 'The theory of the Ancients that work is unworthy of a free man recurs in chivalry', Henri Pirenne remarks in his *Histoire de l'Europe*, p. 113.

[2] It will be said: What about the Apocalypse? But the disasters heralded in the Book of Revelation represent our *punishment* and not our deliverance. It is not death or disincarnation that offers salvation; but the act of grace performed by God.

Active Love, or Keeping Faith

who identify Christianity with Europe commonly overlook. Everything European is not Christian. If therefore Europe were to succumb to its evil genius, it would be through having for too long cultivated the para-Christian or anti-Christian religion of passion.

Should we infer that passion has been *the Eastern temptation held before Europe*? Inasmuch as passion did not spread in our history and culture earlier than the twelfth and thirteenth centuries—and then only thanks to a peremptory impulsion from heresy in Southern France—it turns out that our 'fatal' beliefs reached us out of the Near East and Persia, the regions in which unmistakably the Heresy first sprang up. Yet the same beliefs did not have the same effects in the East? No doubt, but in the East they were not obstructed and attacked as they were among us. *Hence it has been our dramatic luck to have opposed passion with weapons foredoomed to foster it.* Such is the persistent temptation to which we owe our finest creations. But what gives rise to life gives rise also to death. Let merely an accent be displaced, and strenuousness changes its sign. We may at least declare that the religious attitude of Europeans and the institution most typical of their morals—marriage—are now at a point where it is possible to behold this displacement of accent upon which everything depends.

Unquestionably a Christianized European differs from an Oriental in that he has the capacity to delve into the particularity of created beings. There lies the real clue to our faithfulness. The wisdom of the East pursues understanding in the progressive abolition of diversity. We, on the other hand, seek the density of being in the distinct person, and have constantly explored it more deeply as thus manifested. 'The more we understand individual things, the more we understand God', Spinoza says. This attitude amounts to defining my West, and likewise the ultimate conditions of fidelity, the person, and marriage—and of the rejection of passion. It assumes the acceptance of diversity, and that our way of taking hold of the concrete is first to accept its limitations. A Christian takes the world as it is, and not as he may dream that it is. His 'creative' activity thereupon consists in recapturing in the depth of individual things all the diversity of the created universe, and that is how it happened that man at the Renaissance was called a microcosm.

Whatever destroys this essential will, or distracts from it, must compromise fidelity and furnish passion with new opportunities.

It is *our* life and *our* death. Hence the present breakdown of marriage is the least misleading indication of a western decadence. There are of course other indications, and in the most various spheres—the cult of multiplicity, the poetry of escape, the way nationalist passions encroach upon culture—whatever tends to wreck the person. But they are complex and collective happenings which often elude personal apprehension. The indication given by the breakdown of marriage can be brought home to us, and it warns us quite unmistakably. No other sign is more obvious or more everyday, no other is so fully confirmed within our secret selves.

7

Beyond Tragedy

In many respects this book appears to be the account of a gradual decay. It has insisted on the degradation of the myth, on the breakdown of marriage, on the disparagement of convention and of formal modes, on the extrusion of the passionate frenzy into spheres where it may be in course of encompassing the collapse of civilization. All that is fact, and all that holds out a threat to us. Indeed, it is the more perilous in proportion as we ignore or dispute it. Yet my gradual diagnosis of it has repeatedly yielded glimpses of how it might be overcome. For instance, it may be that Europe, after a *crisis* of totalitarianism (and assuming that this is not fatal), will recover the significance of a fidelity that is secured by substantial institutions—to the person's measure. Perhaps, the very excesses of passion will excite a reaction in the guise of new *formal modes*, and there will thus be set up a new classical age. After all, however, is not this anxious concern over the morrow now lining so many brows another of the temptations of passion? Our lives are not staked in the temporal beyond, but in the decisions establishing our faithfulness that must always be taken in the present. Whatever may befall, hap or mishap, the fate of the world matters much less to us than does an understanding of our immediate duties. 'For the fashion of this world passeth away', but out vocation is always *hic et nunc*, in that act performed by the Eternal, thanks to which we grasp our hope.

Two themes for reflection, adumbrated already here and there in these pages, can provide an *open* conclusion. I have striven to unravel certain problems propounded in terms of history and psychology; but the entirely objective observations to which I have been led are not self-sufficient. They call for certain decisions. They introduce a fresh uncertainty which is not altogether as simplified as the passion-fidelity dilemma may suggest. Actually, no problem is ever *understood* till we have foreseen how to solve it and pass beyond it. And it is no good trying to pass beyond the passion-fidelity dilemma by simply denying one of its horns. I have already said, and I insist again, that to doom passion in theory can only be to try to suppress one pole of our creative tension. Actually, such a thing is not feasible. The Philistine who is ready 'to condemn' all passion *a priori* confesses thereby never to have experienced passion of any kind. He is not one who has passed beyond the point of conflict, but one who has not yet reached it. The only advance it can be hoped that he might make would be achieved through the breakdown of his confidence—that is, through his being engulfed in some dramatically passionate experience.[1] But beyond a passion that has been experienced all the way to its fatal dead-end, what can we henceforth have an inkling of? The two themes for reflection I am about to sketch indicate

---

[1] Must we go still further than Kierkegaard went beyond the 'ethical stage'? I sometimes feel, indeed, I sometimes realize, that from the standpoint of the Christian faith there is doubtless nothing to be gained by a 'regulation of morals' for non-Christians. On the contrary, that would be a way of protecting them from the authentic human despair which might bring them to believe. The cure of a soul, not in the sense of middle-class moral hygienics, but in the Christian sense that makes the desired end that an unbeliever should come to believe, ought to make us wish that non-Christians might go right through to the far side of the 'happiness' of passion. But all efforts are directed to keeping them on *this side* of it. So that the only concrete *far side* that they are able to wish for or imagine is the 'disorder of the passions'. But it needs to be added that a man abandoned to his disorderliness experiences a despair for which the remedy may well seem to him to be what St. Paul calls the Law. And it is only by renunciation of the Law *as thus understood* that we can be led to faith.

Beyond Tragedy

two ways of going beyond, consistent with this book, but outside the schematic limits of all exposition.

The first theme is given its bearings by reference to a personal drama the biographical details of which are common property. The event which proved for Kierkegaard to be the starting-point of all his reflection was his breaking off his engagement to Regine. The private causes of the break are still partially mysterious. It was an unsharable and unutterable 'secret' that in Kierkegaard's view obstructed his entering into marriage, because this marriage was to have been happy according to the world. The indispensable *obstruction* to the advance of passion was on this occasion so thoroughly subjective, peculiar, and unamenable to comparison, that its gravity will not be suspected unless with the help of a reference to Kierkegaard's faith. According to him, the relations which man—finite and sinful—can have with his God—who is Eternal and Holy—are exclusively those of a love *fatally* unhappy. 'God creates everything *ex nihilo*', he says, and whomsoever God elects by His love, 'He begins by reducing to nothing'. From the standpoint of the world and of natural life, God thus appears as 'my mortal enemy'. Here we are being brought up against the extreme limit, the pure springs of passion; and in the same moment we are thrust into the heart of the Christian faith! For, behold! the man now dead to the world, killed by infinite love, has to go forward and to live in the world as if he had no more urgent and higher task. 'The knight of faith', when met with in the street, has nothing superhuman about him: 'he looks like a tax-collector', and behaves like any decent middle-class citizen. And yet 'he has renounced all things with an infinite resignation, and if he has recovered all things in the sequel, it is *by virtue of the absurd* [that is, by virtue of faith]. He is constantly leaping into the infinite, but faultlessly and with complete confidence, so that he drops back into the finite, and nothing is noticeable about him but the finite.'[2]

Thus the extremity of passion—death in love—introduces a new life, where passion never ceases to be present, but is under the most jealous incognito; for it is now far more than regal, it is divine. On the analogy of faith, it may thereupon be understood how *passion*—whatever the plane in which it is manifested—attains its true future state and salvation thanks only to that *act* of obedience which is a life steadfast and true. To live 'like everybody else'

[1] Søren Kierkegaard, *Frygt og Baevan* (Fear and Trembling).

321

and yet 'by virtue of the absurd' becomes an offensive piece of deceit in the eyes of any one who does not *believe* in the absurd; but it is far more than a synthesis, and something infinitely more and other than a 'solution', for any one who does believe that God keeps faith, and that love never deceives the beloved.

No doubt Kierkegaard did not succeed in 'recovering' the finite world except in his *awareness* of its loss, a loss that was tremendously fruitful for his genius. He never recovered Regine, but he never stopped loving her or dedicating his books to her. And perhaps it is in the life-work put into those books that he was most truly faithful. We need not seek anywhere but in his unquestionably unique vocation for being a Solitary the explanation of his failure as a man. Others are endowed with some other vocation; they marry Regine, and passion lives again in their marriage, but then 'by virtue of the absurd'. And they are day by day astounded to find that they are happy. Such things are too elementary and too complete for words to interpose their dilatoriness between the question which they raise and the answer returned in our living experience.

The other theme for reflection is perhaps not entirely unconnected with this. It may even be regarded as a particular aspect of the transition back to passion that Kierkegaard describes. At the summit of the spiritual ascent which Saint John of the Cross narrates in the most ardently passionate language, he knows that the soul attains to a state in which it is perfectly in the presence of the 'loving object of love. He calls this mystic marriage. The soul then treats its love with a kind of semi-divine *indifference*. It has got beyond doubt and beyond the point at which separateness seems to be like a rending; it wishes for nothing that its love does not wish for; it is at one with this love in duality, and the duality is now simply a dialogue of grace and obedience. And the desire for the highest passion is thereupon being gratified in the very act of obeying, so that the soul is no longer being cauterized and branded; there is not even any awareness of love, only the happy moderation of acting.

Thus, on the analogy of faith, passion, born of a fatal desire for mystical union, may be regarded as open to being surpassed and fulfilled only thanks to the *meeting* with some *other*, and the admission of this other's alien life and ever distinct person, which, although distinct, holds the promise of unending alliance and begins a real dialogue. Then dread having been banished by response and nostalgia by presence, they both cease to summon the happiness it is expected to feel and savour, cease to suffer, and accept our daylight. It is then that marriage is possible. We are two in contentment.

A last time, however, I shall side with moderation. Married couples are not saints, and sin is not some error which we may renounce one of these days in order to adopt a more accurate truth. We are unendingly and incessantly in the thick of the struggle between nature and grace; unendingly and incessantly unhappy and then happy. But the horizon has not remained the same. A fidelity maintained in the Name of what does not change as we change will gradually disclose some of its mystery: *beyond tragedy another happiness waits*. A happiness resembling the old, but no longer belonging to the form of the world, for this new happiness transforms the world.

21 February–21 June 1938 (Revised 1954).

Appendix

INCONCLUSIVE AND SCIENTIFICO-POLEMICAL POSTSCRIPT

translated by

DANIELLE SALTI

I

Influence and Attacks

This book, written in a few months at the age of thirty-two, has not ceased to question me. Thirty-two years later, I return to it and find that the problems it addressed remain, at least for me, as new as they were then. Here I wish only to reply to some of my critics and correct a few errors, not all of them theirs, as one may well imagine.

At the highest polyvalent and unclassifiable level of wild transdisciplinarity, my book could not fail to provoke contradictory reactions. Labelled in turn as 'fine entertainment' and 'the most important book written on love', as 'fragile authority' and 'the bible of the genre', it has not ceased to influence scores of novelists, poets, and filmmakers during the past three decades, and to shock most scholars. This is because its purpose was to disclose spiritual and emotional phenomena, which a certain type of eminent specialist will always be tempted to view as 'difficulties', obscurities, or incongruities in 'posing the problem', incompatible with the seriousness of scholarship and the compartmentalization of the world, in Faculties.

The increasingly flagrant contradiction between the widening influence of and the constant attacks on my theses would itself prevent me from dismissing the consequences of the book and move on to other things. Sometimes I also experience a deep need to punish certain critical insolences. I thus take this opportunity to burden my book with a postscript that is both technical and polemical, renewing my moral responsibility.

2

Ambiguity of Influences

If I am to believe the confidences of a few authors and the writings of their commentators, but even more the texts themselves, it is especially in the Anglo-Saxon world that *L'Amour et l'Occident* seems to have influenced the work of poets and novelists, while in the Continent, films, ballets, and musical compositions manifested diverse free 'readings' of my book. It is uncomfortable to estimate the dialectical, indirect, or negative influence of a book, even if one limits oneself to the examination of written or plastic works. Thus, young novelists have informed me that they had given up such undertakings because after having read me they understood *too well* what they were doing.

Finally, certain of my themes, explicit or not—such as marriage as a factor of social *neguentropy*, or respect for the Other as different—are invoked with increasing frequency by psychoanalysts, sociologists, and a few innovative American city planners, and return to me as approving echoes emitted by the new generations and some of their gurus. Regarding the influence on the lives of my readers, I can say nothing, aside from the correspondence in which I sometimes become involved *nolens volens*. Devoid of the authority of the confessor, I still share with him the commitment to secrecy. Yet the broadest phenomenon of which my book has been the catalyst—not the cause—may be the present vogue of Catharism, always linked to the evocation of courtly love.

3

Catharist Renaissance in the Twentieth Century

Those who deny my hypotheses to the point of suppressing any mention of my book in theirs are the first to play games on the grounds I surveyed: the presence in the same times and places of the poetry of the troubadours and the vast complex of heresies symbolized by the name of Catharism. It all started in 1937 with the publication of *La Croisade contre le Graal* by Otto Rahn, a young German fascinated by Montségur, where he thinks he recognizes the castle of the Grail, and who died mysteriously in an Alpine waste near Hitler's Eagle's Nest. His two extreme theses are taken from Eugene Aroux and the Sâr Péladan: (1) 'all troubadours were Cathars, all Cathars were troubadours'; and (2) courtly rhetoric was the secret language of heresy. While this is untenable, it evokes an obscure evidence: the impression of having touched, albeit gropingly, the heart of the problem, and that somehow, in the fundamental reality of symbol, *one burns.*

Otto Rahn's manifest errors contributed more toward the understanding of courtly love in its socio-religious genesis than did most of the so-called serious works, which until then had regularly concurred on the limited significance of their subject. From that point of departure, and from something else deep inside me which responds to the delirious in Otto Rahn's thesis—that feverish recognition which has always seized me before the ruins of certain Provençal castles in the dawn, the spiritual horizon of all courtly love—I wrote an outline of the passion/marriage opposition for a young people's magazine.

Daniel-Rops suggested that I write a book on the subject

for a series he edited. But on the day the manuscript was to have been delivered, of which not a line had been written, Rops asked me to yield my turn in the series to a young lieutenant-colonel who had just written *La France et son armée*, a most urgent book, it seemed.[1] Relieved, I went to work, and since I had time to spare, I wrote very fast. After three months in a state of trance and the daily delight of discovery or invention, the book was finished for the summer solstice, the triumph of Day, and that very evening I went to the Opera, where they were showing *Tristan*, that revenge of Night.

Habet Acht! Habet Acht!
Schon weicht dem Tag die Nacht![2]

sang Brengain at dawn, at the sublime point in Act II, and I shall never again hear it without crying—I would be ashamed.

---

[1] Urgent? It was already too late. Charles de Gaulle's book was published a few months later, in June 1938. There was no time to build the armoured forces he required.

[2]

Have a care! Have a care!
Now Night gives way to Day!

And the theme of dawn for the troubadours:

> Gardez-vous, cher guetteur de la tour
> Du jaloux, votre méchant seigneur
> Ennuyeux plus que l'aube
> Nous, en bas, nous parlons d'amour
> Grande peur
> Nous fait l'aube, l'aube, oui l'aube.
>   (Raimbaut de Vacqueyras, *Alba*)

> And watch yourself, watcher of the tower,
> with your jealous, evil-hearted lord,
> more envious than the dawn
> of us who here speak softly, and of love,
> and only fear dawn is near
>   (P. Blackburn's translation in *Proensa:
>   An Anthology of Troubadour Poetry*)

4

Retort to My Critics

First a confession: I knew little, while addressing a lot—
when I undertook to write *L'Amour et l'Occident*. If I
could have measured the extent of my ignorance there
would have been no book, that is certain; this was beginner's
luck. About two-thirds of my readings on Cathars and troubadours, since I have been working on the subject, took place
after publication of the book. This enabled me to correct a
number of errors in the 1956 edition, and allows me to respond to the most peremptory critics of my historical hypotheses.

The dispute over the relations between Cathars and Troubadours (or better, between the complex of Gnostic heresies
and the heresy of courtly love) has become something of a
cause célèbre among scholars, usually at my expense. But I
expect to have the last laugh. Let us start at the beginning.
First, my thesis was reduced to a gross simplification, which
caused it to be discarded as simplistic. Rather than seeing
what is at the heart of the book—the drama between the
'Passion of Night' and the 'Norm of Day' (Karl Jaspers),
between the essential structures of the myth and the existential
choice of marriage—the focus was on what seemed most
spectacular but also most vulnerable: Rahn's thesis according
to which the *trobar clus* performed the role of a secret language
of heresy. This was as easy to cite in a gossip column as to
refute in a specialized journal, without touching upon my
real thesis, which remains: that troubadours and Cathars cannot be understood *separately*, outside of the broad religious—
or psychosocial—phenomenon which includes them and carries them from the twelfth to the fourteenth century. Anyone
who claims that these two movements occurring at the same

time and in the same regions, provinces, and castles, exposed to the same sworn enemies, and both condemned by the church, have 'nothing in common', must carry the burden of proof. Let us examine these proofs, or on their behalf, the arguments presented by both sides.

When my book appeared in 1939, the professors who reviewed it in journals of literary history thought that I was embarrassingly wrong due to the sole fact that I seemed unaware of the current state of the knowledge, or *ignorance*, at the time, on the subject of courtly love. They approached it with the slightly exasperated attitude of the specialist who is paid to know where things are and will not accept any nonsense. Above all, they blamed me for what I had purposely omitted, and overlooked my contribution, which occurred on an entirely different level than that of their expertise. All of this still lingers in bibliographies, yet the 'divagations' denounced by yesterday's masters have become matter of learning for their former students in many universities. Without returning to these early 'refutations', I shall mention a few recent recidivists of an intellectual behaviour which may be nothing but the lay substitute of the 'argument of authority', the invocation of the 'scientific seriousness' replacing that of dogma and tradition.

In the *Histoire littéraire* published in the famous collection called '*la Pléiade*',[3] Régine Pernoud discards with disdain the notion that courtesy and heresy ever had anything in common, even geographic locales.

'We shall mention only for the record a thesis which has had some repercussion among the public at large, and which presented troubadours and courtly poetry as echoes of Catharist heresy. The hypothesis is certainly ingenious, but it has the drawback of being entirely contradicted by the facts: when Catharism began to spread to the mercantile cities of Provence, around 1165, courtly poetry had already been in existence for half a century. This theory rests on a radical ignorance both of Catharist heresy itself, basically a heresy of bourgeois and merchants, and of the essence of courtly poetry.' I am tempted to return the compliment to this eminent historian of the bourgeoisie. To invoke as a single 'fact' which

[3] Vol. III, pp. 25 and 26.

would ruin my theory, the propagation of heresy among Provençal merchants around 1165, is to misconstrue the elementary facts of heresy and courtly poetry—the time and area of their diffusion, both geographic and social. It is a fact that the Heresy spread among the merchants of Provençal towns fifty years after the songs of William of Poitiers: it is the prototype of the 'true little fact', incontestable and uninteresting. Who then, except Mme. Pernoud, has ever believed that the troubadours composed for the merchants of Carcassonne? Courtly love, as its name indicates, was sung in the *courts*, not in the shops. The lords, but especially their spouses, were generally on the side of Heresy, not of the Church. And the Heresy was much more ancient than Mme. Pernoud wishes to believe for the sole purpose of invalidating my thesis. She claims there is no 'serious' proof that Catharism preceded the early troubadours. Alas, the Church did not ask as much: since 1017 in Orleans, 1020 in Tours, and 1025 in Arras it had heretic 'Manichaeans' burnt at the stake. One hundred years later, in 1119, the Church excommunicated in Toulouse their numerous descendants. From 1145, Saint Bernard of Clairvaux preached in Toulouse and the Albigenses missions against heresy and cried out in anguished alarm—but at what? The poor man was obviously unaware that Catharism would appear only twenty years later in those regions. . . .

Regarding those Cathars (who were mostly 'bourgeois', according to Mme. Pernoud, but 'modest peasants or poor artisans' according to Yves Dossat; rich and enterprising merchants according to Charles Bru, but 'humble people' according to P. Belperron) many of my critics state that those 'humble origins' exclude any contact with the poetry in 'langue d'oc', which originated 'from the highest classes of society' (P. Belperron, *Joie d'Amour*, p. 227). Yet it cannot be denied that Raimon V, Count of Toulouse, wrote in 1177 to the General Chapter of Cîteaux to request his help against Heresy which 'has penetrated everywhere': 'The most important people on my estates have been corrupted. The crowd has followed their example.'

The focus is on 'the low birth' of troubadours, poor minstrels of whom one would be at a loss to imagine that they might ever have interacted as equals with the lords of Lan-

Appendix

guedoc or expected anything from the noble ladies they celebrated, and who were for the most part at least 'believers', during the second half of the twelfth century. Most sociological explanations I have read (which agree only in excluding any possibility of encounter between Cathars and troubadours) seem struck with the same congenital weakness: they reason on the basis of clichés they consider incompatible, and which are chosen to that end. Even René Nelli allows himself to write that the troubadours 'expected that Love would grant them a value which was not socially theirs, by right of birth'. And to explain submission to the lady, he takes up the theory of the minstrel who 'loves too high' (it is Victor Hugo's famous 'worm in love with a star'). But Nelli is in the habit of providing us with the facts which will allow us to discuss his own statements: in this case, the biographical indications on the forty-three authors he cites in his *Anthology of the Troubadours* (Vol. II, The Poets). What is the proportion of 'mistrels', bourgeois, or knights among them? Here is the computation:

Unknown origin	4
Minstrels	3
'Very modest origin'	3
Bourgeois	6
Clerics	5
Knights and high barons	22

I am willing to go along with Jeanroy's count of about five hundred troubadours (of whom often only the name is known) and the fact that the minstrels were able to form a strong minority of their cohort. But if René Nelli chose those particular forty-three, it is because he judged them both the best and most representative. They must have set the tone, beginning with William IX, who was 'the greatest prince of France', and his friend Viscount Eble of Ventadour, to Geoffrey Rudel, Prince of Blaye, and Raimbaut, Count of Orange, passing through the four lords of Ussel, who may be from a branch of the Ventadours.[4]

Another procedure of intimidation, more cavalier than pedantic, is used by Canon Delaruelle, who also knows all that

[4] Cf. Jean Audiac, *Les Poésies des quatre troubadours d'Ussel* (Paris, 1922).

must be known—and especially what *must* be ignored—about Catharism. In the journal *Archeologica* (December 1967), he states that my book contains, 'in those passages relating to history, one error per sentence'. The examples he cites are caricatures where the error derives from him. (How could I have said, for example, that '*Tristan*'s passionate love is nothing but Catharism'?) And when he speaks of the Reformation, one would have to point out one error per word.[5] But it would be a waste of time, since our author announces that dogma will have the final word. He states that one cannot, as did historian Charles Schmidt, praise the morals of the Perfect (*perfecti*) if one disapproves of their doctrine, since such a distinction shocks 'a French spirit accustomed to seek a deep coherence in the works he studies, and to believe that dogma rules ethics'. Is it in the name of this 'coherence', or French spirit, or dogma, that the intrepid canon does not hesitate to write that 'there has never been a stake in Montségur'? That is a good piece of news, but it arrives too late for the two hundred martyrs of the sinister camp of the Crématz.

Here again, the sureness of tone is unable to dissimulate an attempt to eliminate the phenomenon (through repression) rather than understand it, and this by means of authority, that dogma which 'commands ethics' and through it the embarrassing truths of history. To those 'integrists' of all systems, I say: if you believe it possible to base the coherence of your person on an external dogma rather than on your own psychological makeup or real faith, well, keep it to yourselves. Do not burn as heretics those who have another system of personal coherence. Or at least do not say that your church, your party, or your sect never burnt them at all.

Now a third variant of the same system of recourse to authority, be it that of science, the church, the party, or the simple customs called 'tradition': this is offered by Mme. Lot-Borodine. Even before the publication of my book (of which she had read advance proofs), she conducted a relentless campaign of pious indignation against it in various journals. She

[5] He claims that Socin—the reformed Italian monk who went to preach his particular heresy to the Poles—was a doctor of the Lutheran Church, and believes that Protestant arguments 'assume an infallible Reason'. ('Reason, that whore!' said Luther.)

Appendix

could not forgive me for having assimilated the Maria of Heresy and the Gnostic Sophia, and this Maria-Sophia to the Catharist Church.[6] Despite my having explained that I invented nothing, that those 'horrors' are in the texts,[7] this lady could not accept the consideration of such a shocking truth. André Gide told Jean Delay that my book had explained for him what his reading of Freud had been unable to do, and Jean Delay devoted twenty-five pages of the first volume of *La Jeunesse d'André Gide* to this account. Mme. Lot-Borodine immediately warned Delay that there was cause for suspicion, a notion which he—visibly impressed—shared with the readers of his second volume. André Gide was doubtless wrong to imagine a clearer understanding of himself through the work of such a suspect author, so malevolently ignorant of what orthodox specialists decided one should think of the Virgin. But what should one think of someone who does not conceive of the Maria-Sophia identity in religious psychology[8] because, says she, Mariology 'excludes' Gnosis?

[6] On the assimilation of Sophia and Maria for the Cathars, cf. Déodat Roché, *Études manichéennes et cathares*, pp. 162-64; and on their distinction (similar to that between the Christ and Jesus), p. 146.

[7] For example, a Cathar declared to the inquisitors: 'Mariam non esse nec fuisse mulierem carnalem sed sectam suam dicunt esse Mariam virginem.' Cf. René Nelli, *L'Érotique des troubadours* (Toulouse, 1963), pp. 222-23. See also in Nelli's anthology *Les Troubadours*, 2 vols. (Paris, 1966), the great Catharist *canzo* (in my opinion) of Peire Cardinal, *Vera vergena Maria*: Maria is the true Virgin, born 'in Syria' but became the Queen seated on the right hand of God, who 'favored her prayers'. Hers is thus, indeed, the role of *Sophia aeterna*.

[8] Cf. *Answer to Job* (Princeton, 1973) by C. G. Jung.

5

A Mystical Troubadour: Henry Suso

The example of the great Swabian mystic Henry Suso will best illustrate the viability of my hypotheses on the series of analogies (assimilations) of Eternal Wisdom-Maria-*Vera Vergena*-Sophia-Church of Love-Lady of Thoughts; and on courtly rhetoric as a congenial language of this unique cult.

In his excellent little book *Suso et le Minnesang*,[9] J. A. Bizet recalls how 'Eternal Wisdom' became for young Suso (following a trance of ecstasy) 'a form of theophany substituting the pure notion of divinity'. From then on Suso, in his works, especially *Vita* and *L'Horologium sapientae*, celebrated the cult of Wisdom, his Lady. 'His courtly mystique . . . is the Germanic equivalent of the "blooming piety" which the last troubadours of Languedoc had vowed the Virgin, or that Clemency which, it is believed, under the mask of Clémence Isaure, would only be another devout personification' (p. 139). And one finds in his works of poetic prose not only all the epithets and specific images, but all the obligatory commonplaces of *cortezia*:

* Quest for the beloved (*inquisicio amoris*), which recalls the theme of the *distant princess*.
* Desire for a *Lady* never seen, one is yet to meet: 'My God, when will I be able to see the beloved, hear the sound of her voice? Which is her face, that contains so many charming treasures?' (*Vita*)
* *Doubt as to the true identity* or essence of the Lady: 'Is she God or human creature, man or woman, secret wisdom or magic force, or what else?' (*Vita*) (If only I had known

[9] J. A. Bizet, *Suso et le Minnesang* (Paris, 1944). See also idem, *Henri Suso et le declin de la scolastique* (Paris, 1946).

Appendix

earlier this sentence of Suso! It would have made the best epigraph to my Book II.) But there is something stranger yet on the same page, when he believes he is seeing Wisdom: 'She was both far and near, above and below, present and yet hidden; she was surrounded yet unattainable. . . . She displayed her power from one end to the other and penetrated all things with her tenderness. When you thought you possessed a beautiful woman, you found a proud adolescent. Now she looked like a wise educator, now she behaved like a magnificent mistress.'

- The theme of the *ring*, pledge of allegiance of the knight henceforth a *servant*. ('Oh beautiful, oh lovable Wisdom. . . . Ah! May my soul receive the ring from You!')
- *The love of lovesickness*, 'the sweet ailment that pleases me', as said a trouvère for all troubadours. And Suso: 'Ein suesses we. . . . ein ellende froede' (a sweet pain . . . a plaintive joy).
- *Love placed too high*, whence the need to keep it secret and mistrust informers or *lauzengiers (merkaere)*.
- The Lady's deceptions to *delay the Prize* and frustrate amorous satisfaction. It is the principle of the *joy d'amors* or *joc*, of the Germans' *minnespîl*—that *ludus amoris* which is both *gaudium* and *dolor* in Suso.
- Finally, the essential *nostalgia* of any passion directed to the absolute, to infinitude: the *senen* which is the *dezirar* of the troubadours and which will be the *Sehnen* of Wagner.

(And even 'coarse words' are not lacking, which for our naïve scholars 'proved the reality' of the Lady!)

Thus, Suso 'kept this wager of singing as a beloved woman the unattainable Good, the God with no mode or name' (p. 54). The more abstract the divine principle became, the more feminine it became. In short, everything that our experts in courtly love, on the one hand, and in mysticism on the other, decreed to be forever incompatible, is there put together, as marvelously mixed as in the lyric of Languedoc. This does not prove, of course, that the troubadours were speaking of Sophia when they praised their Lady; but it does prove that this is not impossible, that their disposition may have been such. The extreme thesis—one I do not defend—which assimilates the Lady in the mind to the Santa Gleyzia of the Cathars, encounters here a serious argument: the demonstration in fact that the procedure implied by this thesis is possible and feasible. To those who may counter that courtly rhetoric could not translate such a Gnosis, my answer is that first they must convince me that Suso never existed, never wrote, never happened.

Moreover, we are told that Suso remained during his entire life a Dominican most faithful to the discipline and dogmas of his order; and that nothing can link him to heresy, if not precisely his forceful denial of the extreme theses of the Beghards and the Frères du Saint-Esprit (p. 164). His recourse to courtly forms would thus tend to show that these have no specific ties nor coherence with heresy. This is a fallacy of begging the question regarding Suso's orthodoxy. His influence on the sect of Amis de Dieu need hardly be recalled, and we know of his training in the religious atmosphere of Cologne, 'bastion of the heretic Beghards' (themselves heirs to the Cathars), and at the feet of Meister Eckhart, where he met Tauler: both condemned by the church, both defended by Suso as faithful to orthodoxy—at least as he conceived of it. Above all, this cult of Wisdom which is a decisive trait of his piety—does he not share it with the heretics? Should we infer from this that Suso was a heretic, or, on the contrary, that the Cathars were orthodox? I maintain they share something more essential than what universal judgments of orthodoxy and heresy would have us believe. Moreover, such labels are quite useless in the understanding of a spiritual message.

6

Troubadours and Cathars

Within a completely different intellectual and spiritual climate, based on an intimate knowledge of the issues, I always value two excellent minds, different from each other and differing from my view—one attacking them head-on with a petulance undiminished in thirty years, the other through implicit reservations and meaningful silences: Henri Davenson and René Nelli.

This is how Professor Henri I. Marrou (Davenson's real name) summarizes our argument—or *tenson* as the troubadours said—in his invaluable little book *Les Troubadours* (1961 and 1971), a debate inaugurated with lively thrusts in the journal *Esprit* in 1939:

'I find fault with that dialectical furor in whose crucible contradictions are abolished and all diversity is reduced to unity: everything merges, mingles, and becomes confounded, not only troubadours and Cathars, but Languedoc courtesy and Celtic legends (pre-Catharist Provence exhibits connections with Gaelic and Welsh Celts), the neo-Manichaean current and Arab influence (too bad if the latter rolls the contrasting waves of al Hallaj and Ibn Dâvoud.) Does not all this come from the East, and ultimately represent the return of a symbolic East in Western man? I particularly challenge the value of an assimilation of the courtly love of the troubadours and a definition of "passion" derived from Wagner's *Tristan* and his Schopenhauer of the purest German romanticism.'

Yes, in this twelfth century of which I have provided a synopsis, less detailed regarding Provence but somewhat more complete for Europe than Davenson's own (pp. 21-44), 'everything merges' and sometimes 'mingles' *in reality*, and

340

it serves no purpose to add that *with me* 'everything becomes confounded': such a misfortune would not alter the facts. To address the main point: Davenson challenges any assimilation of courtly love and passionate love (say of Bernard of Ventadour and Wagner) and concludes that 'to make troubadours the bards of unhappy mutual love, whose key word is "Joy", is a strange absurdity.'

The absurdity I see is the reverse: *Joy* is the key word of the troubadours and it is not 'la joie' in the French sense of the word. The absolute contrast that can be established here between 'our poets of Oc . . . who keep talking of *lum* and *clartaz*' and the 'somber Nordic apologue' rests on a cliché: the joyful troubadour exalting spring, while the 'Bretons', Celts, and other Germanic peoples praise Death.

In René Nelli's great book *L'Érotique des troubadours* (1963) we find the elements of a more authentic vision: 'The idea of death by love is one of the traits which seems to constitute the common substance of Arab and Provençal love' (p. 52). If 'unfulfilled love *as such* can only be expressed as an aspiration to death', one can also maintain that the troubadours 'died of love as we die of thirst' (p. 73). Thus 'the *love/death* of the Arabs seems to correspond to the death by love of Provençal eroticism' (p. 251), and for Guilhem Montanhagol 'as for the old troubadours, the theme of *death by desire*—conventional as it may be—belongs with *Fin' Amors*' (p. 242).

There is more: to die of love, to die at the service of the Lady and, through this service in its extreme form to gain salvation, go to God—is this not a theme common to the troubadours and Arab mystics, representing a medieval dualist or Manichaean heresy? '*Take my life in homage, Beauty of hard pity, so long as you grant to me that by you I shall tend to heaven*', cried Uc de Saint-Circ, even though we read in Massignon regarding al Hallaj that 'to worship God through love alone is the crime of the Manichaeans', and in the anonymous Provençal romance *Flamenca*, Frère Guillem, forced to disguise himself as a priest to approach a well-guarded lady, 'became a Cathar and *served God through his lady*'. The latter seems to mean (at least to the author of the romance) 'that heresy consists in worshipping God through woman'.[10] If

[10] 'Le Génie d'Oc', *Cahiers du Sud* (Marseille, 1943), article by René Nelli on 'L'Amour Provençal', p. 66.

Appendix

this is true, neither the Cathars nor the troubadours are very far from the *endura* of love of which Tristan dies, rejoined by Isolde in 'supreme joy'.

H. Davenson himself indicates (p. 41ff.) the extent to which 'Provence was familiar with the rich material of Brittany . . . the quest for the Grail, Gawain, Perceval, the beautiful story of Tristan and Iseult.' To the examples he provides (Cercamon, Barbezieux, and the romance *Flamenca*) one could easily add twenty.[11] But let us face the difficulty which bears the name of Bernard of Ventadour.

In the poem considered his masterpiece and in which beats the heart of Provençal lyricism, the *canzo* of the Lark, at first all is *lum* and *clartatz*. Simone Weil writes beautifully about the beginning of this song: 'A few poems of the troubadours express joy with such purity that through it appears the poignant grief, the disconsolate grief of the finite creature':

> Quand je vois l'alouette mouvoir
> De joie ses ailes à contrejour
> Qui s'oublie et se laisse choir
> Par la douceur qu'au coeur lui va . . .[12]

(Simone Weil: 'When this country had been destroyed, British poetry recreated the same note, and nothing among the modern European languages has the equivalent of its delights'.) But with the second stanza bursts a Tristanian cry, torn by the love that the poet cannot help but feel for she 'from whom he will never have anything': *She took my heart, she took my self, she took my world, and then she herself vanished,*

---

[11] Bleheri, a Breton bard, lived and sang at the court of William IX of Poitiers: what better proof, more vital and dependable, might one demand of contacts between North and South that owe nothing to Wagner?

[12] Davenson's French translation, op. cit., p. 92, in his excellent chapter on the music of the troubadours. The melody is written out on the same page. For the rest of the poem I have used (with slight modifications) Alfred Jeanroy's French translation.

> When I see the lark stir her wings for joy
> against the sunlight,
> forgetting herself,
> letting herself
> fall
> with the sweetness that comes into her heart, . . .
> (P. Blackburn's translation)

342

leaving me with nothing but my desire and my thirsty heart!' Here is the fatal passion and its avowed narcissim: *'I have lost all power over myself from the day when she let me gaze into her eyes, a mirror that I love so. Mirror, since I have seen myself in you, my deep sighs kill me, and thus I have lost myself like the beautiful Narcissus at the fountain.'*

The recourse to exile is always the image of death: *'Since my love does not please her, I shall never express it again. I am separating myself from my love and denying it. She kills me and I respond with death.*[13] *Since she does not keep me, I am going away, miserable, in exile, I know not where.'*

'Tristan,[14] you will have nothing else from me, since I am leaving, weak, I know not where. I renounce songs and deny them. Far from Joy and Love, I hide.'*

Another *canzo,* which begins, 'My heart is so full of joy':

> Du souci qui me hante
> Où m'abriterai-je?
> La·nuit il m'agite et jette
> Sur le bord du lit
> Je souffre plus d'amour
> Que l'amoureux Tristan
> Qui endura maints tourments
> Pour Iseut la blonde
> Ah Dieu, que ne suis-je aronde
> Pour traverser l'air
> D'un vol par la nuit profonde
> Jusque en sa demeure?[15]

Nothing announces the Wagnerian storms in the pure and doleful melody of Bernard, but the love of infinite desire, the torments endured, exile, and the obsessiveness of death— are they not here, as in *Tristan,* entwined by the deep complicities of vertigo?

---

[13] *'Mort m'a et per mort li respon.'*

[14] This expressive *senhal* may refer here to Eleanor of Aquitaine, Marguerite of Turenne, or maybe, according to Jeanroy, to 'an unknown personage'.

[15] *'Where can I hide myself from the care that obsesses me? At night it tosses and throws me to the edge of the bed. I suffer from love more than the amorous Tristan, who bore many torments for the fair Iseult. Oh, God, if only I were a swallow flying through the air in the dead of night straight to her abode.'*

Appendix

Heaven forbid that I should assimilate and homogenize that which differs! (It would be against my theology, my ethics, and my whole political doctrine.) I am only saying that, from the death by love held to be a great honour by the Banou Odrah, a Bedouin tribe, to the lovers of Cornwall of whom Béroul and Thomas, and then Gottfried and Richard repeat that they were born 'to desire and to die, to die of desire', and passing through the great troubadours of the twelfth century and the great German romantics, there is a continuity which was never formally 'certified', but rather made evident through the poems and their emotional quality. Far from wishing that a given system of historical interpretation should conquer, I seek better to feel, understand, and experience a certain exalted form of existing, a certain adventure of the soul, a 'voyage' into which we have been swept away by the herbal wine of the primitive *romance*, by the poetic and musical experience. It is a question of hearing and not of written or verifiable proof; a question of intuition and receptiveness, not of demonstration.

I read the *Vida* of Rudel, poet of hopeless 'far away love', of whom Petrarch tells us 'that he set the sail and took the oars in search of his death.' I read and relive the emotion of *Tristan*. I propose that this emotion be the sole arbiter for our theses.

'Geoffrey Rudel was a gentleman of great nobility and Prince of Blaye. He fell in love with the Countess of Tripoli, without having seen her, because of the good he heard about her from the pilgrims coming from Antioch; and he wrote of her many a poem with good music and poor words. And such was his desire to see her, that he took to sea. And on the vessel he fell ill and was taken to Tripoli, to an inn, close to death. The Countess was informed and she came to his side—to his bed—and took him in her arms. He knew that it was the Countess and immediately recovered his sight, hearing, and sense of smell; and he thanked God for having sustained his life until he had seen her. And thus he died in her arms; and she had him shrouded with great honor in the Temple. And then that same day she became a nun due to her grief at his death.'[16]

[16] René Nelli and René Lavaud, *Les Troubadours*, vol. II, p. 261.

Troubadors and Cathars

This brings to mind the end of another *Vida*, that of Raimon Jordan, Viscount of Saint-Antonin (twelfth century), 'where we are told that the lady of this troubadour, upon learning that he had been killed in combat, shut herself in a convent of heretic women.' René Nelli concluded that this story 'clearly shows that it was not unusual in good society for a woman of high rank to become a Cathar out of despair in love.'[17]

For years after the publication of my book, I found in the books of René Nelli, devoted either to Catharism[18] or to the troubadours,[19] the most precise and perceptive confirmations or corrections of my hypotheses on the relations between troubadours and Cathars during the twelfth and thirteenth centuries.

While Davenson is not afraid to write that 'no document allows to infer the least collusion between troubadours and Cathars' (p. 144), René Nelli recalls what I emphasized at the outset: that the development of 'Provençal love' was parallel to that of Catharism, in the same regions, and that during at least two centuries the two doctrines coexisted (*L'Érotique des troubadours*, p. 228). And he adds the following: 'In 1250, Catharism had been definitively crushed, but the Church still faced another heresy, "Love", which it knew *had always been in partnership with the former*' (p. 236).

If I were told that the Church was mistaken in blending the two heresies (I believe so too) and that my 'evidence' does not constitute the required 'documents', there is this in René Nelli—beyond the above-cited episode from the *Vida* of Raimon Jordan: 'The documents of the thirteenth century reveal that almost all the ladies of the counties of Toulouse, Albigenses, Carcasses, and Foix, who welcomed and protected the troubadours were, on the eve of the Crusade, if not "Perfect" at least "believers" ' (p. 229).

[17] *L'Érotique des troubadours*, p. 229.

[18] *Spiritualité de l'Hérésie: le Catharisme* (collective work), 1953; *Écritures cathares*, 1959; *Le Phénomène cathare*, 1969; *Vie quotidienne des cathares du Languedoc au XIIIe siècle*, 1969.

[19] A number of articles in *Cahiers du Sud*; a beautiful essay on *cortezia: L'Amour et les Mythes du Coeur*, 1952; then the highly informative thesis *L'Érotique des troubadours*, 1963; and finally, in collaboration with René Lavaud, an abaundant anthology in two volumes, *Les Troubadours*, 1965 and 1966, with original texts and translations, and most useful comments.

Appendix

Some fifteen troubadours were Cathars or at least 'Catharizing', among them Raimon de Miraval, Raimon Jordan, Peire Vidal, Guilhem de Durfort, Pierre Rogier de Mirepoix, and Mir Bernat (pp. 232-33), to whom I do not hesitate to add Peire Cardinal. Nelli admits that one would search in vain in their work for 'the least specifically heretic proposition' (p. 234). (One would search vainly in *Les Fleurs du Mal* for catechism or canons of the Council of Trent set to verse.) Every Catharist troubadour—their number matters little as long as there is at least one—is the living refutation of theories not only on the actual absence, but especially on the theoretical impossibility of 'the least collusion'.[20]

'The Catharist preachers liked to cite the *sirventes* of Peire Cardinal *Clergue si fan pastor*' (R. Lavaud, cited in *E.T.*, p. 223, n.). Whether Peire Cardinal was a heretic (a belief I share with Lucia Varga) or only a sympathizer (as Nelli believes), he was in any case a troubadour: there is thus further 'collusion'. The (belated and Catholic) troubadour Matfre Ermengau, in his *Bréviaire d'Amour*, reproves the last Cathars who 'through the error of heresy censure and vilify matrimony'. All the great troubadours have done that.

Finally, the courtly romance *Flamenca* bears certain traces of Catharism, while the *Roman de Barlaam et Josaphat* may represent a 'collusion' between the gnosticism inherited from the East (see p. 94 above) and courtly morals. Regarding *Flamenca*, we see René Nelli in a cautious retreat in terms of his early texts on Catharism. In 1963 he wrote: 'We do not claim, which would be absurd, that this romance betrays a Catharist inspiration. . . . Yet the poet likens the attitude of Guillem to that of a *patarin* in a manner such that one must recognize that, *in spirit*, Love and Catharism might well be confused on a few essential points' (*E.T.*, p. 237).

The outcome is that the troubadour-Cathar relationship so ardently contested (like the courtly love-Tristan relationship) exhibits a kind of spiritual evidence that no so-called objective method will ever adequately grasp—and even less prove to be inexistent. René Nelli is overwhelmed by such evidence

---

[20] Common sophisms on Cathars-troubadours: X is not a Cathar, since he says nothing more than Y, who is not one. How do you know that Y is not a Cathar? Because he speaks like X, about whom I have just established that he was not a Cathar.

when he views as a poet the situation in Provence in the twelfth century; but he comes close to denying it (with some masochism, it would seem) as a scholar determined to challenge the fussiest of 'specialists'.

Nelli will never exhibit the (false) naiveté of stating like Belperron 'that no source describes the meeting of a Perfect and a troubadour in the same castle' (*Croisade contre les Albigeois*, p. 60), and that the very possibility of such a meeting must be excluded, since they are 'two foreign and even antagonistic elements' (*Joie d'Amour*, p. 220). Nelli knows well that meetings such as those denied by Belperron could not help but have taken place almost daily in the Catharist castles 'which welcomed and protected the troubadours' (*E.T.*, pp. 228-29).[21] Better yet, the meeting of a declared Cathar and a troubadour was confirmed at least once *in a single man*, Guillaume de Durfort, and this example suffices to eliminate the 'impossibility' too often invoked by Belperron, Davenson, R. Pernoud, and others. Nonetheless, René Nelli, regarding Durfort and a few other presumed Cathars, notes that 'one would search in vain in [their] *cansos* . . . for the least specifically heretic proposition. . . . They all remain within the framework of traditional eroticism, or more exactly: the differences which separate them from other troubadours, when they exist, do not correspond to their respective beliefs. *One would have to admit that all troubadours were Cathars or that none was.* It is obvious that all troubadours were not Cathars.' Nelli concludes that 'their religious ideas have had no impact on the content of amorous lyric or that they did not wish that such ideas appear in their theoretical singularity' (*E.T.*, pp. 234-35).

I would be tempted to subscribe to this reasoning (which I have adopted on occasion) were I not aware of a serious flaw of symmetry: 'all or none.' Since in fact *a few were* Cathars. If their belief did not modify their lyric—might it not be that there was no need to adapt their lyric to their

[21] For example, in the castles of the Cabardès, the Minervois, and the Lauragais, where Catharist lords lived—(the Cabaret, Pennautier, Miraval, Laurac, Saissac, Montréal, Aragon, Durfort, Mirepoix, etc.), two great troubadours—Peire Vidal and Raymond de Miraval—also sojourned, as their songs prove. Here are your "sources" and your 'documents'! Cf. Michel Roquebert, *L'Épopée cathare*, esp. pp. 313-18.

Appendix

beliefs, being already congenial and interactive from the start? In that sense one might maintain that *all* troubadours were Cathars *nolens volens*, as one can say that Victor Hugo, Baudelaire, Verlaine, and Rimbaud were Catholics. All *surréalistes* were anarchists, although it is probable that few among them had read Bakunin and Proudhon. And they were all influenced by Freud, although according to sources, only Breton and Dalí had ever met their master. Thus it is in vain that one might seek in the poems of Tzara or Éluard 'the least specifically anarchist proposition' (nor, for that matter, specifically communist, should they change camps). All their poetry is anarchy, from the 'words at liberty' to 'mad love'. Breton never quoted Freud in his poems, yet he considered himself a Freudian and condemned Jung for having deviated from the doctrine (even though without knowing or admitting it, he was closer to the latter through his sense of the sacred, of symbols, and of significant coincidences or synchronicity).

I am not resolving more than Nelli. But, pressed to choose between *all and none*, I would lean toward *all*; Nelli maybe toward *none*. Both terms remain equally incredible—or almost. From where do I get this ultimate reticence? From what unyielding *parti pris*? I confess, I feel less certain of my reasons than of having 'felt' the right answer. . . .

When Davenson, regarding the 'Catharist hypothesis', admits that I have not formally adopted it, but adds that my 'fallacious and charming [book] does not cease to flirt with the idea, *so much so that it ends by imposing itself on the reader like an obsessive temptation*' (p. 142), I say to myself: that is astutely perceived and in tune with my objectives, if it will show that it is impossible both to prove the relation heresy-courtesy and do without it, or to deny it. I like that sentence because it is not only for the reader but for me the author that its content is always renewed! (This also happens when I reread Otto Rahn on Montségur, Luigi Valli on Dante, or Ferdinand de Saussure on the decoding of Latin verse.)

7

Tantrism and Courtesy

René Nelli brings an important contribution on a very technical yet decisive point: I am referring to the *asag*, or *assays*, or *essai*—the test the lady imposes on her suitor, and which was discussed (pp. 115-22) in connection with Tantrism. Davenson rightly noted in the Arabs how the refusal to fulfill desire completely is the most 'refined' way to make it eternal. Thus, Ibn Dâvoud: *'Oh, no, don't promise to love me for fear that forgetfulness will follow.'* Yet in the same phenomenon for the troubadours, he only sees a 'corrupt masochism,' a 'morbid refinement, the low calculations of an unbalanced sensibility' (p. 149), as in Cercamon (1135-45): *'Nothing makes me more envious than an object that always escapes me.'* Or Matfre Ermengau (late thirteenth, early fourteenth century): 'The pleasure of this love is destroyed when desire finds its fulfillment.'

René Nelli, instead of showing moral indignation, seeks to understand the nature and function of the *asag* in courtly behavior, and finds its secret in the 'Joy of love' itself. Let us follow the course of this research in *L'Érotique des troubadours*. The *Joy* of love (or *joy d'amors* in Provençal) is a masculine word whose meaning varies not only with periods—from William IX to Montanhagol—but in the same author depending on the tonality of the poem. First and generally, it is *the exaltation caused by the beloved woman and whose object is love itself.* Sometimes it is simply the joy of living through love, or it is a *game*—flirting or petting. But already in William IX, the *joy* is given through Love 'to he who observes its laws'; and this joy is 'pure' because it depends on a good which one desires but has not (yet) obtained: *the joy of desire.* The meaning of *joy* thus oscillates between *the*

349

Appendix

pleasure of being in love and *the vow to perpetuate desire*, as with the Arabs.

In William IX, the *joy* also becomes a mysterious influx which emanates from the presence and the eyes of the lady: '*All the joy of the world is ours, lady, if we love each other*'. And its beneficent effects are felt on the body as well as the heart of the lover: '*My Lady can cure the invalid with her joy and kill him with her anger. I want to retain her in order to refresh my heart and renew my body, so well that I cannot age.*' Or: '*He will live a hundred years who succeeds in possessing the joy of his love,*' that is, if the man is able to control the rules of desire, exalted by the very restraint imposed by the lady: 'no one can be assured of triumph in love if he does not submit to her will.'

The theme of submission to the lady leads to that of the test she imposes on her suitor: '*My lady tests how and to what degree my fondness goes.*' This test, *assay* or *asag*, would become in the thirteenth century—expressly this time—the heroic trial of chastity 'in bed', *nudus cum nuda*, whose modalities in Tantrism have been described by Mircea Eliade. The *asag* appears then as a kind of technique of *joy*, or the *joy* becomes the erotic game par excellence, which presupposes *amor imperfectus* as a condition not only for *fin' amors* but for 'pure' joy, that is to say, pleasure without procreation.

Whence the countless scenes described in the two great courtly romances, *Flamenca* and *Jaufré*, in the *Romans de la Table Ronde*, and in Wolfram von Eschenbach's *Parzifal*, where the lovers lie together naked, but separated by a sword, or a lamb, or a child; and if they surrender to desire, it is proof that their love is not *fin' amors*, true love. Maybe it was believed, as did the Hindus and Chinese, that desire exalted by delayed pleasure exercised a magic power. 'Chastity—provided that physical desire had been previously aroused—became a benefic force', writes René Nelli, adding: 'A Gnostic theory perhaps disseminated in the West by the Cathars?'

We know that Catharism infiltrated the Beguines and the Beguins of Saint Francis of Assisi since the thirteenth century. Regarding the *asag* viewed as 'erotic magic founded on the storage of the sexual vital principle', René Nelli writes: 'The deposition of Guillaume Roux in the *Liber de Sententiarum Inquisitionis Tholosonae* leaves no doubt as to the existence and diffusion among the Beguins of a similar search for "meritorious" and "salutary" temptation.' Roux declares that according to the Beguins no one may be declared virtuous 'nisi se possent ponere nudus cum nuda in uno lecto et tamen non perficerent actum carnalem'—'if they reveal themselves incapable of lying in bed naked without fulfilling the carnal act' (quoted in *L'Erotique des troubadours*, p. 272).

I have two equally important reasons to insist on the *asag* and its essential connection with courtly *joy*. First, it is in and through the *asag* that the meeting of the *cortezia* of the troubadours and the Gnosticism of the Cathars is not only possible but almost inevitable, even though the motives are different in each case: the troubadours exalted desire; the Gnostics, overcoming it (the ascetism of the Perfect), or allowing it only with the avoidance of procreation. (The restraint imposed on lovers by religious ladies combines both motives to perfection!) This is what I meant when I defined Eros as *'infinite* desire.' Courtly love and Catharism, while remaining distinct heresies—and I completely accept on this score René Nelli's conclusions—could not fail to merge in the domain of actual behavior, which indeed occurred. Second, the *asag* appears linked from the start to the other themes of courtly poetry such as William of Poitiers 'invented' them between 1110 and 1120, but it is proven to have existed shortly before in the same region, in Poitou, within the religious movement led by Robert d'Arbrissel.

8

On the Invention of Love in the Twelfth Century

In his important study of William of Poitiers (*Romania*, April 1940), Reto Bezzola, the author of three basic volumes on *Les Origines et la formation de la littérature courtoise en Occident*, asks one of the most difficult questions in the history of Western literature and manners: the *sudden* appearance, in five or six songs of William of Poitiers, of the major themes that would be present in all the poets of love to follow—the troubadours—'and after them, in hundreds and thousands of poets in all of Europe.' Why did this total and unprecedented creation occur at this time and place?

The great Zurich Romanist, Theophil Spoerri, forerunner of structural analysis of texts, describes at the beginning of his study of William of Poitiers[22] thirteen explanatory systems for our enigma, proposed (at the time of his study) by some forty scholars. Each saw one, two, or three of the many literary, religious, social, or psychological aspects of the problem, but many of these theses cancel each other out by their exclusiveness, and not a single one views the phenomenon as a whole. What then are we dealing with? It is a process, both historical and psychological, of convergence, collusion, and tension, a confusion of limits (achieved by certain mystics); a process placed in the first three decades of the twelfth century; localized in Poitou; and in the course of which human love was to be *declared* and sung, through forms and rhythms borrowed from liturgy. From that time on it never ceased to rival with religious feeling.

[22] Theophil Spoerri 'Wilhelm von Poitiers und die Anfänge der Abendländischen Poesie,' *Trivium*, no. 2 (Zürich, 1944).

On the Invention of Love

This unique process from whence derives courtly love can be traced through the texts and chronicles: *the evolution of forms* in the poetry of William IX. This evolution parallels certain *circumstances of his biography* linked to the Abbey of Fontevrault, that is, to the long rivalry between the count-duke and the monk Robert d'Arbrissel. Here we shall follow Reto Bezzola: no one has more aptly framed in its time and place the resplendent person of William and the marvelously fertile conflict which opposed the duke and the monk.

Poitou and William of Poitiers are less at the origin than at the focal point of the *history* of love in the Western world and the issues it raises. Behind the missionary successes of Robert d'Arbrissel there is the eleventh-century religious evolution in Aquitaine, the secret diffusion and then the success of the anti-Roman Manichaean sects, in which the great-grandfather of William IX—the seventh duke, candidate to the Empire—'took great interest', according to the chronicle around 1050. One century later this movement was to bloom in Provence under the name of Catharism.

And behind William's poetic talent was the secular literary tradition of the courts of Aquitaine,[23] of Bishop Fortunat in the sixth century and his elegant letters to Queen Radegonde, abbess of the monastery of the Sainte-Croix of Poitiers, up to the duke's own aunt, Agnes, wife of the emperor Henry III. She maintained a correspondence with Pierre Damien which shows 'these refined souls already very close to the language of Saint Bernard but also to that of courtly love in its most idealized phase.'[24] From William of Poitiers and his close friends, the Ventadours and d'Ussels of the Limousin, the new poetry spread south to Toulouse and southeast to Provence, with which troubadours are confused in our day, but Dante, who knew, called them 'Limousins'.

Poitiers's Nordic progeny was no less prolific. William's granddaughter Eleanor married Louis VII of France, and later

---

[23] Not to mention little Latin poems in praise of noble ladies and nuns, by Marbode and Baudry de Bourgueil, about which Régine Pernoud, following Albert-Marie Schmidt, makes much ado—even though there is no connection between William's innovative genius and their rhyming platitudes. William must have felt nothing but contempt for those talentless beggars.

[24] R. Bezzola, *Guillaume IX et les origines de l'amour courtois*, p. 166.

Appendix

Henry II of Plantagenet. Desperately courted by Bernard of Ventadour, she gave the Anglo-Norman, French, and later the Champagne world her son Richard Coeur de Lion, a good troubadour, and her daughers Marie of Champagne and Aëlis of Blois, who handed down the secrets of courtesy to the authors of 'Breton romances', the greatest of whom was their thankful friend Chrestien de Troyes.

William was the most powerful prince in the lands that constitute France of today. All his uncles were dukes or kings, his cousins and aunts queens or empresses of England, Burgundy, the Holy Roman Empire. One of his sisters married King Peter of Aragon, the other King Alphonse of Castille. William himself married first Ermengarde of Anjou who, repudiated, became the Duchess of Brittany, and then he married the young widow of King Sancho of Aragon, Philippa of Toulouse. Prolix chroniclers of the time describe him as 'prodigal and adventurer', 'mad womanizer', 'the enemy of all modesty and sanctity', to the point 'that he seemed to believe the world was governed by chance, not by Providence',[25] yet 'audacious, pious, and extremely joyful of character'. He was excommunicated twice: the second time as a result of his flaunted liaison with the Viscountess of Châtellerault, so appropriately named 'Dangerous', whom he set up in a tower of his castle. Yet he was above all a poet. His first poems (or *cansos*) 'sing his gallant adventures in a bawdy, even obscene manner' for an audience of 'gay companions in debauchery' (p. 152). The most important event in his life: he took the cross in the spring of 1101—underwent a crushing defeat at Héraclée, and after several months of captivity at the court of Tancrède and at the hands of the Saracens he returned to Poitiers in the fall of 1102. In the meantime, Robert d'Arbrissel had founded the Abbey of Fontevrault. The duel began.

Born the son of a priest around 1050 at l'Arbressec, Robert d'Arbrissel first became a wandering cleric, uttering violent sermons against the marriage of priests, and later became a hermit in the forest of Craon. His asceticism and eloquence attracted disciples who joined him in his retreat. Communes (we would say) evolved around them. They were granted

[25] Guillaume de Malmesbury, *Història regum Anglorum*.

lands to cultivate. Then Robert was named 'apostolic preacher' by Urban II. He returned to the roads and to his sermons, 'marked by a profound pessimism', denouncing the perversity of a world filled with lies and ignorance among the populace, of murder, adultery among the princes, of simony, and hypocrisy among the priests. It was already the basis of the anti-Roman preaching of the Cathars, the Waldenses, and later of the *fraticelli*. To these vices he opposed true piety, poverty, asceticism, detachment. Throngs began to follow him, composed of thousands of young disciples the chronicles described as 'walking barefoot, dressed in bizarre and torn garments, and notable by the abundance of their beards' ('barbarum prolixitate notabiles'). Women left their husbands and the faithful left their priests to follow Robert. His friends warned him against excessive familiarity between the sexes, of which his roving community was being accused. If we are to believe the rumours at the time, Robert, 'following the example of Eastern ascetics, especially the Syrian, had himself fostered such promiscuity by allowing the women who followed him to live with him and even share his bed—all this to expiate his old venial sins and prove his resistance to sensual temptation'. In Rouen, he walked into a brothel 'to warm his feet' and converted all the prostitutes. They prostrated themselves before him, and soon after he took them to a deserted region where they led a holy life as hermits. In 1101, he decided to create for his followers a colony of 'huts' around a church dedicated—of course—to the Virgin. This became the Abbey of Fontevrault, composed of a large convent of women adjoining three houses of men. The order soon emigrated to Brittany, the Limousin, Périgord and Toulouse, and numbered up to 3,000 monks and nuns.

A letter from Robert: 'You know that everything I have built in this world I did for the nuns, and it is to them that I have offered all the strength of my talents. What is more, *I have submitted to them, me and my disciples, for the good of our souls*'. This was an unheard of novelty which even surpassed that of giving the abbess superior power, not only over the nuns (like the Paraclete of Héloïse at that time), but also over the men of the community.

Very soon Robert's charisma attracted to Fontevrault 'the most famous beauties of Europe', among them Queen Bertrade of France—and a more resounding conversion cannot be imagined. Bertrade had caused the biggest scandal of the time by forcing her lover, Philip I, to repudiate his wife and marry *her*, thereby bringing upon the new couple an excommunication such that 'all the bells stopped ringing when the king and "queen" entered a town or castle.' But best of all, in 1112, Ermengarde of Brittany, first wife of William IX, and then in 1115 Philippa of Toulouse, his second wife, accompanied by their daughter Audéoude, crossed over to the monk's camp, denied William, and took the veil at Fontevrault.

'William IX does not seem to have taken seriously the work of reform of saving wanton girls from hell. If it is true that Robert d'Arbrissel advocated a kind of mystical *assays* between monk and nun, destined to test their Christian virtue and continence in the same bed—one can conceive that William IX, not too religious by temperament, had only seen in those manoeuvres an amiable and hypocritical depravity.'

Thus wrote René Nelli (*E.T.*, p. 100). To these lines, which show that Robert engaged in the *asag* earlier than any of the troubadours and before William mentioned it in one of his poems, let us oppose Bezzola in a more realistic vein:

'Can one believe that William IX, Count of Poitiers and Duke of Aquitaine, witnessed this upheaval of the region's entire aristocracy, this general exodus of noble ladies, including his first and second wives, as well as his own daughter, without batting an eye? It seems very probable that William was deeply affected by the movement of Fontevrault and its stunning success in his own neighborhood' (p. 207).

The first reaction from William at the challenge of this 'stunning success': sarcasm and jest. To parody the abbey of loose girls 'reformed' by d'Arbrissel, he founded at Niort a colony of small houses—'habitacula quaedam quasi monasteriola'—imitating the 'huts' of Fontevrault's beginnings, where he installed courtesans as 'unreformed' as possible, and set up the most expert among them as 'abbess'. The second reaction, according to Bezzola: a dark moral crisis which brings him to ask again 'what man desires most', as he said in one of his songs. 'May it not have been in that condition of inner malaise that he began to oppose to the ascetic mysticism of the time, a mundane mysticism, a spiritual elevation of knightly love, rivalling with the attraction of mystical love and submission to the *domina* disseminated by Fontevrault?'

Suddenly, there was a lyrical blooming, first in the forms of the ecclesiastical *conductus*, then in the Arab *zadjal* and the broad themes of courtly love: the knight's *submission* to the lady in an allegiance of pure love, the *assai imposed by the lady* as a test of true love—all this 'for the good of our souls,' said Robert. And William translated: 'to refresh my flesh and renew my body.' The classical troubadours would say: 'For our salvation through love. I surrender, I commit myself to Her!' Pure grace, inexpressible nostalgia. At the birth of Western lyricism there was a conversion, not of the spirit nor even of consciousness, but of the soul's sudden awakening 'to the sweetness of a new time.'

Through the study of prosodic forms Theophil Spoerri, in the wake of Bezzola, tackled the same problem and presented us with the principle behind his method in a formula reminiscent of our common master Rudolf Kassner: 'Bewusstwerdung ist identisch mit Formwerdung.' This means that awareness of psychic reality is inseparable from its form (plastic or poetic), or that one cannot use a liturgical or literary form without being affected and transformed: no rhetoric is innocent for a poet. The formal process consists of the passage from the Latin verse to the verse in vulgar language, *oïl* or *oc*. This passage occurred through liturgical forms, the ambrosial *hymn* and the *sequence* converging in the *tropes* of Notker, then in the *conduit* (*conductus*) soon made autonomous in the form of *verse* (*versus*) or *song* (*canso*): this secular evolution climaxed between 1100 and 1150 in the prestigious repertory of one of the high locales of medieval music, the Abbey of Saint-Martial of Limoges. And it so happens that the 'lay abbot' of Saint-Martial was none other than William, seventh Count of Poitou, ninth Duke of Aquitaine, and first troubadour of Europe.

William began by imitating, with the intent of parody—against the increasing climate of religiosity of Fontevrault—the forms of the ambrosial hymn, of sequence and conduit. He put his declarations of profane love in the form of a liturgical hymn.[26] Gradually, through the magic of the rhythms

[26] In a letter to me dated August 3, 1955, Roland-Manuel gave me a precious example of these imitations: 'It is clear that the troubadours, who

of melody and word, these forms began to take over the theme of the poems. Unbeknownst to the poet, they acted on him and transformed him. William discovered that love was much more than making love. So much so that in the end he shifted the very movement of the spirit to the praise of the flesh, the fervor of the impulse toward the beyond (expressed in liturgical forms) to the 'sweetness' of the amorous impulse on earth. Origins of Western poetry!

Spoerri follows the dialectic of this contamination and the progress of an original secular spirituality in the detail of the metric of songs I through IX: a profound transference of the impulse toward divine love expressed in the liturgy to the impulse toward the plainest and most basic human love. This was a secularization of the enthusiasm (in the literal sense of 'divine inspiration') which discovers fulfillment and 'salvation' in the love of woman, springtime and the rapture of living the new time, that outpouring of grace in Nature. Here is the strong and trembling song:

Ab la dolchor del temps novel. . .

> Par la douceur du temps nouveau
> Les bois verdissent, les oiseaux
> Chantent chacun en son langage
> Les versets de leur chanson neuve:
> Il faut bien qu'on se mette en quête
> De ce qu'homme désire le plus![27]

And further on in the same song the famous lines:

La nostr' amor vai enaissi
Com la branca de l'albespi. . .

> Ainsi va-t-il de notre amour
> Comme de la branche d'aubépine
> Tant que dure la nuit sur l'arbre,
> Elle tremble à la pluie, au gel.

---

were musicians before they were poets, modelled their verse on the melody. The form of the stanza is musical in essence. The only musical text we have of William of Poitiers uses the same melodic formulas we find in a *versus* of the *tropaire* of Saint-Martial.'

[27] '*In the new season when the woods burgeon and birds sing out the first stave of a new song, time then that a man take the softest joy of her who is most to his liking.*'

On the Invention of Love

Mais l'endemain le soleil luit
Sur la feuille et le rameau vert.[28]

Theophil Spoerri concludes that

'In the songs of William IX there emerges and takes shape what was to characterize the European spirit: all the ardour previously directed to the Other world was now shifted to this one and sought its transformation. The resulting work is finished, but its form expresses the infinite tension of the power which transforms—that no renunciation, no disaster, not even death can stop—and which through all forms, imperfect though they may be, reveals the lure of perfection.'

To Spoerri's beautiful analyses I would like to add the following: if it is true that what he appropriately calls 'the operative magic of liturgical forms' helps to understand the emergence of courtly lyricism in William's work, there is a second formal factor whose action on the poet's consciousness has been as important: Arab rhetoric and its refined eroticism—one of the proven sources of courtesy. William undoubtedly knew the procedures of lyrical composition of the poets he encountered in the Near East during his months of captivity, and then in Spain, in Aragon or Castille with his brothers-in-law, who socialized with Andalusian literati and mixed bands of minstrels: Moorish and Christian singers. There is more: at Saint-Martial itself the music, poetry, and eroticism of the Arabs were well known. In 1019, for example, twenty Moslem slaves from Spain were received by the abbot, who kept two of them in his service and sent the rest to some high lords who would use them as interpreters.[29] (These slaves are often well versed in letters, poetry, and music.) This makes the influence of the zadjal—so often set off in five of William's eleven songs—much less mysterious.

Yet in the creative struggle of all mystique of literature to our day—a struggle which opposed the monk to the count-duke, that is to say Rasputin to Don Juan—we see neither Cathars nor minstrels. Robert was Catholic, William a high lord. Yet it is easy to verify that from the Church's point of

---

[28] *'Our love is like the branches of the hawthorn that creak in the night, trembling from the rain or ice. But tomorrow the sun shines on the boughs and green leaves.'*

[29] Cf. René Nelli, *L'Érotique des troubadours*, p. 50, who cites many other examples of direct Arab influence in Languedoc.

Appendix

view, William IX was the orthodox one—despite having been twice excommunicated. Robert d'Arbrissel—already a Cathar in his sermons and behaviour—was the Gnostic, honoured by the Pope, and the founder of some twenty convents.

Furthermore, Catharist heresy was present in Poitou since its early European expansion. It appeared at approximately the same time as in Orleans, Arras, Liège, Cologne, Reims and Toulouse—early in the eleventh century. In 1028, William V, concerned with the spread of heresy in his estates, gathered a council at Charroux to study the means to fight the 'Manichaeans'. In 1114, Robert d'Arbrissel preached against the heretics in Agen. In 1134, the heretic Henry of Lausanne, banned from Mans, took refuge in Poitiers before reaching Provence. These dates comprise the lifetime of William IX and the whole first generation of troubadours—from Poitou, the Limousin, Gascony, and Charente through Cercamon, the Ventadours, Marcabru and Rudel. We know that Marcabru, protected by the son of William IX, was a student of the monks of Saint-Martial, and Déodat Roché believes that it would be 'timely to research the connections between these Benedictine or Cistercian monks and the Cathars, since the *Poème sur Boèce*, whose unmistakable Catharist inspiration we have shown, could have originated from this abbey.'[30] I quote these 'facts' to show how the stances adopted on heresy—hostile, abbetting, or positive—mean less, in terms of psychic truth and creative dynamic, than does the actual confrontation with the phenomenon.

The noble ladies of Aquitaine rallied around Robert, going further in their religious commitment than the 'believers' of Toulousian Catharism toward the end of the twelfth century. It was also that William had not yet 'converted' to courtesy, and they had reason to avoid him. Later, Peire Vidal would side with the 'believers', even while remaining outside of the sect, while Peire Cardinal would condemn the complaisance of courtly love and ridicule its plaintive poets 'who sing as if they had a toothache'. There are as many different situations and contradictory judgments on the church, heresy, courtesy, their open struggles and secret relationships as there were poets. Some adopt a position of rivalry, others one of con-

---

[30] *Cahiers d'Études Cathares*, no. 9, 1952.

sonance. What matters is that these oppositions manifest themselves and intersect in the same sphere, within the same interplay of psychic forces, at the heart of the same *complex of aspirations and prohibitions*, of soul-liberating heresy and the conservative orthodoxy of the City.

The history of the birth of Love provides three memorable examples. In the duel between Robert d'Arbrissel and William IX the judgments brought to bear on Love—the sense of restraint in the *asag*, the submission and allegiance of man to woman, the very notion of salvation—are often opposed and sometimes hard to compare, but they consecrate and favor the same objects, which constitute the major and fascinating novelty of the period.

Toward the end of the ninth century, a similar relationship, but of higher dramatic tension, existed between the great mystic al Hallaj and the first Arab troubadour Ibn Dâvoud. Both were bards and 'inventors' of a Love that was veiled and secret, chaste and burning, delicious torment and incurable ailment, a beneficent passion which blossomed in death, since 'he who does not die of his love cannot live of it'. Love, for al Hallaj, was directed to God (as to a man), while for Ibn Dâvoud it was directed to a youth (as to a god). And in the name of orthodoxy, the poet would ask the death penalty for the mystic accused of heresy. The two were connected by their conflict and their fanaticism, by a spiritual or poetic field.[31]

Close to William in time and space, a third pair of sworn adversaries, both 'servants of Love', burst into quarrel: Pierre Abélard and Bernard of Clairvaux. Abélard's love songs for Héloïse are contemporary to the first courtly songs of William IX (about 1110). Despite their enormous popularity at the time, they have all been lost, but, there remain the letters of a chastised and repentant 'Tristan' to an 'Iseult' (turned abbess in spite of herself, while obstinately holding on to the dictates of her heart). 'Deus cordis potiusquam operis inspector est' ('God looks into the heart more than into acts'), she wrote. Bernard of Clairvaux, for his part, developed the first Chris-

---

[31] See above, pp. 111-18. In all times and places the great antinomies have been interconnected. Thus *diva* in Syriac, *daeva* in Iranian, *dew* in Armenian (demon). But the same word *dewa* gives *Zews*, *Zeus*, *Theos*, *Deus* in Hindi, Greek, and Latin.

tian mysticism of Love, sublimating the sensuality of the Song of Songs into Marian piety and ultimately making love absolute: 'Amo quia amo, amo ut amem.' His pitiless fight against the theology of Abélard (who died in 1142) preceded his mission in Provence against Catharism (1145)—that heresy which *descended* from the French North (Arras, Reims, Orleans), through Poitou, toward the County of Toulouse, Carcasses and the Albigenses, at the same time as did courtly poetry, born in Poitiers and the Limousin of the Ventadours.

9

Final Imprecation

I shall now reply collectively to the cohort of my adversaries, and seek to sift out certain erroneous formulae which seem to have affected their criticism. *First*, they still believe in relations of cause and effect, dear to those would-be 'scientific' scholars but long abandoned by nuclear physicists. I did not make much of such relations in my first version, and banned them in the second. I find significance only in certain clusters of relations, structures of interaction, sets of forces, in short, certain fields, such as might define the tensions between William IX and Robert d'Arbrissel, or al Hallaj and Ibn Dâvoud—where it is much less a matter of knowing who claims to be the champion of what, than seizing the commonalities in the phenomenon as compared with the relations between troubadours and Cathars, and thus deriving the moral and religious implications.

Second, they want legalistic types of proofs (scientific or experimental proofs being excluded by the nature of the phenomenon under study). One can call to their attention the spatial and temporal coincidence of heresy and courtesy in the same minds and the same conflictual situations. They are not impressed. They remind me of those American judges I have read about recently who dismissed a verdict rendered against five murderers convicted of having killed twelve persons: certain details of the preliminary examination gave rise to some doubt, that is to say, to indefinite dismissal. If the Apostles had presented themselves to our historians in need of proofs on the very night of Pentecost, the latter would have demanded a notarized receipt from the Holy Ghost. Most of them are entirely ignorant of poetic genesis and the psychology of created works. *They only believe what has been 'certified'. Yet poetry never is.* They are only willing to believe those sources expressly presented by an author. Yet true sources are generally unconscious, repressed, or deliberately dissimulated.

Third, not only are they ignorant of the games and ruses of love and creation, but *a fortiori* also of the specificity of poetic, mystic, and religious problems. They think that everything has always existed everywhere in the same way. 'Love, with certain nuances, is the same on all latitudes and periods especially for lyric poets,' wrote Belperron. Yet not one of the great Greek tragedies—I mean of the thirty which remain—has love for its subject. Not one. Does that not mean something?

Fourth, their psychology is at best outdated, linear, and rationalistic, admitting only univocal motives which condemn them almost automatically to credulity or ill-timed incredulity. When they say: that troubadour wrote exactly the opposite from what a Perfect should profess; that Gnostic has declared his aversion toward love and its consequences; that praise of chastity conforms to Catholic morality since it tends to repress desire—I note that they have not understood the nature of the object under study and its intrinsic dialectic. They have not understood the most important thing: the indivisible and complementary union of *certain* antinomic realities—precisely those which concern me here. Not only do they believe that every man who *calls* himself a Catholic, a Cathar, or a leftist, *is* one, and is such in all his actions and words; not only do they believe what is alleged or labeled rather than what is experienced—but they seem entirely ignorant of the complicities of love and hate, chastity and eroticism, desire and anguish, attraction and repulsion, affected indifference and repressed affectivity. They have not realized that the true opposition is not between those who exalt and those who condemn any given element of *cortezia*, but between those who create or endure it and those who make it the subject of their dissertations. The latter alone believe that an explanation can be 'established' in such a domain, as the doctrine of a party triumphs through simple majority. Only he who has conceived of the highest level of meaning may hope to seduce truth.

There is an inconceivable naïveté in certain scholars who, pronouncing 'My Descartes!' as one might cross oneself, refuse to acknowledge the realities of the unconscious and take for granted, beyond any critique, the incompatibility of the will to live and the desire to die, which are one and the same in vertiginous attraction; of the Crusades and the spiritual interaction with Islam; of Cathars and troubadours; of asceticism and burning desire; of delirious mysticism and willing chastity. They have understood nothing about the object of their study: the traps of poetry, the gaps of history, desire in search of an object—the twelfth century, love in general, and love in the twelfth century. At this point many exasperated readers may cry: 'Enough! After all, in your book there are not only troubadours and those Cathars who may or may not have been their brothers. Why dwell on all this? Tell us rather about marriage, the couple's morality, or eroticism!' Indeed, why return to all this? There are many reasons, and I shall begin with the least good of them.

Before the pack of critics barking at my heels in the 'scientific' journals, I have sometimes felt overtaken by a kind of anguish, and wondered: Are they not, maybe, right? On many points of detail it was probable, and on two or three even certain—but on the essentials, on the whole? I reexamined all my arguments and theirs, as well as the old texts. Yet no, they could not all be right since they were divided on every subject (and these were many), so much so that their consensus, which was just about nil, would not exist if it had not been for their agreement against my theses. I confess I was seduced into the game. It is a fascinating game, marvelously gratuitous. We know so little! At every crumb of new information the players make a run for it: 'This is for me!' What sport! (What *desport*, said the Anglo-Norman language).

It is true, there are not only the troubadours, but the troubadours were there in the beginning, because first there was poetry, then the feelings it knew how to express and by this expression, awakened, and then drama appeared. We had been expecting it without knowing it, but from the very moment it *spoke*, we knew. And then there is morality (to which I shall return). The troubadours come first because first there is expression, especially lyrical expression. In the beginning there was Song—the music of the Word—and that is due to the very nature of love, the passionate love I have described, of which it constitutes a first approach. In dealing seriously with this problem, I do not believe I succumbed to some obsession or allowed my scholarly critics to drag me into a field where they may have been better armed. I have attempted to deepen my conception of love, the single subject of this book and true object of my dispute with the scholars. What separates us in these debates is not a difference in knowledge or information but only our conceptions of love, and more than that, our different experiences of passion and poetry. What we have not sought, undergone, experienced in our lives, how might we recognize it across the centuries in men who did not say everything as *we* would, and who otherwise remained silent? We must enter into a consonance of the soul, and this can only be done through the ardent listening of works in which the soul has left traces of its most secret heartbeat and the trail of its impulses.

IO

Misunderstandings on Morals

The moral theses of my book have met with far less opposition—even while they motivated some amusing contradictory opinions. Catholics approved because of my critique of heresy, which seemed to imply a warning against passion; but Gnostics knew where my heart was. Women's magazines approved my defense of marital fidelity, while regretting my exclusion of passion from marriage (which is not so). The American counter-culture applauded my depictions of passion (and, of course, the effects of the love-drug), while regretting my shameless acceptance of Western culture. The unhappily married saw in my book their 'breviary'; the happily married, their leaps over abysses; the divorced, their useless and bitter vindications. Finally, after the war, Jean-Paul Sartre used my book to illustrate the thesis he had attacked before the war and had wrongly accused me of supporting. The texts follow.

Reviewing my book in June 1939,[32] Sartre announced that the book's interest 'resides above all in that it reflects a recent and deeper flexibility of historical method under the triple influence of psychoanalysis, marxism, and sociology'. Then he wondered whether, contrary to what he deemed to be my thesis, *real* passion 'might not have, as a psychological phenomenon, its own dialectic', and whether 'certain *basic structures* of the human condition might not be realized through specific historical condition'. (I thought I had said exactly that.) In short, he blamed me for not having seen that transcendence is, in fact, the 'existential structure of man'. Desire '*naturally* entails its own contradiction, misfortune, and di-

---

[32] This review–chronicle was reprinted in *Situations I*.

alectic'. There would thus be 'no need for a courtly myth in order to explain passion'.[33] In sum, because my book did not recognize that the dialectic of love is in the *nature* of man, it merely constituted 'a fine entertainment'.

Seven years and one war later, after publication of *L'Être et le Néant (Being and Nothingness)*, everything changed. In his 'Présentation des *Temps Modernes*' (*Situations II*) Sartre listed 'the essential issues' which placed him in opposition to Proustian analysis and to the 'legend of the poet's irresponsibility':

'In the first place, we do not accept *a priori* the notion that passionate love is an inborn trait of the human spirit. It may very well be, as has been suggested[34] by Denis de Rougemont, that its historical origin links it with Christian ideology. More generally, we believe that a feeling is always the

---

[33] There is a fluctuation between 'essential' and 'existential' structures that characterizes Sartre at this time. Likewise between internal dialectic and external factors. If the 'dialectic of desire' were enough to create passion, the latter would be universal—which it has not been and is not. It is clear that courtesy, an external sociocultural factor, could only affect latent internal structures which would have remained thus—as elsewhere—without its intervention. (Similar fluctuations, on the same subjects, can be found in the later Freud of *Civilization and Its Discontents*.) But Sartre decidedly goes astray when he provides as an example of what he calls transcendence 'sexual desire itself.' Would not a dog's sexual desire be part of its 'existential structure'? Would it therefore not comprise canine transcendence? Nothing then, in the domain of passion, would distinguish man from dog. It is obvious that Sartre abuses language—deliberately in this instance. What he obstinately calls transcendence (just to annoy theologians?) is only *exorbitance*—man's movement to force himself courageously to step out of himself (to be sexually attractive), to supersede his limits at all cost. There is a revealing phrase in the same article: 'To desire is to thrust oneself into the world, in danger next to a woman's flesh, in danger in the very flesh of this woman.' I am not refuting neurosis, but one is entitled to suspect any general argument derived from this stance. (This critique would likewise be valid in the case of Kierkegaard, who, however, explained himself with convincing humour.) Unfortunately, these kinds of personal observations compose the main chapter devoted to love in *Being and Nothingness*. By itself almost as long as my book, it remains never far from its problems and approaches. . . .

[34] 'Suggested'? Yes, in my whole book! If Sartre views some four hundred tight pages as a mere suggestion, one understands more readily that he should need five thousand pages to *really* deal with a subject, be it as considerable as his hatred of Flaubert—already emulously declared in this same 'Présentation des *Temps Modernes*'.

Appendix

expression of a certain lifestyle and world view common to a whole class or period, and that its evolution is not the effect of some internal mechanism but of these historical and social factors.'

Thus, my book became the first argument that *Les Temps Modernes* opposed to the supporters of an invariable 'human nature' and its 'essential structures'—the same ones Sartre, in *Situations I* had blamed me for neglecting.

The reception of *L'Amour et l'Occident* by its Eastern and Western readers alike has hinged on a number of misunderstandings for which I might congratulate myself because of their positive outcome. The book lives, both loved and hated, after four decades of exposure to all manner of critical storms—personal and public, psychological and political. Yet the greatest misunderstanding is believing that I consider marriage and passion to be mutually exclusive, as had been decided by the courts of love. Such a reading of my book is mistaken. Whether I am congratulated or blamed, it is not what I meant to say.

I wanted to emphasize the contrasts, reinforce the awareness of valid and inevitable antinomies that must be taken into account: movement/security, ecstasy/duration, marriage/passion, to dream of Eros and submit to it or experience Agape and act upon it. Once the nature of the antinomies was better understood, far from vainly attempting to resolve them by eliminating one of the terms, there had to be a decision to live out their drama and chose to experience their ever-changing and surprising tension. My underlying tenet was the following phrase by Heraclitus which, quoted or not, is present in all my books: 'Opposites cooperate, and from their struggle emerges the most beautiful harmony.' In all this I have not changed. I may have matured, perhaps reaching a clearer understanding of the interaction of opposing terms, which cannot survive without one another, and finally conclude in federal alliances, the first model of which is marriage.

II

Passion and Incest

In his book *Prohibition de l'Inceste* (*Incest: The Nature and Origin of the Taboo*) (1905), Durkheim, well before Freud (in *Totem and Taboo*), assumes that culture emerged from prohibitions first imposed on the father's wife and then on the women of the clan as a whole. I would emphasize more today the theme of incest in *Tristan* and its Oedipal aspects (clearly indicated, if not well developed, for example in Chapter 12 of book II). True, Tristan could not have desired his mother, who died in labor. But his sadness derived from this death, as is indicated in his very name and his culpability. And when he *accidentally* bedded with Iseult, who was the promised wife of his 'father', King Mark, his maternal uncle—who performed the father's role among the Celts—he committed and consummated incest, but in a trance, in the phantasmal, dreamlike state provoked by the love-potion, that hashish of the time.

He *conquered* Iseult through a hard struggle. According to ancient custom, he would have had the *right* to possess her, as he had already done—and this was correct, since he had shown himself to be the strongest. It appears that he thereby escaped the Oedipal situation (where the child is always the weakest, and even *too* weak). Yet, because he needed a father, he chose to observe civil law, whereby he became once again the weakest, and he chose to make Iseult the wife of Mark, his true common-law father. At the same time he brought guilt to his love, however legitimized by courtesy, which prescribed that the lover seek a married woman.

The mirror image of the Oedipus complex is well described in the *Roman en prose*. First we see an adolescent Tristan, fourteen or fifteen years old, sojourning with his uncle King

369

Appendix

Mark 'as a foreign man, and he did so well that after a short time there was no damsel at the king's court who did not have him in the highest esteem'. At this time Mark loved Tristan, and was unaware of their parentage. Then Tristan triumphed over Morholt and revealed his royal birth. But, wounded, he went to Ireland where he was nursed by Iseult, and when he returned to the court of Tintagel 'the king established him as the lord and master of his estates and possessions'. Here, without the least transition, the *Roman* tells us: 'Soon King Mark took to hating Tristan, because he feared him more than before.' He therefore sent his nephew 'in search' of Iseult, whom he wanted for his wife, knowing full well that Tristan would be risking his life if he returned to the country of Morholt. Tristan knew this too: 'When Tristan hears this news, he thinks his uncle is sending him to Ireland to die rather than to find Iseult.' Yet he pledged before God 'that he will do everything in his power'. (His Oedipal culpability vis-à-vis Mark, substitute for the deceased father, was heightened by the memory of his mother, whom he caused to die by coming into the world.) Conquered by Tristan's prowess, the king of Ireland finally said to him: 'Tristan, you have done so much . . . I am giving you Iseult *for yourself or for your uncle*.' All those giants, dragons, and traitors that wound him with a poisoned sword, and that he kills—are they not the paternal symbols of the forbidden, to be overcome not without a wound?

The 'father's' vengeance being the castration of the symbolic son through *separation* (loss of the maternal bosom, severance), we understand that Tristan cannot love (in the sense of the German *dürfen*, or permission) unless the object of his love is *distant* (Geoffrey Rudel's *amors de lonh*). The principal dialectical moments of the complex are found in the triangular relationship between Tristan, Mark, and Iseult. These contradictions are manifest in all the episodes of the romance—they *make* the romance: the alternation of nostalgic separations and ecstatic farewells, new separations to avoid social fault, but also to recreate the courtly situation of 'far away love' (anything is better than shared daily existence).

If Tristan had decided to keep Iseult for himself, he would have violated the courtly taboo. If he had bedded her while she was married to Mark, he would have violated the incest

370

taboo, and the whole social order would have collapsed in a dazzling ecstasy. But he chose to respect the feudal order, not wishing to have everything collapse around him. In fact, he violated in turn both taboos—that was precisely his 'bitter torment': whether to rejoin Iseult or remain apart from her; whether to live with her in thè forest or voluntarily return her to the king.

The destructive effects of incest and the elating effects of courtesy converge toward ectasy in death, the end of passional entropy, the voluptuous fall into the undifferentiated—which is nothingness. Tristan had only wanted to keep the dazzling moments of love, those of forbidden passion, and those times of nostalgic desire when one best experiences love in oneself. Supreme dazzlement could only be deadly from then on: it was the death of the Banu Ohdri, the legendary tribe where one died when one loved.

Freud understood it well: no civilization could survive the disappearance of the incest taboo. Neither could courtesy nor passion, we add. But if we have reason to believe that the incest taboo is the minimal law in order that a culture be differentiated from nature,[35] we see that *Tristan*, the poem of the essential triangle (Father/Mother/Son) and the primeval creative situation, is something quite different and much more than an 'epic of adultery': it is the poem of Western culture.

[35] Cf. Claude Lévi-Strauss, *Les Structures élémentaires de la parenté,* 1949.

12

Passion and Allergy

What is unleashed in the anguished but dazzled victims of love at first sight is characterized by the hyperbolic reactions of the whole being to a banal stimulation, which would be *normal* to anyone else, in other words, easy to compensate or neutralize by the obvious response. But now suddenly the lovers' whole being reacts to this stimulation in a general commotion with fever, redness, arrhythmia, or, on the contrary, with a kind of hieratic catalepsy, eyes riveted in mutual hypnosis. They all say that they love to be overtaken by such a fever, by this upheaval of the senses and the soul. Passion is this frightening yet delicious perturbation provoked by the presence of certain beings, for reasons of which they themselves, as well as those who react to their presence, claim to be entirely ignorant. And I believe them. (Later, they will try to rationalize, poeticize, moralize—and there I shall stop believing them.)

In seeking the analogies to this phenomenon at a psychological level, all I find is the mechanism of *allergy*: an excessive reaction to an ordinarily harmless external agent which suddenly, for unknown reasons, provokes on the subject *sensitized* by a first contact a violent overcompensation, such as an overabundant production of antihistamines following a simple mosquito bite. In the legend, this first contact was the first encounter in Ireland, the bath scene. From then on, it was courtly poetry and the Breton romance that would *sensitize* men and women and provoke in them this 'altered response of the organism to substances normally tolerated' which characterizes allergy. The two phenomena, passion and allergy, also elicit the mobilization of the entire nation for an unverified border incident, or a war which kills millions of men to avenge an assassination—which (moreover) suited everyone. At the incitement of desire, suddenly passionate reaction overflows. It makes no difference whether desire be satisfied or not in serious cases (complicated by drugs), such as that of Tristan and Iseult. Passion, once declared, demands much more than this satisfaction. It wants everything, and especially the unattainable: infinitude in a finite being.

The 'normal' response to desire being to make love, or to escape, the passionate (allergic) response is to become prey to a fever that is almost fatal in certain cases, a frenzy which, in turn, elicits cries of pain or ecstasy, drives to crime or to suicide, transfigures the world or devastates it in the eyes of the moaning victim—who nonetheless does not wish to be cured and refuses help. The cure would consist of a confrontation with reality. The equivalent of the antihistamines prescribed in cases of allergy would be to bring the impassioned individual to look at and see the Other, such as he is. This is precisely what the lover passionately refuses to do. He prefers to withdraw from the beloved he might risk to see too well in the sobering light of shared existence.

'It is not love, that what turns to reality.' This courtly maxim means that *fin' amors* is the enjoyment of desire, not of pleasure. Its meaning can be extended to the motivation and creation of most obstacles in the romance—legal, sexual, psychological—all of which turn aside any opportunity to see reality better, they deny proximity. When the affected lovers are constrained to live together, the philtre soon loses its effect. In the extreme, it is a matter of removing the physical reality of the loved one, especially that of the woman where the man is concerned, since there is no symmetry here: I have yet to find a single woman who has sung 'far away love'.[36] Might passionate love be a lovable allergy, a positive, delicious allergy—no better explained to this day than the others?

[36] On this subject see in my *Amour III* (in preparation) the chapter on 'the woman of one's dreams'.

13

Passion and Drugs

The most frequent cause of allergy is contact with, or ingestion of, certain substances. Passion is usually aroused through the sole *mutual presence* of two beings. For Tristan and Iseult such was the case, according to Thomas. But according to Béroul, it was the philtre they drank that unleashed the passion, after a number of 'ineffectual' encounters (even the so erotic bath scene). Not only did the philtre intervene accidentally from the outside, but Béroul limits its effects in time to 'three years'.

Béroul follows closely the 'case history' (as physicians say) of this intoxication[37] which he explicitly blames for the lovers' indiscretion. Let us recall the double confession he puts on their lips (p. 40). Tristan: '*If she loves me, it is by the poison which holds me from leaving her and her from leaving me.*' And Iseult: '*He loves me not, nor I him; except for a herb potion which I drank and which he drank: it was a sin.*'

Béroul's procedure, which *isolates* the legendary passion, allows us to follow its internal dialectic. We find the rhythm of the byword 'a little, a lot, passionately, not at all', which recalls that passion annihilates its object. Its first delicious flame we call the amorous state, is only its veiled form—'a little, a lot'—which links itself to desire, becomes its accomplice, and usually vanishes once its ardour has been satisfied. But triumphant, declared passion burns so strongly that the philtre is activated, and suddenly passion drops to the 'not at all' of the proverb. It is as if ardour had consumed

---

[37] What could have been this drug in the twelfth century? Probably ergot of rye, whose effects resemble those of LSD but are certainly more aphrodisiac.

the *image* of the beloved in the hallucination of the drug ('S'il m aime, c'est par la poison'), and when the lover finds himself before the *real* Iseult, he realizes that she is not the one he has loved.

The role of sea voyages in Celtic legends is well known. In Béroul's romance there are four, and each is related to a story of 'poison', as the *Roman en prose* puts it. Wounded by the poisoned sword of the giant Morholt, whom he has killed, and without hope of surviving, Tristan embarks on an adventure in a boat without sail nor oars, taking along his sword and his harp. The voyage ends in Ireland, where Iseult nurses him back to health. The second voyage, in search of Mark's fiancée, more or less repeats the first. The third resembles what young Americans would call a 'trip': it is the return with Iseult, the scene where the philtre, 'la poison', is drunk. The last voyage is that of Iseult going to her lover in an attempt to cure him of a newly poisoned wound, but this time she is to rejoin him only in death.

A curious difficulty arises upon examining these voyages. Iseult intervenes to cure Tristan of the effects of the poison, at the time of the three wounds related to solitary voyages. Then they are again separated. But when they drink the same philtre together—are they taking the same 'trip' or is this an illusion? It is certainly an illusion in the eyes of the vigilant, convinced that dreamers cannot communicate and that there is no passage from the dream of one to that of the other. But if both lovers share this illusion, does it not become the truth of their passion? One can justly denounce their illusion of reality, yet be unable to touch them: as long as the philtre acts and maintains *l'amistié*, they live the reality of their double illusion.

The analogy of the drug makes clear the irretrievably solipsistic, narcissistic, and segregative character of passion. Those who 'travel' are always alone. Their passion does not touch the reality of the Other, but loves only its own image.

That is why marriage cannot be based on passion.

14

Passion and Marriage

One of the biggest misunderstandings derived from my book consists in repeating that it condemns passion—which is false—because it is the sworn enemy of the institution of marriage and its ethic—which is true. From this it has been inferred that 'love' is incompatible with marriage—which is ridiculous. This is one of those ultracondensed views required by the magazine captions. It is superfluous to repeat here that I entirely disavow it.

I have attempted to establish that since its origins in the twelfth century, passionate love was constituted in hostility to marriage and that the objectives of Eros and Agape are in a relation of systematic antinomy. I wanted to emphasize contrasts and to indicate incompatibilities prior to the choices all men must make in what they perceive as freedom.

I have tried to isolate passion as is done for a chemical compound—the better to learn its properties. I have shown that isolated from its opposite (active love, or Agape), in its pure state, passive or ecstatic, passion is deadly, such as for Tristan and some of the great mystics. There remains to be seen what passion can produce in composition—if it can tolerate it. Pure chlorine is lethal, but sodium chloride is the salt of our meals—of our agapes.

Neither repressive nor Marcusian, I do not purport either to forbid or to authorize. I never said: 'Do this, but not that.' I only said: 'If you do this or that, here is what you will really be doing, these are the types of behaviours you will be following, the mythical structures you will be engaging in.' I do not write to legislate, nor even to advise, but to warn. To help in adopting correct views. If I deserve to be called a moralist, it is insofar as I have sought to make my reader more responsible, freer to chose in full knowledge of the facts and goals.

There may be no sphere where such work is more necessary and where contemporary humanity is in greater need than that of emotion—ignored or vilified by our technological society. So much so that a whole generation is reduced to seeking salvation in evasive, infantile, or tribal behavior, i.e., the drug 'culture', drop-out communes, and societies of free sex.

In light of the latter observation, the obstinacy of my *inquiry on the origins of love* may be better understood. It can provide the clue to more than one erotic or sentimental tradition turned reflex or nostalgia in modern man—all the more bewitching and constraining inasmuch as man is no longer aware of its formerly liberating meaning, and cannot interpret its symbols.

I have attempted to reinvent the origins of passionate love. I have proved that it is dependent on marriage, just as mysticism is dependent on dogma and the ecclesiastic institution, remaining oriented precisely by denying or superseding them.[38] I have shown the mistake of pervasive bourgeois romanticism: *founding marriage on passionate love*, that is, on what denies it from the start. A barely less fatal mistake would be to *exclude passion from marriage*. I have stated this clearly in my first version. I have not changed since, only advanced a little along the same lines. In *Comme toi-même* (*Love Declared*),[39] I suggested that the obstacle which nurtures all passion can be reborn within marriage:

'If it is true that passion seeks the Inaccessible, and if it is true that the Other as such remains the best-defended mystery in the eyes of a demanding love—could Eros and Agape not join in a paradoxical alliance at the very heart of an accepted marriage? Is not every *Other* the Inaccessible, and any woman loved an Iseult, even if no moral prohibition, no taboo symbolizes (for the requirements of the fable and the convenience

[38] Cf. Karl Barth, *Church Dogmatics*, vol. I, 2nd part.

[39] *Comme toi-même*. First edition Albin Michel, 1961. Reprinted as paperback, with the old subtitle now as title: *Les Mythes de l'Amour* (Paris, Gallimard, Idées, 1967). English translation: *Love Declared: Essays on the Myths of Love*, tr. Richard Howard (New York, Pantheon, 1963). British title: *The Myths of Love* (London, Faber & Faber, 1963).

of the novelist) the very essence of the exciting obstacle, the obstacle that will never depend on anything but being itself: the autonomy of the person loved, her fascinating otherness?' This search for the Angel, which is the mystery of the Other, exciting both Eros and Agape—might it not be a third form of love, similar to the mysticisms of spiritual marriage?

The fidelity I advocated (and that many confuse with a policing of lifestyles, repression, or at best self-imposed virtue) is simply the *sine qua non* of any work of art (or life) whose development requires time and great concentration. (There is nothing here revealed through dogma, or that could not be based on the evidence of psychological reality.)

Nor have I changed in admitting with some fervor, in *Comme toi-même*, the nostalgia for Gnosis and its passion, which I was misunderstood to have condemned. In fact, I have never 'condemned passion', and I explained my views on this point in the concluding chapter of my first version of *L'Amour et l'Occident*: 'I have said it and I insist again: to condemn passion as a matter of principle would be like attempting to eliminate one of the poles of our creative tension. It is not possible.'

I wish to condemn nothing and propose no self-mutilation—too much neurosis already takes care of that. I have tried to show the vital contrasts, conflicts, antinomies, which underlie our reality, and to better define these terms. The next step is to internalize the tensions and creatively counterbalance them, far from madly attempting to exclude one of the terms. We do not have that power, and the Devil himself cannot eliminate either good or evil—and not even his own person—from the game.

To infer from my book that passion should or could be obliterated in order that Agape should reign triumphant would be a complete misunderstanding of the inner logic of my thought. All my morals, my passion, and my politics derive from the composition and tension of opposites.

The person, source and end of all moral values, is man, both free and tied to the community by a singular vocation, a vocation which at once distinguishes him from the mass and holds him to the community, within which he alone is responsible for his unique mode of living with others.

The couple is the original social cell, whose basic forces

are two beings with singular, different laws, but who choose to compose a 'union without fusion, without separation, and without subordination'—as is said of the union of the two natures in Jesus Christ[40]—even while the conflict of Eros and Agape animates their days and their dreams.

Finally politics, which is the art of organizing human relations in the city (*polis*), reduces to federalism, which is the art of joining communities only where their union alone can save their autonomy.

Any attempt to eliminate either of the two poles of these tensions, to confound it with its opposite, to reduce it to the law of the Other (whether it be stronger or weaker) through annexation or colonization, or to establish between them any relation of subordination, brings about a totalitarian state and destroys the interest of life. As to the subject of our concern: it is to destroy the existence of essential Love.

1972, 1982

[40] Canons of the Council of Chalcedon in 456.

Index

381

Index

Beatrice, 98, 179
Bédier, Joseph, 15, 23, 26, 31, 128, 136
Bel Accueil, 176
Belges, Jean Lemaire de, 119
Believers, the, 81, 82, 85, 95, 113, 114
Bembo, Cardinal, 252
Bérénice, 200 sq.
Berger extravagant, Le, 196
Bergson, 221
Bernard of Chartres, 89
Bernard of Clairvaux, 131, 133
Bernart of Ventadour, 89
Bernis, Cardinal, 258
Béroul, 20, 23, 26 sq., 44, 48, 123, 127, 128, 131, 136, 143, 175
Bezenval, 211
Bigorne, 187
Black Death, 183
Blanchefleur, 26
Blaye, Prince of, *see* Rudel, Geoffrey
Boccaccio, 236
Boehme, Jakob, 173
Bogomil churches, 78, 109
Bohort, 126
Boileau, 196
Bonet, Honoré, 247
Book of the Blessed Angela di Foligno, 158
Book of the Twelve Beguines, 156
Book of the Two Principles, 79
Borst, Arno, 79, 83
Bouddhisme, études et materiaux, 116
Boulenger, J., 255
Bran, 127
Brantôme, 245
Brengain, 27, 28, 204, 228
Brethren of the Free Spirit, 175
Breton, André, 295
Brinkmann, 77
Britain, 64
Brittany, 40
Brod, Max, 283
Buddhism, 64, 87
Buddhist Tantrism, 80
Burckhardt, Jakob, 252, 254
Burgundy, 249
Cabalistic doctrines, 191
Caldwell, Erskine, 236

Calprenède, La, 193
Calvin, 176, 301
Canzoniere, 214
Carcasses, 85
Cardinal, Peire, 93
Carduel, 28
Carolingian emperors, 73
Carpocratians, 99
Calvacanti, Guido, 167, 177 sq.
Casanova, 211
Casti connubii, 287
Castiglione, Baldassare, 252
Castillo interior, 161, 162
Catharism, 7, 78 sq., 82 sq., 92, 93, 99, 103, 104, 110, 114, 119, 131, 132, 145, 149, 155, 159, 167, 169, 175, 188, 190; *see also* Believers and Perfect
Catharisme, Le, 79, 87
Catharism and troubadours, 82
    and War, 119, 120
    twentieth century, 294
Catharist view of Christ, 169
    view of love, 134
Celtic myth, 62, 123, 190
Celtic myths and Arthurian romance, 127 sq.
Celtes, Les, 62 sq., 127 sq.
Celts, 62 sq., 72, 124
Cent Nouvelles Nouvelles, Les, 186
Cercamon, 120
Cervantes, 189
Chamfort, 209
Champagne, Countess of, 34
Champmeslé, Marie, 202, 203
Chanson de geste, 33
Charles VIII, 253
Chastellain, 20, 249
Chastity, 59, 60, 114, 118, 120, 185, 248
Chateaubriand, 63, 174, 183, 222
Chénier, André, 222
Chess, 111, 112
Chivalry, 20, 22, 31, 47, 246 sq., 254, 270
    and marriage, 32
    decline of, 250
    feudal, 32, 33, 35, 60
    later history of, 188

382

Index

Index

385

Index

Index

Index

Index

Index

West-Östliche Mystik, 154
William of Poitiers, 83, 88, 106, 110,
   117, 118
Woman, 63, 64, 74
   Catharist attitude to, 79
   Christian attitude to, 312, 313
   emancipation of, 294
   Italian, 252
   medieval attitude to, 76, 77
   place of, in Germany, 291
   standardized beauty of, 282, 283
   types of, 291
Works of Ossian, 189

Yeats, W. B., 189
Yoga, 70
Yoga, The Method of Reintegration, 116

Zadjal, The, 106
Zarathustra, see Zoroaster
Zardusht, see Zoroaster
Zend-Avesta, 103
Zerlina, 52
Zetkind, 289
Zola, 186, 232
Zoroaster, 65, 102
Zwingli, 176

393

About the Author

Born in Switzerland in 1906, Denis de Rougemont participated in many of this century's most important intellectual movements. He was one of the founders of the "personalistic" movement of the thirties, directed French broadcasts over the Voice of America during World War II, and was in the forefront of the postwar interest in European unification. De Rougemont helped found an impressive number of European cultural organizations, and served as president of the executive committee of the Congress for Cultural Freedom and director of the Centre Européen de la Culture in Geneva.

De Rougemont is best known in the United States as the author of the influential works, *Love in the Western World, The Devil's Share,* and *Love Declared.* He also wrote a great many other widely translated books, articles, and pamphlets on politics, philosophy, theology, and literature.